TATA

TATA

The Global Corporation That Built Indian Capitalism

Mircea Raianu

HARVARD UNIVERSITY PRESS
Cambridge, Massachusetts
London, England
2021

LIBRARY OF CONGRESS CATALOGING-IN-PUBLICATION DATA

Names: Raianu, Mircea, 1987– author.
Title: Tata : the global corporation that built Indian capitalism / Mircea Raianu.
Description: Cambridge, Massachusetts : Harvard University Press, 2021. |
Includes bibliographical references and index.
Identifiers: LCCN 2020048905 | ISBN 9780674984516 (cloth)
Subjects: LCSH: Tata Group. | Capitalism—India—History. | International business
enterprises—India—History. | India—Economic conditions.
Classification: LCC HC440.C3 .R35 2021 | DDC 338.8/8954—dc23
LC record available at https://lccn.loc.gov/2020048905

Contents

TATA

Introduction

> You wake up in the morning to a Titan alarm, have Tata Tea
> for breakfast, call your office on Tata Indicom, go to office in a
> Tata Indica, and lunch at the Taj. After work, you may shop at
> Westside or have a cuppa at Barista. This list could go on. Yet,
> the first thing that comes to mind when we think of this great
> organisation is trust and commitment.
>
> —T. R. DOONGAJI, former managing director, Tata Services

> We all watch Tata Sky, we surf the net with Tata Photon, we
> ride in Tata taxis, we stay in Tata Hotels, we sip our Tata tea in
> Tata bone china and stir it with teaspoons made of Tata Steel.
> We buy Tata books in Tata bookshops. *Hum Tata ka namak
> khate hain.* We're under siege.
>
> —ARUNDHATI ROY, author and activist

These two snapshots of everyday life in early twenty-first century India
mirror each other.[1] Both describe the products and services of one corporate group, Tata, as inescapably ubiquitous. Both speak directly to a middle-
class urban citizen-consumer (Doongaji's "you," Roy's "we"), the prototypical
neoliberal subject of an economy unshackled by market reforms since 1991.
After all, only a select few Indians can afford to have lunch at Bombay's ma-
jestic Taj Hotel, built by the founder of the Tata dynasty during the colonial
period, or to sip tea from bone china. But the ubiquity of the Tata brand is
invoked to starkly different ends. For Doongaji, a faithful servant of the group,
what matters is the ethical compact of "trust and commitment" between the
corporation and the citizen-consumer. Indians trust the quality of Tata products and value the group's dedication to social responsibility. Roy, a sharp critic
of contemporary capitalism, draws the opposite conclusion. The Hindi phrase
Hum Tata ka namak khate hain literally translates as "We eat Tata's salt." The
metaphor of "eating the salt" has a long history in the political culture of the
subcontinent, connoting loyalty and patronage. During the Mughal period,
its use functioned as a "ritual of incorporation" binding conquered subjects to

the emperor.[2] It also featured in a television advertisement for Tata Salt, "Maine is desh ka namak khaya hai" ("I have eaten the salt of this country"), as a way to celebrate the group's nation-building role.[3] Roy's usage of the phrase suggests that the private corporation has become a sovereign power in its own right. Citizen-subjects are "under siege," their relationship to capital no longer mediated by the welfare state and its promise of a more just and egalitarian future.

Why is the scene of a life lived entirely in a Tata-branded world so easily depicted and so intimately familiar to audiences in India as to require little explanation or justification? What accounts for the gulf between the celebration of corporate giants like Tata as stewards of a prosperous economy and the condemnation of corporate greed as suffocating democracy? These questions are, of course, not unique to India. The spectacular ascendancy of corporate power is a truly global phenomenon. Corporations care for us, feed us and clothe us, surveil us and discipline us, ever more intensively. Yet, they also appear increasingly unstable and vulnerable, coming under severe public scrutiny in the wake of the 2008 financial crash, widening income and wealth inequality, the harvesting and misuse of private data, and the ongoing climate and pandemic crises.[4] India stands out as an extreme case, having seen the explosive emergence of a billionaire class of "crony capitalists" and a fraying social fabric over the past few decades. For many Western observers, India has now entered its own "Gilded Age," unfolding much as its namesake in the United States once did.[5] However, there is one major difference in kind that often goes unnoticed. The companies that dominate the economies and societies of North America and Western Europe today are not the same as the monopolies of bygone eras. In India, Tata has been at the top of the corporate pyramid for the better part of a century. It is as though the Vanderbilts and the Rockefellers themselves, not simply their modern equivalents, owned Amazon, Apple, and Google. The "creative destruction" posited by Austrian economist Joseph Schumpeter as the driving force in the history of capitalism seems to have stalled in India.[6]

Numbers tell only part of the story. In 1931, shortly before the end of colonial rule, Tata was the largest business group in India in terms of paid-up share capital and total assets. It was also the only Indian-owned group in the top fifteen, the other spots occupied by the British expatriate managing agencies. In 1958, a decade after independence, Tata was still in first place fighting for supremacy with the rival Birla group. The top of the table was unchanged on the eve of liberalizing reforms in 1991, this time with new contenders for the crown the Ambanis not far behind. Today comprising one hundred subsidiary and affiliate companies operating in over eighty countries, Tata arguably remains India's wealthiest and most powerful group.[7] As one analyst succinctly puts it, "no other company anywhere has dominated the history of its national industry as the house of Tata has done."[8]

The evolving composition of Tata's portfolio is equally, if not more, significant. In the time of founder Jamsetji Nusserwanji Tata (1839–1904), the group began as one of many merchant families in the port city of Bombay, making their fortunes in the cotton and opium trades across the Indian Ocean. Through Jamsetji's pioneering entrepreneurial efforts in textiles, iron and steel, and hydroelectric power, Tata ascended to the commanding heights of the national economy by the time of Indian independence in 1947. Subsequently led by the dashing and cosmopolitan Jehangir Ratanji Dadabhoy Tata (1904–1993), the group expanded into new sectors such as chemicals, aviation, and automobiles. More recently, under the chairmanship of the reserved and technocratic Ratan Tata (born 1937), information technology has been the group's most consistently profitable division, keeping it afloat when manufacturing businesses have faltered. Not only does Tata's historical trajectory reflect the broad transition from trade to industry to services, but it also contains all these phases at once, rarely shedding the weight of the past. Tata is thus a microcosm of Indian capitalism, both synchronically and diachronically.

Despite being led by members of an extended family for most of its history, Tata was unusual among Indian corporate groups even in this respect. It employed professional executives and talented nonrelatives from an early date, relied on more transparent methods of financing than their competitors, and maintained extensive social and economic ties across community boundaries—a noteworthy cosmopolitan ethos in a business environment segregated according to race, caste, region, and ethnicity.[9] Tata also avoided the worst excesses of the prevailing form of corporate governance in colonial India, the "managing agency" system, which enabled the formation of conglomerates composed of many unrelated companies. Under this system, a small number of individuals controlled boards of directors and extracted hefty commissions regardless of profitability. But while managing agencies may have been useful in promoting enterprise in a capital-scarce market by acting as guarantors of trust for reluctant investors, they were also plagued by corruption and inefficiency. Tata made it a principle to charge commission only on profits rather than sales, eliminating one of the most perverse incentives.[10] Rather than standing for difference, Tata approximated the ideal type of the bureaucratized and rationalized managerial corporation—all the while serving as the most recognizable face of Indian capitalism.

This book will show how Tata's exceptional characteristics evolved gradually and contingently. It was not until the early 1930s that the group ceased to rely on a far-flung network of trading companies run by family members for financial and technical assistance. Around the same time, practices of scientific management imported from the West were introduced in the textile mills in Bombay and the steel town in Jamshedpur but never without compromises or countermeasures. Family and community ties remained important, often generating controversy when the financial reputation of the group was on the line, or when its philanthropy came under question in the Parsi (Indian Zoroastrian) community to which they belonged. The Tatas' ideas of ethical or socially responsible capitalism, common to many businesses in "emerging markets," were not organic outgrowths of traditional religious values and norms, nor natural responses to mass poverty and a weak state.[11] They were produced through unpredictable and intermittent flows of knowledge and expertise, as well as a conscious process of adaptation and experimentation.

Between the Nation and the World

When renowned Mexican poet and diplomat Octavio Paz visited India in 1951, the first sight that struck him was "the silhouette of the Taj Mahal Hotel, an enormous cake, a delirium of the fin-de-siècle Orient fallen like a gigantic bubble, not of soap but of stone, on Bombay's lap." This ornate hotel, located on the shores of the Arabian Sea in the heart of the preeminent colonial metropolis, was one of Jamsetji Tata's passion projects. Exemplifying the group's contradictory history, it served both as a symbol of nationalist self-assertion and a mark of openness to the wider world. It is often said that Jamsetji decided to build it because he had been denied entry into a British-owned hotel. The myth persists despite historians demonstrating that overt color bars were rare in Bombay and many Parsis had already opened smaller hotels before Tata. The other revealing myth about the Taj is that it was built facing away from the sea because the builders could not read the architect's plans sent from Paris. To Paz, the mistake seemed "a deliberate one that revealed an unconscious negation of Europe and the desire to confine the building forever in India. A symbolic gesture, much like that of [Spanish conquistador Hernán] Cortés burning the boats so that his men could not leave." In reality, the design was meant to maximize sea breezes and the entrance to the hotel changed location over time.[12] But the alluring myth persists and reinforces the notion of a rigid boundary between colonialism and nationalism, which could only be trespassed by mistake.

Tata maintained close ties with global markets while also fulfilling nationalist aspirations for the advancement of *swadeshi* (self-sufficiency) through industrialization. But like the rumored architectural plans for the Taj, its history has been lost in translation, falling victim to reductive analysis. One tendency has been to read Tata's position as "structurally induced" by its strategic relationship with the colonial state. In a spatially fragmented economy where regions were often more closely connected to distant markets than to each other, and where British managing agencies dealing in cash crops for export (jute, indigo, and tea) controlled the majority of capital, Indian business was left to develop in a few sectors with potentially more lucrative internal markets (cotton textiles, iron and steel).[13] To exploit these narrow openings, fledgling industrialists like the Tatas needed government support in the form of protective tariffs. Conversely, their subordination to foreign capital is said to have made them natural allies to nationalist movements.[14] Beyond India, the formation of large, diversified business groups on the "periphery" of the world economy is seen as a rational response to "institutional voids" and other constraints such as political instability, technology gaps, and underdeveloped markets.[15]

In such volatile environments, business groups ensured their survival by cultivating an almost symbiotic relationship with imperial and national states. For example, the Egyptian economy in the aftermath of British rule was dominated by "rival coalitions of investors," composed of interlocking agrarian, commercial, financial, and industrial elites. Conglomerates like the 'Abbud group had access to both the state and foreign capital in their entrepreneurial pursuits, but the main source of rents was always the state. A similar dynamic unfolded in Mandatory Palestine, where Arab businessmen responded flexibly to the rise of nationalism.[16] In Korea under Japanese imperial rule, large vertically integrated *chaebol* groups like the Koch'ang Kims combined trade, banking, and manufacturing. They owed their success to a shift in Japanese policy toward supporting indigenous industry in the early 1920s. The balance of power between the Kims and the Japanese imperial state was overwhelmingly tilted in favor of the latter.[17] In China under semicolonial conditions, textile entrepreneurs like the Song family were repeatedly forced to accommodate authoritarian and interventionist states, not always successfully.[18] In the long run, many of these groups fell victim to expropriation, decline, or marginalization accompanying political transitions.

Although not unique in occupying a liminal position between empire and nation, Tata also kept its distance from the state in both its colonial and postcolonial avatars. The group carved out a unique "niche" for itself by separating the economic and political dimensions of *swadeshi,* giving only tepid support to the Indian National Congress while proudly assuming the mantle of industrialization in the service of the nation-in-the-making. It enjoyed "the best of both worlds" until World War II and independence, when this niche began to disappear. Rivals like G. D. Birla, who had openly supported and financed the Congress during the years of the independence struggle, moved closer to the corridors of power in New Delhi. As the restrictive "License-Permit Raj" took shape, the Tatas found themselves excluded from planning decisions, their further expansion restricted. This was partly because the basic industries they had pioneered, from steel to chemicals to hydroelectric power, fell under the exclusive purview of the developmental state.[19] Yet, the group survived the transition to independence, held off the threat of nationalization, and maintained its position at the top of the corporate pyramid into the late 1970s, when the state laid down its regulatory weapons and embraced the private sector in a concerted push for growth.

This book argues that Tata was able to preserve and sustain a significant degree of autonomy over time due to three principal factors: transnational financial connections, first with East Asia and then with the United States; control over land, labor, and natural resources within India; and networks of scientific and technical expertise cultivated through strategic philanthropy. All three factors, in different ways, conferred upon the group certain attributes of sovereignty in the interstices of state power.

State and Corporation

The Empress Mills was Jamsetji Tata's first major industrial venture. It was located in the dusty town of Nagpur in central India, far away from the metropolis of Bombay and the glittering lights of the Taj Hotel. A visitor approaching the mills in 1930 captured the separation of economic and political *swadeshi* in the following rapturous description:

> Any stranger who happens to see the huge yellow walls on both sides of the Jumna Tank, the call chimneys, the heavy motor lorries & the adjoining bungalows, forms an opinion that the Empress Mills is a State. If he is more inquisitive and enquires further, he is led only to confirm his former opinion. Because, though it has no

freedom in the political sense, if you take into consideration the existence of the Mills for the past two generations & more, the thousands of workpeople, servants, peons employed there, the schools, dispensaries & model villages they have provided for their workpeople, you will find that it is not merely an industry, but has become a rich State by itself.[20]

Although not politically independent or legally sovereign, the textile mill was a state-in-miniature by virtue of the wealth it produced, the services it provided, and the social relations it engendered. Tata functioned both as a "surrogate state" laying the groundwork for future economic development by opening up of the interior of India to mineral extraction and industrial production, and a "state within a state" governing domains of its own in enclaves such as company towns and model villages.

The concept of the corporation as state or as "private empire" has been widely applied, from Robert Clive's East India Company in the eighteenth century to King Leopold's Congo Free State in the nineteenth century to Rex Tillerson's Exxon Mobil in the early twenty-first century. When shorn of context, it tends to obscure the specific legal and political conditions of possibility for the commodification of sovereignty.[21] States and corporations are locked in an agonistic relationship, "a kind of *doubling*, in which the fate of state sovereignty and corporate power are conjoined and also in conflict."[22] The challenge is to show how this relationship has been "doubled" differently across time and space. The modern state itself may be seen as one corporate form triumphant over others, which were reduced to the economic realm alone. The British East India Company (EIC), like its powerful Dutch counterpart and rival, had been a "body politic on its own terms," exemplifying a "hybrid" early modern form of sovereignty that became obsolete with the interlinked rise of the nation-state in Britain and the colonial state in India.[23] In literary theorist Gayatri Spivak's vivid formulation, the EIC grew into "a misshapen and monstrous state that, although by definition chartered by the state of Britain, burst the boundaries of the metropolitan or mother-state."[24] By the end of the nineteenth century, this was an anomaly whose time was thought to have passed.

What, then, did it mean for a corporation to become state-like just as the nation came into being? The colonial government that succeeded and superseded the EIC after 1858 produced a territorially bounded economy through a range of institutions and practices, including transportation and irrigation infrastructure, a reformed currency, and the standardization of accounting procedures. In turn, nationalists reinforced the "divide between an internal, national economic space enclosed within the borders of a state and a foreign, international economy that existed beyond state territories."[25] Both colonial officials and nationalists presumed that the integration of India's economic space would be undertaken by the state, not by private capital—still less so by one group above others. As M. G. Ranade, a prominent figure in the nationalist school of political economy, declared in 1892, "The State is now more and more recognized as the national organ for taking care of national needs."[26]

In this moment of realignment, Tata's "pattern of diversification went even beyond a simple logic of the firm to become the first attempt at some kind of systematic economic planning in the Indian context."[27] Tata furthered the incorporation of India as a territorial economic body through forms of material infrastructure (textile mills, steel plants, hydroelectric dams) and what I term knowledge infrastructure (universities, research centers, laboratories). These nation-building initiatives were only loosely connected with one another and evolved along largely separate paths. Taken together, they ensured that flows of private capital would come to govern entire fields of economic activity. Territorial closure, marked by "deglobalization" and the encasement of production and consumption within the borders of the nation-state, accompanied the internal expansion and consolidation of capitalist "social forms"—notably large, diversified, and relatively stable corporate groups like Tata.[28]

Law was a crucial mechanism behind this dynamic, undermining the unitary sovereignty of the state from within at every turn. The Land Acquisition Act (1894) and the Charitable Endowments Act (1890), two influential laws still on the books in India today, were originally meant to bolster the power and reach of the colonial state. They also allowed Tata to acquire vast swaths of land and establish philanthropic trusts through the codification and reproduction of exceptions. Tata's assumption of the trappings of sovereignty within a fluid and unstable legal matrix, rather than a vernacular "ethos" inherently incommensurable with abstract "market governance," underpinned its conflicts with both the colonial and the postcolonial state.[29]

Economic nationalism, expressed as *swadeshi* in India, domiciled and integrated "translocal" elites like the Tatas within the nation-state form.[30] This process, far from complete and always contested, formed a small part of what Austro-Hungarian economic thinker Karl Polanyi famously termed the "great transformation." Nineteenth-century globalization was anchored by bankers and high financiers who were "subject to no *one* government" and embodied a "metaphysical extraterritoriality."[31] With its disintegration, a different breed of capitalists bound by national borders was forced to play by a new and uncertain set of rules. The terms of engagement between state and capital remained open, in the interplay of extraterritorial finance and territorial nationalism, the dominion over land and labor, and the distribution of philanthropic gifts and the circulation of ideas. In India, as elsewhere, corporations like Tata mediate great transformations, putting a human face on the abstractions of capitalism, including the market, class, and property.[32] By fashioning themselves as sovereigns on par with the state, with workers, consumers, and citizens as their subjects, they leave open vital spaces of contestation and claims making.

A Note on Archives

During the Gilded Age in the United States, groundbreaking journalist Ida Tarbell set out to write one of the first in-depth investigations of a modern corporation, John D. Rockefeller's Standard Oil. It was then a new and timely subject for research, which she could justify simply by virtue of the sources available. Tarbell observed that "there is in existence just such documentary material for a history of the Standard Oil Company as there is for a history of the Civil War or the French Revolution, or any other national episode which has divided men's minds."[33] In our own time, the business history of India and South Asia has experienced a resurgence as part of a wider global interest in the history of capitalism in emerging markets. The opening of dedicated corporate archives allows for more fine-grained firm-level research, enriching a field long dominated by a select few private papers and traditional state archives in London and New Delhi.[34] Tata has left behind a longer paper trail than any other Indian business but has not yet been the subject of a comprehensive academic history.

This book is the first to mine the records of the Tata group, including internal correspondence, board minutes, account books, legal documents (wills and court cases), memoirs, newspapers, and advertisements. These records are held in two sites separated by more than a thousand miles: the Tata Central Archives (TCA) in Pune and the Tata Steel Archives (TSA) in Jamshedpur. The TCA is located on the leafy campus of the Tata Management Training Center in Pune's most upscale neighborhood. Unlike many state archives in India, its holdings are meticulously preserved and made accessible to researchers with minimal bureaucratic hassle. Since it opened to the public in 2001, TCA has acted as a source of best practices to other business groups in

FIG. I.I. Russi Mody Centre for Excellence, Jamshedpur, April 2014. © Mircea Raianu.

the process of creating their own in-house archives. By virtue of its location, TCA also doubles as a venue for inducting new Tata managers in the history, culture, and ethos of the group. However, the primary objective of establishing an archive in the first place was its "evidential value." The prestige and finances of the group were at stake if reliable documentation could not be produced in response to legal challenges that might arise.[35] The TSA in Jamshedpur is housed in the Russi Mody Center for Excellence, amid imposing Masonic pyramids and columns designed by famed Parsi architect Hafeez Contractor (Fig. I.I). It performs similar functions as the steel company's public face and a repository of useful evidence.

The independent researcher working in the Tata archives is little more than an interloper in a far-reaching web of knowledge and power. The archives would surely exist even if no outsider visited them. What, then, justifies their display of openness and transparency? Corporations reproduce their power and authority over time through the constant "reinvention of history and collective memory."[36] Archives embody a powerful impulse to present oneself to the public and to posterity, analogous to the way a state chooses to selectively open its bureaucratic records to citizens as a prerogative of sovereignty. Indeed, corporations that most closely resemble states keep "the most state-like archives."[37] In the Tata case, some key sources, including the personal papers of founder Jamsetji Tata and his sons, have been lost, destroyed, or deliberately concealed to preserve the group's reputation. The researcher must circumvent a strong "gatekeeper" effect and restrictions on access, analogous to states' invocation of secrecy powers.[38] However, Tata is somewhat exceptional even in obeying this logic. Other business families and groups in South Asia take an altogether different course, shielding their history completely from outsiders. The past is often a collective resource to be used by and for the community, not a public currency.[39] By recognizing some external claims to knowledge, the archives themselves further legitimize Tata as an institution of national and global standing.

Corporate "storytelling" extends beyond archives to related public-facing initiatives such as commissioned histories, popular books by journalists, and business school case studies using carefully curated sources. One approach to "hegemonic" archival sources is to read them "against the grain" to uncover "the accidents, crises, and failures that are inevitably part of a corporation's past."[40] Hagiographies of the Tata group proliferate in multiple genres, cementing a master narrative of the group as the bearer of an unbroken tradition of nation-building and socially responsible capitalism.[41] While remaining mindful of archival silences and erasures, my own approach has not been to counter this master narrative in the vein of an exposé. I have chosen to read the archives "along the grain" or on their own terms, as "condensed sites of epistemological and political anxiety rather than as skewed and biased sources."[42]

This is a history written in the conditional tense, registering what was tried and failed or what might have been, dead ends as well as successful resolutions. I reconstruct the conversations, deliberations, and decisions made by several categories of actors, paying close attention to "medium" thinkers: a layer of pragmatic knowledge brokers who seized upon and diffused certain ideas and practices within the group.[43] In the first half of the book, this role is played by B. J. Padshah, founder Jamsetji Tata's trusted right-hand man, whose imprint was felt on all aspects of the group's early history, from finance to labor relations and philanthropy. In the second half of the book, it belongs to Minoo Masani, an ex–trade unionist and politician turned adviser to the Tatas, whose activities encompassed public relations, management training, and consulting from the 1940s to the 1970s. A range of scientists and experts, from the physicist Homi J. Bhabha to the architect Otto Koenigsberger, and talented senior managers such as A. D. Shroff and Russi Mody, likewise traversed several domains within the group. Political leaders, including firebrand socialists like M. N. Roy and Jayaprakash (JP) Narayan, left their mark as allies or enemies. Workers at all levels, from trade union leadership to the shop floor, literally built Tata companies and townships. Their collective action and struggles for a more humane and equitable economic order decisively shaped the group's history by forcing it to live up to its stated ideals.

This is not an elite story of great leaders imposing their vision from above, nor a tale of subaltern resistance that looks up at the corporation from below, but an eye-level immersion in the "black box" of information exchange within the group.[44] My aim is to disaggregate Tata as a stable and unchanging entity, bringing attention to the many ways in which people "enact" corporations as "collective subjects" through everyday conflicts and decisions.[45] Throughout the book, my shorthand use of "Tata" or "the Tatas" should be read as metonymic of the combined actions of the many people who made and remade the corporation over time.

Structure and Outline

The book is divided into six chapters, along both chronological and thematic lines. The first part (chapters 1–3) spans the century before World War II, whereas the second part (chapters 4–6) covers the period from the late 1940s to the late 1970s. My choice of World War II rather than independence as the main temporal divide is deliberate. The war redefined the relationship between state and capital, exposing the limits of separating economic and political *swadeshi* as a viable long-term strategy. It also sparked a larger geopolitical struggle for influence in South Asia between Britain, the United States, and the Soviet Union, opening a new terrain of maneuver to Indian big business. Intensified war production and growing labor unrest accelerated the selective import of transnational expertise in industrial relations, urban planning, and social science. I have chosen to end in the late 1970s because the Emergency declared by Prime Minister Indira Gandhi brought the overt conflict between big business and the state to an abrupt end, sacrificing regulation on the altar of boosting productivity. The Emergency also broke apart the alliance between big business and oppositional socialist politics, paving the way for market reforms and reglobalization in the following decade. It is perhaps no coincidence that the Tata archives dry up considerably at this point.

Within each part, I stress two additional critical moments that anticipated these two major turning points. The first is the global economic crisis of 1920–1921, which contributed more than any other event to the orientation of Indian business toward internal markets and the decline of an earlier system of finance based on long-distance trade. On the ground in the steel town of Jamshedpur, the resulting economic contraction caused the first wave of strikes and the deployment of transnational expertise to address the labor problem. The second is India's foreign exchange crisis of 1957–1958, which tempered the hostility between big business and the postcolonial state and recast competing visions of capitalist and socialist development in a Cold War frame. This was also the year of the last direct challenge to the Tatas' control over Jamshedpur, in the shape of a Communist-led strike, and the beginning of a long period of relatively stable labor-management relations.

The six chapters may be read as mirrored pairings, corresponding to the three main strands of argument. Chapters 1 and 4 tell the political and economic story of Tata's expansion, with an emphasis on transnational financial connections with East Asia and the United States. Chapters 2 and 5, centered on Jamshedpur, explore shifting modes of corporate governance, from legal struggles to secure sovereign control over land to the interplay of paternalism and scientific management in labor control. Chapters 3 and 6 trace the institutionalization of philanthropy, the networks of expertise it generated, and its eventual mobilization against the state through the political language of "corporate social responsibility."

Chapter 1, "Becoming *Swadeshi*," explores the origins of the Tata group in the cotton and opium trades across the Indian Ocean in the mid-nineteenth century. Complicating narratives of a neat transition from mercantile and industrial capitalism, the chapter shows how the success of the textile and steel companies managed by Tata Sons, the main holding company in Bombay, depended on financial connections and overseas market access cultivated by two lesser-known trading companies, R. D. Tata & Co. in Shanghai and Hong Kong, and Tata Limited in London. The global crisis of the early 1920s, followed by the Great Depression, led to the sudden demise of these two companies and a sustained drive to capture domestic markets. In parallel, the group faced political pressures from Indian nationalists to resolve the contradiction between their *swadeshi* claims and reliance on foreign finance and technology. The crisis forced the sale of major assets to American and British concerns and enhanced the need for tariff protection from the colonial state. If Tata eventually became a "monopoly house" in a protected national economy, this was due to the contingent failure of an earlier strategy of expansion rather than a foregone conclusion.

Chapter 2, "Governing Land and Labor," describes the consequences of the group's turn to resource extraction in the interior of India. The first part focuses on the process of acquiring land for the Tata Iron and Steel Company (TISCO) plant. Between 1909 and 1919, the company secured private leases from local *zamindars* (landholders) while relying on the colonial Land Acquisition Act (1894) to secure absolute tenurial rights. In doing so, TISCO took on the functions of employer, landlord, and municipal government in the proprietary steel township of Jamshedpur, exercising a flexible but fragmentary form of corporate sovereignty challenged from above by the state and from below by workers and residents. The second part of the chapter outlines the evolution of labor control and welfare policy in TISCO through the work of visiting experts from the Department of Social Science and Administration at the London School of Economics. The company resisted expert recommendations for improving working conditions on the grounds of exceptionalism and difference, centered on the figure of the *adivasi* (aboriginal / tribal) worker. Following a series of violent strikes in the 1920s, Jamshedpur became a flashpoint for wider anxieties about integrating "primitive" labor in a "modern" industry.

Chapter 3, "Worlds of Philanthropy," follows the transition from local and community-based charity to cosmopolitan and nation-building projects. It argues that Tata philanthropy was distinct from but deeply connected to the group's vision of economic *swadeshi*. Founder Jamsetji Tata's interest in technological innovation inspired his decision to establish the Indian Institute of Science (IISc), India's first research university devoted to science and engineering. Protracted negotiations between Jamsetji's heirs and recalcitrant colonial officials over the endowment of the IISc were resolved by the application of the Charitable Endowments Act (1890). This outcome set the precedent for a "handover" pattern whereby institutions initially funded by Tata charitable trusts were brought under state control, but it did not alleviate tensions between corporate philanthropy and state sovereignty. The Tata Trusts became conduits for transnational flows of scientific expertise. The Tata Institute of Social Sciences (TISS) blended practical social work and social science research. Commitments to medical research for leukemia and radium therapy led to the creation of the Tata Institute of Fundamental Research (TIFR), cradle of India's atomic program. After independence, philanthropy was subordinated to the needs of group companies and competed more directly with the state in service provision.

Chapter 4, "National Capitalists, Global Wars," returns to the narrative of Chapter 1, beginning on the eve of World War II with the unresolved contradiction between the Tatas' economic nationalism and their reliance on foreign capital. The chapter tracks the shifting strategies of the Tatas in the context of declining British influence and growing Soviet-American competition, particularly the quest for private foreign investment as a counterweight to centralized state planning. This chapter argues for the importance of foreign capital as an overlooked "extraterritorial" dimension to the political economy of decolonizing India. Despite their fears about each other's designs on the subcontinent, British and American officials only took an interest in India's planned industrial development after the involvement of the Soviet Union. Soviet aid to public sector projects attracted American capital to India, which ended up strengthening the Tatas more than any other group. The chapter concludes with Tata's successful approach to the World Bank in 1957–1958 to finance the expansion of the steel plant at Jamshedpur as the cash-strapped Indian state suffered from a debilitating foreign exchange crisis.

Chapter 5, "Between Paternalism and Technocracy," rethinks the transition from paternalism as an ad hoc mode of labor control, influenced by ingrained beliefs about exceptionalism and difference, to scientific management as a more systematic and replicable set of interventions. In response to widespread labor unrest in the aftermath of World War II, TISCO once again sought guidance from foreign experts, including urban planners and industrial psychologists. At first, management established a personnel department to deal with workers directly, followed by a turn to collective bargaining with a docile company union. The inadequacy of these measures was brutally exposed in the last violent strike in the history of the company in 1958, but an unstable mixture of paternalism and technocracy subsequently achieved industrial peace in the long run. In parallel, information exchanges among group companies in the mid-1950s created a shared corporate ethos, which reflected the compromise between paternalism and managerialism in labor policy. The chapter concludes with a look at the Tatas' public relations efforts, focusing on artworks and photographs depicting the *adivasi* body at work in the Jamshedpur steel plant, which deliberately mirrored statist tropes of social progress through industry.

Chapter 6, "The Social Responsibilities of Business," connects the internal codification of ethics and values within the Tata group, discussed in the previous chapter, with the wider political mobilization of Indian business from the late 1950s to the late 1970s. Big business in this period was confronted with the rise of bureaucratic planning, a restrictive licensing system to curb monopoly power, and the occasional threat of nationalization. The Tatas responded by drawing on a disparate set of ideas, including Mohandas K. Gandhi's concept of "trusteeship," democratic socialism, and free-market liberalism, to enhance their legitimacy. The key figures who made this intellectual convergence possible were the Gandhian leader JP Narayan and his friend Minoo Masani, a close adviser to the Tatas. This chapter follows a series of initiatives spearheaded by JP and Masani, which defined the practice of corporate social responsibility (CSR) in India as a set of voluntary codes and commitments. Tata broke from the Gandhians by the time of the Emergency in 1975–1977, preferring to sponsor concrete local projects such as model villages and slum resettlement schemes and embracing the state's authoritarian productivity drive.

A brief epilogue follows each of the three major strands of argument into the aftermath of the economic reforms of 1991, when Indian capitalism began to trespass the borders of the nation-state once more. It shows how the unraveling of the postwar status quo revived older conflicts over the risks of overseas expansion, the extent of corporate sovereignty over land and labor, and the responsibilities of companies to local, regional, and national communities.

1

Becoming *Swadeshi*

Early in 1864, a young Parsi merchant from Bombay named Jamsetji Nusserwanji Tata set sail for England, carrying a set of bills of exchange backed by a consignment of Indian cotton. By the time the ship docked in Liverpool, the price of cotton had fallen so quickly that the bills became worthless. Unexpectedly forced to manage the liquidation of his father's firm, Jamsetji took time to observe the workings of the textile mills in Lancashire, the heartland of the Industrial Revolution. When he returned to India a few months later, he found Bombay in the grip of a disastrous financial crisis. The whole of the city, Jamsetji's first biographer later recalled, "was sitting on the stool of repentance, with sackcloth and ashes; while the disconsolate creditors held *Dharma* at the door of their ruined debtors."[1] Out of this chastening experience arose India's own Industrial Revolution, more modest and limited in scope than its British counterpart but all the more impressive for the constraints it had to overcome.

The outbreak of the Civil War in the United States in 1861 launched a speculative frenzy among Indian merchants eager to supply Britain's cotton needs following the naval blockade of the American South. As the tide turned in favor of the Union around 1864 and shipments resumed, the ensuing price collapse devastated not only Bombay but also Liverpool, Egypt, and other farflung outposts of the global "empire of cotton."[2] In response, many Parsi and Gujarati merchants diversified into manufacture. Within two decades, the skyline of Bombay was dotted with the smokestacks of cotton mills owned and operated by Indians. Few as they were in number, India's industrialists emerged from the colonial port city, posing a challenge to long-standing Eurocentric assumptions about the origins of modern capitalism. Max Weber's *General Economic History* (1923) firmly held that "capitalism in the west was born in the industrial cities of the interior, not in the cities which were centers of sea trade." Parsis typified the religious minority exempt from ritual restrictions of caste and guild systems, much like European Jews. But they were not yet ready to make the full leap from commerce to the rational organization of production Weber regarded as fundamental to modern capitalism.[3]

No single figure was more closely identified with that leap than Jamsetji Tata. Building on substantial but fickle fortunes made in the cotton and opium trades, his firm led the way in the industrialization of India: first in textiles, then in more capital-intensive and technologically complex sectors such as iron and steel and hydroelectric power. Contemporary admirers saw him as embodying the spirit of *swadeshi* or self-sufficiency "long before Swadeshism was boomed in Bengal" as a self-consciously nationalist movement at the turn of the twentieth century.[4] Instead of boycotts and bonfires of imported cloth, hallmarks of the movement, Jamsetji Tata struck a blow for India's freedom through sheer entrepreneurial ambition. Yet in many ways, he was an imperfect standard-bearer for the nationalist cause.

What did it mean to be *swadeshi* in late colonial India? The term encompassed multiple meanings, holding together the economic and the political in uneasy tension. The most ostensibly modern section of Indian big business, led by the Tata family, turned out to be the least overtly nationalist. Their attitude to the major campaigns led by the Indian National Congress in the 1920s and 1930s, which involved the mass mobilization of workers and peasants, swung between cautious engagement and open hostility.[5] Economically, being *swadeshi* meant producing goods for home consumption and, as far as possible, training Indian technical staff to assume responsibilities previously held by foreigners. The Tatas made slow progress on this count, employing American, British, and other European professional managers to a greater extent than their rivals. The markets for their products, from cotton cloth to pig iron and finished steel, were truly global. A clear shift toward domestic markets did not take place until the mid-1930s, when Tata joined other big business houses in pursuing a rapprochement with the Indian National Congress and acting in concert against foreign business interests. In the wake of another unexpected financial crisis, they adopted a new strategy of internal consolidation at the expense of maintaining financial and trading connections beyond India's shores. Tata became *swadeshi* belatedly and contingently, not as a foregone conclusion.

The Tatas' ambivalence toward nationalism may be explained by the technical complexity and high capital requirements of their pioneering ventures, which required a broader outlook from the start. Nationalist *swadeshi* rhetoric, which drew increasingly strict boundaries between the nation and the world, has obscured the persistence of commercial and financial connections beyond the British Empire, particularly with China, Japan, and the United States.

Historians have focused their attention on shifts in tariff policy in London and Delhi, or on different factional business associations in Bombay and Calcutta and their relationship with expatriate British managing agencies.[6] The impact of other players who forged global connections, such as trading companies, Marwari intermediaries, and foreign technical experts, has been neglected or imperfectly glimpsed.

The post–Civil War crash and the transition to industry in the late 1860s halted Tata's involvement in trade only temporarily. Two little-known subsidiary companies, R. D. Tata & Co. in Shanghai, Kobe, and Paris, and Tata Limited in London, made possible the firm's expansion and diversification. Legally separate from the parent firm in Bombay and acting in a semiautonomous capacity, these companies facilitated the export of cotton and pig iron, remitted profits, and helped finance large, capital-hungry enterprises in India such as the iron and steel plant and the hydroelectric power companies. Maintaining a widely dispersed network of agents and go-betweens, many of them family members, enabled Tata to overcome the constraints of a colonial economy even as it increased exposure to volatile global markets. Vulnerable to speculation and fraud, Tata & Co. and Tata Limited were ultimately costly failures, which restricted the scope of the parent firm's activities beyond India.[7]

Since Tata and other urban capitalists could never establish full control over the movement of goods "from field to factory or port," they depended on Marwari intermediaries to connect them with inland markets.[8] Shrewd merchants and bankers originating in the deserts of Rajasthan, Marwaris controlled key entrepôts throughout central and northern India and grew rich through complex futures trading in commodities. Colonial officials and business rivals alike regarded them with suspicion. Marwaris' secretive, familybased business culture was seen as governed by custom rather than law, thereby distorting "true" market practices.[9] Yet, even firms organized on the joint-stock principle and trading on the nascent Bombay share market resorted "to the bazaar and to social networks" when necessary, frequently engaging in speculative behavior.[10] Behind the scenes, Marwaris permeated the Tata organization as selling agents, partners, and shareholders. Their importance only came to light during moments of financial crisis, when account books were thrown open and reckonings had to be made. As Tata sought to cultivate a reputation for fiscal probity and capture internal markets for themselves, Marwari intermediaries were gradually displaced.

The final piece of the puzzle of Tata's remarkable rise to prominence was a continual recourse to American expertise and technology. Early nationalists pursued closer relationships between fledgling Indian enterprises and the United States as a means of countering British domination. From World War I to the Great Depression, the American connection allowed the Tatas to circumvent restrictive colonial state policies and save troubled companies from mismanagement and bankruptcy. In turn, Tata served as a key point of entry for American influence in India, which grew more intense during World War II as independence neared. But India was not brought into the fold of an informal "American technological empire" without resistance.[11] Political controversies swirling around the Tatas' reliance on foreign capital and expertise exposed the contradictions between lofty *swadeshi* aspirations and the harsh constraints of industrialization in a colonial setting.

Houses on the Sand

The origins of the Tata fortune are shrouded in myth and rumor, particularly in relation to the opium trade. Jamsetji Tata, born in 1839, belonged to a Parsi priestly family from the small town of Navsari in Gujarat. His grandfather was the first member of the family to move to Bombay, where he served as a minor revenue clerk for an *inamdar* (permanent revenue holder) on the island of Salsette and ran a small shop on Bazargate Street in the Fort area.[12] It was his father, Nusserwanji, who first took to business on a larger scale. During the British occupation of the Persian Gulf port of Bushire in early 1857, which incurred "extraordinary" expenses for troops and ships sent from India, Nusserwanji made a handsome profit as a contractor.[13] Young Jamsetji was brought into his father's firm soon after, gaining valuable knowledge of the China trade. Nusserwanji opened branches in Hong Kong and Shanghai, importing Indian cotton and opium and exporting Chinese tea, silk, and gold.[14]

Parsi merchants like the Tatas owed their success in the China trade to their inheritance of the "maritime tradition" of the Indian Ocean, "connecting Aden with Canton in their own ships."[15] As the East India Company consolidated its hold over the subcontinent in the late eighteenth century, overseas traders displaced the typical "portfolio capitalist," whose wealth was derived mainly from revenue farming and the mobilization of military resources on land.[16] Enterprising Parsis, as master shipbuilders on the western coast of India, readily took advantage of the new commercial environment to assemble a different kind of portfolio. Through the consignment system, they formed lucrative partnerships with British firms, shipping opium and cotton from the

Indian interior to China. The most prominent Indian merchant of his time, Jamsetjee Jeejeebhoy, worked closely with the British agency house of Jardine Matheson & Co. None had moral qualms about what was, in essence, state-sanctioned drug trafficking. The nature of the commodity had no bearing on prevailing "gentlemanly capitalist" ideals.[17]

Such close partnerships became more unequal over time, as Indian merchants depended on bills of exchange issued in London to remit their profits. By the time the Opium War broke out in 1839, the year of Jamsetji Tata's birth, British firms increasingly dominated the China trade.[18] The Parsis' middleman role was also eroded by the advance of the railway, steamship, and electric telegraph, which made communication with the Indian interior easier and enabled the rise of new intermediaries like the Marwaris.[19] Parsis had at their disposal various strategies to safeguard their position. Kinship networks helped to restore credit and ensure the survival of firms in difficult times. It might even be possible to speak of a single "loosely organized Parsi company at work" in mid-nineteenth-century Bombay.[20] Sending agents and family members abroad helped reduce dependence on London bills and solved the problem of remittances that had plagued Jeejeebhoy's generation.[21] Nonetheless, the risks of long-distance trade remained serious. When global cotton prices came crashing down at the end of the Civil War, just as young Jamsetji was on his way to England, few in Bombay would be spared the consequences.

One of the earliest extant archival records of Tata's business dealings affords a unique glimpse into the intricacies of the China trade. This was a suit filed in the Court of Chancery in London in 1865, brought by Nusserwanji and Jamsetji Tata alongside five other Indian merchants of Shanghai, Hong Kong, and Bombay against the London firms of Springfield, Son & Nephew and Lindsay & Co. The plaintiffs alleged that they had drawn two bills of exchange, worth £10,000 in total, for delivery of 605 bales of cotton on the ship *Lalla Rookh* to Springfield, with Lindsay as an intermediary. The consignment was never made, "the cotton market having begun to decline," whereupon the plaintiffs requested Lindsay to remit the balance of £4,496 to Springfield. After Lindsay went out of business and "suspended payment," Springfield refused to abide by the original agreement and threatened "to endorse, part with, or dispose of the said Bill of Exchange . . . for value to some other persons or person, and to apply the proceeds thereof to their own use." This left Nusserwanji Tata liable for the full amount to the Bank of Hindustan, China, and Japan, Limited.[22] The only non-Parsi merchant listed among the plaintiffs was a Marwari, Cheniram Jesraj, who served as the Tatas' opium broker and whose firm would later hold the selling agency for the Tata textile mills.[23]

The outcome of the case is not known, but it reveals the fragility of trust in a volatile market and the lack of transparent and reliable mechanisms of financing. Keen observer of Indian affairs Karl Marx described bills of exchange as a form of "fictitious capital," their rise and fall in value wildly disconnected from the assets they backed.[24] In moments of crisis, the global trading system made possible by the circulation of bills of exchange was exposed as fundamentally speculative, no matter the actors involved. The collapse of British firms in China affected even those Indian merchants who were responsibly trying to honor their commitments. Closer to home, one of the partners in Nusserwanji's firm was the ambitious Jain broker Premchand Roychand, who channeled profits from the cotton boom into real estate, especially land reclamation. By virtue of his control of the Bank of Bombay, Premchand stood at the center of a web of speculation. The failure of his bank reverberated through both the Indian and British business communities in the city, leading to the temporary exit of the Tatas from the China trade.[25] Premchand's spectacular rise and fall was later reduced to a cautionary tale of thwarted ambition, overshadowing deeper structural forces at work.[26]

The Tatas could have been just another casualty of the crash, never to be heard from again, if not for another fortuitous military commission. Nusserwanji Tata won a contract worth Rs. 40 lakhs to supply Sir Robert Napier's expeditionary force, deployed from British India against the ruler of Abyssinia in 1868.[27] Napier's campaign was both a military success and a logistical disaster. Total costs ran up to £8 million (more than double the original estimate), of which £5.5 million were spent in India. The army overpaid for everything from mules and camels to coal and rice. A House of Commons committee appointed to investigate the matter found that Indian merchants swiftly cornered the market and raised prices "within 10 minutes" after the Bombay government finalized the list of necessary supplies.[28] Anti-corporate activists in India today often invoke the opium trade to unmask the Tatas as colonial collaborators and undermine their claims to nationalism. Critical scholars point to the absence of records dealing with the opium trade from the Tata archives as a smoking gun.[29] However, the real scandal at the root of the Tata fortune, recognized as such by contemporaries, was insider trading and corruption in a nineteenth-century version of the military-industrial complex, revealing the nexus of Indian capital and imperial power.

Nusserwanji swiftly rebuilt his firm, opening a branch in Hong Kong with the assistance of his brother-in-law Dadabhai, who had remained active in the opium trade. This partnership came to be known as Tata & Co. Upon Dadabhai's death in 1876, Nusserwanji and Jamsetji withdrew from the company, but the father rejoined in 1880 against the son's wishes. Jamsetji thought the China branch was "too remote for efficient supervision," turning his attention to opening several textile mills in India. It was only in 1883, when Dadabhai's son Ratanji Dadabhoy (R. D.) took over, that Tata & Co. was put on a sound footing.[30] R. D. continued to trade in opium, petitioning against regulations proposed by the Hong Kong Legislative Council in 1887 along with six other Parsi and Jewish merchants.[31] The two sides of the family were brought closer together upon the formation of Tata & Sons as a managing agency controlling the mills in 1887, with R. D. and Jamsetji's two sons Dorabji and Ratanji as partners (Fig. 1.1). Tata & Sons, while legally distinct from Tata & Co., was deeply connected to its trading counterpart by more than blood. The success of Jamsetji's mills in India depended on finding new markets for the export of cotton, bypassing the colonial state's restrictive tariff policies and the monopoly of British shipping.

Tata's much-heralded transition to manufacturing in the late nineteenth century was shaped by global forces transcending the territorial boundaries of British India, even as it prefigured a long-term shift away from oceanic trade. The Empress Mills, opened by Jamsetji in 1877 (the year of Queen Victoria's coronation), was located at Nagpur in the Central Provinces, hundreds of miles from Bombay but closer to the fields where cotton was grown. This was a truly pioneering decision that set Jamsetji apart from his rivals, who remained clustered in the major coastal cities.[32] Yet, it also entailed an equally significant outward-facing move, as Jamsetji sought to challenge British domination of the Indian market by playing imperial powers against each other. He first looked to build in the French enclave of Pondicherry, with a view to capture colonial markets in West Africa. As late as 1899, he submitted a memorandum to the French minister of colonies proposing a similar arrangement at Mahé on the Kerala coast.[33] Nothing came of these plans. Instead, Jamsetji opened his next mill in Bombay in 1886, where he aimed to produce cloth for export to China. He chose to name it the Swadeshi to follow the prevailing political winds (the Indian National Congress had been founded the year before). But it was clear that any self-styled *swadeshi* enterprise needed to expand globally. The new mill failed to make a dent in China at first, as

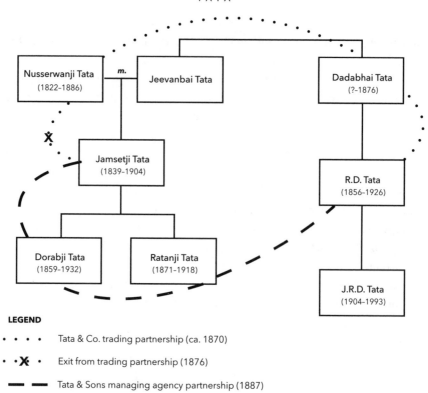

LEGEND

• • • • Tata & Co. trading partnership (ca. 1870)

• • ✘ • Exit from trading partnership (1876)

▬ ▬ Tata & Sons managing agency partnership (1887)

FIG. 1.1. Simplified Tata family tree showing evolution of trading and agency partnerships, ca. 1870–1887. Mircea Raianu, "Trade, Finance, and Industry in the Development of Indian Capitalism: The Case of Tata," *Business History Review* 94, no. 3: figure 1. Used by permission.

sales lagged and customers complained of the low quality of the cloth. Jamsetji's agents in the Middle East found a solution by procuring finer varieties of cotton from Egypt. Without them, the Swadeshi would likely not have survived.[34]

Tata was now on a collision course with the colonial government, which imposed tariffs to preserve India as a captive market for Lancashire textiles. In 1894, Tata & Sons lodged a protest against the imposition of higher excise duties on finer yarn (40s. count and above), which they decried as "a fatal blow" to the development of a manufacturing process "still in its experimental stage." India needed to produce competitive export-quality cloth, all the more urgent since "China itself has entered the lists as a producing instead of being merely a consuming country, and Japan still more so."[35] Bombay millowners wished to seize these markets before it was too late, deploying the resources and contacts of their affiliated trading companies to challenge Britain's monopoly of the high seas in Asia.

In the absence of a direct shipping route between to Japan, Indian merchants were forced to contend with a cartel led by the British Peninsular and Oriental Steam Navigation Company (P&O), which controlled the route via Hong Kong, charging high fixed prices and setting a maximum limit of bales per month that could be transported. Seizing the opportunity to simultaneously reduce the transaction costs for his mills and strike a blow for India's commercial and strategic autonomy, Jamsetji Tata boldly proposed a new shipping line as a joint venture between his firm and the Nippon Yusen Kaisha (NYK) in 1893. Tata & Co., which had opened an office in Kobe two years earlier, assisted in the negotiations for lower rates and a minimum quantity of freight.[36] "If we secure," Jamsetji wrote, "anything like a hundred thousand bales of cotton, and, say, about two thousand chests of opium, it will be greatly to the advantage of our trade, to excite our opponents to lower their rates as low as possible."[37] The mention of opium is significant because the P&O had reserved the exclusive right to ship the drug, which made up the largest share of its profits. It also highlights the complementarity of collaborationist or "comprador" trade and nationalist industry, categories that made little sense in the interconnected system of nineteenth-century globalization.

The new Tata Line was short lived, undercut by a ruthless price war with the P&O (referred to by Jamsetji as the "war of freights") and by the hostility of the British government. His fellow Bombay millowners "deserted" Jamsetji in his hour of need, following the appearance of anonymous letters in the press condemning the arrangement.[38] One of the gravest charges, strongly refuted by Tata & Sons in the pages of the *Indian Textile Journal*, was that the line "had been started from interested motives," namely to give Tata & Co. preferential treatment in the cotton trade. The relationship between the two companies had to be thoroughly disavowed:

> Capital has been made of the resemblance between the titles of the two firms coupled with the fact that one partner of our firm [R. D.] is also partner in Messrs. Tata & Co. Beyond this, there is or has been no connection whatever between these two firms, whose line of business is entirely distinct. . . . It is not contended that we are putting Messrs. Tata & Co. on especially favorable terms as compared with other shippers.[39]

Given R. D.'s active role in securing the agreement with NYK, this line of defense was not very convincing. Tata & Co.'s presence in China and Japan had been a key asset in the race for new markets, but it ended up threatening the security and credibility of Tata & Sons in Bombay.

The episodes recounted here in the guise of an origin story—the military commissions in Bushire and Abyssinia, the devastating post–Civil War crash, and the failed shipping line linking Kobe and Bombay—point to a consistent underlying extraterritoriality in the Tatas' expansion. If their history is told from this perspective, abandoning *swadeshi* industry as the inevitable end point, a slightly altered picture emerges. At the "high noon" of the British Raj, Indian businessmen succeeded in the first instance not by inscribing themselves within the anticipated economic boundaries of a territorial nation-state but by aggressively going global. Financial connections with distant markets would play a crucial role even in the Tatas' most celebrated nationalist projects, the iron and steel plant and the hydroelectric power companies.

Financing Dreams

Toward the end of his life, Jamsetji Tata devoted his energies to realizing two long-standing dreams: generating hydroelectric power for the Bombay mills and building India's first integrated iron and steel plant. Jamsetji saw an opening for indigenous enterprise to take the lead in harnessing the subcontinent's rich mineral resources. For nationalists, there was no clearer example of the perverse incentives of colonial political economy, which kept India poor in the name of comparative advantage in exporting primary commodities. As Mahadev Govind Ranade put it in the landmark *Essays on Indian Economics* (1899), "nothing strikes the stranger who studies Indian economy so much as the contrast between the bounty of Nature and the poverty of man in the matter of this iron industry." The colonial state's failure to encourage domestic production to supply the railways was a "golden opportunity" passed up at the behest of British manufacturers.[40] Beginning in the early 1880s with the viceroyalty of Lord Ripon, officials took half-hearted and piecemeal steps to reduce dependence on steel imports. But the interests of British India and the Empire at large appeared contradictory, resulting in policy paralysis.[41] Some economic historians point to unfavorable "conditions of factor markets," such as the high cost of fuel and transportation, as the primary reason why the iron and steel industry never took off.[42] Overcoming these political and economic constraints required an extraordinary entrepreneurial effort.

A keen supporter of the Indian National Congress, particularly its Liberal Bombay wing led by Ranade, Pherozeshah Mehta, and Dadabhai Naoroji, Tata shared its overarching commitment to industrialization as a way of stemming the "drain" of wealth from India.[43] He took Japan, where the new Imperial Iron and Steel Works at Yawata had opened with much fanfare in 1901, as a model for how a poor Asian country could develop rapidly.[44] Naoroji, a fellow Parsi and chief exponent of the drain theory, was more circumspect. He warned Jamsetji that "any comparison of India with Japan in any economic matter or for enterprise, trade etc. is unjust to India. India is being bled. It has no resources."[45] Political self-determination was the essential precondition to economic self-sufficiency. Ranade's *Essays* likewise could only envision the state ("the largest consumer, and the largest capitalist and manufacturer in the country") as the sole driver of industrialization within a bounded national economic space.[46] However, in keeping with the paradoxically globalizing nature of *swadeshi*, Jamsetji recognized that capital and technical expertise for such a complex venture could only come from abroad.

Indian business in the colonial period faced a "serious scarcity of long-term capital" due to the limitations of the formal stock exchange and banking system.[47] Unsurprisingly, Jamsetji and his sons looked to the London money market at first. Naoroji disapproved, telling Jamsetji that it was "a matter of grief that you should become the instrument of enabling foreigners to carry away the natural wealth of India." He instead proposed an alternative, asking if it was possible to "raise the million you want from the Indian Princes."[48] In response, Jamsetji declared himself "anxious and willing to utilize Indian capital" and asked Naoroji to "recommend any chiefs and princes" who might be interested in purchasing shares of the new company. But in order to follow "strictly commercial principles," he steadfastly refused to borrow in India "at a higher rate . . . than in Europe or America."[49] At this juncture, a sound and profitable *swadeshi* scheme of this size and complexity necessarily required looking abroad for finance. The economic and political meanings of the term were in conflict.

The rulers of the princely states were unlikely backers. Left in quasi-sovereign control of vast areas of land by the British, mainly in the less economically developed interior, they lived comfortably on agricultural rents and had not demonstrated much interest in industrialization thus far. But in their very "political separateness," they offered potentially lucrative untapped markets and resources for Indian business.[50] Appealing to the princes played multiple sovereign powers against each other, as Tata had done with the Pondicherry mill and the NYK shipping line.[51] When the Tata Iron and Steel Company (TISCO) was publicly floated in 1907, just as the *swadeshi* movement in Bengal was coming to an end and nationalist passions were running high, it received an enthusiastic response. All eight thousand original shareholders were Indians, but ownership was highly concentrated, with 13 percent of the share capital in 1911 held by the rulers of fifteen princely states. The entire first debenture issue of £400,000 was subscribed by Maharaja Scindia of Gwalior, while the *diwan* of Bhavnagar State, Prabhashankar D. Pattani, sat on the company's board of directors.[52] The rest was in the hands of a small circle of Bombay millowners seeking alternative investment opportunities during a slump in the Chinese cotton market.[53] This outcome has been interpreted either as an unambiguous triumph of the *swadeshi* spirit or as a cynical ploy to exploit a favorable political climate.[54] The extraterritorial dimension, particularly Tata's failure to attract support in the City of London, has been overlooked.

Recognizing that investment markets were interconnected, Tata never offered "discriminating terms" because "Indian capital would find profit in subscribing with a view to immediate selling out in England."[55] But London financiers showed no interest in the proposition, a stance commonly attributed to racial prejudice or commercial narrow-mindedness.[56] A more immediate obstacle was their reluctance to invest in India and preference for China, Latin America, and other areas of Britain's informal empire.[57] As R. D. Tata, assisting in the negotiations from the offices of Tata & Co. in Paris, ruefully complained, "Show me one instance where a capital of the magnitude we want was invested in India by English financiers for industrial and mining enterprises and I will show dozens of instances in which they invested in wild goose schemes in all parts of the world."[58] The conflict that mattered was not along racial lines but one between metropolitan capital and the colonial state. R. D. was informed by contacts in London that "Rothschild [and others] will have nothing to do with a country whose Government will not allow them to make money."[59] Above all, prospective British partners feared competition with Tata & Co. in East Asia. R. D. was advised to use his influence in Japan in hopes that "a Chinese concern supported by Tata and worked through Japs, would be hospitably received by the London money-market," but to no avail.[60]

The colonial government did eventually throw its weight behind Tata but for its own strategic reasons and in a characteristically hesitant and limited manner. The viceregal administrations of Curzon and Minto and the India

Office under Secretary of State George Hamilton had grown alarmed by a flood of steel imports from Germany, Belgium, and the United States. Jamsetji Tata skillfully deployed arguments against laissez-faire orthodoxy to press his case. In 1901, calling attention to the formation of J. P. Morgan's US Steel cartel, he warned that it was "impossible to withstand the blow aimed by this American Combination at the Free British Trade unless Great Britain in her own interests adopt the American policy of protective tariffs."[61] TISCO obtained major concessions, including a reduction in railway freight and a guaranteed order of 20,000 tons of rails.[62] However, the government refused to allow Sir Thomas Holland, director of the Geological Survey of India, to formally advise the company. As one official wrote, Tata "desired to emphasize publicly the good feeling of the Government," but "the gratification of such a desire, if it exists, is the very thing we should specially avoid."[63]

Neither the impetus of *swadeshi* nationalism nor the fortuitous shift in colonial state policy fully explains the emergence of TISCO. They must be considered together in a global context. The fate of the new company depended on the export of pig iron to East and Southeast Asia even more than on securing guaranteed orders for finished steel.[64] Due to low input costs for coal and iron ore, TISCO was much more competitive in pig iron, rapidly becoming the world's cheapest producer.[65] In its formative years, the company deliberately set out "to avoid coming in violent conflict with foreign imports" and "to distribute a variety of our goods widely in markets overseas." The shipping arm of the Mitsui *zaibatsu*, the Mitsui Bussan Kaisha, was granted a monopoly on foreign sales of pig iron up to 1913, with Tata & Co. facilitating the deal.[66] Three years later, TISCO management decided that Mitsui was making disproportionately large profits and moved to appoint a salesman of their own "attached to the Tata firms in the East," who would "push on the sales of the company's pig in China, Japan and other countries."[67] The establishment of a *swadeshi* industry entailed an expansion in overseas financial and commercial ties, in turn enhancing the importance of the trading companies.

Realizing Jamsetji Tata's other great dream, the generation of hydroelectric power, set in motion a similar process. Much like the Empress Mills and TISCO, this venture sought to open new resource frontiers in the hinterlands of the colonial port cities. Jamsetji proposed damming a valley at Lonavla in the Western Ghats, "to run the Tramways of Bombay, to supply as much electric lighting as may be required in Bombay, and to have a balance over for the supply of power in a few cotton mills, and sufficient for small local industries."[68] Electricity grids in colonial India at the turn of the century were rudimentary and fragmented, unlike the unified and heavily subsidized railway network. A few multinationals, including the American General Electric (GE) and the German AEG, and around ten small British engineering firms operated power stations in the major cities at low capacity (ranging from 1,000 to 3,000 kW).[69] Jamsetji's proposal to generate over 30,000 kW addressed an unmet need from the textile mills. But in an echo of the "war of freights," he encountered apathy among his fellow millowners and stiff resistance from the Bombay Electricity and Supply Company (BEST), which held a license to run the tramways and provide residential and street lighting in the city. The two companies came to an agreement at the end of 1906, whereby BEST would purchase electricity at low fixed prices from Tata and hold a monopoly on distribution to consumers below 225 kW.[70] Bombay's fragmented electricity grid evolved as a "series of nodes" disconnected from each other and the surrounding countryside.[71]

The Tata hydroelectric concerns also struggled to raise the required capital of £1.5 million. A "syndicate" of expert consultants was formed for this purpose, including Robert Miller, an influential promoter who had previously floated lighting concessions for Delhi and Lahore on the London market, and Alfred Dickinson, an engineer who had designed the tramways of Birmingham, Cape Town, Hong Kong, and Singapore.[72] One of the syndicate's first steps was to try to persuade the gaekwad of Baroda to join. Already subscribed to the steel company, the gaekwad was reluctant to spread himself too thin and take on an additional burden.[73] Princely backing was pursued in tandem with a broader appeal to foreign financiers, especially in the United States. At the very same moment as TISCO turned away from London to the Bombay market, the panic of 1907 put New York out of reach for the syndicate. Because "negotiations in the one country would necessarily interfere with the negotiations in the other," the Tata Hydro-Electric Company was floated with exclusively Indian capital.[74] Its shareholder profile resembled that of TISCO, boasting an impressive roll call of Indian princes. Subscriptions included "40 lacs of rupees from Gwalior; 10 lacs from Baroda; 12 lacs from Mysore . . . and 20 lacs from Bhavnagar."[75]

The princes, including the reluctant gaekwad, had finally come forward in response to an appeal by the governor of Bombay, George Clarke, who let it be known that "it was a pity Indian investors did not do their best to help a really Swadeshi Scheme." Clarke, a former military engineer, supported the project for both personal and political reasons. He told Dorabji Tata that "he knew what London City financiers were" and wished to help him get "out of the hands" of the syndicate. The undercurrent of antipathy between the colonial state and metropolitan finance remained strong. As Dorabji saw it, the company's "flotation was assured chiefly through the interest the Governor took in it." The princes' involvement had the added benefit of proving "they were loyal and believed in the stability of the British Government" in a tense political climate, as the *swadeshi* movement in Bengal came to an end and the Morley-Minto constitutional reforms were introduced.[76] Princely rulers' financial reserves offered an escape valve to both Indian capitalists and beleaguered colonial officials.

The government's priorities had shifted gradually, if not to outright support of industrialization, then at the very least toward selectively co-opting *swadeshi* rhetoric for their own ends. A few years later, Clarke's successor Willingdon insisted that Tata Hydro was "really an Imperial venture" accomplished through "co-operation and joint efforts of Indians and English." The initiative and capital had come from the Indian side, easily surpassing in a few years the combined efforts of British firms to promote electrification over the preceding two decades. Yet, British and American contractors were responsible for the majority of the works.[77] The same was true of TISCO and the steel industry. No *swadeshi* enterprise could ever remain detached from the wider worlds of empire and global finance. The interests of Tata, the colonial state, and the princes would not have aligned without the initial failure of the steel and hydroelectric companies to secure financial backing in London and New York, a failure largely extrinsic to both Tata's ambitions and shifts in state policy.

"As the Romans Did"

After Jamsetji Tata's death in 1904, his sons Dorabji and Ratanji and cousin R. D. were faced with a series of momentous decisions about how best to carry on his legacy. The firm now managed a far more diverse portfolio than in its early days, necessitating a thorough reorganization. In family and business matters alike, their guide was B. J. Padshah, Jamsetji's right-hand man and trusted adviser. Padshah was a brilliant polymath, an ex-college vice principal who dabbled in mathematics and Theosophy.[78] The family was caught between Dorabji's conservative instincts and R. D.'s ambitious plans for expansion, with Padshah as the mediator. Putting the steel and hydroelectric companies on a sound footing required sustaining connections with global markets without endangering the parent firm's reputation and credit.

The relationship between the trading and industrial branches quickly grew strained under the weight of these competing imperatives. R. D. argued that Tata & Co. should obtain TISCO's selling agency in Calcutta, whereas Dorabji viewed this linkage as a source of unnecessary risk.[79] Padshah informed R. D. that "the general policy is one of curtailment in all departments . . . on the chief ground that the brothers wish to feel that they are not burdened with too much responsibility." Padshah found a creative solution to bring their interests together:

> Tata & Sons live on Mill commissions; there is not much room for new partners there; I, therefore, revert to an idea which I have encountered in several minds since the death of Jamshedji—the amalgamation of Tata & Co. & Tata & Sons, under the style of Tata, Sons & Co. (The word Sons will largely add to the goodwill of the firm. The Marwaree seems an incongruous element in such a firm).[80]

It is telling that Tata & Co.'s Marwari agents, who had played such a vital role in the China trade, would be excluded from the new firm on the grounds of respectability. In the tight-knit Bombay business community, with a formal share market still in its infancy, capital flows "chased individual family names" rather than responding to the performance of specific companies.[81] To protect the firm's reputation, the Tata name had to remain unblemished.

Padshah's scheme for amalgamation rested on the three partners holding equal shares. He reassured R. D. that even though the brothers would "bring into the firm bigger credit than you, and bring in the large profits of mill agencies . . . you will be bringing in the great agency business of Tata & Co. including the new schemes" then under way.[82] R. D. was contemplating a wide range of new investments in mills, real estate, and mines in India and Singapore. Padshah advised him to dampen his enthusiasm and think of the firm as an expanding empire, using lessons from ancient history:

> There have been Empires and Empires, the Romans built slow, but firmly planted their foot on all the ground they acquired. The Arabs rode through huge realms on the whirlwind and the storm and when they were barred by ocean or mountain range, they found that the conquered peoples had already risen in their rear. Plant your indus-

trial Empire with the organising precision of the Roman, and not with the fever of the Arab.[83]

For Padshah, the Tatas' future would be secured by treading carefully between unbridled expansion, championed by R. D., and Dorabji's preference for retrenchment. Although the personalities involved may seem to fit crude stereotypes, with R. D. as the speculative trader and Dorabji as the austere industrialist, the fundamental problem was one of corporate governance. Making R. D. a partner in the original managing agency agreement in 1883 while he retained control of a semiautonomous trading company made formulating a coherent strategy of expansion difficult.

As a result of the exchanges, the managing agency firm in Bombay was renamed Tata Sons and a new overseas subsidiary was established in 1907. Headquartered in London, Tata Limited was simultaneously an independent trading company dealing in jute and pearls, the main selling agency for Tata cotton in Europe, and a procurement channel for machinery, technical expertise, and market information for TISCO.[84] It also performed the role of London banker for the textile mills, remitting profits on cotton shipments to the Levant, Egypt and Europe, which had been previously routed through third parties such as the Ottoman Bank at Istanbul, the Imperial Ottoman Bank at Smyrna, the Banque d'Orient, and the Crédit Lyonnais.[85] The new company thus represented complementarity between trade and industry, without introducing any significant organizational innovations or safeguards. Operating on a similar scale as Tata & Co. in China and Japan, Tata Limited was equally vulnerable to market downturns.

Dorabji Tata looked askance at these developments, as both Indian and British business faced a worsening economic climate. Tata & Co. suffered heavy losses in the pearl and rubber trades and was only kept afloat through Dorabji and Ratanji's help. In 1913, Dorabji warned R. D. that the brothers "always live in dread lest speculation or incapacity or mistakes on the part of a partner or agent might land us into trouble and disgrace," as happened to many others around them. Their "greatest anxiety in the office" was to "keep the fact of your [R. D.'s] position from the knowledge of all and sundry." Reputation was secured through extended kinship networks in which women played a key role. Dorabji worried that his financially "puritanical" wife, Meherbai, and her relatives "might crow over us and say 'well you need not talk; your family's commercial morality is not anything like what you boast of about it.'"[86] This was not the last time that the family found itself needing to save face. The wide mandate of Tata & Co. and Tata Limited to trade independently would soon come back to haunt the Bombay firm.

Boom and Bust

The outbreak of World War I temporarily alleviated fears of bankruptcy and ruin. Indian business stood to benefit from the curtailment of imports and the encouragement of domestic industries for defense purposes. TISCO's entire output was placed at the disposal of the colonial government, which allocated steel across the empire on the basis of need and the condition of oceanic communications. Rails from India were sent to Mesopotamia and Egypt, given the risk of interception by German submarines if diverted to France.[87] In India, TISCO offered to build a benzol (motor fuel) distillation plant for the Department of Explosives as part of a planned expansion of capacity.[88] Other Tata companies were also poised to reap the rewards of collaboration. The Ministry of Munitions in London inquired about the manufacture of anti-gas respirators from coconut shell charcoal at the newly opened Tata Oil Mills in southern India. The director of the Geological Survey of India reached out to the Tata Hydro-Electric Company regarding the possibility of supplying electric power for aluminum production.[89] Tata's contribution to the war effort earned it enormous goodwill in official circles. Victory in Mesopotamia, the viceroy pronounced in 1919, would not have been possible without the steel company's assistance.[90]

Military contracting in the service of the British Empire had come to the rescue once again, this time on an even grander scale than the nineteenth-century expeditions to Persia and Abyssinia. Yet, Tata's relationship with the colonial state remained fraught. With the entry of the United States into the war and the mobilization of additional resources across the Atlantic, shipments of essential machinery for the steel plant "could not be placed in the first rank of urgency." As Dorabji Tata put it in his chairman's speech to the TISCO general meeting in October 1917: "The war has taught us all a great and terrible lesson. It brought home to us our utter helplessness and dependence on foreign machinery and foreign goods."[91] While calling for protectionism and a more interventionist industrial policy, the Tatas were not averse to strategically invoking the principles of free trade to protest these wartime restrictions on the purchase of equipment. In 1916, a frustrated Padshah sent a message to London warning that "if the Board of Trade are very anxious to keep up its export and prohibit at the same time the export of machinery . . . they must not complain if we go to America, as an alternative."[92]

The steel and hydroelectric companies were forced to balance their entrenched preference for American technology with competing pressures to participate in a closed British imperial economy. The low quality of coking coal at TISCO forced management to adopt the "duplex" process in use at Buffalo, New York, and Gary, Indiana, combining a Bessemer converter with an open-hearth furnace for additional purification. This made the steel slower and more expensive to produce.[93] TISCO's willingness to adopt the higher standards of British Standard Specification Steel (BSSS) demanded by the Government of India for the railways also contributed to higher production costs.[94] Similarly, GE supplied the transmission lines for Tata Hydro because British manufacturers had no experience with the high voltage required (110,000 V over 60 miles from Lonavla to Bombay). Yet, the company "favored Great Britain so far as circumstances could permit," placing 66 percent of its orders through GE's British subsidiary, the Thomson Houston Company.[95]

Despite these compromises, the Government of India demanded that equipment for the second hydroelectric plant in the Andhra Valley be purchased exclusively from firms within the empire.[96] The British trade commissioner lobbied the Bombay government in support of the restriction, stating that he had been "very much impressed by the absence of British Machinery" at Tata Hydro due to the influence of American engineers.[97] The Tatas firmly rejected this clause as "a negation of the present free trade and fiscal policy of the British Empire."[98] At Padshah's urging, Tata Hydro agreed to grant "a definite percentage of their total electrical business" to GE, since they were more "up to date" than any other competitor.[99] The American connection was both technologically necessary and strategically useful, serving as a lifeline against the colonial state's reluctance to craft a new industrial policy.

During the war, the government appointed the Indian Industrial Commission to investigate ways of raising domestic production capacity, inviting Dorabji Tata and other business leaders to serve as members. The final report, released in 1918, made for pleasant reading in Bombay. Recognizing that "the old *laissez-faire* doctrine is as dead as Queen Anne," the commission recommended transforming India into "the arsenal of the East" by stimulating a true "industrial revolution."[100] Such confident assertions masked ongoing hesitation over what the new policy would entail. The report said precious little about whether large- or small-scale industries would be favored or whether financial control would be devolved from London to Delhi. The point was not lost on the commission's most ardently nationalist member, Pandit Madan Mohan

Malaviya, who submitted a bristling minute of dissent. He was proven right when expatriate British businessmen joined hands with civil servants intent on preserving the flow of "home charges" to London to water down the policy to a select few "discriminatory" tariffs.[101]

Tata nonetheless stood to benefit from the new protectionist regime, limited as it was. The end of the war caught B. J. Padshah in a buoyant mood, even as he found himself increasingly marginalized from the decision-making process in Bombay. Writing from the offices of Tata Limited in London, he put forward a comprehensive plan of expansion and consolidation that would elevate the firm to the status of a national institution:

> If the Tata firm become an organ of public service widely recognized, if the Tata firm include more & other than Tatas, if the Tata interests include so many ordinarily conflicting businesses, that a parallelism between Tata interests & the interests of the general public cannot be avoided, if Tata finance be the finance of a large wealthy & able group (preferably international), what is there to fear?[102]

Shedding his earlier caution, Padshah proposed entering a range of "fascinating business," including wool and silk mills, hydroelectric power generation for coalfields, aluminum and cement manufacture, irrigation, land reclamation, railways, tramways, and aerial transport. He became convinced that expansion could be achieved systematically, reprising his favorite historical analogy when advising R. D. "to do it with alert intelligence as the Romans did by securing each inch of ground won. They, the Romans, planted <u>Colonies</u>; I ask you to plant subsidiaries."[103]

As before, the success of postwar expansion depended on securing stable long-term financing. Padshah proposed the creation of the Tata Industrial Bank for this purpose, inspired by similar organizations in Japan and Germany. Indeed, at the height of the war, he visited the internment camp at Ahmednagar "to suck the brains of the scientific enemy."[104] Unlike R. D.'s preference for quick profits in commodity trading, the bank would promote investments in essential infrastructure. As Padshah explained, "urbanization of rural localities will bring urban civilization into villages—electric power and light and transport, roads, motor lorries, schools, hospitals, well-built cottages, stores and thus breathe new life into villages."[105] This vision was not as autarkic as it might initially appear. The bank would provide a "direct connection with the London Money Market, and be able to tap its vast resources" for the benefit of rural India.[106] Its branches would extend from the imperial capital (London) to coastal urban centers (Bombay and Calcutta), inland entrepôts (Kanpur and Hyderabad), and the outer reaches of British India's sphere of economic influence (Rangoon and Basra).[107] The bank would also further the integration of trade and industry within the Tata firm. For example, a planned joint investment between the bank and Tata Limited in a dyes company was not only "very remunerative in itself" but would also help TISCO "with inside knowledge about dyes manufacture at Sakchi [Jamshedpur], a project which the Directors of the Steel Company have been anxious to bring into existence."[108]

The bank did not fulfill these lofty ambitions. Shareholders protested that its investments were almost exclusively Tata related, rather than contributing widely to the growth of new industries, and that it did not employ enough Indians.[109] At the second general meeting in June 1920, the directors reported only two Indian managers of *mofussil* (upcountry) branches but promised to train "sub-assistant accountants" in Bombay and Calcutta. They claimed that each attempt to post an Indian manager to the *mofussil* was "met with a request from the Indian mercantile community to send an English officer."[110] The incursion of formal banking, backed by urban capitalists such as the Tatas, into the traditional domains of rural moneylenders provoked widespread resentment.[111] Rival financiers also mobilized against the new venture, seizing on the wave of public criticism to engineer the amalgamation of the bank with the Central Bank of India in 1924. Most of Padshah's schemes were left unrealized, including the dyes factory at Jamshedpur. As a company insider later recalled, it was all for the best: "Thank God, Tatas did not touch any of these projects otherwise . . . the result would have been disastrous when bad times came."[112]

The swift downfall of the Tata Industrial Bank did not take place in a vacuum. The global deflationary crisis of 1920–1921, sparked by governments' desire to restore the soundness of their currencies after wartime spending sprees, brought the entire firm to the brink of collapse.[113] Tata Limited was especially hard hit, facing a chronic shortage of liquidity as commodity prices came crashing down. From April to November 1921, the company drew several short-term bills of exchange from London investment bankers Kleinwort & Sons, backed by £82,415 in future jute sales to Germany and by 7,125 unsold bales of jute held in warehouses in Barcelona and Bilbao. Tata Sons in Bombay agreed "to hold ourselves liable for all the consequences of their default or failure to meet such engagements."[114] The global jute market collapsed by the end of the year, forcing Tata Limited to call up its remaining capital.[115] Shortly thereafter, "serious irregularities" in the account books came to light. The managing director, H. F. Treble, had kept Tata Limited's dealings in cotton "concealed from Bombay and camouflaged in the Balance-Sheets . . . because his own personal transactions had been irregularly financed through the firm." Treble then destroyed the incriminating records to cover his tracks.[116]

Tata Limited was doomed to failure by more than just the vicissitudes of markets or the greed of its employees. It had been forced to operate under the untenable contradiction of being legally distinct from Tata Sons while collecting agency commissions on the parent firm's behalf. The decision to register a separate company in London rather than a formal subsidiary was taken because "the partners did not desire to run any risk of rendering themselves liable for assessment on any part of their respective Bombay profits" by the British income tax authorities. Tata Limited was advised "to conduct the business of the company as not to present any appearance of an agency" and to ensure that its correspondence with Bombay reflected this fiction.[117] Following "the stoppage of all trading business," Tata Limited relied exclusively on revenue from agency commissions, which was no longer forthcoming as Tata companies experimented with new ways of distributing products and capturing markets. The Tata hydroelectric companies refused to pay full commission for transactions in debentures and securities on the London money market. The newly formed TISCO sales department in Calcutta left Tata Limited "entirely at sea as to their requirements, method or policy" regarding sales of pig iron in Europe.[118]

The failures of the Tata Industrial Bank and Tata Limited signaled a decisive shift in the firm's overall strategy and spatial orientation. Whereas the bank called into question the Tatas' nationalism, Tata Limited severely damaged the family's financial reputation at a moment when TISCO was desperate for long-term capital.[119] Treble's fraud in particular confirmed Dorabji's deep-seated apprehension about trade:

> My feeling always was against undertaking any business that had to be carried on at a great distance from the head-office as I always felt that we could not have the requisite control over it. That is why I always felt shy of the China & Japan business especially after the losses incurred by our representatives in those places. . . . I shall be a crore, if not more, rupees to the bad including the losses made by

Tata Ltd., London, during the last 3 years. And I believe that the cause is that we are doing much more business than we ought ever to have undertaken, and for which we are dependent on outsiders for management.[120]

R. D.'s and Padshah's enthusiasms had carried the day, but Dorabji's repeated warnings about overextension turned out to have something of a prophecy about them. The global financial crisis of the early 1920s, along with political pressures from an increasingly assertive nationalist movement, would circumscribe the firm's expansion within the territorial boundaries of India.

The Difficulty of Being Swadeshi

In April 1920, the *Bombay Chronicle* published "The House of Tatas: Its Future and India's Prosperity," a damning exposé subtitled "A Danger to Jamshedji's Life-Work." The anonymous author claimed to be a "Friend of the Family" with special knowledge of the inner workings of the Bombay head office. The article began by recounting Jamsetji's painstaking efforts to raise a business house that once enjoyed "no special place of honour" to a position of unchallenged preeminence. At the time of writing, Tata's financial interests were "bigger than those of any State and in a couple of years they will be as big as the budget figures of a great Presidency." However, the author warned that Jamsetji's successors were jeopardizing his illustrious legacy. R. D. Tata's cosmopolitanism came under special scrutiny, as "a French subject and married to a French lady" (see Chapter 3) who could not be reliably looked upon to "maintain any National sentiments connected with the House." The author reserved his greatest scorn for B. J. Padshah, "a dictatorial professor" who "professes a deep national life, but in practice has little faith in the capacity of Indians for any responsible positions." Padshah's preference for recruiting foreign personnel betrayed his belief "that the white-skinned blonde is a better man to control our destinies than a dusky Indian." How sincere, then, was the Tatas' appeal to *swadeshi* sentiments? The article concluded by recommending the establishment of "a great Indian Industrial Tata Service" to train indigenous management cadres and technical experts as a "bulwark against foreign industrial invasions."[121]

The criticism in the *Bombay Chronicle* may have come from the proverbial disgruntled employee, but it clearly stung. As the Indian National Congress launched the Non-cooperation movement in the spring and summer of 1920, a campaign of mass resistance under the charismatic leadership of

Mohandas K. Gandhi, the Tatas found themselves on the defensive regarding their employment of foreigners. An anonymous letter to the editor in the *Bombay Chronicle* defended Padshah against the charge of "nervous veneration for the 'white-skinned blonde,'" claiming he was "an embodiment of the best of our national aspirations." Recruiting foreigners in upper-level management positions was unavoidable, the letter claimed, because "in highly technical services, we have still to depend on expert knowledge."[122] Dorabji Tata made a similar point at one of the "stormy" shareholder meetings of the Tata Industrial Bank, asking "the critics whether they would prefer not to have an industry at all or have an industry with the aid of foreign technicians."[123] But these arguments failed to hold sway in a charged political atmosphere.

TISCO was on the front lines of the battle over Indianization. As early as 1913, when the plant was barely one year old, the Calcutta-based nationalist periodical *Modern Review* lamented the lack of qualified Indian employees and the bias toward American engineers.[124] A strike by foreign or "covenanted" workers in August 1920, one of the first rumblings of labor unrest at TISCO, increased the sense of urgency felt by management to correct the imbalance.[125] One year later, the Jamshedpur Technical Institute (JTI) opened with much fanfare, promising to cultivate Indian talent along the lines of the successful apprenticeship scheme at the Empress Mills. The curriculum combined practical and theoretical training, attracting more than 2,600 candidates from across India in its second year and offering a viable alternative to colonial engineering colleges.[126] The ratio of covenanted to Indian labor employed in the Jamshedpur works fell by two-thirds within three years. R. D. Tata boasted to his close friend, the nationalist leader Motilal Nehru, that the number of Europeans employed in the sheet mills was reduced from 240 to 60 by reorganizing shifts.[127] Yet, management conceded that the JTI was "gradually drifting away from the main object," only turning out qualified job candidates below the rank of foreman.[128] The highest echelons remained the exclusive preserve of Americans until the following decade.

Apart from being laggards in Indianization, the Tatas were also charged with selling off what had effectively become national assets. The American connection, which had served them well as a counterweight to the colonial state, became a full-blown scandal. A few months after the incendiary "House of Tata" article, the *Bombay Chronicle* published a short follow-up titled "A Tata Contract." TISCO had agreed to supply the total output of its new bar mill to the Truscon Steel Company of Youngstown, Ohio, for the manufacture of reinforced concrete buildings. The article claimed this monopoly would "spell a great disaster to the economic interests of the country, throwing Indian industries at the mercy of a foreign firm." TISCO's acting general manager, S. M. Marshall, was blamed for the decision. The agreement with Truscon fell through due to the Americans' unwillingness to compete with Belgian imports, but the company's reputation suffered.[129] TISCO was willing to take the risk in the first place because its financial position was rapidly deteriorating, with few good options for disposing of surplus product during the postwar slump. In a memorandum to the Government of India in 1923, the company announced it was "in danger of being extinguished for want of working capital."[130] Protective tariffs on steel imposed the following year provided some respite, but the future was clouded with uncertainty. Rumors spread that Dorabji Tata was contemplating selling the TISCO agency to an American group, either GE or US Steel.[131]

The hydroelectric companies' position was not much better. As shareholders began to default, the Tata Power Company requested a £1,000,000 guarantee on purchases of plant and machinery under the Trade Facilities Act, hoping to induce British engineering companies to invest.[132] Support in London was lukewarm due to fears of American competition, as well as to the perceived "intense anti-English feeling of the Parsee section of the community" in the aftermath of the Non-cooperation movement.[133] In 1925, the three Tata electric companies, whose finances were in varying shape, were amalgamated into what was optimistically billed as "one of the safest investments in the world."[134] TISCO's main consultant in New York, Charles P. Perin, opened negotiations with the Electric Bond & Share Company (holding company of GE) for the sale of the managing agency. The Americans suggested forming a new entity, "Tata Super Power Ltd.," which would undertake all further expansions such as "developing a large steam plant on the Jherria Coal Fields or in that neighbourhood, and running a line to Jamshedpur and to Calcutta" to supply the steel plant and jute mills.[135] Following preexisting industrial corridors would bring the operations of different Tata companies closer together. But this integration of national economic space would unfold under foreign control, running counter to Padshah's earlier vision.

Rather than triumphantly inaugurating the era of *swadeshi* industry, it now appeared to outside observers that Tata facilitated creeping Americanization. Intense conflicts over the proposed sale broke out within the Bombay head office. Lady Tata, Ratanji's widow, confronted Perin: "I used to think you were a friend of the family—I now look upon you as our worst enemy." When Perin asked, "What have I done now?" she sternly replied, "Trying to introduce foreign capital and eliminate the Tatas."[136] Women were meant to uphold the reputation of the firm, as Dorabji's wife, Meherbai, had done a decade earlier by chastising her husband over speculative losses, but their influence had waned. By 1929, as the companies' situation continued to deteriorate, the directors were "of one mind" to proceed with the sale. The final agreement awarded a majority share to the American consortium in exchange for Rs. 37 lakhs, with the power to appoint four directors: two American and two Indian, for "the necessary local colour." Effective control over the power companies passed out of the hands of Tata Sons until 1951.[137]

The agreement was met with considerable hostility in the press. Prominent board member Purshotamdas Thakurdas warned that "the introduction of Americans in the Agency . . . would militate a lot against the house of Tatas which was so far considered to be a national house."[138] The Bombay Municipal Corporation passed a resolution demanding the government take steps to prevent the electricity license falling into the hands of an "alien syndicate."[139] Influential businessmen close to the Congress, led by G. D. Birla in Calcutta and Thakurdas in Bombay, came to fear a new type of semicolonial dependence, with the United States merely displacing the British Empire.[140] Despite a lack of consensus within the nationalist movement on the desirability of allowing foreign capital in *swadeshi* enterprises, there was a difference between technological dependence (begrudgingly tolerated at TISCO due to the complexity of the industry) and outright managerial control. Even as successive crises pushed the Tatas to abandon overseas trade and turn to internal markets, that very same perilous global financial landscape forced them to rely on their American connections more than ever before.

Up the Country

The chain of events leading to the Tatas' withdrawal from overseas trade began with R. D. Tata's death in 1926. For many years, R. D. sustained the family's connections to the wider world. During the war, he relocated to Japan with his family and was awarded the Order of the Sacred Treasure by the emperor in 1918, "in recognition of his signal services to Indo-Japanese trade and marine transportation."[141] His son Jehagir Ratanji Dadabhoy (J. R. D.), who later became chairman of the group, grew up in England, Japan, and France—an unusually cosmopolitan background even at the time. R. D.'s will left behind extensive landed property in Shanghai's French Concession, valued at £21,132, and made special provision for J. R. D. to succeed him as a partner in Tata Sons. It also granted power of attorney in Shanghai to Bejan Dadabhoy Tata, one of the few members of the family who stayed on in China to manage two successful cotton mills until the Communist takeover in 1949.[142] Apart from this small remnant of the family's presence in East Asia, the Tatas' trading past would fade into obscurity.

An investigation of Tata & Co.'s balance sheets after R. D.'s death revealed a staggering amount of debt, which put the parent firm in a difficult position. In 1930, young J. R. D. informed the Tata Sons directors that his father's estate was "in an insolvent condition" and could not cover the Rs. 2.5 lakh gap between assets and liabilities. The company's principal creditors included the Yokohama Specie Bank (YSB) and Taiwan Bank in Japan, the Hong Kong & Shanghai Banking Corporation (HSBC), and the National City Bank of New York. The banks "had been mislead [sic] relying on Tata name, and if Tata Sons took up the attitude that they had nothing to do with R. D. Tata and Co., they would be justified in law but would leave a bad impression on the minds of the Bankers in different parts of the world." The "similarity of name" acted as a virtual guarantee for investors. As one Marwari merchant from Calcutta put it, "I always thought that so long as Tata Sons Ltd., was there, it would be quite safe to trade with R. D. Tata & Co. Ltd." If Tata Sons did not assume these debts, its industrial interests would be adversely affected:

> In Japan and the United States and even in Shanghai, people do not know the difference between R. D. Tata & Co. and Tata Sons Ltd. Already there are reactions on us. Tata Iron and Steel loan which we wanted to negotiate through the National City Bank of New York, finds difficulty because of R. D. Tata & Co. mess up. Our Tata Iron & Steel Co. pig iron negotiations in Japan were also questioned because of what had happened to R. D. Tata & Company.[143]

Keen to safeguard their most lucrative market for pig iron exports in the face of competition from the Soviet Union and a new blast furnace in the puppet state of Manchukuo in northern China, the Tatas needed to maintain good relations with Japan from a position of relative weakness.[144]

The Japanese banks drove a hard bargain and forced Tata Sons to guarantee Tata & Co.'s losses up to 85 percent.[145] The directors agreed to the harsh terms for both practical and "sentimental" reasons, "in consideration of keeping Tata name unsullied."[146] Privately, Chairman Nowroji Saklatvala was furious that "the Japanese Banks who owe practically their whole position in India to the

Tatas and in a great measure to poor R. D. have shown no gratitude for all that has been done for them."[147] His complaint reflected the Tatas' diminishing role in commercial linkages between India and Japan, which had once challenged British imperial hegemony in Asia. After the liquidation agreement was signed in 1930, Tata & Co. ceased all trading and went out of existence. This was not the only possible outcome. When British trading companies failed in the same period, they were often bailed out by London banks with deep pockets.[148] With less cash on hand and no comparable access to the London money market after the failure of Tata Limited, the Bombay firm could not follow suit.

In addition to its repercussions on financing for the steel company, Tata & Co.'s collapse left the "position of our Marwaris . . . considerably shaken."[149] Marwari names abounded on the list of the company's shareholders, including Cheniram Jesraj, the Tatas' stalwart collaborators since the days of the opium trade. Their debts were settled through informal assets held by families, such as an emerald necklace worth Rs. 50,000/- given by "Mr. Sitaram's grandmother" to be used as collateral in case a "dispute between C. J., and Messrs. R. D. Tata Co. Ltd" should arise.[150] Tata directors in Bombay had expressed unease at their companies' involvement with Marwaris for many years and used the crisis as an opportunity to enact a clean break. The Empress Mills at Nagpur sought to dispense with their Marwari selling agents, Jamnadhar Potdar & Co., due to the accumulation of "doubtful debts" on the company's balance sheets. They were to be replaced with a "special representative" deputized from Bombay.[151] Meanwhile, the Birlas and other leading Marwari families began to purchase controlling shares in British jute and coal companies, crossing the divide between the "bazaar" trade and modern industry.[152] Birla would, in time, challenge Tata's position as the largest and most powerful business group in India.

The Great Depression of the 1930s affected Indian industrialists less than the crisis of the early 1920s, mainly because they had grown less dependent on the world economy. The government enacted a harsh deflationary policy, resisting calls to devalue the rupee in order to preserve the system of fixed exchange rates with the pound sterling. The Indian countryside, denuded of capital as formal and informal credit markets froze, suffered greatly from commodity price fluctuations. But tariffs protected industrialists and even allowed them to expand into new sectors such as sugar, paper, and chemicals.[153] Conversely, imperial protectionism sharpened conflicts with British capital and pushed them closer to the nationalist movement. The Ottawa Conference of 1932 put the final nail in the coffin of free trade and gave preference to British manufactures. The Mody-Lees Pact of 1933 lowered duties on imported British cloth to ward off Japanese competition. Both caused an outcry among nationalist businessmen and drove them into an alliance with the Congress.[154] Taking recourse to global trade and finance, as Tata was inclined to do in difficult times, was no longer politically feasible. This left domestic markets as the only way forward.

During the Depression, Tata companies began to rely on their own agents at the expense of local intermediaries and introduced landmark organizational innovations such as the TISCO sales department. The company established its own network of depots and stockyards and enacted prohibitions on resales and forward contracts, which increased its bargaining power over local dealers and merchants. In the long run, this spatial reorientation toward the interior enabled collective action by big business in support of a protectionist national state.[155] In the short run, it led to accusations of monopolistic behavior by smaller merchants and manufacturers. In 1931, the Bihar and Orissa Industrial Conference passed a resolution calling for the removal of TISCO's protective tariffs. The company allegedly charged small pig iron producers Rs. 65 per ton while exporting at Rs. 30 per ton, a blatant case of discrimination "in favour of European Concerns and Foreign Industries and to the detriment generally of Indian Concerns and Indian Industries."[156]

Controversies over Tata's *swadeshi* credentials multiplied as representatives of the Congress were elected to devolved provincial legislatures. When the concessional freight rates agreement between TISCO and the Bengal-Nagpur Railway came up for renewal in 1932, TISCO faced an outpouring of "wild and extravagant statements" in the Legislative Assembly, necessitating "constant and continuous propaganda work."[157] According to one pointed complaint in the assembly, the low freight rates enjoyed by TISCO "deprived the people of Bihar and Orissa from carrying on business in pig iron in their own land," rendering "the advantages of the Tatas being in their midst" null and void.[158] In response, TISCO insisted that "we are an all-India concern with no provincial bias whatever."[159] The company was keen to demonstrate how Jamshedpur's location in Bihar was beneficial to the province as well as to the nation. This search for a new political language of legitimation foreshadowed Tata's postindependence conflicts with a democratic and federal Indian state.

The turn to domestic markets depended on other factors beyond organizational innovation and the changing balance of power between big industrialists and smaller merchants within India. It also resulted from the failure of an earlier strategy of expansion based on active partnership and cooperation between semiautonomous trading and industrial branches. The financial crisis of the early 1920s decisively shifted the spatial scale at which Tata companies operated but did not eliminate their dependence on foreign capital and expertise. This can be seen in the curtailment of Tata Limited's mandate to trade independently, the bankruptcy and liquidation of Tata & Co., the displacement of Marwari partners, the sale of the hydro agency to the Americans, and the rise of the TISCO sales department. Embarking on a "transformative" evolutionary path from trade to industry may have forced Indian capitalists to transcend their mercantile origins, but this took a very long time even in the paradigmatic Tata case.[160] A fundamental contradiction lay at the heart of the *swadeshi* imperative. To build a self-sufficient national economy through industrialization required cultivating complementary global networks of trade and finance, which were more vulnerable to systemic shocks. A wide constellation of relationships stretched beyond the British Empire, from the Indian Ocean to China, Japan, and the United States, through which Indian capital moved, multiplied, and occasionally disappeared.

2

Governing Land and Labor

In the winter of 1932, while vacationing in India, the American writer and agriculturist Louis Bromfield accepted a spontaneous invitation to visit the Tata steel township of Jamshedpur. As he looked out the window on the overnight train journey from Calcutta, Bromfield imagined himself traveling back in time. Crossing from Bengal into Bihar, he wrote, the countryside "grew wilder and wilder, the villages smaller and farther apart, the lonely farms little more than clearings in wild jungle." The people, too, "grew smaller, harder, darker, more savage in appearance. . . . In a few hours' ride we had come back to the very beginning of mankind." Suddenly, this reverie of the past was interrupted by a vision of the future:

> There appeared in the sky ahead of the train and a little to the left an immense glow with billowing clouds of smoke tortured and churning over and over in shades of rose and scarlet and gray and black. It was the kind of night spectacle sometimes provided by volcanoes like Stromboli but more often by great steel cities like Mannheim or Pittsburgh or Birmingham.[1]

Bromfield's account, cast in the mold of familiar Orientalist tropes, typified the reactions of visitors to Jamshedpur who marveled at the "spectacle" of full-blown industrialization in an unlikely, remote corner of the world. He drew stark contrasts between the Tata steel plant and the jungles and villages surrounding it, and between its "savage" indigenous workforce and up-to-date machinery. Jamshedpur was analogous to the well-known urban centers of the Industrial Revolution in the West, both an exotic curiosity and an instantly recognizable, quintessentially modern space.

Located at the confluence of the Kharkai and Subarnarekha Rivers in the province of Bihar and Orissa, approximately 250 kilometers west of Calcutta, Jamshedpur was ideally positioned to take advantage of the key natural resources necessary for steel production (coal, iron ore, limestone, and water), as well as of a steady supply of local labor from the *adivasi* (aboriginal / tribal) population. It was the first company town established by Indians and the site of the first successful experiment with heavy industry in the interior of the subcontinent. Company towns have long served as "outposts introducing industrial capitalism into previously unexploited territory."[2] Embodying modernity as a break in space (a factory and planned township out of the jungle) and time (industrial production as a developmental advance in a largely agrarian society), Jamshedpur prefigured the utopian "new town" movement in the mid-twentieth century while reproducing many of the inequalities and exclusions of the nineteenth-century colonial city.[3]

Tata's pioneering foray into steelmaking marked a turning point in the spatial reorientation of Indian capitalism away from the coastal world of export trade. The "interior" was perceived by nationalists and colonial administrators alike as a "repository of hidden wealth and resources."[4] However, the advance of modern industry threatened to disturb the existing social order and undermine the state's commitment to render the landscape "productive and secure for the formation of stable village communities."[5] Colonial land law was still in the process of formation, caught between these contradictory impulses. The passage of the far-reaching Land Acquisition Act (1894) allowed for compulsory dispossession for the benefit of private companies if they fulfilled a "public purpose," which usually meant infrastructural improvements such as railways and ports. Even though the distinction between public and private was murky and ill defined, the state remained the "supreme landlord."[6] If companies like the Tata Iron and Steel Company (TISCO) were allowed to administer vast tracts of land under the "public purpose" clause, this supremacy risked being undermined. At the provincial level, the Chotanagpur Tenancy Act (1908) was meant to protect the customary rights of *adivasi* cultivators by expressly prohibiting the transfer of land to nontribals. Its passage was part of the countervailing tendency to forestall the decay of a settled agrarian order.

By exploiting these ambiguities and contradictions, Tata seized the weapons of colonial "lawfare," deploying them against the weak while also turning them against the state.[7] From 1909 to 1919, Tata cemented control over the space that became Jamshedpur in stages. Some villages were left undisturbed, only to be acquired later. Others were immediately displaced, with recalcitrant tenants facing a barrage of lawsuits. Through this process, TISCO became a quasi-sovereign power, simultaneously acting as employer, landlord, and municipal government. Neither the colonial state nor its postcolonial successor was ever able to undo this anomalous arrangement. The Jamshedpur model of private urban governance proved exceptionally resilient. It represented a flex-ible, heterogeneous form of corporate sovereignty, dependent on the state in some respects but fiercely resistant to it in others.

Once the boundaries of the city had taken shape, the problems of urban planning and worker welfare urgently demanded attention. Foreign "cove-nanted" employees (American, British, and German) lived in leafy bunga-lows adjacent to the plant. Skilled Indian workers occupied permanent quar-ters on acquired land nearby. But no one quite knew what to do with the largest number of workers, local *adivasis*, who were thought to be inherently mobile and unsuited to urban life. Tata managers sought guidance from outside ex-perts, including former colonial bureaucrats such as F. C. Temple, author of the first urban plan for Jamshedpur, and a team of social scientists from the London School of Economics (LSE) led by Sidney and Beatrice Webb. But no coherent strategy for dealing with *adivasi* labor emerged. On the one hand, visionary schemes such as Temple's hexagonal "coolie town" attempted to pre-serve the fundamental essence of the village within the town. On the other hand, management insisted that *adivasis* could never permanently settle and should be allowed to roam at will. The same reticence characterized the com-pany's attitude toward the regulation of working hours, improvements in labor efficiency, and other welfare measures. Although Tata managers prided them-selves on introducing an eight-hour day in advance of a legal mandate, they also maintained that the altered rhythms of steel production in a tropical cli-mate rendered established practice in the West irrelevant to India. In partic-ular, TISCO delayed the imposition of Taylorist scientific management until the late 1920s, when a wave of strikes led to the formulation of a more sys-tematic labor policy.

What did Tata's bold experiment with industrialization in a "backward" re-gion mean? Was the company pointing the way toward India's economic future by training unskilled workers to operate sophisticated machinery, and by creating a model urban space for them to live in? Or did it reproduce the worst features of contemporary global capitalism, intensifying exploitation and segregation in a society that was already profoundly unequal? There was much to admire in what Bengali sociologist Benoy Kumar Sarkar called Tataism—a powerful force for unleashing India's economic potential and catching up to the West. But TISCO's record of turbulent labor relations in its first few de-cades of operation told a more conventional story. The company appeared in multiple avatars, as both an agent of modernization and a traditional sover-eign exercising power through dependence and patronage.

A Public Purpose

The search for a suitable location for the Tata steel plant involved negotiations with the colonial state at several levels, from the highest ranks of the India Office to lowly district commissioners, and with rulers of princely states large and small. Under Viceroy Curzon's administration, the Government of India relaxed its strict regulations on mining in order to encourage the development of domestic industry.[8] Both Indian and British companies leaped at the opportunity, entering into aggressive competition with each other. Around 1900, Jamsetji Tata sent his son Dorabji and his nephew Shapurji Saklatvala to pursue all possible leads on raw materials across India. They found themselves in the midst of a speculative frenzy, reporting back to Bombay that "everybody is mad with some mining project or another." Some of the most valuable resources were discovered in princely territory, requiring companies to navigate multiple overlapping layers of sovereignty, not always successfully. Despite the friendly overtures of the acting financial secretary to the nizam of Hyderabad, who was "most favourably inclined towards us," Tata lost the race for a prospecting license in the state to a rival concern, Parry & Co., supported by the British resident.[9]

With early investigations in southern and central India yielding little result, the Tatas' search came to focus on the forested hills of the Chotanagpur Plateau. During the early years of East India Company rule, this region was seen as a wild frontier impervious to military conquest and pacification. It became a "zone of anomaly" where policing, land settlement, and revenue collection were devolved to a dense "political society" of powerful *zamindars* (hereditary landholders) and other intermediaries, rather than being governed through uniform laws and bureaucratic institutions.[10] Here, the Tatas found an ally in the maharaja of Mayurbhanj, the largest and highest ranked of the Orissa Tributary States, who had taken an interest in developing mineral resources as a way to bolster his own legitimacy.[11] In 1904, the Bengali geologist P. N. Bose, then in the employ of the maharaja, brought the rich iron ore deposits in the Gurumahisani District to the attention of the Tatas.[12] After several false starts, a final site was selected near the village of Sakchi on the Bengal-Nagpur Railway, at the "point of minimum transportation costs" for iron ore from Mayurbhanj and coal from Jharia. Proximity to Calcutta ensured access to both domestic and foreign markets.[13]

Company histories narrate this outcome as the culmination of a teleological process of finding the perfect location, characterized by brilliant insight and intrepid risk taking.[14] Even the most critical accounts of TISCO praise Jamsetji Tata and his associates for their "entrepreneurial ability" in going where others feared to tread.[15] Their choices were nonetheless heavily constrained by political, legal, and resource geographies. An earlier, equally promising site was abandoned in order to avoid potential resistance from the Kol *adivasi* inhabitants. Here, the local deputy commissioner proved "inflexible in the matter of the rights of the Kols, and is averse to dispossessing 700 families whose rights over the lands he considers to be of a peculiar nature."[16] In the wake of several large-scale *adivasi* uprisings against the Raj, culminating in Birsa Munda's millenarian revolt of 1899, colonial officials cast themselves as protectors of customary rights.[17] This was not simply a matter of administrative exigency but was part of a longer transformation of the state's role in the region.

The Permanent Settlement, which created a fixed class of *zamindar* proprietors in Bengal, had been extended westward throughout the nineteenth century. Under the prevailing *khuntkatti* system of joint ownership in Chotanagpur, rights to land accrued to unbroken lineages descending from the original *adivasi* cultivators who cleared the jungle. Over time, local rulers were brought into the fold of Hinduism or "Sanskritized." Some of them acquired the title of *zamindar* in the landholding hierarchy. The colonial state depended on *zamindars* to maintain order in this "zone of anomaly" but grew alarmed at their arbitrary power. Exorbitant rents and rising indebtedness among *raiyats* (cultivators) accelerated land sales and the degradation of customary tenures. The landmark Chotanagpur Tenancy Act (1908) "consolidated and suspended all previous agrarian legislation for the province," with the status of the *pradhan* (village headman) coming under the protection of the law for the first time. The act expressly prohibited the alienation of tribal lands and provided for a regular survey of tenancy and occupancy rights.[18] Codification of these rights widened the scope of "what could be recognized as a legal entitlement well beyond property in the land's rent alone"—that is, below the *zamindar*'s claim at the top of the hierarchy.[19] This strand of colonial legal thought stood in tension with the concurrent expansion of the state's eminent domain powers.

Tata's preferred site for the steel plant at Sakchi was located on the Dhalbhum *zamindari* estate. According to the first revenue survey, this estate offered "a striking example of the decay of the ancient village system of the aboriginal tribes." Out of a total of 1,686 villages, headmen were recognized in just 943. Of these headman villages, only 30 percent preserved the customary *khuntkatti* system.[20] Tenants complained of "oppression, excessive enhancement [of rents], and underhand practices." In 1904, the heavily indebted seventy-nine-year-old *zamindar* leased his entire estate to a private syndicate known as the Midnapore Zamindari Company.[21] This was a rare British managing agency that invested in land, monopolizing forest produce and supplying raw jute to the mills of Calcutta. It could only make a profit from the bankrupt estate by "increasing rents enormously" and "disregarding existing customary rights." The company's managers refused to recognize village headmen and *khuntkatti* tenure altogether, claiming absolute proprietorship.[22] The commercialization of land in the region had thus reached a new stage with the intrusion of organized capital in rent extraction, which justified the pressing need for protective legislation.

Tata arrived on the scene in early 1908, while the survey of the Dhalbhum estate was still under way. The steel company applied for 3,564 acres under section 41 of the Land Acquisition Act at a rate of Rs. 13 per acre, offering Rs. 12,000/- in compensation to the expropriated *raiyats*. To government officials, the area appeared "prima facie excessive," so they stipulated "a conditional and not an absolute transfer." The land would be put up for resale in case the company failed to construct or maintain the specified works in time, with the right of first refusal retained by the government.[23] TISCO's response to these "unprecedented" restrictions was to emphasize the "public purpose" of the steel plant, arguing that the transfer should not be any "less permanent or less absolute than if the Government were acquiring the land for themselves."[24] Tata's lawyers reasoned that officials felt "oppressed by the consideration that this case is an exceptional one as it deals with a large tract of country and it is sure to be quoted as a precedent hereafter so they wish to provide for possible rights which after all may not really exist."[25] The Dhalbum syndicate had advanced a similar claim about the nonexistence of customary rights but only for the purpose of raising agricultural rents in its established capacity of *zamindar*. Using the land for industry entailed outright displacement, with the company acting in the place of the state as the apex sovereign.

There is a widespread belief in the region today that Tata worked behind the scenes to delay the implementation of the Chotanagpur Tenancy Act in order to carry out the acquisition.[26] No clear evidence of lobbying exists, nor would it have been likely to leave a paper trail in the first place. The company archives do preserve one letter from the resident engineer, W. O. Renkin, warning the board of directors "that the new Chota Nagpur Tenancy Act will make considerable trouble unless land acquired is declared as being exempt from it; this is purely my opinion and is offered as a suggestion only." At the top of the first page, a barely legible scrawl in pencil calls for "quick action" on the matter.[27] In the end, Clause 43 of the Chotanagpur Tenancy Act did specifically exempt "land acquired under the Land Acquisition Act, 1894, for the Government or any Local Authority or Railway Company."[28] TISCO was none of these things but rather a new kind of entity legislators had not yet considered—an Indian private company that could make a legitimate claim to fulfill the "public purpose" clause.

Operating on the assumption that the Land Acquisition Act extinguished all other rights, TISCO pursued a dual strategy of directly acquiring land in some areas and assuming the title of *zamindar* in others. Following a series of protests and complaints by *raiyats* to the district commissioner, which resulted in an undisclosed amount of crop compensation payments, resistance was minimized by deliberately skirting the more populated settlements.[29] TISCO secured a leasehold over twenty-one additional villages from the Dhalbhum syndicate, which were not part of the "actual acquired land" but could be "later acquired through Government much easier than now."[30] TISCO thus inserted itself into the complex and rapidly changing agrarian structure of Chotanagpur as a powerful intermediary. Other companies in the region adopted the same strategy. As *zamindars* discovered that minerals were more profitable than land, "the new extractive industry blended with the prevailing agrarian system as a kind of subsoil agriculture."[31] However, this "blending" did not occur smoothly. Frequent disputes over rights and royalties could rarely be adjudicated by existing legislation. Companies sought to simplify land tenure regimes by expropriating rival claimants, while simultaneously profiting from the ambiguity of the law to consolidate their position.

The *pradhans* occupying "waste" or common lands in the villages of Sakchi and Beldih, whose rights were explicitly protected by the Chotanagpur Tenancy Act, proved to be the single most intractable obstacle for TISCO in its early years. At first, there was a clear recognition of the limitations imposed by the original agreement: "The Company cannot eject or oust the Prodhans so long as they pay the stipulated rents and carry out the terms of the Pottah [lease]." They were to be "treated with kindness and firmness as it is to their interest to be on friendly terms with the Company."[32] But as the steel plant came up and the population of the town grew, TISCO began to take a harder line. The company brought a lawsuit against the *pradhan* of Beldih in 1912, on the grounds that he had subleased land and erected buildings "unlawfully and without our consent." The resulting settlement was "a menace to the sanitation of Sakchi and further occupies the only suitable ground upon which the northern town [where European and American staff lived] may be extended."[33] The *pradhan* of Sakchi, also facing a lawsuit, argued that the company was not legally entitled to his land "without paying a proper compensation," since he had been "all along in undisturbed possession and enjoyment of the said land and by exercising his permanent right thereon."[34] In court, TISCO selectively used provisions of the Chotanagpur Tenancy Act against the *pradhans*. Unauthorized sales and transfers of land were prohibited under section 46 of the act, while "subletting for building purposes" was illegal under section 21.[35] The law was a double-edged sword, obstructing as well as enabling the company's claims.

Individuals who settled land on their own and constructed unauthorized buildings revealed the patchwork of multiple sovereignties at Sakchi. One contractor in particular, Babu Ramdas, was a thorn in the company's side for many years. In addition to a permanent lease of 50 *bighas* (around 25 acres) held directly from the deputy commissioner, he obtained a temporary lease of another 50 *bighas* for a brickfield. At first, the general manager was confident that "we can always put pressure on the employees living in Ramdas's quarters to vacate them if necessary," but his patience soon ran out.[36] In July 1917, the directors in Bombay announced a sweeping change in policy: "As a general rule, we would prefer that all the areas included in our lease from the Dhalbhum Syndicate, without exception, should be acquired under the Land Acquisition Act" in order to "ensure the perfect safety to our Company for the future."[37] TISCO's appetite for land was growing due to the wartime boom in profits and the need to expand and modernize the steel plant to accommodate increased production. The new policy meant that pending ejectment suits against the *pradhans* could be safely dropped, "as the compensation we might have to pay according to the Land Acquisition Officer's estimate will be considerably less than the cost of further litigation."[38] Ramdas's entire plot was acquired and leased back to him, making his tenants wholly dependent on the company.

The conflict between TISCO and the numerous intermediaries standing in its way did not depend exclusively on the internal contradictions of the law. The company's ultimate legal right to eject undesirable occupants was never successfully challenged in court. As is often the case when orderly expropriation encounters resistance and subversion, the "clarity and simplicity of the law" mutated into a "material struggle" over compensation.[39] A fully bounded enclave could not come into being in Jamshedpur until this everyday struggle came to an end. Meanwhile, colonial officials learned from their mistakes and resolved not to surrender the state's sovereign claim to land and mineral resources whose value was becoming more and more apparent.

A Sovereign Space

During the second round of acquisitions in 1917, TISCO applied for an additional 12,215 for extensions of the plant, employee housing, and leases to subsidiary companies. The price of land had risen from Rs. 13/- per acre to Rs. 133/- per acre and was projected to increase still further.[40] Partly in order to control costs, the company demanded the right to expedite further purchases without continual recourse to the government.[41] In response, the deputy commissioner of Singhbhum, A. Garrett, wrote a long memorandum urging the "reconsideration of the whole question of the land acquisition . . . at Sakchi as part and parcel of the whole mining field." This question had not been properly addressed because the lands and minerals in the region were "not the property of the State." Garrett was concerned both by lost revenue and the problems of law and order posed by a restive mining population. He summarized the status quo as follows:

> At Sakchi the situation is a mass of anomalies with a mixture of rural, regular Government, and private police and choukidars [watchmen] in a Municipality that is no Municipality. Everywhere we have given away that real command and control which should be the price of every concession, statutory or otherwise.[42]

The "mass of anomalies" Garrett described was a consequence of the layered and contested sovereignty of the region, where resources could be brought in tax-free from princely to British territory (as in the case of iron ore shipped from Gurumahisani to Jamshedpur), companies ruled over their own private fiefdoms, and the reach of the law was fragmented, incomplete, and twisted by corruption. His solution was for the state to "acquire the properties on its own behalf, and give them out on lease to the Companies concerned," which would be "an infinitely nearer approximation to the real intention of the legislature and the plain meaning of the [Land Acquisition] Act than the present system."[43]

Garrett's memorandum articulated the profound contradiction inherent in applying the Land Acquisition Act to private capital, which undermined the unitary sovereignty of the state. In other parts of India and the world, extractive industries operating through private concessions created unstable zones of exception or "anomaly," which were ultimately brought under state control. In the coalfields of Assam, mining companies struck ad hoc deals with tribal leaders, forcing the government subsume various "acts of exchange" under the logic of the contract and of territorial sovereignty.[44] In the roughly contemporary case of Venezuelan oil, access to subterranean resources through profit sharing ultimately enshrined the state as "national landlord" and custodian of "national wealth."[45] Garrett and other officials hoped a similar outcome would transpire across India, but the colonial state had found itself outflanked by private companies. The early 1920s represented a moment of reckoning with the inadequacies of the law, at times taken to extremes. When the third Tata hydroelectric power company applied for the use of the Land Acquisition Act in 1921, the collector of Poona proposed levying a royalty on water. Just like gold mines, the "rain-flooded valleys of the Western Ghats" were "unique natural assets of the country, for the exclusive use of which Government should demand a due return." Tata no longer deserved exceptional privileges because the "pioneer period of doubt as to the feasibilities of the schemes is over."[46]

A similar argument was used against the steel company during the second round of acquisitions. The Maude Committee, appointed by the Government of Bihar and Orissa in 1919 to investigate the growth and administration of Jamshedpur, held that "the application of the Act has been unduly extended to cover cases in which land is required for private industrial concerns such as the Tata Iron and Steel Company," whose business was now deemed "only indirectly useful to the public." Unless the act was amended, the committee recommended establishing a board of works, a local government authority far better equipped to acquire land in an orderly fashion and assist the dispossessed tenants.[47] This constituted the strongest challenge yet to TISCO's de facto sovereignty over Jamshedpur, ironically precipitated by the company's own claim that "we constitute a large Municipality, and as such we are a public body and entitled to the operation of the Land Acquisition Act."[48] This attempt to assuage the government's doubts about the applicability of the "public purpose" clause backfired. Land became the main vehicle of a protracted struggle for control over the town and nearby villages.

Following the Maude Committee's report, TISCO agreed that a board of works should be constituted to perform "administrative functions" but without the power to alienate property.[49] In 1924, the provincial government nominally declared Jamshedpur converted the board of works into a notified area committee, a step that normally (but not necessarily) preceded the declaration of a municipality.[50] TISCO refused to recognize this body as an independent authority, which meant that no public property technically existed in Jamshedpur. With a population around fifty thousand, the town attracted growing numbers of shopkeepers, clerks, lawyers, and other service providers in addition to workers for the steel plant and subsidiary companies. The government established a court, hospital, jail, and police station, which residents could not reliably access because the few roads the company had built were "expressly declared to be private" and closed at least once a month. Local resident lawyers actively petitioned against these restrictions.[51] Chief Town Engineer F. C. Temple, formerly the sanitary engineer for the Government of Bihar and Orissa, authored the first urban plan for Jamshedpur in 1919, laying out an integrated road system based on the old village cart tracks.[52] Temple urged the directors to open the roads, if only for reasons of self-interest: "Assuming that Govt. declares the roads public, & that is almost a certainty if we do not, & assuming that Govt. resumes comparatively large areas of land for residential purposes . . . we should run the very serious risk that the next NAC would no longer have a Steel Co. majority."[53]

The directors were inclined to agree with Temple, recognizing that the situation was untenable. As the postwar boom came to a crashing halt, TISCO requested government assistance for the town's upkeep in the form of a guaranteed loan. A slow devolution of municipal authority would bring a measure of financial relief to the cash-strapped company.[54] John Peterson, a TISCO director and former civil servant, conceded that "a private town of this size owned by a private corporation is a thing unknown in any other country in the world and we should be very glad indeed to be relieved of the responsibility of it"—a statement that would have been unthinkable only a few years earlier. Peterson proposed making the roads public, giving the notified area committee the power to tax "the general public" (but not the company itself) to pay for infrastructure and sanitation, and completing the transition to a municipality in ten or fifteen years "when the Town is educated up to it."[55]

The government agreed to the proposal, subordinating the principle of unitary sovereignty to the practical task of ensuring law and order in a climate of increasing worker unrest. As Deputy Commissioner of Singhbhum J. R. Dain put it in 1927:

It is clearly undesirable that a private company, almost uncontrolled by Government, should be the one and only authority in a large modern town. It is particularly wrong that a company supplying essential public services, like water, power and light, should not be subject to the law which ordinarily controls such services, and be able to enforce their will and get rid of undesirable persons by refusing supplies. On the other hand a democratic form of Government would be dangerous in Jamshedpur, and the Company must always have a large voice in the administration of the town.[56]

Dain's position on the question of Jamshedpur's municipal status thus inverted his predecessor Garrett's argument, made a decade before. To keep democratic self-rule at bay, private governance was an acceptable substitute for the state's exercise of police power. Corporate and state sovereignty typically "merged into one" in frontier zones of resource extraction.[57] In Jamshedpur they continued to function side by side, each a proxy for the other.

And the Law Won

Throughout the following decade, TISCO slowly consolidated its dual role as *zamindar* and municipal authority while operating under strict legal and financial constraints. The growth of Jamshedpur was limited to the area between the rivers Kharkai and Subarnarekha. The need for further acquisitions continued to plague town administrators, as the Maude Committee had predicted. In order to detect and prevent the spread of "slum areas," the directors commissioned an aerial survey, a novel technique used across the British Empire for both counterinsurgency and routine planning. The view from the air revealed a total "reality that demanded improvement and development" for the first time, confirming the fundamental defects of Jamshedpur's growth.[58] A report by army engineer P. G. W. Stokes, completed in 1937, recommended acquiring an additional belt within a two- to three-mile radius to control rising land values. "Had the original planner of Jamshedpur been gifted with omniscience," Stokes wrote, "he would have planned it in concentric rings, with the lowest class dwellings nearest the works, and the highest class furthest."[59] Instead, the residential neighborhoods for skilled workers and middle management, known as the Northern Town, were located next to the factory due to the need to skirt the more populated villages during the original acquisition process. Overcrowded *bastis* (slums) within the acquired area and the "unsanitary" village of Jugsalai just outside its boundaries, where an independent *pradhan* speculated in land, exacerbated the problem.[60]

Jugsalai could not be more different from the sedate suburban utopia of Jamshedpur's Northern Town a few miles away. One TISCO employee later recalled that "people did not dare to walk alone" in Jugsalai, "for fear of dacoits and ferocious animals even in day time."[61] It was also a site of subversion and resistance, where workers could organize away from the watchful gaze of the company's spies.[62] TISCO made little progress in dealing with the village because it would have "cost a good deal of money" to acquire the land and administer its population.[63] When the government decided to construct a bridge connecting the north bank of the Subarnarekha with Jamshedpur, the deputy commissioner suggested "taking steps to prevent the growth on the north side of the proposed bridge of an area which might develop the unsatisfactory features of Jugsalai." Land would be acquired across the river as a buffer zone, but the company would not be allowed to use it "for industrial development or as a substantial source of profit."[64] It was a vicious circle; as the company expanded, undesirable fringe areas emerged, which would then have to be purchased at a higher cost. Jugsalai was Jamshedpur's antithesis, a shadow space produced by the model urbanism it now threatened through the rise in prices.

Within the notified area, by contrast, the newly constituted town department became "a great productive asset" to the company, implementing the first systematic survey of land values to enhance the income derived from rents. The town revenue budget showed that municipal services were in constant deficit, but land and house rents showed a healthy profit.[65] Converting semiautonomous cultivators into dependent ratepayers was a tried-and-true administrative strategy in colonial India. When the government acquired lands in the Punjab for the construction of New Delhi a decade earlier, it offset lost agricultural revenue by allowing tenants to remain on the land upon payment of rent.[66] In this respect, both state and corporate sovereigns obeyed the logic of the market.

To maintain its tenuous profitability, the town department began to sue for arrears of rent in its capacity as *zamindar* under section 234 of the Chotanagpur Tenancy Act.[67] The company's suits imposed a crushing burden on the tenants that found expression in organized political action. A speech by peasant leader Swami Sahajanand, delivered before the Singhbhum District Kisan Conference in 1939, described the "horrible sufferings (*bhayankar kashton*)" of the villagers within the acquired area, including rent payments up to four times higher than in nearby districts. Villagers complained that "we enjoy no benefits of any kind from this municipality," which was intended exclusively for TISCO staff and permanent workers.[68] Their holdings were also eroded by acquisitions on behalf of subsidiary companies, sanctioned by section 50 of the Chotanagpur Tenancy Act. Some *adivasi* cultivators refused to accept compensation from contractors and sowed crops over disputed plots. This kind of nonviolent resistance adopted the techniques of the Civil Disobedience movement led by Gandhi and the Indian National Congress in the 1930s.[69] Sahajanand's activism in Jamshedpur linked these small-scale struggles with regional and national politics, at the very moment when TISCO's tariff protection was coming under fire in the Legislative Assembly for displacing Bihari traders and merchants (see Chapter 1).

The precise legal status of Jamshedpur's residents became a point of contention once again during the second government survey of Dhalbhum in 1934. TISCO requested the exclusion of the entire notified area from the survey, which would have denied tenants the protections of the Chotanagpur Tenancy Act and facilitated the enhancement of rents. Since "all traces of the original boundaries between the various villages in this area had disappeared," the company argued, Jamshedpur contained only urban residents. The government did not agree, finding "a large number of agricultural holdings within the notified areas" and accusing the town department of not creating the "record-of-rights" required by the act. Tenants and the company filed an equal number of competing petitions against each other, leading to a flurry of court cases. TISCO eventually conceded that the act applied to the entire area, regardless of municipal status, allowing the survey to proceed.[70]

Was Jamshedpur then a city, or a collection of villages with a factory in their midst? The question remained open. In 1937, an amendment to the Chotanagpur Tenancy Act in the Bihar Legislative Assembly sought to grant "protection to 'Raiyats' owning homesteads from ejectment on account of arrears of rent." This amendment would, the general manager submitted, "vitally affect the administration of acquired areas in Jamshedpur" by interfering with the company's right to terminate leases. Although acknowledging the continued existence of prior tenants whose rights were protected, he insisted that "the greater portion of the agricultural lands in Jamshedpur are held by persons who are not raiyats in the popular interpretation of the word" but employees who had been given small plots of land for vegetable gardens. Any land "held for residential or business purposes has to be subject to regulations and by-laws of a municipal nature," which would be undermined if these tenants were to claim the status of cultivators.[71] The Chotanagpur Tenancy Act, however instrumentalized, continued to obstruct TISCO's full control over land. As before, the company freely invoked the act to exercise the authority of *zamindar* but denied jurisdiction when it came to the rights of tenants. The reinvention of categories such as *raiyat* and urban resident was one of many strategies available for working through and around the law.

Encountering Expertise

The rapid expansion of Jamshedpur after the second round of acquisitions drew urgent attention to labor problems. As the city came up, the rural economy of Chotanagpur was in an extended crisis. Harvest fluctuations on a commercializing agrarian frontier led to widespread dependence on credit and loss of access to land. Thousands of *adivasi* migrants moved to mines, factories, and tea plantations throughout eastern and northeastern India, including the new steel plant.[72] TISCO employed unskilled or "coolie" labor from nearby districts, often recruited by duplicitous traffickers working closely with *zamindars* and princely rulers.[73] Skilled workers, many of them trained in railway workshops and other industrial establishments, were drawn from across India and assigned to departments along the lines of caste and ethnicity: Bengali clerks, Punjabi foremen, Bihari blacksmiths, and so on. Although seasonal migrants to the Bombay textile mills maintained strong ties with their home villages, workers in Jamshedpur were more likely to become exclusively dependent on industry.[74] This put significant pressure on the company to provide housing and welfare programs.

Jamsetji Tata left behind few concrete instructions about what his planned township would look like. In a letter written from the United States in 1902, undoubtedly influenced by prevailing "garden city" ideals, he advised his son Dorabji:

> Be sure to lay wide streets planted with shady trees, every other of a quick-growing variety. Be sure that there is plenty of space for lawns and gardens. Reserve large areas for football, hockey and parks. Earmark areas for Hindu temples, Mohammedan mosques and Christian churches.[75]

This passage is often quoted as an illustration of Jamsetji's exceptional foresight, but it offers scant evidence of decision making about the planning of Jamshedpur after his death. The town's population was assumed to be cosmopolitan, and facilities for recreation and worship were given priority. Beyond those basic principles, it was left to Jamsetji's successors to work out the details.

At first, the directors in Bombay were too preoccupied with technical matters to give much thought to urban planning or worker welfare. The exception was the indefatigable B. J. Padshah, the intellectual architect of the firm's expansion (see Chapter 1). As early as 1914, he proposed setting aside 1.5 percent of TISCO's net profits for "introducing among the working classes improved diet and better clothing within the limits of caste, religion, custom and income."[76] The qualifier was important. Padshah paid close attention to advances in the discipline of sociology in Britain, especially to in-depth studies of urban poverty by Charles Booth, Seebohm Rowntree, and Patrick Geddes.[77] He was convinced that the rapid industrialization of India made a thorough knowledge of the social sciences imperative. Rigorous research would help employers, statesmen, and reformers determine how "the social life of the people may be corrected." Studying the environment, birth and death rates, disease, family structure, caste, village conditions, and more had "a profound bearing on the value and efficiency of the individual as a social unit."[78] Padshah envisioned recruiting the best and brightest minds from the West to make Tata into model employers. But it was an apparently unrelated philanthropic gift that allowed the steel company to become a conduit for transnational expertise.

In 1912, Jamsetji's younger son Ratanji awarded £1,400 per annum to the London School of Economics for the general purpose of "preventing and relieving poverty and destitution." The Department of Social Science and Administration at LSE, supported by the Tata grant, attracted a "bizarre" and "wildly improbable" mixture of British intellectuals, from the voluntarist Charity Organisation Society (COS) to the ethical socialist R. H. Tawney and the Fabian collectivists Sidney and Beatrice Webb.[79] As part of a wider "cult of the business man" in Edwardian Britain, the Fabians believed that private fortunes could be tapped for the benefit of "national reconstruction." As Beatrice Webb wrote, their strategy was to "detach the *great employer*, whose profits are too large to feel the immediate pressure of regulation and who stands to gain by the increased efficiency of the factors of production, from the ruck of small employers or stupid ones."[80] During their tour of India in 1912, the Webbs were especially impressed with the Tatas: "Compared to other Plutocracies, these Indians are aristocratic, in appearance, manners and cultivation; and far superior in personal distinction, to Government House or the Indian English official world."[81] Ratanji Tata's subsequent offer to endow a poverty research unit fit neatly into the Webbs' elitist worldview. Here was a progressive employer willing to advance the cause of "efficiency" through social science.

In the first few years of its existence, the LSE department carried out a series of rich empirical studies on topics such as the effects of minimum wages in various industries, industrial housing, the health and feeding of schoolchildren, and women's housework, mainly in East London.[82] Beyond the source of funding, it had no connection with the empire, India, or Tata until 1917, when Padshah requested the head of the department, E. J. Urwick, to form a committee "to advise on the appointment to Social Welfare Work at the Steel Works."[83] The report of this committee, which included the Webbs, Urwick, and the liberal sociologist L. T. Hobhouse, criticized the company and led to sharp disagreements about the meaning and purpose of industrial welfare.[84] The mutual understanding between employer and expert broke down when the Tatas called upon social scientists as a source of practical advice.

The report began with a memorandum by Padshah, who advocated organizing the town into "self-contained" neighborhoods governed by *panchayats* or "mass Meetings of resident men and women within the same caste system." The aim was to counter the destructive and atomizing tendencies of modern industry by reviving "the old Indian village-life which was based on ideals of co-operation and self-sufficiency."[85] Sidney Webb's contribution echoed Padshah's concern with social and environmental influences but in a noticeably sharper eugenic tone:

> The creation of a new town population, newly gathered from all parts, of mixed races, with diverse standards and customs of hygiene, morals and religion, without provision for the education of the young or the recreation of adults, presents one of the gravest of social problems. It is not merely a question of social improvement. It may easily prove to be one of preventing actual deterioration, physical and moral. . . . With such a population the level of industrial efficiency would imperceptibly become lower year by year.[86]

Anxieties over the adaptability of migrant workers to the altered rhythms of industrial labor and cosmopolitan urban life permeated the report. Padshah's optimistic vision of a synthesis between tradition and modernity and Webb's declinist warnings were two sides of the same coin.

One of the most contentious sections of the report was the "Memorandum on Fatigue" by Urwick and Hobhouse, which proposed a thorough investigation of the "effects of the length of shifts and of the total number of hours per day."[87] TISCO prided itself on introducing eight-hour shifts in 1912, well before it became a legal requirement anywhere in the world. This was not unique among Indian employers and could be partly explained by climatic factors, but it stood out as a bold and progressive move.[88] While acknowledging TISCO's advances in this regard, Urwick and Hobhouse pointed to Lever Brothers' soap factory at Port Sunlight, which had experimented with a six-hour day to promising results. Citing the time and motion studies of Frederick Winslow Taylor in American steel plants and wartime investigations of "muscular or nervous strain" by the Ministry of Munitions in Britain, they also recommended mandatory breaks of ten to fifteen minutes every four hours. The memorandum critiqued irregular patterns of work, particularly unauthorized rest periods. Women "coolies" in particular, who made up around one-sixth of the workforce, took "surreptitious breaks for themselves which the foremen are compelled to wink at."[89] What the investigators observed was in reality a practice of "everyday resistance" to punishing conditions in factories, also common among women in the Bombay textile mills. Indian employers generally regarded the lowest skilled workers as "free agents" who came and went as they pleased and worked at their own pace, conveniently using this tendency to resist rationalization and standardization of working hours.[90]

A companion report by Dr. Harold H. Mann of the Poona Agricultural College on housing and welfare in Jamshedpur made similar recommendations but went further in proposing a weekly day of rest. Like Urwick and Hobhouse, Mann was impressed by the *adivasi* women who performed a variety of "loading and unloading" tasks in the coke oven and traffic departments. They were "on the whole healthy and happy people" and "one of the most attractive features of the Works." But because women lived in villages several miles away, they often came early or stayed overnight and brought their children along. They could sometimes be seen "bathing in the warm waste water from the blast furnaces." Workers had no space inside the plant to spend their two-hour break, which was scheduled in the middle of the day when the heat was most intense.[91] To remedy this state of affairs, Mann called for "careful scientific inquiries" to determine "the best length of working hours for each shop or type of operation in a steel works *under Indian tropical conditions.*" Going through the rolls systematically, he found an exceptionally high turnover rate due to absenteeism. In August 1918, for example, 6.8 percent of monthly paid employees were discharged for "irregular attendance," which Mann surmised was mainly due to untreated illness. Making allowances for prevailing notions of Indian difference, he concluded, "It is, as all authorities agree, a sign of inefficiency that the change of workers in an industrial concern should be frequent and large. Here they are enormous."[92]

Sidney Webb praised the Mann report as "both comprehensive and conclusive" in making it evident that "the whole structure of welfare at Jamshedpur was not so far advanced as they had supposed."[93] Padshah reacted swiftly and defensively, declaring that the experts' reports were "one-sided" and ignorant of local conditions. Lever's thirty-three-hour week at Port Sunlight, cited by Urwick and Hobhouse as a model, might be well suited to England "for men who work very strenuously," but "not for the more or less compulsorily leisurely work in a tropical climate." Padshah favored breaking up the eight hours to take into account the heat of the midday sun, for meals and "rest or stretching or drill." But the nature of steelwork itself complicated the straightforward relationship between efficiency and output posited by the experts. In a blast furnace, Padshah explained, "output depends on the charge and on the period of reaction, which cannot be altered by the reduction of hours of labour." As to the role of welfare in the alleviation of worker discontent, this was "an illusion, particularly in a tropical country, where work, hours of work, heat, nervous tension, mosquitoes, dread of disease, want of accustomed social amenities, are greater sources of discontent than can ever be dispelled by measures of what is called welfare."[94]

Padshah's arguments echoed Bombay millowners' well-worn appeals to nature and culture, while creating a secondary line of differentiation between TISCO and other industries. To take another example, Mann had found that the company provided housing for only eight thousand workers and their families, out of a total population of fifty thousand. He contrasted the cleanliness and order of nearby villages to the squalor and overcrowding of the town's "coolie lines," rows of rude shacks where residents complained of filth, unbearable heat, and lack of green space. He proposed building one-story, two-room houses with a central courtyard, arranged in decentralized "village colonies."[95] Padshah's response invoked climatic, racial, and medical ideas in circulation at the time to posit the "coolie" as a unique laboring subject:

> I sent to Mr. Wells [the general manager] a report of the Sociological Society of England in which one of the most capable scientists of the day had contended that modern model houses for coolies in

the tropics had killed the dark population with the white plague. . . .
When you dissociate them from this open air life, when you put
them in chawls and tenements, when you provide them with so
much room at a high rent that they are tempted to sub-let, you produce, you create conditions for phthisis [tuberculosis] among men
who have no congenital powers of resistance to it.[96]

The multistory *chawls* or tenements built on the cheap for Bombay's mill-
workers were indeed notoriously unsanitary and overcrowded, contributing
to high rates of tuberculosis along with the ingestion of cotton dust on the
factory floor.[97] But Padshah conflated the specific limitations of the *chawl* with
company-provided housing in general, asserting that any kind of confinement
would be destructive to *adivasis* both medically and financially. In their ignorance and simplicity, they would be "tempted to sub-let" by having ownership
over more space than they were naturally accustomed to.

Padshah's mode of reasoning may appear to be a textbook case of special
pleading, but it has much in common with the Webb Committee's reliance
on empirical social scientific investigation. The visiting experts accounted for
climatic and social-cultural difference and shared, to a great extent, Padshah's
faith in distinctly Indian institutions like the *panchayat* to produce social order
in the new township. Yet, they were met with a form of managerial counter-
expertise rooted in the same epistemology. Their recommendations, however
modest and carefully worded, were rejected out of hand as unsuited to local
conditions. Inconvenient facts, such as evidence that heat deaths affected Indian and foreign workers equally, were left out.[98]

The housing problem, inseparable from the land question and Jamshedpur's
contested status as a municipality, occupied TISCO management's attention
in the following years. Town Engineer F. C. Temple devised a creative solution in his 1919 urban plan. Like Mann, Temple admired the traditional *adivasi* way of life: "Most of the tribes of these parts are a clean people, provided
they have plenty of space and are not overcrowded. Their villages in the districts, built of brushwood and mud, are models of neatness and cleanliness."
In order to replicate these attractive features in an urban setting, Temple designed an experimental "coolie town" in Sonari, at the confluence of the
Kharkai and Subarnarekha Rivers. It followed the "well-known work by Herr
Rudolf Müller of Vienna, who designed a system of hexagonal planning which
gives great convenience for services, such as water supply and drainage." The
hexagons had the added advantage of providing ample courtyard space in-

FIG. 2.1. Hexagonal "coolie town" in Sonari, Jamshedpur. Reproduced from a copy of
F. C. Temple's *Report on Town Planning*, 1919, at the Frances Loeb Library, Harvard
Graduate School of Design.

cluding bathing tanks, latrines, and a plot where residents could gather their
own mud for building houses (Fig. 2.1).[99]

Temple's idiosyncratic scheme brought together transnational high modernism and localized primitivism. Its inspiration was Rudolf Müller, an obscure Austrian engineer who joined the brief worldwide craze for hexagonal
planning. Rejecting the aestheticized City Beautiful movement and its precepts of long axial roads, green space, and neoclassical architecture, Müller
drew on patterns found in nature (honeycombs, insect eyes) for the purpose
of improving delivery of basic municipal services. In a short article titled "The
City of the Future" (1908), Müller admitted that hexagons were not necessarily pleasing "as a city dweller, but as a system of water engineering and
sewage engineering." They may not have responded to "the wishes of the population" in Vienna but were worth trialing in certain districts.[100]

A sanitation engineer himself, Temple leaped at the chance to prove that
Müller's plan could be realized in faraway India, where it would fulfill the
imagined desires of "primitive peoples" for group living. In a presentation to
the Town Planning Institute in London, Temple stressed the usefulness of
the scheme as a technique of control and a first line of defense against the
physical and social degeneration of the *adivasi*. Members of the institute
praised his efforts to make Jamshedpur into a testing ground for the latest

planning trends, which could then be brought back to the metropole. One respondent suggested that the hexagonal layout could be a "most useful method of dealing with the ways of the slum dwellers" in Britain because "they could make their own mess in their own place." Another placed the emphasis on difference, observing that Jamshedpur was "not like a town, an English town," with "civic centres and vistas and architectural features," but a mere "collection of villages."[101] As in the legal debates over municipal status and taxation, Jamshedpur could not be imagined as a full-fledged city, only as a liminal space at once rural and urban, primitive and cosmopolitan, traditional and modern. The company's right to control and order space was the only constant.

The Ends of Welfare

Experts and managers shared a deep ambivalence toward *adivasis*, seen as naturally virile and pure races who had to be disciplined without destroying their innate health and physical strength. Even rank-and-file TISCO employees rhapsodized about the strange and wonderful spectacle of the *adivasi* body at work. S. Modak, who served as a timekeeper in the company's brick department during the early years, recalled:

> The men put on a small loin cloth and the women had small loin cloths like napkins of four cubits in length hung from their waists to the knees. Their upper bodies were completely bare. These labourers tied their attendance cards to their necks and the time keepers while punching these cards for attendance sometimes touched the bodies of the women without any objection from them. Their favourite songs were in Bengali, "I shall die and shall be reborn as the wife of a Time Keeper", "Ah, the Tata has much money and I shall not drive the bullock carts any more in Sakchi", "Ah, the Tata's electric lights are burning the whole night without oil."[102]

Modak's description lays bare a clearly unequal power relationship, with the supervisor free to touch women's bodies without their consent. Unlike the higher skilled workers, who were carefully segregated by community, *adivasis* were perceived as naively free of bodily shame and ritual taboos. Imputed fantasies of reincarnation as sexual partners to upper-caste men served to partially restore a familiar sense of hierarchy.

Surprisingly, given Modak's role as timekeeper, he did not engage in the kind of harsh moralistic condemnation of idleness that suffused the legitimizing discourse of the British Industrial Revolution.[103] *Adivasi* workers simply could not be subjected to the regime of clock time like their counterparts in the West. Of course, this had the added benefit of making regulations of working hours redundant. The relative absence of time discipline in Indian capitalism has been the subject of extensive historiographical debate. Employers ruled through hierarchical deference, paternalist blandishments, or raw physical violence rather than through rigidly enforced time sheets and attendance rolls. But the same could be said of most capitalists around the world, who worked through the "primordial loyalties" of ethnicity, religion, or kinship rather than destroying or diluting them.[104] Moreover, the considerable variation and change over time in managerial practices, even within a single company, belies easy conclusions about the nature of labor control in India as a whole. If the very first visits by government factory inspectors in the early 1880s were treated as "a frontal assault on the principle of the sovereignty of mill owners," by the 1920s, companies like TISCO were learning to share sovereignty with outside experts.[105]

International regulations affecting India's prestige in the world, the availability of more sophisticated and adaptable systems of scientific management, and above all, the outbreak of major labor unrest began to slowly change employers' minds. In 1919, the inaugural conference of the International Labour Organization (ILO) met in Washington, DC, aiming to counter the global spread of worker radicalism in the aftermath of World War I and the Bolshevik Revolution.[106] India was a founding member and the eighth most industrialized country represented in the ILO. The conference recommended implementing a universal six-day week and prohibiting the employment of women at night in coal mines. Representatives of leading Indian metallurgical concerns gathered at Jamshedpur in 1920 to state their categorical opposition. A day of rest might be appropriate for the textile mills, TISCO management submitted, but the nature of the steel industry "compels us to work on 365 days of the year and for 24 hours each day." The ILO's attempt to globalize regulations ostensibly failed to take account of the "relations between Indian industrial labour and agriculture and of the frequency of religious festivals," which made even simple record-keeping impractical. Moreover, TISCO employed a large number of "aboriginals or women of the lower classes who are in less need of benevolent protections than women elsewhere."[107] Liberal social reformers (many of them elite women) represented in the ILO focused on the plight of female labor in mines and factories, constructing an opposition between wage work and reproduction. In response, employers highlighted the "animality" of the *adivasi* woman, whose body could easily withstand both hard manual labor and childbirth.[108]

Not long after dismissing the recommendations of the Mann report in line with his colleagues, Padshah found himself opposing them on the question of the weekly day of rest. In a blistering attack on the company's official position, he invoked "the tradition of the Tata Iron & Steel Co. to take a broad and generous view of labour problems so as to be an example to others." Stubbornly refusing to implement the day of rest, when it had been accepted by other industries in India and Britain and recommended in Washington, DC, "would stamp the Steel Company's attitude as reactionary."[109] With regard to women working overtime at night, "we have been almost convicted of breach of law," which had already "produced a disagreeable impression" in the eyes of the world.[110] Padshah made his case using language that would, in time, become a Tata slogan: "One is in business for profits, but not for profits only."[111] Town Administrator S. K. Sawday, taking a hard line, dismissed Padshah's arguments by pointing to the "amplitude of leisure" enjoyed by workers on the loosely enforced eight-hour shift. Higher wages were unnecessary and undesirable for the same reason. The worker only wanted "recreation, time to go to the bazaar and to see his friends." As for night employment in the mines, Sawday insisted there was "no semblance of compulsion" involved: "Women don't work unless they want to. If there was any sort of hardship they would stop."[112]

Assumptions that workers in Jamshedpur were fundamentally content with their lot were shattered by the outbreak of the first major strike in February 1920. Increases in the cost of living due to postwar inflation affected all residents of the city, including the foreign "covenanted" employees. Indian workers' longer list of complaints included compulsory overtime, a rise in accidents after the expansion of the plant, racial discrimination and abuse on the shop floor, the lack of a representative town council, and Sawday's "arbitrary" rule over Jamshedpur.[113] The strike was initiated by Punjabi foremen and Bengali clerks, the most educated and highly skilled workers. They quickly established connections with the Indian National Congress in Calcutta and organized a formal union, the Jamshedpur Labour Association (JLA).[114] The company's initial reaction was both tone deaf and heavy-handed, using the language of paternalism to inspire loyalty without granting any concessions. On March 1, the American general manager T. M. Tutwiler addressed the workers "in the spirit of a father," pledging to personally take up their complaints with the directors, but his words did not have much effect.[115] On March 15, a group of Punjabi strikers attempted to stop a train carrying women "coolies," who had returned to work, out of the plant. Sawday lived up to his despotic reputation by ordering the police to fire on the crowd, resulting in five deaths and twenty-one injuries.[116] The strike ended soon after, but the illusion of consent was broken. The combination of workplace and urban grievances, the sharpening of regional and occupational divisions, and the company's vacillating response would become defining features of labor unrest in Jamshedpur.

Over the next few years, TISCO struggled to cut costs and improve productivity despite the grant of preferential tariffs. Increased workloads, irregular pay, and several rounds of retrenchment sparked mounting resistance. Continuing racial tensions and the enhancement of rents in the town added fuel to the fire, culminating in the outbreak of the largest strike in the company's history in 1928. This time, it was led not by a small minority of foremen and clerks but by a wider cross-section of skilled and semiskilled workers. They included crane drivers and *adivasis* in the rail finishing mills, who gave speeches in the Santhali language calling for solidarity with their Hindu and Muslim brethren. These workers approached Maneck Homi, a Parsi lawyer and son of a former TISCO employee with a grievance against the company, to represent them and form a rival union to the JLA. Managers and union leaders alike were dumbstruck, refusing to believe that mere "coolies" could act on their own and speak for themselves.[117] Women's prominence in the struggle came as a particular shock. They gave militant speeches and fought off strikebreakers with brooms, stones, and bodily refuse. From objects of protection during the previous strike, they became agents of resistance. Management decided to remove women from the workforce altogether once the agitation subsided, thereby meeting the ILO's demands from earlier in the decade.[118]

The company embraced expertise reactively and belatedly. Town Administrator S. K. Sawday, the workers' nemesis, became an unlikely champion of reform. He represented TISCO at the Third International Committee of Scientific Organisation of Labour in Rome in September 1927, shortly before the strike erupted. Impressed by the widespread adoption in the West of the principles of Taylorist scientific management, Sawday concluded that "a good many of them are applicable to us." Higher wages and a measure of collective bargaining would have to be accepted as part of the package. Arguments about *adivasi* workers' distinct habits, which Sawday himself had used against Padshah, were abandoned:

> At the present day, I think it can be argued that the coolie labour or at any rate the aboriginal coolie has no desire to improve his standard of living and if he earns more money, merely works less, and takes more leave for going home. Even then, we must remember that only certain parts of the world believe in work for the pleasure of working, and if the aboriginal spends more time in his own village after getting more money, that is his idea of raising the standard of living, and if he care to spend his money on leisure rather than food or clothes, it is none of our business.[119]

Sawday proposed an efficiency enhancement scheme (EES), which introduced a standardized wage structure and "payment by results." TISCO also established departmental shop committees, composed of workers appointed by both management and the union, in a tentative first step toward industrial democracy.[120] Crude assertions of difference in dealing with workers were giving way to a more complex interplay of localized paternalism and transnational expertise.

Machines in the Jungle

Even after embracing the basic desirability of "rationalization" through the EES, management did not abandon old habits of thinking with difference. Workers' ostensibly preindustrial mentalities were seen as the chief threat to the stability, productivity, and efficiency of the factory. The annual Hathyar Puja (tool worship) day, when cranes and locomotives were garlanded with flowers and received offerings as if they were deities, proved that workers "did not come to terms with the machine on the basis of even an elementary understanding of its working principles."[121] Both Indian and foreign experts who wrote about the Jamshedpur plant stressed the need to cultivate a stronger "machine sense" among workers, especially *adivasis*. Doing so would realize the full potential of industrialization and transform India from a backward colony to a modern nation.

The report of the Royal Commission on Labour in 1931 clearly articulated this agenda. Anthropologist Margaret Read's *The Indian Peasant Uprooted* (subtitled *A Study of the Human Machine*), which translated the dry findings of the commission into evocative prose, imagined how a typical migrant worker must have felt upon arrival in a textile mill:

> The machine with all its parts, some of them fenced for protection, seemed to him a monster, noisy, dangerous, and just alive enough to make the same movements over and over again with no pause and no change. Nothing in his previous experience with the cattle in the fields helped him to understand this machine creature and its ways.[122]

Read and the commission did not advocate converting villagers into a full-fledged proletariat entirely dependent on the factory, endorsing standard climatic and eugenic arguments about the enervating effects of heat and indoor confinement. But they brought monetary incentives to the forefront: "The wages paid to the worker supply his power as a human machine. Generally speaking, high wages mean high power in the human machine, low wages low power."[123]

Compared to the Bombay millowners, who still resisted the imposition of uniform scales of wages and grades, TISCO had made greater strides toward "rationalization" by the early 1930s.[124] The steel company had the opportunity to create a new kind of laboring subject whose rebellious enthusiasms would be dampened and whose aspirations for a better life would be fulfilled. Sheer skill was never thought of as an impediment to achieving the reconciliation between man and machine. As early as 1882, the report by German geologist Ritter von Schwartz, which had originally inspired Jamsetji Tata, argued that iron and steel production was well suited to India because it required "more quickness of movement and manual cleverness" rather than brute physical strength.[125] Indeed, adivasis' "natural precision of hand and eye" was the stuff of legend, evidenced by the remarkable accuracy of the rail straightening process (done mechanically but judged by the eye).[126] The rapid technical progress achieved at TISCO in just a few decades was plain to see. Sir Thomas Holland, a former director of the Geological Survey of India who advised the company, recounted, "I have seen labourers at Sakchi, who only a few years ago were in the jungles of Santals without any education. They are handling now red hot steel bars, turning out rails, wheels, angles of iron, as efficiently as you can get it done by any English labourer."[127]

Much like their foreign counterparts, Indian social scientists imbued TISCO with a radically transformative potential. The proximity of Jamshedpur to Calcutta allowed a new generation of Bengali economists and sociologists writing in the aftermath of the *swadeshi* movement, most notably Benoy Kumar Sarkar and Radhakamal Mukerjee, to study firsthand the progress of a pioneering industry.[128] On a visit to Jamshedpur as a member of the Bihar Labour Enquiry Committee in the late 1930s, Mukerjee was "astonished . . . to see a woman control driver at a crane in charge of her skilled and responsible task" while earning only Rs. 1 per day. Echoing Holland's assessment, this proved beyond any doubt that "the Indian industrial worker who is often treated by the employer as a part-time agriculturist can rise to his full stature as a machine-tender, comparable in his efficiency to his compeer in the industrial countries in the West."[129] Benoy Sarkar pointedly complained that to many "foreign observers," TISCO was "still appearing as an exotic 'unsuited to the tropics' . . . nothing more than an object of international curiosity."[130] Modern industry offered a new way of being in the world for Indians, free from the stigma of backwardness. Sarkar confidently declared, "The spirit of Tata is abroad and Tataism has come to stay. The tonic of machinery has commenced functioning in no unmistakable manner."[131]

For this "tonic" to have its desired effect on the patient, it had to be administered correctly. The lack of standardized occupational designations meant that experienced and capable Indian workers were deemed only "semiskilled" in the company hierarchy, which prevented them from obtaining higher wages and taking on greater responsibilities.[132] Mukerjee and Sarkar believed that rationalization "alone holds the key to the successful utilization of machines by men." But TISCO management was found wanting in its application. Intensifying workloads without offering a strong social bargain in return in the form of higher wages, Mukerjee warned, added up to "a perverse view that does not augur well for the increase of efficiency and output in the Indian steel industry."[133] Sarkar, too, struck a note of caution: "So with retrenchment and unemployment in one hand and higher wages and efficiency in the other the directors of the Steel works are consciously educating the people of all ranks to the double-edged sword of rationalization."[134]

What did Jamshedpur and the machines mean to the workers themselves? Perspectives from below are nearly impossible to access without intermediation. The *adivasi* song in praise of electricity recorded by the timekeeper Modak ("Ah, the Tata's electric lights are burning the whole night without oil") provides a clue. Anthropologists studied many such folk songs in the 1950s and 1960s, interpreting them through the lens of modernization theory as expressing a radical rupture between old and new. The following example, collected by Martin Orans, is meant to show the aspirational appeal of the city:

Kalka and Manpur are dark
While Holy (*holi*) Bistupur (main section
   of Jamshedpur) is light.
The train moves, the whistle sounds,
Tata coolies are dressed to go.
By day the bus, by night the train
khokokok' the big train has arrived.
O my friend, my old friend, bundle your
   things, let's go to Tata,
khokokok' let's climb aboard the big train.[135]

Along with electric lights and furnace fires, which pierce the primeval darkness of the jungle, the train inaugurates modernity by compressing space and accelerating time. This imagery, mirrored in Bromfield's travelogue that opens this chapter, corresponds to the trope of the "machine in the garden" as defined by critic Leo Marx. It is no coincidence that the noisy intrusion of a locomotive in a rustic landscape, a recurring scene in American art and literature from Hawthorne and Thoreau to Faulkner, also appears in Satyajit Ray's iconic film *Pather Panchali* (1955).[136]

The advent of industrial capitalism is laden with both promise and peril, eliciting a wide range of responses, from wonder and desire to fear, anxiety, and anger. At the height of the 1928 strike, trade unionist Abdul Kader described Jamshedpur as *"Andheri Nagar* (City of Darkness), ruled by an *Andha Raja* (Blind King)."[137] This language was especially powerful because it directly challenged the benign view of Jamshedpur as a city of lights pointing the way to India's industrial future (as in Bromfield's vision) and a spectacle of desire for the *adivasi* (as in Modak's memory of the song). We can only surmise it would have resonated with his audience.

Given the frequency of industrial accidents, the harshness of the climate, and the worsening social tensions in the town, rituals and rumors helped make sense of routine unpredictability and danger. In May 1929, soon after the end of the strike, word spread that the construction of a railway bridge over the Kharkai River required the kidnapping and sacrifice of 160 children to propitiate the machine gods. A hostile crowd threatened the contractor's life and stoned General Manager Keenan's car. Over the next two days, "a large number of coolie labourers on the Kharkai bridge, and also in Messrs Tatas works, absented themselves" from work. By way of explanation, colonial officials noted in the margins of the file that Jamshedpur was "built more or less out of nothing with an indigenous population largely aboriginal, but itself having a large cosmopolitan population."[138] Jamshedpur's dual "aboriginal" and "cosmopolitan" character was to blame. Concentrating diverse ethnic and religious groups in a tightly bounded and ordered space, as Sidney Webb feared, could amplify rather than dispel superstitions.

Protests against alleged human sacrifice for the construction of public works articulated a deeply felt "shock and disgust" at the abstraction, homogenization, and disenchantment of space.[139] From the perspective of *adivasis* who were forcibly conscripted into working on the bridge and whose livelihoods were under threat from TISCO's insatiable appetite for land across the river, the rumor provided an outlet for resistance soon after the escape valve of the strike closed. But it also echoed long-standing beliefs about the power of local rulers to strengthen and sanctify their fortifications by burying children underneath their walls. Similar stories circulated during the construction of railways, dams, and steel plants well into the twentieth century.[140] Since TISCO had legally assumed the role of *zamindar* alongside the command of labor, it came to bear the many burdens of sovereignty. The company could be a benevolent paternalistic ruler, ensuring that sacrifices would not be made in vain, or a blind king leading his subjects to destruction.

3

Worlds of Philanthropy

After Jamsetji Nusserwanji Tata's death in May 1904, the satirical news-paper *Hindi Punch* ran a revealing cartoon alongside his obituary. Seated with hands clasped together in reverent prayer, Jamsetji's words flow upward from his mouth in a plume of smoke: "Great Hormuzd [Ahura Mazda, the high deity of the Zoroastrian faith]! Giver of Light! For Thy Glory! In Thy Service! In Thy Keeping!" He is flanked by several stately female figures: one recognizably dressed in Parsi style, another whose trident evokes the Hindu goddess Durga, and the third wearing a sash that reads, "Charity." A number of objects are strewn around Jamsetji's feet, including a horn of plenty marked "Mr. Tata's Benefactions," a compass, a set of laboratory flasks, and a micro-scope enveloped by the words "Scientific Research Institute" (Fig. 3.1).

By juxtaposing cosmopolitan religious tradition with the cutting edge of modern science, the cartoon depicted Jamsetji's philanthropy as a bridge be-tween earlier mercantile charity in India, which was largely community based, and the needs of a modern nation. As the accompanying obituary commented, "his was not the charity that the average Parsi affects, but it was charity all the same, the truest kind—charity that helps to create not destroy, to regen-erate not demoralise, and he dispensed it, regardless of caste, colour or creed, without ostentation, without the accompaniment of trumpets and without the ulterior object of self-glorification and titled renown."[1] The oblique reference to "titled renown" alluded to an intense political controversy brewing over Jam-setji's endowment of the Indian Institute of Science (IISc), his single most important philanthropic bequest. The colonial government suspected that Jamsetji was merely using it as a means to obtain a title of nobility for him-self, in keeping with the perceived tendency among wealthy Indians to align charity with self-interest.

Jamsetji's philosophy of "constructive philanthropy" anticipated the devel-opmental needs of the nation-in-waiting, putting him at odds with the colonial state. His vision of economic *swadeshi,* in which private industry would build the material infrastructure of the Indian economy through textile mills, steel plants, and hydroelectric dams, also entailed a complementary infrastructure

FIG. 3.1. "One More Name in the Scroll of Fame," Jamsetji Tata obituary cartoon. Reproduced from a copy of *Hindi Punch*, May 22, 1904, at the Tata Central Archives, Pune.

of knowledge production and exchange. The IISc would reshape the educational field in much the same way that the Tata Iron and Steel Company (TISCO) transformed industry. The government embarked on its own project to promote modernization through technical education, finding in Tata an unexpected competitor. Officials were slow to grasp the appeal of "constructive philanthropy" and learn how to co-opt it. But this did not make the institute, any more than the steel plant, an unambiguously nationalist project. Ultimately, it was state sovereignty that made the IISc possible through the application of the Charitable Endowments Act (1890), just as the "public purpose" clause of the Land Acquisition Act secured TISCO's control over Jamshedpur.

Like the firm's industrial and commercial enterprises, Tata philanthropy transcended the boundaries of community, nation, and empire. It relied on the transnational movement of ideas and experts, some of them closely involved in technology transfer and labor control in the service of Tata companies. Investments in applied social science, beginning with Ratanji Tata's endowment of the poverty research unit at the London School of Economics (LSE) and culminating in the establishment of the Tata Institute of Social Sciences (TISS) in Bombay, were deeply connected with the need to manage diverse and restive labor forces in the Jamshedpur plant and Bombay textile mills. But the Tatas' giving cannot be directly mapped onto the firm's changing economic interests, nor did it mainly serve to bolster the family's social or community standing. Philanthropy and economy progressed along separate tracks, intersecting at crucial moments only to reveal the gaps between them.

In French sociologist Pierre Bourdieu's influential formulation, "economic and symbolic capital are so inextricably intertwined that the display of material and symbolic strength . . . is in itself likely to bring in material profits."[2] Bourdieu's concept of "symbolic capital" built on the earlier work of Marcel Mauss, who applied his study of the gift as a "total social fact" in ancient and tribal societies to market economies in the early twentieth century. To forge inclusive welfare states in which policies such as social insurance would avoid the "wounds" inflicted by unreciprocated charity, Mauss argued, "we can and must return to archaic society and elements within it."[3] Large-scale corporate philanthropy with explicitly "public" and nation-building aims held the promise of performing such an integrative function in the modern world. Yet, its relationship to the market was profoundly contradictory. British colonial jurisprudence attempted to draw rigid boundaries between profit making and altruism, interpreting the Indian mercantile gift as *extra commercium* (outside commerce) and thus characterized, as Bourdieu would have it, by "a willful misrecognition of its own calculatedness." At the same time, by subjecting the gift to the modernizing test of "public utility," the law demanded the kind of quantification and rationalization only the market could provide.[4]

In an attempt to wrench apart the reproduction of capital and the reproduction of families and to sequester the gift from the market, donors' wishes were sometimes altered beyond recognition. The estate of Tamil notable

Pachaiyappa Mudaliar, who died in 1794, was used to fund secular educational institutions only after courts reinterpreted his will to conform to "modern requirements" of what a philanthropist should be.[5] Despite lingering official distrust, the Parsis appeared to have internalized these requirements more than other communities. Since the early nineteenth century, Parsi merchants had funded the construction of schools, colleges, libraries, hospitals, and other works of "public utility," taking the lead in the "joint enterprise" of making modern Bombay in partnership with the colonial state.[6] Economic and philanthropic collaboration mirrored and reinforced each other. In 1838, Sir Jamsetjee Jeejeebhoy used his opium fortunes to endow a general hospital in Bombay "in the best interests of humanity." Yet, he was also the first of several distinguished Indians to be awarded a hereditary baronetcy, which allowed him to evade restrictions on the posthumous settlement of property.[7]

Recent scholarship has rejected the crude distinction between "naked instrumentalism and religious piety" inherited from colonial legal discourse, pointing to the existence of flexible and heterogeneous gifting practices across the medieval, early modern, and modern periods. Temples used donations as collateral for loans, whereas merchants used religious endowments and joint family assets as capital reserves.[8] What colonial law attempted to break apart, the historian must put back together. Self-consciously cosmopolitan, modernist, and technocratic from the start, Tata philanthropy aroused suspicion precisely for blending utilitarianism and market logic too closely. If not quite market driven, it remained market adjacent through the persistent connections with Tata enterprise. Philanthropy was embedded in a distinct *swadeshi* construct of the protonation through semiautonomous institutions of knowledge production.

Tata philanthropy remains an inconvenient case study, all too easily interpreted through the instrumentality-piety dichotomy. For many in the fields of business and management studies, Jamsetji's giving is reducible to his community identity as a Parsi and the basic ethical precept of *Humata, Hukhta, Huvarshta* (Good Thoughts, Good Words, Good Deeds). According to this literature, Jamsetji's acquisition of wealth was always tied to a long-term vision of development and thus lay outside the realm of the market.[9] This conforms to the colonial tendency to understand Indian philanthropy only "in its difference, as *ethnic,* that is, as the expression of a timeless culture."[10] A rival narrative presents his efforts as a catalyst for the modernization, professionalization, and bureaucratization of philanthropy in India. By replacing the community with the nation as the object of giving, and by employing transnational expertise and managerial methods of governance, Tata laid the groundwork for the ascendancy of the results-oriented and market-driven nongovernmental organization sector.[11]

Both narratives make use of comparisons with the general-purpose foundation in the United States, especially the Big Three of Carnegie, Rockefeller, and Ford. Jamsetji and his sons deliberately modeled the Tata Trusts on these foundations, both conceptually and organizationally. This influence undoubtedly set them apart from both other Indian philanthropists and the colonial model of utilitarian but circumscribed giving.[12] But while the Gilded Age titans were presumed to have turned to philanthropy in order to expiate the sins of capitalism or simply to evade taxation, Jamsetji Tata is presumed to have "acted of his own free will."[13] The tangled relationship between the Big Three and the state, first on a national then on a global scale in the age of "development" and Cold War ideological rivalry, offers the most fruitful terrain of comparison. Widely dispersed and loosely connected "knowledge networks" were not merely tools to accomplish foundations' instrumental goals, which changed over time and under various political pressures. These networks were "both a *means* of hegemony as well as an *end in itself,*" populating a landscape of elite actors who shaped knowledge production and governance across the public-private divide.[14] Most Tata-founded institutions were smoothly handed over to the new Indian state after independence in 1947, but their origins as private benefactions continued to matter. Networks could and did take on a life of their own.

A Landed Gentleman

Jamsetji Tata distinguished himself from his contemporaries, as the *Hindi Punch* cartoon and obituary indicated, by a resolutely scientific disposition in business and in life. In his first industrial venture, the Empress Mills, Jamsetji was an early adopter of the ring spindle, a method to improve spinning used by the most advanced operators in Lancashire and New England. Few Indian millowners followed his example. By contrast, in Japan, foreign technology was quickly indigenized with the *gara-bo* (rattling) spindle and Toyoda automatic power loom, which partly explains why the Japanese textile industry began to outcompete India's at the turn of the century.[15] For the hydroelectric and iron and steel projects, Jamsetji carried out an extensive correspondence with metallurgists, chemists, and engineers from Britain, the United States, and Germany, always on the lookout for the best and most recent innovations.[16]

Jamsetji's enthusiasm for science extended beyond the realm of production. During the plague outbreaks ravaging western India in the late 1890s, he took up the cause of a promising vaccine developed by the Russian Jewish bacteriologist W. M. Haffkine, spreading "the gospel of inoculation" among his family, servants, and friends. Before his son Dorabji's marriage, he insisted that the bride's father submit to the vaccine immediately upon arrival at Esplanade House, appealing to him "as an educated man, whose business it was to set an example for others."[17] Although many colonial doctors in the Indian Medical Service questioned Haffkine's claims and rumors spread about the vaccine's potentially harmful effects, Jamsetji led a committee that conducted a large-scale observational trial among Parsis, conclusively showing a substantial reduction in mortality.[18] The Empress Mills set out to inoculate the majority of its four-thousand-strong workforce in September 1899, and did so again during subsequent outbreaks.[19] To be sure, controlling plague was also a matter of economic self-interest. When the disease first reached Bombay, many mills were forced to close. Thousands of workers fled the city; those who remained could bargain for higher wages and resist managerial authority. Employers joined hands with colonial officials to make the city safe for business again.[20] But vaccination competed with forced quarantine and slum demolition as preferred techniques of mitigation. Jamsetji's wholehearted support made a powerful public statement in its favor.

Agricultural experiments, many of them connected to Jamsetji's growing real estate portfolio in and around Bombay, are equally noteworthy for their breadth and ambition. His former land manager recalled a variety of initiatives, including turtle rearing, a poultry farm in his hometown of Navsari, horse stables in the hill station of Panchgani, and several reclamation projects in Bombay. The vast Mahim River scheme involved moving all cattle out of the city and establishing "Buffalow, Cow and Sheep-breeding farms on an elaborate scale on scientific lines." Jamsetji proposed acquiring 2,800 acres of land in the north of Bombay island and planting "special salt bushes to serve as fodder for buffaloes," which he thought would improve the quality of the animals' milk. He even purchased the entire nearby village of Anik "solely for his own edification and pleasure" as a laboratory for salt bush cultivation.[21]

Most significantly, Jamsetji promoted long-staple Egyptian cotton, which was superior to Indian cotton but grew only under drier climatic conditions. He reported good results from a personal plot at Navsari, which yielded "400 lbs. of pure lint per acre in one season," and planned more experiments with the American Sea Island variety.[22] In an influential memorandum on the subject, published in 1893, Jamsetji called for nationwide trials, which could become "a source of great amusement as a rational pastime" even for India's "poor and starving submerged class."[23] He also used the firm's connections with Japan to promote the circulation of agricultural knowledge, establishing a silk farm near Bangalore staffed by a Japanese expert, Mr. Ozu, and using imported machinery. The colonial Department of Agriculture judged that the Tata Experimental Farm produced "some of the best silk in India" and briefly attempted to emulate its achievements.[24]

Idealistically, Jamsetji envisioned both large landowners and millions of small cultivators adopting his scientific mindset and following his entrepreneurial example. Pragmatically, Jamsetji's appeal was concerned with the commercial future of the industry. In the 1890s, Bombay millowners faced increasing competition in the China market from Japanese exports, not least due to the kind of technological leaps Jamsetji had taken at the Empress Mills but others had failed to emulate. In the end, due to the apathy of the colonial state and the magnitude of his commitments elsewhere, Jamsetji's contribution to the modernization of Indian agriculture remained marginal. His first biographer, Wacha, lamented a lost opportunity: "On the whole his views on irrigation and agriculture were of a sound and practical character, and it is a pity that Mr. Tata did not expound them for the benefit of the country in his own exhaustive way as he had done in reference to matters industrial."[25]

If his agricultural experiments were something of a dead end, the lands purchased by Jamsetji would eventually bear fruit through their sheer monetary value. For many Parsi merchants of his generation, real estate offered a promising new outlet for investment after the decline of the opium and cotton trades.[26] As plague drove the population of the city north into new suburban developments, Jamsetji lobbied the government on behalf of tenants who built houses on village plots and wished to be assessed at lower rates of taxation.[27] His own strategy was to buy up as much "vacant land" as possible throughout the islands of Bombay and Salsette, at low prices ranging from 3–12 annas to Rs. 1/- per square yard, convinced that they would "one day be worth 1000 or 2000 fold its original price." He then refused to sell to any private buyer, no matter the offer, unless "compelled by the Government" through the Land Acquisition Act.[28] Here was another instance of colonial law enabling private capital accumulation. But unlike the situation in Jamshedpur, Tata was a beneficiary rather than a victim of speculation. After his death, Jamsetji's sons inherited a diverse real estate portfolio, concentrated in Bombay but extending to Navsari, Nashik, Panchgani, and the hill station of Ootacamund in South

India (see Appendix). The family's great benefactions were made possible in the first instance by the sale of these lands.

A Contested Inheritance

The Indian Institute of Science took shape at the confluence of national, imperial, and global forces. The idea came to Jamsetji after listening to an address by the governor of Bombay in 1889 bemoaning the deficiencies of Indian higher education. During his travels to the United States in connection with the iron and steel project, he became fascinated with the research university model pioneered at Johns Hopkins in Baltimore through private philanthropy, and grew determined to replicate it.[29] A chance encounter with the Bengali monk Swami Vivekananda on a steamship from Japan to Chicago in 1893 strengthened his resolve. An ardent nationalist and modernizing religious reformer, Vivekananda was on his way to the inaugural Parliament of the World's Religions, where he became an instant global celebrity. Perhaps apocryphally, he is said to have asked Jamsetji why the Tata trading companies imported matches from Japan and urged him to start more factories in India in order to "prevent the national wealth from going out of the country."[30] Invoking Dadabhai Naoroji's "drain" theory, as its author did when trying to persuade Jamsetji not to seek foreign financing for the steel plant, shows that the precepts of *swadeshi* were not yet self-evident and had to be carefully cultivated.

During their encounter on the ship, Jamsetji found that his ideas for the institute resonated with Vivekananda's plans for promoting technical education through a new social service organization, the Ramakrishna Mission. He aligned the quest for pure research with the religiously inspired work of the mission: "no better use can be made of the ascetic spirit than the establishment of monasteries or residential halls for men dominated by this spirit, where they should live with ordinary decency, and devote their lives to the cultivation of sciences—natural and humanistic."[31] Vivekananda returned the favor, writing in the pages of his periodical *Prabuddha Bharata,* "Mr. Tata's scheme paves the path of placing into the hands of Indians this knowledge of Nature . . . that by having the knowledge, they might have power over her and be successful in the struggle for existence."[32] In a departure from the "joint enterprise" model of collaboration, what began as a government appeal to local elites to improve education came to be mediated through intellectual and institutional channels far beyond the imperial relationship.

In 1899, Jamsetji submitted a concrete proposal to the government, drawn up by his faithful lieutenant B. J. Padshah after an additional fact-finding tour across Western Europe and consultation with nationalist leaders. Its most significant feature was joining the gift for the institute with the settlement of the family estate. Jamsetji would donate Rs. 30 lakhs worth of his Bombay properties, yielding Rs. 1.25 lakhs per annum for the institute. His descendants would be allowed to draw on the same fund for their maintenance, giving them a stake in the success of the venture. The proposal justified this unusual structure of the endowment on strictly utilitarian and technocratic grounds. Because "property Trusts are very difficult to manage and liable to abuse," Jamsetji explained, "my descendants will become a sort of hereditary managers with liabilities to the Governing Body."[33] This arrangement would, in theory, ensure the responsible governance and long-term financial health of the institute.

Such an endowment required the passage of special legislation to overcome the "rule against perpetuities." At the time, colonial law prohibited the settlement of property "either by a transaction *inter vivos,* or by will, on a person who is not in existence at the time of the transaction."[34] The *Tagore v. Tagore* case (1872) and the Transfer of Property Act (1882) expressly prohibited the vesting of property in the future for "nonexistents," in order to prevent "unproductive accumulation" in Hindu Undivided Families (HUFs). Property was meant to circulate freely in the market, unfettered by the "dead hand" of the testators.[35] Rare exceptions had been made only in favor of two Parsi merchants granted the title of baronet, Jamsetjee Jeejeebhoy and Dinshaw Petit, but not without considerable anguish. In 1893, Petit was allowed to settle property consisting of his mansion and Bombay Municipal Corporation bonds yielding 1.25 lakhs per annum (coincidentally the same amount as Jamsetji's estate) to prevent his family's "dignity from falling into poverty or disrepute at any future time."[36] Officials were wary of generalizing these exceptions. They scrambled to parse the intricacies of diverse Hindu and Muslim legal traditions, which often provided for expanded family claims to property, and render them commensurate with British legal precedent.

The stringent rule against perpetuities took shape in the context of "a rising capitalist economy." In the notorious case of *Thelluson v. Woodford* (1805), a merchant involved in the West India sugar trade had set up a trust that would continue to accumulate after his death for the exclusive benefit of his descendants. This led to the passage of an eponymous act to prohibit others from following his example. Colonial legal advisers were well aware of this case and expressly cited it during the debates on the Jeejeebhoy and Petit settlements.[37] On the one hand, the prevailing government policy was to consolidate and secure the estates of large *zamindars,* who would benefit from a relaxation of the rule. Whereas in England, it was "obviously desirable to prevent the land from getting into the hands of a few families who would be practically monopolists, in a vast country like India . . . the best landlords are the great *zamindars.*" Representatives of the Tagore family and Bengali landholders' associations naturally agreed.[38] On the other hand, the rapid ascent of an Indian commercial elite whose wealth no longer lay primarily in land reinforced the need for the rule. The government had "no interest, or very little, in the maintenance of modern families to whom titles have been given of late for services of a public nature, chiefly for liberal donations of money to objects of public utility"—that is to say, merchant philanthropists like Jeejeebhoy, Petit, and Tata.[39]

The odds were thus decidedly against the proposal as originally drafted. Padshah made a valiant attempt to persuade officials that some strands of personal law did provide for joint settlements, as long as they fulfilled a charitable public purpose:

> The proposal to create the Joint Trust is on the lines of the Mahomedan system of Wakf, recognised by British Indian Law as valid for one-third of her Majesty's subjects in India. In case of non-Mahomedans, the law acquiesces in the creation of Trusts exclusively for the benefit of public charities; and would not presumably object if designated persons were made hereditary stewards on a remuneration specified in the Trust Deed.[40]

Waqfs were indeed a partial exception to the rule against perpetuities, nominally permitted under Muslim law but increasingly subject to the same limitations on the disposal of urban real estate and commercial securities. The Zoroastrian legal tradition in Iran made no distinction between family endowments and public charities. Many Zoroastrians used *waqfs* to protect their property after the imposition of Islamic law, although there is no evidence of continuity between these practices and the development of Parsi personal law in India.[41] In any event, Padshah did not fully develop this argument, allowing the utilitarian and market-based logic of Jamsetji's offer to stand on its own merits.

Legal opinion on the matter within the government and the India Office was divided. Some were willing to concede that "the public interests involved, the enterprise and enlightenment of the family for which provision is to be made, and the exceptional display of a wise public spirit, render this a special case."[42] Others saw in the proposal a dangerous precedent that should not be encouraged: "Mr. Tata has committed a blunder very similar to that committed by the Jubbulpoor millionaire Gokul Dass . . . he has started by coupling together what he is ready to give & what he wants to get in such a way that no amount of ingenuity can ever separate them."[43] The Marwari merchant and landowner Raja Gokuldas had styled himself a princely ruler and sought legitimacy through philanthropic largesse, sponsoring a women's hospital in the Central Provinces in response to an appeal by the viceroy's wife in 1885. Behind the scenes, he was involved in negotiations over the question of how to settle property in the HUF, seeking to protect the customary rights of joint family heirs. Local officials publicly praised Gokuldas but regarded his pretensions to higher status with deep suspicion.[44]

Was Jamsetji another Gokuldas, a mere arriviste angling for a title and exploiting legal loopholes the state had unwittingly left open? The viceroy, Lord Curzon, certainly thought so. "Old Tata was even more interested in his family endowment settlement than in his Research Scheme," he concluded.[45] There was little evidence to support this cynical assessment. In fact, one Parsi baronet in Bombay privately tried to convince Jamsetji to accept a title as a condition of passing the special legislation, but he steadfastly refused to consider it.[46] When the government's hostile attitude became known, nationalist public opinion rallied to his side. Sister Nivedita, Vivekananda's disciple, objected to Curzon's insinuations in the Calcutta newspaper *The Statesman:* "So far from Mr. Tata's trying to involve the Government of India in a scheme for the benefit for his own children, he is willing to risk starvation for his children in order to secure the benefit to the Nation which he desires to confer upon it."[47] The dispute exemplifies the larger tension between colonial sovereignty and indigenous philanthropy. A joint settlement was unacceptable because it violated newly instituted boundaries between public and private, and between the gift and the market. Yet, the application of the rule against perpetuities in this case was *not* due to anxieties about vernacular gifting practices incommensurable with British law. The very transparency, legibility, and utilitarian logic of Jamsetji's proposal made it potentially subversive.

Contemporary developments in the United States help clarify the distinctiveness of the Tata case. Andrew Carnegie, John D. Rockefeller, and other

Gilded Age benefactors also attempted to establish general-purpose foundations with a wide mandate to promote scientific research and education. Yet,
they ran up against the "dead hand" precedent protecting the claims of blood
relatives on family fortunes. The test case here was Samuel Tilden's gift of the
New York Public Library in his 1884 will, which was challenged by his im-
poverished heirs. The Tilden Act, passed by New York State in 1893, gave
trustees freedom to modify the scope and character of philanthropy according
to changing circumstances.[48] The Tilden Act paved the way for the advent of
the modern multipurpose foundation, but its purpose was to stop families limiting the scope of philanthropy. By contrast, colonial law expelled the family
from the trust in order to impose more stringent restrictions on the uses to
which gifts could be put. The institute was controversial precisely because it
fulfilled a priori the narrowest standard officials could devise.

The demand for passing special legislation was dropped after Jamsetji's
death, and the grant was registered under the terms of the Charitable Endowments Act (1890). This far-reaching law facilitated the creation of trusts devoted to "relief of the poor, education, medical relief and the advancement of
any other object of general public utility," placing them under government
oversight.[49] In the service of "an abstract public of beneficiaries," not bounded
by kinship, religion, and community, the state assumed ultimate "trusteeship"
over its subjects while at the same time upholding "nonintervention in indigenous gifting practices."[50] Jamsetji's claim to the abstractions of the market
and "public utility" destabilized but failed to dislodge the principle of state
sovereignty.

However, registration under the Charitable Endowments Act did not put
an end to the controversy. From the start, officials warned that the institute
"may degenerate into a sort of almshouse for the maintenance of Brahmin &
Mahratta agitators, and that therefore a supreme control by Government ought
to be insisted upon as a sine qua non."[51] The question of its location sparked a
new round of legal battles, undermining colonial sovereignty in a different way.
Jamsetji was forced to abandon Bombay, the traditional home of Parsi philanthropy under the old framework of collaboration, due to "the opposition
of the Parsi members [of the Municipal Corporation] who wished that their
own community would exclusively benefit by his liberality."[52] A generous offer
of a site near Bangalore from the princely ruler of Mysore offered a way out.
Along with Baroda, Mysore was one of the leading progressive princely states
committed to modernization through education and industry.[53] Locating the

institute in Bangalore would allow it to operate away from the watchful gaze of the authorities, signaling the Tatas' commitment to nation-building over community interest.

To facilitate the application of the Charitable Endowments Act to the Bangalore site, two conditions were imposed. First, "the site of the Institute should be so dealt with by the Mysore Government *as, if possible, to make it part of British India.*" But there was considerable confusion as to whether Mysore had provided merely "for the cession of jurisdiction, and not of sovereignty."[54] This distinction was important because it determined which laws would apply within the boundaries of the institute: Mysore's or those of the British Civil and Military Station?[55] Colonial officials feared that "this area, being exempt from the operation of all laws, would soon become an Alsatia," the disputed border territory between France and Germany. Ultimately, it was decided that legislation then in force in the station, as well as the jurisdiction of its courts, would apply wholesale to the site.[56] The institute had not quite become a privately governed zone of exception, like the steel township of Jamshedpur described in the previous chapter. But it was now free from Curzon's attempts to centralize government control over higher education through the Indian Universities Act of 1904.[57] In both cases, with varying degrees of success, private capital and philanthropy carved out a semiautonomous sphere of operation by taking advantage of fragmented and layered sovereignty.

The second condition of applying the act, with more adverse implications, was a drastic reduction in the academic scope of the institute. Following the Johns Hopkins model, Padshah originally proposed three branches: a scientific and technical department, a medical department focusing on the study of tropical diseases, and a philosophical and educational department housing the study of history, statistics, philosophy, and other humanistic and social scientific disciplines. The government recommended the establishment of just three branches (chemistry, experimental physics, and biology), comprising only a small part of Padshah's plan. Moreover, the experimental research carried out by the institute would have only a tangential connection to India's industrial development. Padshah and the first director, the chemist Morris W. Travers of University College, London, clashed repeatedly over the mandate of the institute. Frustrated, Travers asked the government to determine once and for all "whether the Tata Brothers were donors of the endowment or are handing over the properties and income in fulfillment of a trust"—a clear statement of the "dead hand" problem. But the Law Department was not inclined to reopen the question of the founder's intent. Travers resigned in 1914, blaming Padshah for his excessive meddling.[58] The Indian Industrial Commission, convened after World War I, expressed the government's disappointment with both the location and academic scope of the institute, finding that "its value to the industries of India is reduced by its distance from the places in which they are carried on."[59]

Dorabji Tata refused to give up on medical research, in accordance with his father's wishes. Jamsetji had once contemplated installing the bacteriologist Haffkine as the first director of the institute, indicating the importance he attached to the study of infectious diseases. Curzon's opposition put an end to that idea as well. Dorabji proposed the creation of a School of Tropical Medicine in Bombay with a wide research mandate and attracting highly paid faculty from Australia and the United States. The Government of Bombay preferred a more practical and circumscribed scheme, with the Tata endowment funding buildings rather than salaries, and finally withdrew its support in 1922.[60] A bitter Dorabji linked the fate of the Indian Institute of Science with the failure of the school in a sweeping indictment of colonial apathy:

> For over 20 years, in spite of protests from Indian Public men, my father and I sought the co-operation of Government in such matters. But I regret to have to say that in every instance we did not meet with the support we hoped for from Government. The Indian Institute of Science at Bangalore took years to establish, and is still not in a satisfactory condition. . . . From all this I can only come to one conclusion, namely, that if Indians want higher education and scientific knowledge they must depend upon themselves.[61]

In this belated embrace of *swadeshi* radicalism, Dorabji admitted that the Tatas' readiness to cooperate with the colonial state, even after all the troubles they had faced, may have been a mistake.

Nationalist opinion was divided on how to interpret the achievements of Tata philanthropy. The poet Rabindranath Tagore, a living embodiment of the *swadeshi* spirit, told a British newspaper:

> But every Indian feels, and every candid student of India must admit, that you have conceived it to be your interest to keep us weak and have discouraged education. In the laboratories you dislike us to acquire science and to pursue research. The Tata Foundation is

an illustration. Here at last, we thought, India's opportunity had come. But the Government has taken control of it and killed it, and that splendid gift is now barren and worthless.[62]

From a cause célèbre at the time of the joint settlement dispute, the institute had become a cautionary tale. Other spokesmen for *swadeshi* were more sanguine, depicting the Tatas as agents for Indian progress and worthy equivalents to their American counterparts. The Kashmiri Urdu poet Kaifi exclaimed, "Let every man be like a Carnegie, and every Indian be the image of a Tata."[63] The Bengali physicist Meghnad Saha made the same comparison between Tata and Carnegie in the pages of his journal *Science and Culture,* as part of an appeal to Indian business to fund scientific research.[64] The sociologist and economist Benoy Kumar Sarkar observed that the "Carnegie spirit as embodied in educational and humanitarian benefactions may be virtually as old as Indian culture itself." India had "her Carnegies, big, medium, and small," including the monks of the Ramakrishna Mission. In this respect, Sarkar claimed, "the East is qualitatively, if not quantitatively, at one with the West."[65] Tata philanthropy was simultaneously understood as vernacular, with roots stretching deep into the mythico-spiritual past; as global, connecting India to the latest scientific and technological developments in the West; and as laying the groundwork for the nation-in-waiting.

Philanthropy and Community

Jamsetji Tata defined "constructive philanthropy" in the following well-known quote: "What advances a nation or community is not so much to prop up its weakest and the most helpless members, as to lift the best and most gifted so as to make them of the greatest service to the country."[66] This was self-consciously different from traditional practices of Parsi charity in Bombay. Donations to fire temples, schools, *dharamshalas* (rest houses), and *baugs* (low-cost housing colonies) served to provide employment, education, and spaces of worship to community members while reinforcing the status of elites and distinctions between Parsi and non-Parsi.[67] The J. N. Tata Endowment for the Higher Education of Indians, a scholarship established in 1892 to give concrete expression to his philosophy, was initially open only to deserving Parsi students but only a few months later "extended so as to include [in] its operation any Natives of India besides Parsees including Native Christians having Indian domicile."[68] The IISc was located in Bangalore in overt defiance of community leaders' preference for Bombay. The Tata Trusts endowed by

Jamsetji's two sons would follow this path, becoming ever more capacious and cosmopolitan in order to meet nationalist aspirations for an all-India infrastructure of knowledge production.

Ratanji and Dorabji died in 1919 and 1932, respectively. Their wills clearly express their priorities and approaches to philanthropy. Ratanji's income from real estate and shares in the holding company Tata Sons were vested in a trust "for the advancement of Education Learning and Industry in all its branches" and "for the relief of human suffering or for other works of public utility." The trust struck a balance between national and community needs: "The objects to be aided by the funds should be public and general in preference to sectional unless in the latter case they tend to contribute to the general well-being and advancement of my own community [the Parsis]." Ratanji's will also prioritized the question of "the proper subjects of charity and how the benefits contemplated by particular charities might be realised to their fullest extent." Above all, the trust would be guided by the "fresh light that is thrown from day to day by the advance of science and philosophy on problems of human well-being."[69] This concern was already evident in his sponsorship of the LSE Department of Social Administration (see Chapter 2). Dorabji's will cast an even wider net than his brother's, offering support to charities "for the benefit of all communities" and "of a general character" and excluding "gifts or donations to relieve individual distress."[70] The activities of the Dorabji Tata Trust were confined to India at first but quickly took on a global character. The very term *Indian* was broadly defined to "include Indian communities abroad whether in Kenya, America, South Africa or any other place."[71]

Whereas Ratanji was more inclined toward the humanities and social sciences, Dorabji's main passion was medical research. Undeterred by the failure of the School of Tropical Medicine, he established a fund for leukemia research in honor of his wife, Meherbai, who died of the disease one year before him. The Lady Tata Trust was the first philanthropic organization in the world exclusively devoted to the little-understood blood cancer. It drew on the advice of experts from London, Paris, and Berlin and reserved scholarships for students by "zones": two from England, one each from Germany and France. Around four-fifth of grants went to European researchers, and the trust resisted pressures to refocus on India. The Dorabji Tata Trust thus promoted the "internationalization" of science, even at the expense of building up Indian capacities in certain areas.[72]

Whatever their differences, the brothers shared a fundamentally cosmopolitan perspective in their giving. During his lifetime, Ratanji donated to causes transcending national and imperial borders. His most notable gift was a political contribution of Rs. 25,000 to support Mohandas K. Gandhi's campaign for the rights of Indians in South Africa. Ratanji's help came at a critical moment when Gandhi's movement was desperate for funds and many of his colleagues were tempted to compromise with the Transvaal government.[73] In his correspondence with Gandhi, Ratanji stressed the global implications of the struggle. Failure, he wrote, "will be considered tantamount to an acknowledgement by us of our inferiority to the white races. What effect this would have in future in the treatment of our countrymen by the whites in various parts of the world, could easily be imagined."[74] In 1913, while chairing a committee appointed to raise additional funds for Indians in South Africa, Ratanji made a donation of Rs. 1,000 for the families of those killed in the Balkan Wars. A few years earlier, he also offered to assist "the poor Parsis of Iran" after attending a lecture at the Society of Arts in London.[75] Ratanji's philanthropy was thus informed by multiple anticolonial, pan-Islamist and pan-Zoroastrian imaginaries.

Even the most seemingly esoteric and inward-looking of Ratanji's interests must be viewed through a global lens. In 1912, he agreed to finance the Archaeological Survey of India's excavations at Pataliputra in Bihar, with a view of making acquisitions for his extensive art collection. The archaeologist in charge of the dig, the American D. B. Spooner, uncovered what he believed to be the audience hall of the ancient Mauryan emperor Ashoka. Spooner observed numerous similarities between the pillars of this hall and the ruins of Persepolis in Iran. With Ratanji's encouragement, Spooner published a theory of common origin between the Zoroastrians and the Mauryas, thus simultaneously globalizing the most ancient and glorious of Indian civilizations and indigenizing the Parsis. Rumors spread that Spooner's findings were nothing more than a "*quid pro quo* to ascribe the glories of Chandragupta and his capital to the Parsis of old," in an obvious attempt to flatter his patron.[76] But Ratanji's attraction to the theory cannot be ascribed to mere communitarian blinders. His father was similarly enthralled by archaeology, becoming convinced that in the Gujarati village of Sanjan, site of the Parsis' first arrival in India, "some buried treasure or some remarkable relics of our Zoroastrian religion will one day come to be unearthed." Jamsetji's quest for ancient ruins was inseparable from his geological investigations for the iron and steel project.[77] Ratanji, too, sought to use the tools of modern scientific inquiry to discover what was Indian, and who was Parsi, in the world.

At first glance, Dorabji appeared more inclined than his brother to police community boundaries. But he did so within the same framework of empire-wide race relations informing Ratanji's correspondence with Gandhi, rather than making an argument from orthodoxy. When his cousin Ratanji Dadabhoy (R. D.), head of the Tatas' trading company, announced his intention to marry a French woman, Suzanne Brière, Dorabji expressed his fervent opposition. He told R. D. that "as the question of the young lady being of a different race goes very few of us would have any objection on religious or other similar grounds. The trouble is all racial &. . . in India such marriages are more than a mistake and absolutely criminal."[78] For his part, Jamsetji was "quite at a loss to understand" his son's objections and gave his blessing to the marriage.[79] As in business matters, Dorabji's excessive caution proved prescient. The union sparked a massive public controversy over whether the new Mrs. Tata could become a Parsi and have access to community institutions. In the landmark case of *Sir Dinshaw M. Petit v. Sir Jamsetji Jeejeebhoy* (1908), the Bombay High Court ruled that full conversion was impossible because Parsis had become an Indian community analogous to a Hindu caste and were not simply members of the Zoroastrian faith living in India. The judgment affirmed orthodoxy up to a point, allowing Mrs. Tata's children (including future chairman Jehangir Ratanji Dadabhoy [J. R. D.] Tata) to become Parsi. In effect, men could marry outside the community, but women could not.[80] The courts thus enshrined new distinctions into law without definitively settling the question of who was a Parsi.

The Tata family fell squarely on the "reformist" side of the burgeoning community divide. Both brothers strongly denounced superstition and blind adherence to custom in their wills, in line with Parsi elites' desire to distinguish themselves from Hinduism in the aftermath of the *Petit v. Jeejeebhoy* case.[81] Ratanji's wife, Navajbai, was to "move about and mix in society as she has been doing in my life time and dress and deck herself quite regardless of the custom to the contrary prevailing among the Parsis."[82] Dorabji likewise stipulated that his funeral expenses should not be "unnecessarily wasteful or made only for show or out of regard for such superstitious customs as have crept into our faith but which do not conform to the true tenets of our religion."[83] The brothers promoted female education in order to rationalize religious practices and gender norms. Ratanji donated to the Zoroastrian Girls' School Association and to the Seva Sadan, a social work organization founded by Behramji Malabari, the famed Parsi campaigner against child marriage. He also left Rs. 15,000 in his will for the promotion of "hospitals, work-classes, industrial houses and institutions of a like character for females in any part or parts of British India."[84] In a slightly more conservative and paternalistic vein, Dorabji offered to finance a survey of women's education in the Bombay Presidency "to imbue girls with a sense of responsibility for duties which as wives, mothers and members of Society, they will have to perform."[85] His wife, Meherbai, was active in campaigns for prohibition, women's suffrage, and the abolition of child marriage and *devadasi* (temple dancing, associated with prostitution). She notably spoke in support of the Sarda Act (1929), a landmark law that raised the age of marriage for girls to fourteen and symbolized the coalescence of women as nationalist political subjects.[86] Following the lead of contemporary reformers, the Tatas believed in systematic top-down solutions to social problems, including the perceived decay or decline of their own community.

During the Great Depression, the single most pressing issue facing the Parsis in Bombay was precisely the one that traditional charity was designed to address—namely, the relief of urban poverty and unemployment. Some business families, such as the Wadias, intensified their efforts to build low-cost housing. Others spearheaded a "back to the land" movement of agricultural colonies. The industrialist Ardeshir Godrej established an experimental farm in the lush green hills near Nashik to cure unemployed Parsis of the "parasitic life in Bombay."[87] Anxieties over economic decline were increasingly racialized. The community's perceived overreliance on charity was thought to create a permanent beggar class, sapped of vitality and entrepreneurial spirit. Victorian-era moralizing distinctions between the "deserving" and "undeserving" poor were recast in an aggressively eugenic mold. The state of Parsis in Bombay, as one letter to the *Times of India* put it, offered an "unparalleled example of mass degeneration."[88] Meherbai Tata took up this rhetoric, condemning "the stupid attitude of poor Parsis, both men and women, of refusing to do manual work to earn an honest living" and comparing the "foolish and ridiculous" Parsi charities in Bombay with "the wretched dole system" that contributed to the "steady deterioration of the working classes" in England.[89]

In this dire atmosphere, complaints that the Tatas were not doing enough for their fellow Parsis came to a boiling point, threatening the family's standing in the community. The Dorabji Tata trustees firmly refused a call to set aside Rs. 3 crore "for the exclusive use" of the Parsi poor, "in view of the fact that theirs was a cosmopolitan trust."[90] Instead, the trusts took the lead in the rationalization and systematization of charity. The Bombay Parsi Panchayat (BPP), the apex community body, began keeping a centralized register of applicants. In 1935, the Ratan Tata Trust commissioned Jal F. Bulsara, the general secretary of the BPP and an adviser to the Godrej farm, to more thoroughly investigate the problem of urban poverty using these data. The study aimed to help Parsis "regain and retain a normal level of physical and intellectual efficiency" and to ensure that "inefficient, unhealthy, and unintelligent never-do-wells are not to swarm the army of the unemployed." Bulsara's main recommendation was to start an employment bureau and an industrial institute in Bombay, supported by the Ratan Tata Trust, where Parsi men and women "could receive wages not doles."[91] As had become typical, the trustees framed their role in universal terms, insisting that they "have not frittered away money on causes just because they were communal, but because they were genuine matters of distress and required urgent relief which it was the duty of any Trust cosmopolitan or otherwise to help from a purely humanitarian point of view."[92] But their interventions remained thoroughly enmeshed in community dynamics and beholden to the intellectual currents of the day.

The Uses of Knowledge

The Tata Trusts' fight against inefficiency and degeneration extended beyond the Parsi poor to the broader labor force in Bombay, exposing the underlying connections between philanthropy and industry. The Tata Institute of Social Sciences (TISS), founded in 1936 in Bombay as the first all-India professional school of social work, evolved from Padshah's original proposal for the Indian Institute of Science.[93] Knowledge production was most instrumentalized in the realm of social scientific research, where it could be put to use in mediating tensions between labor and capital. The LSE department's work in Jamshedpur offered an unhappy precedent in this regard, exposing major gaps between expert recommendations and managerial practices on the ground. The mission of TISS was to adapt foreign expertise to Indian conditions in the service of social harmony and, ultimately, the salvation of industrial capitalism as a whole.

As the Ratan Tata Trust took the lead on charity organization among Parsis, the Dorabji Tata trustees commissioned an American missionary and social worker, Dr. Clifford Manshardt, to draw up a list of projects "of genuine importance to the national welfare."[94] Manshardt began his career tending to the needs of Eastern European immigrant workers in the South Chicago steel district, where he realized "the futility of attempting to do welfare work with men who were physically exhausted." Their bodily, spiritual, and communal needs had to be taken care of together. Manshardt came to Bombay in 1925 to lead a slum settlement called Nagpada Neighbourhood House, under the auspices of the American Marathi Mission.[95] The first settlements, such as Hull House in Chicago and Toynbee Hall in East London, were ambitious "class-bridging" projects that brought the urban poor into direct and sustained contact with middle- and upper-class reformers guided by an ascetic ethos of service. In Bombay, similar projects run by the Social Service League and the YMCA provided only basic services, such as literacy classes, gymnasiums, medical clinics, and crafts and sewing classes for women.[96] Nagpada was the first fully residential settlement aiming "to bring together the diverse elements of the neighbourhood into a homogeneous whole," in Manshardt's words. It would take on "the role of an interpreter, explaining the neighbourhood to the outside world, and the outside world to the neighbourhood."[97]

When called upon by the Dorabji Tata trustees for advice, Manshardt seized on the opportunity to expand his vision even further. Rather than the multiplication of individual settlements like Nagpada, he proposed the creation of a research bureau "for a continuous investigation of fundamental problems," including unemployment, the purchasing power of the Indian peasant, and "waste and efficiency" in industry.[98] His main inspiration was the Russell Sage Foundation in New York City, established in 1907 by the widow of a railroad magnate for "the improvement of social and living conditions" in general. The foundation combined diverse strands of social work, including settlement houses and charity organization societies, with social research techniques such as surveys, household budgets, interviews, and documentary photography. In doing so, it brought together Gilded Age corporate philanthropy and the emergent Progressive reform movements.[99] Impressed by this model, the trustees decided to establish a graduate school of social work on the premises of Manshardt's Nagpada House. It would offer extensive theoretical coursework and also train welfare workers, labor officers, and factory inspectors.[100] By combining the ascetic spirit of service with the rigor of academic research, the new school could claim affinity with the philosophy of national regeneration through education expressed by Jamsetji Tata in his correspondence with Swami Vivekananda, arguably more than the truncated IISc.

The practical emphasis on improving welfare work and industrial relations at the new school, renamed TISS, was, in part, an immediate necessity. The Bombay Trade Disputes Conciliation Act (1934) mandated the appointment of labor officers in factories, as strikes swept through the Bombay textile industry and Communist-backed militant trade unions captured the loyalty of the workers. Social service organizations fashioned themselves as mediators able and willing to control labor, while denying they were handmaidens of capital.[101] Manshardt claimed that the Nagpada settlement was "the friend of both employer and labourer," not shy "to criticize either party" and standing "squarely for industrial justice."[102] Defending this neutral stance against critics from the left, he argued that the liberal educator's "concern for humanity is no less genuine than that of the Marxist," except in the belief that "changing men and institutions is a long time process." Manshardt urged his students "to be social servants in deed, but over and above this to be social engineers."[103]

The leadership of TISS saw itself as undertaking a fundamental reconstruction of Indian society, primarily understood through the hoary conceptual prism of "efficiency" and degeneration. As in Jamshedpur, a framework of difference framed sociological inquiry into India's peculiar modernity. The assistant director, Dr. J. M. Kumarappa, explained, "The present day communal conflicts, confusion and social inefficiency arise to a large extent from the breaking up of the old Indian social institutions by the impact of Western Modernism."[104] In his convocation address to the first batch of graduates in 1938, the prominent Bengali sociologist Radhakamal Mukerjee explained, "Industrialisation is changing the whole pattern of relationships in the making of a living; but the caste and joint family relationships and attitudes are not in accord with the demands of Industrial living. Thus misfits, maladjustments and sufferings accompany anti-social attitudes and behavior."[105] TISS researchers interpreted the assertion of women's rights after the Sarda Act, including calls for the abolition of polygamy and the legalization of divorce, as evidence of a loss of "social cohesion" and the "disintegration" of the "family unit." The solution was to use social science to restore and refashion communitarian bonds dissolved by changing property relations.[106]

Anxieties about civilizational malaise and decline were by no means unique to India in the 1930s. In Britain, eugenic ideas gained a widespread appeal across the political and disciplinary spectrum, alongside prophecies of the impending demise of capitalism by the Webbs and others.[107] At the Russell Sage Foundation, sociologists advanced theories of technological and cultural "maladjustment" in order to safeguard the legitimacy of corporate capital.[108] The most direct parallel to TISS was perhaps the Escola Livre de Sociologia e Política, established in 1933 by leading Brazilian industrialists who viewed scientific inquiry, preferably under the guidance of foreign experts, as the panacea for class struggle.[109] Given these commonalities, it is tempting to critique TISS for failing to develop an authentically indigenous knowledge framework and relying on an imperfect "translation" of Western concepts and methods.[110] However, TISS social scientists did posit a uniquely Indian rupture between ancient values and modern industry, manifested in the traumatic displacement of caste and kinship by class, and of the village by the city—the very same phenomena that preoccupied the Webbs in Jamshedpur. These ideas of indigeneity and difference ultimately served to uphold managerial discretion and the denial of workers' rights.

Science and State Power

Meanwhile, the Dorabji Tata Trust forged ahead with the advancement of medical research, where harnessing the power of the atom was the pioneering frontier. Building on their existing leukemia initiative, the trustees turned their attention to radium as the most promising therapy for cancer in general. They planned to build a full-service treatment hospital in Bombay equipped with facilities for cutting-edge research, seeking advice on best practices from the Curie Research Institute in Paris, the Manchester Radium Institute, the Rockefeller Foundation, the Cancer Hospital in London, the Cleveland Clinic, and the Memorial Hospital in New York.[111] Like other Tata-funded institutions, the hospital would bring modern science to India while also contributing to global scientific knowledge from India. Unlike the IISc or the ill-fated School of Tropical Medicine, it would be run exclusively as a "Tata show," without the cooperation or support of the colonial government.[112]

The trustees' first step was to ascertain whether radium was "actually proving itself to be as effective an agent against cancer as it was originally hoped." This powerful and versatile element was thought to possess a vitalizing force, making it an ideal weapon against cancer. But the "radium craze" dampened in the United States by the early 1920s, as concerns about overexposure mounted amid a series of much-publicized deaths.[113] The main expert the trustees consulted, John W. Spies of the Peiping Medical College in China, asserted that radium was most effective "in cases of cancer of skin, mouth, lips and cheek," which happened to be the prevailing types in India.[114] As a tabula rasa for the study of cancer, the subcontinent was an ideal laboratory to test radium's efficacy and perhaps salvage its reputation. Moreover, Spies hoped that the hospital would also exert its "influence on the masses" by inculcating a "cancer-cure sense" among "men and women of all walks of life." He wanted Indians to become "radium-conscious" and approach the hospital without fear.[115] Differences over finance eventually led to Spies's departure, but his overarching vision endured. The Tata Memorial Hospital (TMH) opened with much fanfare in 1941, the first of its kind in the subcontinent. The staff was wholly Indianized within a few years, vindicating the trustees' strategy of building a world-class institution on their own.[116]

The procurement and study of radium at TMH brought the Dorabji Tata Trust into the burgeoning field of atomic research through overlapping scientific, philanthropic, and kinship networks. In 1940, the physicist Meghnad Saha of the Palit Laboratory at the University College of Science, Calcutta, approached the trustees to finance the construction of a cyclotron, a particle accelerator invented by Ernest O. Lawrence at the University of California, Berkeley. Ernest's brother John, a medical researcher also at Berkeley, was searching for a breakthrough in the treatment of leukemia through the production of phosphorus radioisotopes in the cyclotron. The Dorabji Tata Trust agreed to donate Rs. 60,000 to Saha, in view of the close connection between cyclotrons, radium, and cancer treatment.[117] Separately, the trustees pledged an equal amount toward the establishment of a Cosmic Ray Unit at the Indian Institute of Science led by the Parsi physicist Homi J. Bhabha, who was related to the Tata family by marriage (Dorabji's wife, Meherbai, was his paternal aunt).[118]

On the eve of World War II, therefore, the Dorabji Tata Trust supported atomic research in universities from Bangalore to Calcutta but had not yet embarked on an institution-building program of its own. That changed in 1942, when Bhabha left Bangalore and returned to Bombay to be closer to his extended family. The war catalyzed the growth of state-sponsored research infrastructure, leading to the establishment of the Council for Scientific and Industrial Research (CSIR) under chemist S. S. Bhatnagar, but progress was slow.[119] An influential report by A. V. Hill of the Royal Society, published in 1944, noted that the lack of support for scientific research from the government left "a great opportunity for the Indian benefactor" to step in.[120] In this context, Bhabha wrote to Chairman J. R. D. Tata about the possibility of the trusts sponsoring "pure" research in physics on a larger scale, citing the lack of scientific manpower in India and the rapid progress on this front made by the United States and the Soviet Union during the war. J. R. D., who had also pushed the trustees to fund the TMH, "whole-heartedly" supported the scheme.[121] Keenly aware of the history of strained collaborations with the colonial government, Bhabha recommended a joint venture, stressing that "financial support from Government need not, however, entail Government control."[122]

At first, the trust was reluctant to abandon its existing commitments in Bangalore and Calcutta for a "one-man affair" with uncertain chances of success. But Bhabha's relocation offered the unexpected chance to absolve the Tata family in the eyes of the Parsi community and the citizens of Bombay for the decision to locate the IISc in Bangalore. Moreover, the experience of TISS had shown that even an initiative "built round one individual—Dr. Manshardt" could attain a "recognised place for itself" as a national institution. The trustees agreed to support Bhabha, as long as the government assumed part of the financial burden and a clear "handover" strategy was put in place. The trust could no longer "keep on initiating and maintaining new projects unless the maintenance of its earlier projects is passed on to the state or responsible bodies."[123] Other sources of finance were considered but not forthcoming. J. R. D. privately wrote to a fellow Parsi industrialist, Ness Wadia, requesting a grant for the endowment of a chair in astrophysics. Wadia replied that his family trust had "no authority to use the funds except for housing for poor Parsees," underscoring how unusual the Tata Trusts' nation-building approach really was in the philanthropic landscape of Bombay.[124]

The Tata Institute of Fundamental Research (TIFR) opened in 1945, funded through a "tripartite agreement" between the Dorabji Tata Trust, the Government of Bombay, and the Government of India. The institute was first housed in temporary quarters near the Taj Hotel, then moved to a scenic promontory at the southernmost tip of Bombay, overlooking the Arabian Sea. This valuable piece of real estate was obtained from the Ministry of Defense through Prime Minister Jawaharlal Nehru's personal intervention. Upon the accession to power of Nehru's Indian National Congress government in 1947, Bhabha took on the official role of chairman of the Atomic Energy Commission of India (AECI). In this capacity, Bhabha worked tirelessly to ensure the primacy of TIFR in the national nuclear research program, marginalizing both the IISc in Bangalore and Saha's laboratory in Calcutta. Bhabha's unique position and proximity to Nehru resulted in the atrophy of TIFR's independent research mandate in physics and its eventual subordination to the AECI.[125] From the point of view of the wider scientific community, the Tata Trusts facilitated centralization and the concentration of power in knowledge production. The fact that TIFR was an offspring of private capital, later adopted by the nation-state, continued to matter in myriad ways.

The close relationship between Bhabha, the Tata Trusts, and the government experienced a few strains in the early years of TIFR. The most significant concerned the name of the institute, which Bhabha fought to keep against domestic political pressures to downplay the contributions of private philanthropy to the nation. At the foundation stone laying ceremony in January 1954, S. S. Bhatnagar acknowledged that "we have been blamed for connections with the Tatas in this project by some to whom richness of any kind is an obsession."[126] Since the trustees did not provide the majority of the funding, they could not stop the government from changing the name if it proved politically expedient to do so. Yet, Bhabha explained to Nehru that "the name of the laboratory acquires a significance of its own independent of any association with the name of the founder." He gave the example of the TIFR School of Mathematics, which had no direct connection to the atomic program but quickly achieved an independent "international reputation" and was on track to become the "Princeton of India."[127] Changing the institute's name would dilute its hard-earned credibility in the international scientific community.

On the other side of the ledger, retaining the name would draw attention to TIFR's ongoing relationship with different Tata companies. Tata Inc., the group's New York trading branch, regularly assisted in making purchases of sensitive laboratory equipment from American manufacturers.[128] Cold War economic and political pressures threatened the autonomy of the institute, testing Bhabha's deeply felt commitment to scientific exchange and communication across borders.[129] In 1950, he invited the physicist Bernard Peters, who had been accused of Communist sympathies and denied a job at the University of Rochester at the height of McCarthyite hysteria, to work with the TIFR cosmic ray unit.[130] American diplomats and hardline anticommunists in India began to suspect, wholly without foundation, that Bhabha was a "fellow traveler."[131] In 1951, J. R. D. Tata and the trustees expressed their alarm at Bhabha's plans to visit the Soviet Union and TIFR mathematician D. D. Kosambi's active participation in the Soviet-backed World Peace Council. In response, Bhabha declared himself ready to sacrifice the name if necessary:

As a high level academic institution there must be as much intellectual freedom in the Tata Institute of Fundamental Research as there is in any British University and unless this freedom is assured you will not get men of the caliber that there should be in the Institute. I quite sympathise with the feeling that from a commercial or business point of view the association of members of the staff with things like the Peace Movement or delegations to Moscow may be embarrassing for their American connections, but in this case there seems to me to be no alternative but to change the name of the Institute, a point we have often discussed and which Jeh [J. R. D.] strongly favours.[132]

Bhabha's hardheaded pragmatism and internationalist idealism were two sides of the same coin, allowing him to walk a fine line between representing the Indian state, the scientific community, and the interests of his corporate patrons.

D. D. Kosambi posed the most serious challenge to this delicate balancing act. His outspoken Marxist views and public condemnation of atomic energy caused increasing friction with Bhabha, culminating in his sacking in 1962. From the very beginning, Kosambi was under no illusions about who pulled the strings at TIFR:

> In this country, a considerable portion of the business community is all for war, though they pay faint lip service to peace. I have decided to take prominent part in the peace movement. . . . As one result, I face dismissal—not immediately, I believe, but eventually. The warning has been given not only by the director of my Institute (a rank opportunist) but by the real power behind him, one of India's biggest leaders of industry and finance![133]

Although Kosambi was prescient enough to anticipate the hostility he would face as a result of his political activities, his downfall had as much to with his standing in the academic community. The final straw for Bhabha was Kosambi's claim to have proven the Riemann hypothesis, one of the most difficult unsolved problems in mathematics, in the obscure *Journal of the Indian Society of Agricultural Statistics*. Leading international mathematicians dismissed Kosambi's proof, and his colleagues feared the impact of a "scandal" on the school's reputation.[134] With Kosambi gone, conflicts that occasionally arose between Bhabha, the trusts, and the government were dealt with behind closed doors. The name remained unchanged.

Despite becoming an arm of the state, TIFR continued to develop connections with other Tata-funded institutions. In 1948, the AECI established a cell biology unit in the laboratories of the TMH to study the "biological effects of radiation." The hospital cooperated with TIFR on worker safety in the radium department, while TIFR assisted the physics department at TMH.[135] Bhabha's personal appeal to his friend Irène Joliot-Curie secured the services of a young French physicist trained in the calibration of radium and X-rays for the hospital.[136] When the administration of the hospital was transferred to the Government of India in 1957, the culmination of its own "handover" trajectory, it fell under the aegis of Bhabha's Department of Atomic Energy.[137] This was not a natural outcome of Bhabha's centralizing tendencies or his role as a state actor. Everyday scientific networks forged between the two institutions made it possible.

Research at TMH also intersected with the concerns of TISS. The Rockefeller Foundation and the Dorabji Tata Trust funded investigations of human blood groups beginning in 1944. Just like variation in cancer types made India into an ideal laboratory for clinical study, caste endogamy was thought to create "experimental groups ideally suited for work on the problems of human heredity." This research was thought to be urgent in view of the rather optimistic prediction that caste would disappear "within a generation." TMH later assisted with "genetical and anthropological surveys" of tribal populations in western India to determine the incidence of hereditary diseases such as thalassemia and sickle cell anemia. These surveys were conducted as a joint venture between TISS and the United Nations Bureau of Social Affairs, which also promoted "the development of India's national family planning movement on a sound and scientific basis" through localized contraceptive trials.[138]

As was the case with the Ford and Rockefeller Foundations, the Tata Trusts' entry into family planning and population research was "purely institutional," guided by their affiliated experts.[139] But it was no coincidence that this was a key priority for the postcolonial Indian state as well as J. R. D. Tata's passionate personal cause.[140] In the early 1950s, the chairman frequently corresponded with Lady Rama Rau, president of the Indian affiliate of Planned Parenthood, about the latest advances in contraceptives, from oral pills to soluble tampons and hormonal treatments. Echoing Jamsetji's faith in the plague vaccine, J. R. D. was convinced that only science could provide an "effective answer" to population growth that went beyond both "western mechanical methods" and the "Gandhian method of continence."[141]

Social science and medical research led to the cancer hospital, then to atomic energy and back to social science. The simple, linear narrative promoted by the Tata Trusts—private money provides the initial seed for the state to cultivate—made persuasive claims to a distinctly "pioneering" and nation-building role. But this narrative obscures the partial autonomy of networks of knowledge production and exchange, which followed unpredictable and circuitous paths. The prestige of the Indian Institute of Science, TISS, TMH, and TIFR owed more to their independent academic reputation than to the guarantee of the Tata name, but their origins as private benefactions left a lasting mark on their evolution.

Philanthropy and the Nation

Before independence, Tata philanthropy sustained intellectual and institutional networks beyond community, nation, and empire, bringing the world to India and India into the world. The trustees prided themselves for their contributions to "national regeneration during a period when the State in India paid little heed to nation-building activities."[142] With most of their institution-building projects placed on a sure footing, the trustees pondered the new directions they could take in an altered political landscape, characterized by the emergence of a welfare state with a duty to provide for citizens' needs and rising hostility toward private enterprise. The relationship between philanthropy and economy, which had been mostly kept at arm's length during the colonial period, had to be rethought and redefined.

The question of publicity in particular divided the trustees. J. R. D. Tata argued that spreading the word about their good works made a crucial difference to profitability: "The Firm which produces the bulk of the Trusts' income directly and indirectly, will now more than ever be affected by its prestige with the public and with the political parties of the country and by the goodwill it is able to generate." Fellow trustee Prof. R. Choksi countered by drawing an essential distinction between the two spheres of activity: "The primary object of the Trust is charity, not the creation of goodwill." Whereas Tata companies may have needed to "keep themselves constantly before the public . . . it does not follow that the Trust does." Choksi was "not convinced that discreet publicity is really discreet."[143] The trusts would be compromised in the court of public opinion if they appeared to serve an economic interest. They performed a nation-building role that did not quite overlap with that of the Tata companies.

In the background of this discussion lay the crucial decision taken by Dorabji and Ratanji to vest their shares in the main holding company in their eponymous trusts. By 1947, the trusts held over 80 percent of the share capital of Tata Sons. This allowed the trustees to plausibly claim that in its very structure, Tata was different from other businesses: "Wealth is given in solemn trust for public welfare." Although unusual in India, the arrangement was not unique among the first generation of big philanthropists elsewhere. The trustees themselves noted that the Ford Foundation held 90 percent of stocks in the Ford Motor Company.[144] However, based on the experience of the Big Three in the United States, which faced a serious political backlash, the survival of this structure was far from a given. In the Cold War era, the Ford Foundation came under attack for promoting socialism, internationalism, racial integration, and other "un-American" ideals through its sponsorship of social scientific research. Following several congressional investigations, the Tax Reform Act (1969) prohibited foundations from owning a majority stake in corporations.[145] Indian income tax legislation exempted the Tata Trusts from a similar ban in view of their long record of service to the nation-in-the-making. Under the Bombay Public Trust Act (1950), the majority shares in Tata Sons held by trustees were managed by passive government appointees who did not interfere in the relationship between companies and trusts.[146]

Increased public scrutiny nonetheless demanded a novel approach to philanthropy. Independence brought a notable change in resource allocation from large-scale institution building to rural development and direct service provision on a local level. The decision to hand over the TMH to the government in 1951 was initially taken in order to free up funds for an experimental scheme of rural reconstruction in collaboration with TISS.[147] The Dorabji Tata Trust created a rural welfare board to sponsor cooperatives, "model villages," and land reclamation projects near the Tata Chemicals plant at Mithapur, Gujarat, and in the Mulshi Valley close to the Tata Power Company dam. The board functioned as a "private agency supplementing the work of the Government," particularly the Gandhian Community Development program.[148] During one youth training session at the Mulshi site, an external observer from the Rockefeller Foundation observed with satisfaction that "the Tata name was only mentioned once at which time the Trust was referred to with respect to the Rural Welfare Board's withdrawing from the area after a period of year." This was meant to encourage an attitude of "self-help" and "self-ownership" among the villagers, who would take over the work of the board staff and eventually stand on their own two feet.[149]

The Rural Welfare Board occupied the middle ground between J. R. D.'s and Choksi's positions in the debate on publicity. Although superficially a continuation of Jamsetji's "constructive philanthropy," this kind of intervention was more modest in scope, more deliberately self-effacing, and more acutely responsive to Tata companies' quest for legitimacy as landlords and employers in rural areas. On a national level, it would be expressed in the political language of "corporate social responsibility" (see Chapter 6). There may be little evidence of overt "political ideology and dogma" in the trusts' turn to rural development, but politics and philanthropy never constituted entirely "distinct domains."[150] As the trustees recognized, "the State in a sense is impersonal in its programmes of human welfare, and it is here that the personal touch of the private organisation can make a significant contribution."[151] Tata philanthropy would continue to play a "pioneering" entrepreneurial role in areas the state did not yet reach. But it would also shadow the state along the way, reminding the public of the contrast between the donor's "personal touch" and the bureaucrat's heavy hand.

4

National Capitalists, Global Wars

In March 1944, Messrs. Wadia Gandhy & Co., the Tatas' Bombay solicitors, sent a strongly worded letter to the politician M. N. Roy. It concerned
an allegation Roy made in a pamphlet titled *Indian Labour and Post War Reconstruction*, published two years before at the height of World War II. He
had accused Tata of deliberately subverting the war effort in order to help the
Indian National Congress. "The few cases of serious interference with production," Roy wrote, "were engineered by the industrialists themselves including the Tata Iron & Steel Co. Ltd. Even in those cases, the workers did
not fall in line willingly. Mills and plants were closed down, and all sorts of
devices adopted in order to keep the workers away."[1] In August 1942, after
Mohandas K. Gandhi launched a mass campaign known as the Quit India
movement and the entire Congress leadership was arrested, Tata Iron and
Steel Company (TISCO) workers did go on strike in solidarity. Roy was convinced that Tata management at all levels, from the boardrooms of Bombay
House to the factory floor in Jamshedpur, was complicit in the strike. The solicitors warned Roy that he would be sued for libel if he did not make a full
apology and withdraw the pamphlet from circulation.

A *swadeshi* radical, ex-member of the Comintern, and fiercely original
thinker, M. N. Roy was a peripatetic figure then on the fringes of Indian politics. His uncompromising support for the war was consistent with his outward-
looking vision of Indian nationalism, which required subordinating, at least
for a time, the anticolonial struggle to the global fight against fascism. To
spread this message among the working classes, Roy established the Radical
Democratic Party (RDP) and the associated Indian Federation of Labour
(IFL).[2] The IFL was active in Jamshedpur under the leadership of Maneck
Homi, the scourge of Tata management during the massive 1928 strike, the
last time the company's authority in Jamshedpur had come under serious
threat. It was Homi and his men, marginalized by the Congress-backed Tata
Workers' Union (TWU) in the intervening years, who led Roy to see the company's hand behind the events of August 1942. The Tatas, whose flagship
plant churned out steel vital to the defense of the British Empire in its hour

of greatest need, suddenly found themselves on the defensive regarding their commitment to the war effort. At the same time, if they distanced themselves too hastily from the cause of the imprisoned Congress leadership, they risked losing all credibility with the likely government-in-waiting. The case served as a flashpoint illuminating the messy process by which Indian big business negotiated the transition from empire to nation-state.

At first, the substance of the case appeared rather thin. Roy had already inserted an erratum in the pamphlet deleting the offending clause ("including the Tata Iron & Steel Co. Ltd."), because "the attitude of some other industrialists, particularly some of the Ahmedabad Millowners, was responsible for a more prolonged interference with production."[3] Unlike TISCO, the Ahmedabad millowners were openly allied with Gandhi and the Congress, so they presented an easier target. Similar rumors spread about Lala Shri Ram in Delhi and G. D. Birla in Calcutta, who felt intolerable pressure from below to take a stand in defense of nationalism while keeping their factories running.[4] But even after the publication of Roy's erratum, the Tatas' solicitors insisted on an apology. Labour Member B. R. Ambedkar, the prominent Dalit leader then serving on the Viceroy's Executive Council, offered to mediate while passions were still running high.[5] Roy refused to budge, perceiving the stakes of the case to be far greater than the accuracy of the pamphlet itself: "We have plenty of evidence to support the opinion expressed in the book. But our defence will be political."[6] The aim was to expose how big business was "hedging its bets" in serving the needs of two masters.

Roy never got the chance to test his arguments in court. With the end of the war in Asia and the acceleration of negotiations over the transfer of power, the case lost its immediate relevance and subversive potential. In December 1946, the Tatas made the first conciliatory move, offering to "forego the expression of regret if the defendants would admit that their statement was incorrect," given "the time that has elapsed and the completely altered political situation today." In September 1947, just one month after independence, Roy issued a tepid not-quite-apology: "I have been assured by you that the Company did not engineer the strike referred to in the said passage, and I accept the assurance."[7] The matter was quietly laid to rest.

The postcolonial forgetting of the Tata-Roy case parallels the fading from memory of World War II in India, long subsumed in the triumphant master narrative of independence. As the war has come back into view in recent historiography, the business response to the Quit India movement lies at the heart of a contentious debate on the role of Indian capitalism in the process of decolonization.[8] Was the business class as a whole guided primarily by anticolonialism, and did its economic interests genuinely converge with Prime Minister Jawaharlal Nehru's agenda of statist planning? Or is the "national bourgeoisie" a mythical construct that masks capitalists' deep-seated obstruction of the state and self-interested demands for protected markets? The debate originates in a split within the Communist parties of India in the 1960s over how to categorize and interpret the emergence of a powerful indigenous business class under colonial conditions.[9] One camp holds that capitalists were driven primarily by "the desire to *free the economy from foreign domination*," which animated their support for the Quit India movement and later calls for a strong developmental and protectionist state.[10] The other emphatically rejects the notion of any "genuine desire on the part of Indian business to launch a developmental state," emphasizing the reactionary need to maintain legitimacy in the face of popular mobilization during Quit India and the ascendancy of the Congress left. As soon as these threats subsided and organized labor was effectively "demobilized," capitalists fought tooth and nail against state control.[11]

Both schools of thought invoke the pressures of worker and peasant movements from below, divisions within the Congress between left and right, and the uncertainties around the future regulation of foreign capital, yet do not examine how specific groups responded to these factors over time. Both rely on an aggregate construct of the "national bourgeoisie," giving pride of place to the Calcutta-based Marwari jute magnate G. D. Birla as its main spokesman and the Federation of Indian Chambers of Commerce and Industry (FICCI) as its institutional expression. The Tatas are seen as a marginal political outlier, uncomfortable with overt political nationalism but ultimately obeying the logic of class interests when it counted.[12] Even scholars who acknowledge "substantial differences" between the Tata and Birla factions maintain the spotlight on FICCI as the main actor.[13] The shifting balance of power between big business (understood as a singular entity), the colonial state, and the nationalist movement continues to be studied as a domestic drama unfolding within the anticipated boundaries of the nation-state.

Beginning with World War II, preexisting political differences along a binary colonial-anticolonial axis transformed into a more diffuse scramble for proximity and access to the state, using foreign capital as a medium. In this sense, Indian political economy was both "domiciled" and "globalized" in a new way. As in Egypt after the end of formal British rule, investment and policy decisions shifted to the scale of the nation-state, but foreign capital remained a vital resource used by business groups to strengthen their position. This did not make them any more or less "national" in character.[14] Deep factional divisions within the business community also accompanied state-sponsored developmentalism in Argentina, with capital goods importers and commodity exporters pitted against each other and often divided among themselves.[15] The undeniable organized strength of Indian big business and its orientation toward domestic markets have obscured the persistent destabilizing role of foreign capital.

The Tatas' shifting stance on protectionism and state control of industries cannot be explained as a function of class interest alone, not least because of their relatively greater reliance on foreign technical expertise and machinery. This had always been true, going back to the establishment of the steel plant and hydroelectric power companies and the challenges of World War I and the Great Depression (see Chapter 1). As the group expanded into new capital-intensive sectors, from chemicals to aviation to automobiles, it was also forced to navigate a profound geopolitical upheaval. The constraints on national development imposed by the decolonization and Cold War competition from the early 1940s to the late 1950s are by now well recognized.[16] But India's passage from British colony to playing field of superpower conflict, first between Britain and the United States, then between the Soviet Union and the United States, also created strategic opportunities. Despite having lost ground in East Asia, Tata leveraged its remaining global linkages to London, New York, and Washington, DC, in order to carve out a space of maneuver independent of the corridors of bureaucratic power in New Delhi. The "extraterritorial" connections that had kept them afloat during the colonial period were repurposed for new political ends.

Empire's Arsenal

On the eve of the war, Indian big business as a whole found itself in a tenuous position, hemmed in by the colonial state's rigid economic policy on the one hand and a restive nationalist movement on the other hand. Protective tariffs, which kept companies like TISCO afloat, were offset by adherence to harsh fiscal discipline and a continued tendency to favor export-oriented British managing agencies. Above all, the Government of India was intent on preserving the "home charges" that paid for the maintenance of the imperial system. Finance Member James Grigg, a dogmatic anti-Keynesian who replaced the more sympathetic George Schuster in 1934, viewed the Congress right and businessmen like G. D. Birla as the real threat to British rule, not the "millions of peasants whose grievances are entirely economic."[17] Fearful of a potential cross-class alliance between Indian elites and the masses, the colonial state chose to present itself as a defender of agrarian interests.

G. D. Birla's efforts to realize such an alliance should have borne fruit in this antagonistic climate. Instead, he faced an unexpected setback when the Congress left's charismatic leader Jawaharlal Nehru gave a speech to the party's Lucknow session in March 1936 calling for "the advancement of socialism." Led by the Tatas and their allies, including a young banker named A. D. Shroff, twenty-one Bombay businessmen signed a manifesto condemning the speech. This was an attempt to forge a common front among the urban and rural propertied classes—not against the British but against socialism. Birla criticized the rashness of his colleagues, proposing to discipline the left with the help of Congress moderates rather than engaging in direct opposition. His would prove the more prudent view, as government policy soon pushed all factions closer to the Congress. In 1939, an Indo-British trade pact imposing a duty on raw cotton was defeated after a rare show of unity among the representatives of big business.[18]

The entry of multinationals such as Dunlop and Imperial Chemical Industries (ICI) into India caused further resentment, limiting avenues for expansion and diversification opened up by the Depression. German, Japanese, and American firms began to secure greater shares of Indian markets at the expense of British managing agencies, which lost their dominant position just as India's balance of trade began to shift toward the import side. The outbreak of war in 1939 theoretically created "new incentives to Indo-British collaboration," since both business communities "had to deal with the state as purchaser, regulator, or patron on a vast scale."[19] Recalling World War I, Indian business hoped to once again enter new sectors such as automobiles, aircraft, shipbuilding, and armaments, this time insisting on majority control and steadfastly opposing further inroads by multinationals.

The experience of Tata Chemicals, the group's latest venture, illustrated the risks and opportunities at play. In early 1937, the *dewan* (prime minister) of the princely state of Baroda in western India suggested the acquisition by Tata of an existing salt works near the port of Okha for the production of soda ash and caustic soda. This was a logical step forward, given the group's pioneering track record. As with steel and other basic infrastructure, the production of soda ash was seen as "a test of the material progress of a country."[20] However, the new company simply did not have the resources to compete with the powerful multinational ICI and was forced to come to an early agreement with its rival over markets and prices.[21] Supply of technical equipment was another serious problem, as it had been for TISCO and the power companies during World War I. Despite an inbuilt preference for American suppliers, Tata Chemicals had "no option" but to buy specialized components manufactured only in Germany.[22]

For Tata, the war intensified old conflicts, exposing the unresolved contradictions between political and economic *swadeshi* and between national, imperial, and global forces. Entry into this field raised thorny ethical and political dilemmas. Jal Naoroji, Tata Chemicals' representative in London, wrote to Bombay on the subject of "the ethics of the poison gas trade," with the experience of the previous war in mind. He was firmly of the opinion that "it shouldn't be done" and that "we should not send out the raw material in such a form that anyone else can do it." But Naoroji perceptively recognized that "this position is merely theoretical, because the same might well apply to steel or glycerine, which we send out without any qualms of conscience."[23] TISCO faced these contradictions head-on during the Quit India strike, when rebellious foremen informed the general manager that "they had no intention of manufacturing steel which would be turned into bullets and then used against their countrymen."[24]

It is difficult to determine precisely what happened in Jamshedpur in the summer of 1942. Much of the surviving archival evidence was compiled in preparation for M. N. Roy's trial that never was, rendering it inherently suspect. Roy's principal source of information was a report authored by a member of Maneck Homi's IFL. The report described a public meeting held by the Congress-affiliated TWU on August 9, when news of the arrest of the nationalist leaders reached the city, calling for a *hartal* (stoppage). Only about 10 percent of the workers joined in, staying away from work while foremen provided excuses for them. Faced with an apparent lack of enthusiasm, the TWU planned to call a full-blown strike after the distribution of the annual profit-sharing bonus at the end of the month, conflating economic and political issues. This was necessary because many workers, especially Muslims and *adivasis* (aboriginals/tribals), did not know "what is the strike for and what the grievances against the Company are." According to this narrative, they were duped or pressured into acting against their own interests. To mobilize workers, the TWU preyed on widespread fears of sexual assault by soldiers stationed in Jamshedpur. Women "were threatened that if they go within the works they would be harassed and insulted by the military soldiers within the Works."[25] A petition from May 1942 described how ten soldiers entered an employee's house while he was away on duty at the collieries and "began to molest the women." Such incidents made workers justifiably "scared and panicky." But the outrage was certainly selective, breaking down along the lines of caste and class. The petitioners themselves admitted that "many other cases in which the soldiers molested some of the *rejas* [female coolies] of the Company" were not reported because "sufficient proof was not available."[26]

What evidence did Homi and the IFL provide for management's collusion with the TWU and manipulation of workers' fears? The report claimed that General Superintendent P. H. Kutar was put in charge of organizing meetings in support of the war effort but dragged his feet and kept silent ("in purdah" or female seclusion, Homi sarcastically wrote).[27] Kutar then reportedly "called the 'C' class apprentices some 5 or 6 days before the strike and asked them to keep aloof" from the works, promising that no disciplinary action would be taken against them. On August 20, leaflets in support of Quit India "were typed by the typists of the Company with the typewriters openly in the General Office." Most damningly, the first meeting to organize the strike "was held in the bungalow of Mr. [M. D.] Madan," the assistant superintendent of the steel melting shop. According to the report, the general manager refused to take action against the foremen and supervisors involved in this meeting.[28]

The middle ranks of TISCO management were unlikely nationalist heroes. Whereas the authority of the "jobbers" in the Bombay textile mills depended on cultivating community ties in working-class neighborhoods, foremen were technocrats who owed their position to formal recruitment from elite educational institutions and had few organic connections with the workers.[29] They wrestled with both high-minded dictates of conscience, as Naoroji had done, and professional ambitions. T. M. Shah, identified as the president of the "Jamshedpur Strike Committee," was an MIT graduate who had once been refused an engineering job with the Tatas and later found work in the TISCO power plant after starting a small contracting business. Like other rebellious foremen, Shah saw no contradiction between his "technological vision" of progress, embodied in the Tatas, and his strongly held nationalist convictions, embodied in the imprisoned Gandhi.[30] Because dissent came from within the managerial hierarchy, Quit India threatened the steel company's legitimacy as a *swadeshi* enterprise more than the upheavals of the 1920s, which had followed a more predictable script of workers pitted against bosses on "bread-and-butter" economic grievances.

How the strike ended was every bit as suspicious as how it began. On September 3, TISCO director Ardeshir Dalal issued an appeal through the company's new radio relay system. He began by conceding that "in any other circumstances a political strike would stand self-condemned and call for the strongest measures, but the present situation is altogether exceptional and I am prepared to make allowances for it." He then promised to personally take up the cause of the imprisoned Congress leaders with the viceroy in Delhi, along with Chairman J. R. D. Tata. Yet, Dalal also stressed that loyalties to country and company were inseparable, "because only by helping to win the war can India ensure and retain her independence." If the workers refused to listen to reason, he threatened to bring in relief labor from Calcutta to man key posts under the Essential Services Ordinance.[31] The combination of carrot and stick worked to defuse the situation without serious outbreaks of violence, and the plant soon returned to normal. For Homi and Roy, the quick success of Dalal's two-faced appeal clearly demonstrated that "the Company could have prevented the whole mischief" in the first place.[32] But they could not provide incontestable evidence of coordination between the upper echelons of management and supervisory staff during the strike.

TISCO's defense rested on the surprising nature of the events and the calculated forbearance of its response. The general manager reported that he had received the first indication of the strike "only 8 hours ahead of its actual occurrence." Charge sheets were not issued "in order to avoid excitement and provocation," which was what the foremen wanted anyway.[33] Contrary to Roy's accusations, management was not opposed to adopting "scorched earth" methods in the event of a Japanese invasion. But suddenly closing a steel plant was "not so simple as shutting down a Cotton Mill." It would damage the furnaces, severely disrupt production, and cause enormous financial losses. Nonetheless, management drew up a secret plan to decommission the plant and transport some equipment to Nagpur by a special train.[34] It is worth noting just how finely this claim split the difference between the nationalist and loyalist positions. G. D. Birla and FICCI loudly protested the government's contingency plans to demolish factories in Calcutta, which would set back India's development by destroying "all the good work that we have done in a generation."[35] Tata's response had to show enough willingness to deny the enemy access to the plant but not to the extent of giving up the industrial infrastructure that was, after all, its calling card as a *swadeshi* enterprise.

Management also maintained they had pursued "a policy of sympathy and conciliation at every turn" to ensure workers remained at their posts.

Defending his involvement in the strike, General Superintendent Kutar explained that he had been instructed by the general manager to meet the troublesome C-class apprentices in his office and let them know "if they felt in their heart of hearts that they should observe a hartal to register their protest, they could do so for a day or two." Kutar then told the apprentices that they were different from the students in schools and colleges taking part in the Quit India agitations, since the company paid for their education and would secure them jobs. But if they chose to stay away from the plant for political reasons, "they should do so quietly." Kutar admitted that supervisory staff had tried to influence the workers. M. D. Madan "was stopped from visiting departments other than his own" but not necessarily "warned to stop strike propaganda." Apart from verbally dissuading the foremen not to strike, it was not clear "what other measures were taken."[36]

It is easy to see how such noncommittal action fueled conspiratorial thinking. Had this information ever come before the courts, Roy's case might have stood a chance. Management's "opportunism" and vacillation is evident at every step. But this does not prove that workers were duped into acting against their class interests.[37] Their attitudes toward nationalism were equally as ambivalent and contradictory as their employers'. A glance at the mass of vernacular pamphlets circulating in Jamshedpur at the time reveals both intense support of and opposition to the Congress. Rumors of a Japanese invasion and the impending collapse of the colonial state conveyed an "impression of fragility" that emboldened resistance and sharpened social tensions.[38] One two-page leaflet titled "Rivers of Blood Flowing through Jamshedpur" vividly described how striking foremen were arrested, "tied with ropes and taken round the homes and *chawls* [tenements] of the workmen" to set an example. Images of bodily suffering abounded: "Red hot nails are being pierced into their mouths, nose, ears and bodies." A Hindi-language poster warned that the government "wants to blow up factories after putting labour inside," a horrific embellishment of the "scorched earth" policy. On the other side, Muslim League and IFL literature condemned Quit India as a venal ploy by "Marwari and Gujarati businessmen" to "establish the rule of aristocrats, capitalists, Zamindars, stockholders, profiteers, etc. so that they may reap all profits and the poor may starve." The Adivasi Mahasabha used similar language to persuade sweepers to return to work.[39] Long-standing religious, caste, and ethnic differences were momentarily expressed in new political idioms. Fears of big business complicity in a nefarious plot cut both ways, dividing workers and capitalists alike.

The Quit India strike was indeed a decisive turning point in Tata's history, not because TISCO management was somehow behind it. Rather, it violently exposed the contradiction of profiting from a steel plant that supplied the British Empire's war machine while simultaneously serving the cause of national development. The careful separation of economic and political *swadeshi* they had cultivated for so long became untenable. If the immediate response was typically noncommittal, the horizons of possibility had narrowed. Sooner or later, the Tatas would have to choose a side. As in previous moments of crisis, transnational financial and geopolitical connections offered a way out, restoring a balanced field of power and ensuring their long-term survival.

The Americans Are Coming!

The prospect of increasing American involvement in India divided big business every bit as much as the dramatic events of August 1942. An internal memorandum for the Tata Sons statistical department found that due to the difficulty of obtaining machinery from Britain and Europe, the "only country which can fill up the gap in our import trade is U.S.A."[40] The Tatas were decidedly in a minority in welcoming this prospect. FICCI leader Purshotamdas Thakurdas warned that foreign multinationals would use the war as a pretext to further exclude Indians from their share of the spoils. A. D. Shroff, the young banker who had led the charge against Nehru after the Lucknow speech, joined Tata as a financial adviser in 1940. He condemned Thakurdas's warning as "a downright Congressman's utterance" and "a clumsy attempt at the usual double-dealing game at which he always plays."[41] More than any other single factor, differences on foreign capital undermined the tendency toward unity and concerted political action among Indian businessmen.

The controversy over the American Technical Mission, headed by diplomat Henry F. Grady, brought these differences into sharp relief. The mission arrived in India in the spring of 1942 to make ostensibly nonpolitical expert recommendations on strengthening Indian industry as part of the Allied war effort. President Roosevelt's representative, Louis Johnson, who was known to be friendly to the nationalist cause, gave his emphatic assurances that the mission was "not here to introduce American capital" and "not concerned with the commercial and economic relationships that may exist between India and the United States."[42] In response, FICCI issued an official communiqué warning "the Indian public and the commercial community to be vigilant."[43] American help was welcome but only in the form of essential plant and equipment under Indian control. Thakurdas refused outright to meet with the mission, but G. D. Birla believed there was "a very important political value" in at least getting to know the Americans.[44] Johnson's and Grady's protestations aside, the importance of the mission lay first and foremost in the political domain. Its main advocate in Washington was India's agent general Girja Shankar Bajpai, whose aim was to draw the United States deeper into Indian affairs in order to accelerate independence negotiations.[45] Birla's instinct was to go along with this strategy, even if he gained no obvious economic advantage from it. The assumption that Indian businessmen spoke out as a united class against the mission does not bear scrutiny.[46]

The Grady Mission spent five weeks in India, visiting only Bombay, Calcutta, and Jamshedpur. With regard to the steel industry, it recommended the expansion of TISCO plant capacity and the procurement of additional equipment and production engineers from the United States.[47] The Government of India agreed to spend Rs. 143 lakhs on extensions to the Jamshedpur plant, absorbing 50 percent of the total cost and arranging the import of American machinery under the Lend-Lease Act.[48] For this reason, the Tatas could not join their colleagues' public condemnation of the mission as a Trojan horse for American imperialism. Nor could they give the impression of supporting it too enthusiastically. M. N. Roy had spotted the bind they were in, making the lukewarm response to the Grady Mission a centerpiece of his case. Tata solicitors' reply to this particular charge was understated, simply noting that the mission "had expressed themselves satisfied" with the steel company's participation in the war effort.[49] The problem faced by Tata, Birla, Thakurdas, and the various factions they represented was not the desirability of American involvement per se, which could be downplayed in public, but how to position themselves behind the scenes in order to benefit from the seemingly inevitable geopolitical ascent of the United States.

For its part, the colonial government not only disregarded the Grady report but actively suppressed its findings about the underdeveloped state of Indian industries. The British were clear-eyed about the long-term consequences of the mission: "Once a start has been made along this road there can be no turning back. Industries equipped with American plant and organized by American technicians must in the future turn more and more to the United States for renewals, replacements and future developments." But officials could take consolation in the fact that "the American team and the Indian personalities they met do not seem to have mixed very well." They noted with satisfaction that "Grady and Co. and Birla and Walchand and Co. take as low of a view of each other respectively as you and I take of both lots—

which is saying something!"[50] In Washington, Bajpai bitterly complained that Indian businessmen were "reactionary and self-seeking and it was they who had spread the first rumours designed to discredit our technical mission before its arrival in India."[51] His plans to foster closer Indo-American ties had temporarily stalled. The US military, wary of the political instability caused by the Quit India movement and the prospect of an imminent Japanese invasion in the summer of 1942, refused to sanction the export of a new blast furnace for TISCO. The promised extensions to the Jamshedpur plant never materialized.[52]

The failure of the Grady Mission affected the Tatas more than anyone else. During the course of the war, they had come to be associated more with the expansion of American interests than with the nationalist cause. A widely felt affinity with the United States as a counterweight to the British Empire was evident across their operations. In late 1942, TISCO middle managers still smarting from the defeat of the Quit India strike expressed their discontent by displaying American war propaganda, including copies of the Declaration of Independence and lyrics to the "Star-Spangled Banner," "under the glass surfaces of their desks."[53] In 1944, a German newspaper made special note of this tendency: "If the U.S.A. show such a lively interest in Tata, this is not solely due to the American capital invested there, but it is particular because of their hope that they can pit the political strength of India against England, with the help of Tata."[54] The article went on to recall Tata's long history of using financial connections with the United States to circumvent colonial state policy and secure their industrial base, going back to the early days of TISCO and the power companies. It was with this history in mind that British officials and the Indian public reacted to the landmark Bombay Plan, typically seen as the moment of arrival of the "national bourgeoisie."

Eight Indians

Published in 1944 and 1945 in two parts, the Bombay Plan was jointly authored by eight leading businessmen: J. R. D. Tata, G. D. Birla, Purshotamdas Thakurdas, Lala Shri Ram, Kasturbhai Lalbhai, and three senior Tata executives (Ardeshir Dalal, A. D. Shroff, and John Matthai). The plan put forward a bold vision for India's future economic growth, proposing to double per-capita income in fifteen years through an aggressive investment program and controversially endorsing the principle of state control of basic industries.[55] Although economists issued dire warnings of an "inflationary spiral" as prices rose, businessmen embraced Keynesian deficit financing and advocated using

India's accumulated "sterling balances" in London, money borrowed by the British government from the Indian taxpayer to fund the war effort.[56] The authors made an emotive appeal to patriotic duty in support of the plan. In J. R. D.'s words, "that there should be widespread poverty and misery in a country so lavishly endowed by Providence with man-power, talent and natural resources is an intolerable paradox and a disgrace which should fill us with shame and anger and a burning desire to wipe out this terrible wrong done to our people."[57] By taking on the burden of alleviating poverty and promoting development, big business positioned itself as "a proxy for the nation."[58]

Tata played an outsized role in researching, financing, and publicizing the Bombay Plan, drawing on the group's wide-reaching intellectual networks and institutional resources. Its principal author was economist and Tata director John Matthai. He had been a student of Sidney Webb at the London School of Economics (LSE), where he wrote his doctoral thesis on village government in British India, around the same time as the Webbs introduced social scientific expertise to Jamshedpur (see Chapter 2). P. S. Lokanathan, editor of the *Eastern Economist* and Birla's lone appointed expert, also had a doctorate from LSE. The plan's embrace of deficit financing and familiarity with the ideas of John Maynard Keynes was due to this academic background.[59] The Tata Sons statistical department was responsible for research and data collection. The public relations department, headed by Minoo Masani, supervised translations of the plan into vernacular languages, with J. R. D. Tata paying one-third of the costs. In London, Beram Saklatvala of Tata Limited took the lead in countering criticism in the British press.[60]

An illustrated pamphlet by Masani set out to introduce the plan to a popular audience. It opened with the following questions: "Some time in 1943, eight Indians got together and started worrying about the state of affairs in India. They were all rather well-fed, well-to-do, well-educated and well-looked-after people. So one wonders why they should have bothered. Was it due to what is called a social conscience? Was it another method of swelling their profits?"[61] Historians have been unable to definitively provide answers. Did the plan mean that Indian big business had come into its own as a responsible and mature capitalist class, or were there ulterior motives at work? The intellectual influence of the Bombay Plan on postindependence political economy is undeniable. The first two five-year plans under Prime Minister Nehru shared its emphasis on rapid growth through heavy industry, import substitution, and investment reallocation ("forced saving"). But the practical influence of businessmen on policy making drastically declined as the state took near-complete control of the planning process.[62] This has led some commentators on the economic right to condemn the authors of the Bombay Plan for their shortsightedness. By conceding so much power to the state, they had "dug their own graves" and "should have known better."[63] Others in the same camp more generously view the plan as a lost opportunity, blaming Nehru for freezing out the private sector.[64] On the left, the plan has been interpreted either as a triumph of "bourgeois ideological hegemony" allied with nationalism, a transformative attempt to create a truly "enterprising" business class, or a cynical rearguard action to maintain the legitimacy of an "old élite and their version of capitalism."[65]

In its own time, as the undercurrent of defensiveness in Masani's question suggests, the Bombay Plan was fiercely contested by all shades of Indian political opinion and by the colonial bureaucracy in New Delhi and London. Contemporary critiques may be grouped into two broad categories: suspicion of interested motives and the lack of priority given to certain issues. The authors certainly spoke for only a narrow segment of the business community, not for the many thousands of small traders, manufacturers, and moneylenders.[66] They prioritized industry over agriculture and consumer goods, whereas the problems of land reform and foreign capital were given only cursory treatment. After the publication of part I, G. D. Birla realized that the authorship of the plan was the underlying cause of the "real hostility" it faced, telling J. R. D., "the main target of attack is the businessman and the critics treat yourself and myself as a symbol of the business community. The Communists, the Socialists, the British vested interests and our own government all seem to be on common ground."[67] Perhaps this showed that the plan had struck a chord, but it also doomed it as a blueprint for a political project.

On the right, many Indian and British businessmen resented the ideological concessions to the state. Tracy Gavin Jones, a Kanpur industrialist, protested to Thakurdas that "government expenditure should be confined to the establishment of Hydro-electric Power Stations and Armament factories. All other industries should be undertaken by private enterprise."[68] Millowner Padampat Singhania accused the plan of playing into the hands of the colonial authorities: "all our attention at the present moment should be directed towards mobilizing public opinion for gaining more and more control over vital industries as private enterprises and not providing the British Government an argument that we too want State-owned industries."[69] M. D. Darookhanavala, a former Tata employee and protégé of B. J. Padshah then working as a clerk in the Central Bank of India, penned the most impassioned excoriation of the plan. Inspired by an "accidental reading" of Austrian economist F. A. Hayek's newly published *The Road to Serfdom* (1944), he lamented the loss of the group's entrepreneurial spirit and unique *swadeshi* identity. It was, Darookhanavala wrote, a "painful spectacle almost humiliating and distressful" to see the House of Tata becoming a "glorified and later a miniature edition of the National Government . . . a department of the state working under the orders of the Supreme Council of Planners servile in behaviour, with a complete self-effacement of their personality and their individuality."[70] Masani took such criticisms to heart, including references to Hayek and the dangers of "total planning" in the promotional pamphlet. By 1945, Keynes's star had begun to wane, which may have contributed to the authors' change of attitude toward state control soon after the release of part 2.[71]

On the left, the plan was seen as a desperate attempt to preserve the capitalist system in the face of an upsurge in radical politics. M. N. Roy took aim at both "capitalist greed and economic nationalism," putting forward an alternative "People's Plan" giving priority to land reform, the modernization of agriculture, and the purchasing power of ordinary consumers.[72] The most in-depth critical appraisal by economists P. A. Wadia and K. T. Merchant saw the Bombay Plan's abandonment of "individualism" and "unregulated competition" as a necessity of the times, without "any *radical departure* from the methods of production and distribution characteristic of the present economic organisation." Wadia and Merchant conceded that deficit financing might overcome the miserliness of colonial economic orthodoxy, but decisions on how to spend this "created money" could not be left to the capitalists alone. The plan's blind spots were most evident in the proposals for land reform, which involved the consolidation of holdings through cooperatives and the eventual creation of a class of "peasant proprietors," rather than the outright legal abolition of *zamindari* (hereditary landholder) tenures.[73]

Colonial officials responded to the Bombay Plan in a cautious and ambivalent manner, drawing on both sets of critiques. Economic Adviser T. E. Gregory, an anti-Keynesian closely allied to Finance Member Grigg in the late 1930s, dismissed the plan's profligate financing scheme and centralizing tendencies in a lengthy note.[74] After reading it, Secretary of State Leo Amery wrote to the governor-general: "We do not want to encourage a purely destructive attitude towards this Plan, whose boldness and initiative are praiseworthy, but it seems desirable that comments like those of Gregory should be ventilated in order to avoid Plan becoming regarded as sacrosanct." He suggested "confidentially" supplying copies of the note to the editor of *The Economist*, "with permission to use in his own way the ideas contained in it."[75] The resulting article forcefully criticized the plan for its neglect of agriculture, which should have "first claim on post-war resources," and its recourse to "autarky," which "will not allow advantage to be taken either of foreign capital or of the international division of labour."[76]

However, Gregory's arguments by no means held unanimous sway inside the corridors of Whitehall. During the war, when the Soviet Union was both an ally and a rival to the British, many in the Indian Civil Service found an increase in centralized bureaucratic power "psychologically appealing."[77] Amery tended to view the plan with equanimity. Its Soviet-style ambition could be politically useful in driving a wedge between big business and the Congress:

> It is the bigness of the Russian conception and the enthusiasm behind it and not only its ruthless and autocratic methods that insured its success and I wouldn't despair of India pulling off a big thing. . . . Politically it may be a very big thing if it does catch hold, even if only to the extent of making Birla & Co. bored with Congress political intransigence.[78]

Other officials argued that the implications of following the Soviet model rendered the plan far less subversive than it might have seemed. After all, if India adopted a truly centralized planned economy, "the lives of Messrs. Tata, Birla etc. would become uninsurable."[79] The colonial state was faced with an existential dilemma—should it continue to preserve India as a source of agricultural exports and playing field for British capital, as Gregory and *The Economist* advocated, or should it become a strong developmental state that could meet Indian aspirations halfway and ensure the empire could compete with the Americans and the Soviets?

The Soviet example also weighed heavily on the planners' minds. During the research stage, Thakurdas sent Matthai clippings from M. N. Roy's *Independent India* weekly on economic data from three Soviet republics, which "makes a telling support for the Plan which you have drafted."[80] Sometime in 1943, J. R. D. himself took note of the following contrast:

> While in Soviet Russia inequalities of income are encouraged and used as a means of increasing national production and the shouldering of responsibility, which I think is the right thing in a country

whose primary need is still increased production, in advanced cap-
italistic countries like the U.K. and the U.S.A. the trend, under
pressure from the labour movements, is in the opposite direction. . . .
I am therefore all in favour of the Soviet concept for India.[81]

Developmental leaps of the magnitude envisioned by the Bombay Plan required the concerted exercise of state power, if not outright authoritarianism.
Not for the last time, big business endorsed a strong state to control labor and
increase productivity. Wadia and Merchant seized on this line of thinking,
referencing the infamous Stalin-era practice of offering special incentives to
the hardest workers to ridicule the plan's authors: "They regard Stakhanovism
as an equivalent of the profit motive." If the plan really wanted to follow the
Soviet lead, it would not seek to create a class of "peasant proprietors" but
would promote collectivized "large scale farming with modern technological
appliances."[82] Even the ultraorthodox Gregory agreed that "the U.S.S.R. authorities were probably right in their instinct that it was necessary to reduce,
and not strengthen, individual landholding rights."[83]

The plan's authors faced essentially the same dilemma as the colonial
state—how to balance political centralization and economic openness, particularly with regard to the preservation of private property and the regulation of foreign capital. Here, the contours of their specific business interests
mattered considerably. The Tatas owned a number of key infrastructural assets especially vulnerable to nationalization, including steel, power, and air-
line companies. They were willing to back land reform only as long as it did
not set the dangerous precedent of expropriation without due process. Between
1946 and 1948, both J. R. D. and Thakurdas (on behalf of FICCI) lobbied the
Constituent Assembly against zamindari abolition without compensation.
J. R. D. warned that going down that path would lead to "a complete collapse
of private industry in the not too distant future." The fundamental right to
property was duly enshrined into the Constitution, curtailing the new Indian
state's ability to enact fundamental reforms.[84]

Historians' perception of the Bombay Plan as a bid to capture and monopo-
lize domestic markets tells only half the story. The countervailing need for
capital goods from abroad also required state support but of a different kind.[85]
Contemporary critics realized the significance of "the international aspect"
of the plan. Dr. Gyanchand, professor of economics at Patna University, observed that the authors had "created what is really a mistaken impression that
they are aiming at national self-sufficiency." The plan included foreign loans

of up to Rs. 700 crore among the sources of finance, with the caveat that the funds should be free of "political interference." Gyanchand thought this did not go far enough, urging that "all further private investment of external capital should cease and foreign assistance should be available in the spirit of true international co-operation."[86] Of course, nothing could be further from the authors' minds. By leaving the door open for the entry of foreign capital, they hoped to open up a space of maneuver independent of the Indian state. The Tatas had pursued this strategy in the past and were now promoting its utility to the private sector as a whole.

Viewed in its proper context, the Bombay Plan was a tentative first step by big business as a collective unit in the political arena, rather than the culmination of the "national bourgeoisie" coming into its own or a craven surrender to the state. It was certainly designed to tilt the scales within the Congress Party away from the left, and to bring the Tata and Birla factions closer together for this purpose. Rhetorically, it used the language of technocratic and managerial expertise in which the Tatas had been comfortable for decades. However, by wholeheartedly throwing their resources and prestige behind the plan, the Tatas may have overplayed their hand. The wartime crisis forced them to uncharacteristically merge economic and political *swadeshi*, stepping over the line into uncharted territory. Within a few years, their alliance with the Birlas and relationship with the state had broken down, and a familiar pattern of autonomous action took hold.

Going It Alone

In the United States, the Bombay Plan was received with considerable enthusiasm. The *Baltimore Sun* struck a bullish tone, claiming that the sterling balances in London would enable India "to enter world markets not as a country in debt to her international neighbours in general and Britain in particular but as a creditor country with exchange surpluses available for large scale purchases." The *Washington Times Herald* recalled the interwar period, when India traded more with Germany and Japan than with the United States. With both defeated countries "out of the world markets for some years to come," the way was now open for the United States to "start planning improvement in trade with India and not doze along until one fine day when business balance sheets show British lead on us even longer and clever commissars of USSR are taking over the rest of the trade that was once Germany's and Japan's."[87]

In the summer of 1945, an industrial mission led by J. R. D. Tata and G. D. Birla set out with high expectations of turning these international commercial rivalries to India's advantage. J. R. D. was convinced that "the greatly expanded British engineering industry will be extremely anxious after the war to supply plant and machinery to the markets of the world and will go all out to compete with America and other countries in such markets."[88] British officials quickly connected the dots between the Bombay Plan and the mission, noting that the Rs. 790 crores earmarked in the plan for industrial development would have to be spent abroad. They were keen to appear receptive so the Indians would not be "thrown into the arms of the Americans" but predicted that it was "most unlikely that equipment on anything like this scale would be obtainable from this country in so short a period following the war." The mission's hopes were further dashed by a shortage of foreign exchange, which would become a recurring problem.[89] In the United States, Tata Chemicals did strike a deal with Virginia-based Mathieson Alkali Works for the exchange of information about the manufacturing process and on-site training of Tata employees.[90] Yet on balance, the mission returned largely empty-handed. It was a sign of many frustrations to come.

Despite sharp criticism from Gandhi, and from smaller traders and manufacturers calling for protectionism, the industrial mission marked the high point of unity for Indian big business.[91] In private, tensions were brewing. J. R. D. went so far as to say that "we are definitely not a delegation or a mission, but a group of individual industrialists and business-men. . . . We are not moving about or functioning as a single group."[92] He rejected Birla's suggestion of sharing technical advisers among the different members of the mission, believing this was nothing but a pretext for the Birlas to gain valuable commercial intelligence about their rivals.[93] A. D. Shroff was in complete agreement, adding, "I am sure you must have heard rumours that Birla is contemplating coming into Steel industry after the War."[94] The amicable division of spoils between India's two industrial giants, which had so far kept them at arm's length from each other, no longer held. Far from a petty side show, these mutual suspicions grew into a long war of attrition for the control of internal markets and inflows of foreign capital.

Birla fired the first salvo in 1946, when he decided to enter the crowded field of air transport. Flight was close to J. R. D.'s heart since his childhood years in northern France, living next door to famed aviator Louis Blériot. An intrepid pilot himself, he shepherded the fledgling Tata Air Lines from its beginnings as a night airmail service in the early 1930s to a leading passenger carrier, fighting the colonial government's indifference and fierce competition from Imperial Airways at every step. Renamed Air India, the company was one of the few in the industry to survive and thrive without a government subsidy.[95] By the end of the war, it carried around one-third of total passengers and two-thirds of domestic freight and mail. But as routes expanded and new entrants rushed in, the sector as a whole began to suffer. Losses mounted and the government kept issuing more and more licenses in order to reduce companies' profitability.[96] Airlines were also considered essential infrastructure and thus prime candidates for nationalization.

To justify his decision to set up yet another venture in a hopelessly crowded market, Birla played the nationalist card. His newspaper, the *Hindustan Times,* ran an article accusing existing companies of being "anti-national in outlook" and "prone to employ foreign personnel often in preference to Indians."[97] J. R. D. was outraged, reminding Birla that it was "the policy of leading business firms in India not to add to the many difficulties already facing all of us as a result of social and political trends, by entering into avoidable competition with each other."[98] Birla replied that greater competition was inevitable and the Tatas, by extension, were monopolists: "Friends rightly argued that if India was to advance on the line of the Bombay Plan and if the quickest possible progress was to be the target, India's size and distances demanded a much wider interest in air transport . . . whether we interested ourselves or not, this business, it appeared, was no longer to remain a close confine of a few." He denied that the *Hindustan Times* had specifically targeted Air India but could not resist mentioning "the impression that even in Tatas Parsees were preferred to non-Parsees. This, I suppose, could not be true. All the same, the impression was there."[99] Time would prove them both right, but the Tatas had much more to lose. Birla read the political winds more astutely, realizing that Air India could not sustain its dominance for long, whereas J. R. D. correctly predicted that nationalization would be the inevitable result of new entrants into the sector.

The flurry of organized business lobbying around the time of independence temporarily papered over these divisions and secured important gains. The Bombay Plan may have been a dead letter, but the Congress left was also in full retreat. In January 1948, a policy subcommittee composed of Tata executive and soon-to-be finance minister John Matthai and the Gandhian leaders Jayaprakash (JP) Narayan and Shankarrao Deo advocated bringing "existing undertakings in areas reserved for the state" into public ownership within five years, along with a mandatory ceiling on capital dividends and the expansion of cottage industries and cooperatives. FICCI howled that these proposals were "tantamount to an act of virtual expropriation." They were shelved with the help of Deputy Prime Minister Sardar Valabhbhai Patel, the standard-bearer of the Congress right.[100] In April 1948, the conciliatory Industrial Policy Statement sought to reassure big business about the threat of nationalization and promised a crackdown on labor unrest. Mild regulatory measures inserted into the Industries (Development and Control) Bill in 1949 provoked threats of an "investment strike" across the entire private sector.[101] The government continued to back down. In April 1949, Nehru issued a statement welcoming foreign investment for big industrial projects and relaxing requirements for Indian majority ownership of joint ventures.[102] Birla went to bat for the government, declaring his willingness to approach American investors on Nehru's behalf, as he did during the prime minister's awkward first visit to the United States that same year.[103]

Meanwhile, the Tatas kept their distance from the government and grew determined to secure foreign investment privately. In November 1948, as capital for Tata Power and other group companies dried up, A. D. Shroff opened a back channel of communication with the UK trade commissioner. He bemoaned the "wild, loose, and uninformed talk of nationalization," expressed regret for the departure of "many of his British friends in commerce and industry," and "made a strong appeal for capital goods for India and for the export to her of British experience and 'know how.'" The British did not take the bait. Shroff's alarmism, officials scoffed, "reveals the usual blind spot Indians have about the export of capital goods from the United Kingdom." British businesses did "not appear to share Mr. Shroff's view that there is no future for capitalism in that country."[104] Surveying the domestic battles over industrial policy, London felt assured that "the dark economic background is not without its patches of sky"—namely, "a realistic and stiffening attitude on the part of Government and the political parties towards indiscipline among labour."[105] This attitude of self-satisfied complacency extended to business dealings. When a bidding war for the extension of the Tata hydroelectric power station at Bhira broke out, the English Electric Company quoted a price much higher than their American competitors, Westinghouse and General Electric, in the mistaken belief that the old imperial masters would always have a leg up.[106]

Despite ample incentives to compete with the British, the Americans moved equally slowly. Given that India would never obtain large-scale aid along the lines of the Marshall Plan for Western Europe, Shroff believed American private investors could only be enticed "on the basis of a business proposition." The best course of action was not to deputize the likes of Birla to speak for the government but to encourage "responsible Indian businessmen, either individually or in a group," to "put forth specific proposals worked out in detail and offering attractive investment possibilities."[107] When brought together face-to-face, Shroff was convinced that Americans and Indians would shake hands on a good deal, leaving politics aside. J. R. D. Tata pursued this strategy during a visit to the United States in 1950, with little success. On the whole, American investors remained wary of the risks involved in collaborating with the Indian private sector, whose position was judged too precarious due to the ongoing threat of nationalization and Nehru's socialist rhetoric. This was more of a concern in Washington than in London as Cold War paranoia reached a fever pitch.[108]

Businessmen collectively bent industrial policy in their favor when it came to avoiding nationalization and disciplining labor but found it harder to secure state support, or at least a favorable political dispensation, in their pursuit of foreign capital. In the long run, British and American investment would prove crucial for carving out a sphere of independent action from the Indian state—for the Tatas above all others. Conversely, the state would require another kind of foreign intervention, from the Soviet Union and its allies, to counter capitalist influence and regain the freedom to plan.

Steel Duel

Nehru's announcement of a massive expansion of India's steel capacity was met with predictable indifference on both sides of Atlantic. Their heightened fears of each other's intentions notwithstanding, British and American officials failed to grasp India's developmental needs as an economic or political opportunity. Birla privately urged the prime minister to consider importing half a million tons of American steel every year until capacity could be built up.[109] But Nehru encountered "a considerable lack of interest" in Washington, "mainly because the U.S. steel industry regards India as a potential valuable dumping ground for their own products." The World Bank was also reluctant to support new projects under government control.[110] In London, a cash-strapped British government struggling with its own postwar reconstruction wrote down the sterling balances until they were practically useless to the Indians, exacerbating the new nation's foreign exchange shortage.[111]

While Nehru scrambled for funding, exploratory reports on steel expansion were commissioned from three consulting firms, the British ICC and the American Koppers and McKee. The consultants suggested establishing either one million-ton plant or two plants with 500,000 tons capacity each.

For reasons of strategic "dispersal," sites in Orissa and Madhya Pradesh (formerly the Central Provinces) were preferred to Jamshedpur and the Damodar Valley in Bengal, where most of India's known coking coal and iron ore reserves were concentrated. The Tatas publicly supported the single million-ton plant but simultaneously applied for a Rs. 200 million ($23,000,000) loan to finance the expansion of TISCO, most of which would be spent in the United States for machinery.[112] Privately, J. R. D. urged General Manager Jehangir Ghandy to refrain from criticizing the alternative proposal for multiple plants and to "not indicate complete hostility to even the principle of state enterprise in this field." Given capital shortages and the precarious labor situation throughout the country, they "would not be prepared to undertake at [their] own risk and cost the establishment of a new major steel plant."[113]

Having abandoned the path of overt resistance, J. R. D. declared himself willing to entertain "the possibility of Government wishing to entrust to the Tata Iron and Steel Company . . . the management of a new steel works which they might build in future."[114] This "joint enterprise" model became the Tatas' preferred way of engaging with the planning process. They would offer their expertise in exchange for capital investment and demand to be entrusted with day-to-day management. The inspiration was Air India International, created after the nationalization of foreign routes in 1948. The government held 49 percent of the shares, with an option to acquire an additional 2 percent, while Air India and its shareholders held the rest. J. R. D. Tata willingly served as chairman of the new corporation and poured his time and effort into making it a success.[115] Here was perhaps the purest expression of the Bombay Plan's quest for state support without state discipline.

A warning sign against the feasibility of this model going forward came in the summer of 1953, when the government finally undertook the complete nationalization of airlines. J. R. D. may have seen it coming in his earlier exchanges with Birla, but the move still came as a shock. He expressed his outrage to Nehru, who was at a loss to understand J. R. D.'s reaction. The prime minister reminded him that "as a matter of general policy, we have always thought that transport services of almost all kinds should be State-owned."[116] Similarly, Minister of Communications Jagjivan Ram depicted nationalization as a pragmatic necessity. He reassured businessmen that it should not be taken as "the triumph of any particular economic philosophy over another" but as the "culmination and final flowering" of their entrepreneurial efforts.[117] J. R. D. naturally did not see it that way but agreed to retain the chairmanship of the new domestic carrier Air India in the spirit of "service to the country," following "the highest traditions of the Founder" Jamsetji Tata.[118] To the shareholders, he was defiant, insisting that he was not opposed to consolidation or reorganization of the sector but that the government should have followed "the model of joint private and State enterprise" adopted at Air India International. Fending off new attacks from Birla, he told his rival that only "the hard fight put up by the Tatas" had secured favorable compensation terms for everyone in the industry.[119]

In the autumn of 1953, J. R. D. resumed his war of words with Nehru. He complained that TISCO had been excluded from the negotiations leading to the contract with German combine Krupp-Demag for the construction of the first new steel plant at Rourkela in Orissa. The prime minister coolly replied, "Of course, it would have been a good thing to consult Tatas. But the consultation could only have been about the quality of the firm we were approaching and not about the technical details which have not yet been settled, or about the financial arrangements."[120] J. R. D. pressed TISCO's case with Production Minister K. C. Reddy, rejecting the strategic importance of dispersing steel plants "in the atomic age" by pointing out the proximity of Orissa to Jamshedpur and claiming that the government should "leave it to the Tatas to create the additional steel capacity which they could have done at a fraction of what it would cost on a new site."[121] But he could not arrest the marginalization of the Tatas in New Delhi. When push came to shove, Nehru asserted the state's right to independently negotiate contracts and make planning decisions, a stance made easier by the German offer.

To be sure, the state was far from a singular entity, nor did it put forward a coherent ideological vision. Competing power centers emerged, each pursuing their own agenda. Big business had a powerful ally in Minister of Commerce and Industry T. T. Krishnamachari (TTK), who fought Reddy's Ministry of Production and C. D. Deshmukh's Ministry of Finance for control of the planning process.[122] In 1954, with construction in Rourkela already under way, the question of financing the second steel plant at Bhilai in Madhya Pradesh took center stage. TTK advised Nehru to eschew complete nationalization, both as a matter of principle and due to the shortage of foreign exchange for the Second Five-Year Plan. "With regard to industrial property if we move left," he argued, "we are not going to augment the scale of expansion of industries." TTK placed his hopes on a delegation led by B. M. Birla, G.D.'s brother, who was busy wooing bankers in the City of London. Although the terms were "not satisfactory," TTK advised using Birla's negotiations "as a medium" to open the project to private financing.[123] The Madhya Pradesh government, stung by the rejection of Bhilai in favor of Rourkela as the site of the first plant, was also talking to Birla and offered to contribute Rs. 25 crore.[124]

These overtures to private business contradicted at least the spirit of the Industrial Policy Resolution of 1948, which reserved steel for the public sector. It was one more indication that the rhetorical bark of Nehruvian socialism was far worse than its bite.[125] Rather than precipitating a showdown between the state and big business, steel expansion sparked competition within the private sector over who could best secure and manage inflows of foreign capital, a game the Birlas were better positioned to win. While they toiled in London, A. D. Shroff was in New York trying to charm American investors. He worryingly reported back to J. R. D. that G. D. Birla had "made a studious effort to run down Tata in general and you in particular" during his visits to the United States. Birla had even told Eugene Black, the president of the World Bank, that "Tata could be ignored, as other interests, including himself, were very enthusiastic about expansion of their industrial interests as they fully backed and approved of the government's industrial policy."[126]

The Soviet proposal to finance the Bhilai plant arrived like a thunderbolt, shattering both the Tatas' and Birlas' hopes. It had been negotiated in secret through the shadowy dealings of Kedar Das, an obscure businessman with personal connections to one of Nehru's ministers. The Soviets offered an extremely low interest rate of 2.5 percent to be repaid over twelve years, with which City of London financiers could not compete. Birla was left in the lurch, and the British sounded the alarm about this "most unexpected development." According to intelligence reports, Nehru's decision to accept the offer was taken "without any full consideration on initiative of Ministry of Production who throughout have fought for a Government plant and do not mind at all from what source the necessary finance and technical help is provided." TTK was reportedly "very embarrassed" and "inwardly furious that the Ministry of Production had been able to pull a fast one."[127] His attempts to take control of planning process by bringing in the private sector came to a screeching halt.

The turn to the Soviets had more to do with bureaucratic power struggles and internal policy paralysis than with high-minded Nehruvian nonalignment. Although its ideological implications would be endlessly dissected in London and Washington, the offer functioned much like German assistance for Rourkela a few years earlier. The Soviet lifeline temporarily freed the state from dependence on private financing, conferring a substantive degree of autonomy in making planning decisions.[128] In the long run, the arrival of Cold

War economic competition on Indian soil exacerbated turf wars between the various ministries and provincial governments, slowly eroding the entire planning apparatus. For big business, it was merely the latest in a series of "opportunities to use international resources to fight domestic battles."[129] Upon receiving news of Bhilai, the Tatas' main concern was to safeguard their American lifeline. E. T. Warren of Tata Inc. in New York wrote to J. R. D.: "If an agreement is reached between the Indian Government and the Russians for this plant I feel rather certain that a great deal of the 'open-sesame' this office has had for entry and information from the American Steel Industry will be closed to us."[130] He need not have worried. The flow of Eastern Bloc aid to public sector projects in the wake of Bhilai rapidly drew American capital and expertise to India, which ended up strengthening Tata more than any other group.

Annus Mirabilis, 1958

On the ground, Bhilai was a spectacular propaganda triumph for the Soviets. Unlike Rourkela, which suffered from severe construction delays and labor conflicts and failed to meet its production targets, the new plant was completed on schedule and functioned relatively smoothly from the start. Journalist Taya Zinkin of the *Manchester Guardian,* who visited both sites, pronounced Bhilai a "recipe for success," Rourkela one "for failure." German personnel left a bitter impression, their technical competence marred by drinking, womanizing, and a general disregard for local sensibilities. There were stark differences in pay and status between the Germans and their Indian counterparts, while patents and trade secrets were jealously guarded. By contrast, the Russian engineers lived frugally under "strict discipline," threatened with a return passage home "if they molest local women, appear on the job drunk or are generally disorderly." Zinkin described the relationship between Indians and Soviets as "cordial if cool—the very prototype of polite coexistence." Surprisingly, the language barrier helped ease tension by allowing each side to curse out the other without giving offense.[131]

American officials keeping an eye on the progress of the steel plants observed that by giving ultimate financial and administrative responsibility to Indians, the Soviets had assumed "the role of helping Big Brother and advisor rather than as the superior and the boss." As a result, there was "a great feeling of fraternity" between them.[132] Ved Mehta's firsthand reports from Bhilai in the *New Yorker* amplified this impression with tales of camaraderie and self-sacrifice reminiscent of TISCO's early days, with no trace of the racialized terror of hard-knuckle American managers like Tutwiler and Keenan. The melodramatic story of junior chemical assistant Sisir Chakravorti's friendship with the blast furnace engineer Ivanovich was typical:

> Somebody had saved my life. I got up, looked—and looked straight into the eyes of a hefty Russian with a round red face where anger and sympathy struggled over the surface of a usual joviality. . . . He approached me, caught hold of my arm, and asked in broken English, "You hurt?" I will never forget that tone. My oldest of acquaintances could not have shown a more genuine sympathy than was expressed in those two words uttered by an unknown giant foreigner. I smiled, clasped his hands, and said, "No. Thank you."

Later, Ivanovich was crushed by a falling piece of equipment while saving another Indian worker. As he lay dying in the hospital, he muttered with his last breath in Russian, "Is my brother saved?"[133] Rather than a mere practical benefit, as in Zinkin's account, the language barrier made possible the expression of a transcendent laboring masculinity. American readers approaching the story in a Cold War frame of mind must have been terrified.

The Soviet leadership had done everything in its power to ensure Bhilai's success. Nikita Khrushchev, who confessed to knowing virtually nothing about India apart from a few Orientalist stereotypes of exotic tigers and diamond caves from a nineteenth-century Russian opera, took a personal interest in the project. He placed V. E. Dymshitz, a capable engineer who had worked on the massive steel plant at Magnitogorsk in Stalin's time, in charge of the operation. Labor unions that looked to Moscow for guidance were kept under a tight leash to minimize unrest.[134] To speed up the pace of construction, the Soviets assented to the use of British, German, and American equipment, including Otis elevators and Krupp cranes purchased with precious foreign exchange.[135] A former TISCO manager who advised the Ministry of Steel was delighted with the arrangement. "Give me a deal with the Commies every time!" he exclaimed. "To begin with there is no hankey pankey about trade secrets, patents, etc. They may violate the secrets of others, but *you* get the benefit of their violation and *you* remain correct. . . . They do not use their working here to indoctrinate; not a bit of it; they are far too busy working."[136] The fundamentally nonideological character of the project was evident at every turn, as was the Soviets' weak position. They knew they could not outcompete the West in the sheer amount of foreign aid, seeking instead to open new trade channels with a friendly country through targeted and carefully managed projects. But in the "feverish imaginings of American policymakers," Bhilai was a gateway to full-blown Communism.[137]

The Tatas' pressing need to implement their two-million-ton program (TMP) extensions at Jamshedpur allowed the United States to regain lost ground through financial and technical participation in the Indian steel industry. TISCO had first sought a loan from the Export-Import Bank in 1955, soon after the announcement of the Soviet offer for Bhilai. The US Embassy in New Delhi "strongly recommended the granting of special or favorable terms . . . as a means of countering the favorable terms provided in the Soviet proposal." But negotiations foundered over the high cost of equipment, which the Tatas had tried to mitigate through some form of "invisible" aid or subsidy. J. R. D. Tata refused to go to the World Bank "since according to the regulations of that institution the loan would have to be guaranteed by the Government of India, thus undermining the purely private nature of the venture which Tata wishes to maintain."[138] This was in keeping with the Tatas' entrenched preference for seeking foreign investment entirely outside government channels, but going it alone no longer made sense.

Less than one year later, J. R. D. returned to Washington and applied for a government-backed loan from the World Bank, which would allow TISCO to buy equipment "on worldwide bids and save a great deal."[139] The $75 million loan was approved, as American officials realized they had driven too hard a bargain in the past. Central Intelligence Agency (CIA) director Allen Dulles told President Eisenhower that "it was going to be very hard for the United States to compete with cheap Soviet money as had been shown by our attitude toward a loan to the Tata interests."[140] With Eisenhower's approval, the National Security Council even proposed abandoning the long-standing reluctance to support public sector projects.[141] Although familiar anxieties of red tape, corruption, and the possibility of nationalization remained, American companies concluded that "the prospects for a decided improvement in the climate for foreign business activities in India are probably better now than at any time since the independence of India."[142] Bhilai had cracked open the floodgates of American aid, which would soon drown out the Soviets as a multinational consortium pledged $350 million in general (not project-based) assistance. Politburo member and diplomat Anastas Mikoyan freely acknowledged that "help from the Soviet Union obliges the US to increase its own grants." Indian businessmen had asserted their crucial intermediary role in managing flows of foreign capital. Even the Soviets were forced to negotiate with Birla and others deputed to Moscow by Nehru, just as the Americans had to deal with Tata.[143]

In this context, the Indian state's attitude toward the private sector in general shifted dramatically. The guarantee of the World Bank loan to TISCO took place around the same time as G. D. Birla led another government-sanctioned industrial mission to the United States. The discovery in 1958 of a yawning gap of $700–$900 million in India's foreign exchange reserves undermined policy autonomy and further sanded the edges off Nehru's promises of building socialism. Licensing restrictions were lifted, as more and more industries in "reserved" sectors were thrown open to private investment.[144] The Ministry of Finance emerged victorious from the internecine battles in New Delhi, leaving the Planning Commission and rival ministries in the dust. By 1961, foreign capital accounted for 32 percent of all fixed investment in the private sector.[145]

For big business, 1958 was a rare moment of unity, recalling the heady days of the industrial mission at the end of World War II. This time, due in no small part to the Cold War, they found both a more receptive audience in Washington and London and a more pliant state back home. As the British political economist Michael Kidron argued in an insightful contemporary study, foreign capital had provided Indian business with "a toe-hold of extraterritoriality from which to confound the planners in every aspect of their work."[146] This "extraterritorial" dimension is often absent in debates about the "national bourgeoisie," which remain narrowly centered on the moment of independence. For the Tatas, connections with the United States preceded and outlasted that moment. They allowed the group to regain some of the ground lost to the Birlas and the bureaucrats after the disappointments of earlier in the decade, when Air India was nationalized and TISCO was bypassed in the expansion of steel capacity. National capitalists were forged in the crucible of global war.

5

Between Paternalism and Technocracy

In October 1944, an ordinary typist in the Tata Iron and Steel Company (TISCO) accounts office named A. Gowtama Rao sent a long, unsolicited note to Chairman J. R. D. Tata, titled "Shape of Things to Come—Jamshedpur as in the Year 1954." Presented as "an extension of the Wellsian vision for the future," a reference to popular science fiction author H. G. Wells, the note outlined an intriguing speculative history of the steel town into the following decade and beyond. Rao claimed his bold predictions bore "poetic kinship to the great welter of plans and super plans for the world and the steel industry" accompanying the end of the war. The note begins by recounting a concerted drive for industrial development, inspired by the recently published Bombay Plan. In Rao's vision, Tata is destined to take on "big housing schemes and mass electrification" and to develop into a "quasi-NRA" (President Franklin Roosevelt's National Recovery Administration). The United States appears as both a model to follow and an ally to cultivate, in line with the expectations raised by the Grady Mission: "The Tatas and the American Lease-Lend firms came to an agreement which was in the nature of a complementary effort, the Americans to work in the higher strata of the steel industry, for a time and a partial monopoly of aeroplane and automobile industries for a little more." Tata is uniquely positioned to use its extraterritorial connections to ensure that India will develop free from the stranglehold of British domination. The specters of socialism and state control, very much on the horizon at the time of writing, are banished from the narrative.

Rao's note also explores the relationship between capital and labor in Jamshedpur and life in the city. Strikes predictably follow the end of the wartime production boom, just as in 1920–1921. But management is willing to meet "reasonable" union demands for a thirty-six-hour week, a halt in retrenchments, and a reorganized labor bureau to implement a consistent hiring policy. A "very sensible agreement" is reached with the Tata Workers' Union (TWU) in 1952, which subsequently becomes a "permanent feature of the company administration." Through the "studied and liberal approach both by the Employer and Union, the psychology of the Steel Worker is shaping itself into a healthy and robust optimism." Standards of living in Jamshedpur improve dramatically. Supplies of vegetables and milk increase, maternity centers open, and "the old rickety bodies and jaded faces of an ill-nourished population" disappear. The housing problem is resolved by replacing the "monotony of the old regimented police barracks" with "architectural variation" and modern household amenities. In these and many other ways, Rao declares, "a tranquil era of industrial harmony and prosperity has come to stay." He adds another literary flourish with a reference to Percy Bysshe Shelley's poem about the Egyptian pharaoh Ozymandias, "whose statue on the sands of Egypt speaks eloquently of the glory that was once Alexandria at its peak." In a similar way, Jamshedpur is destined to stand as an eternal monument to twentieth-century industry, science, and technology.[1]

No response from J. R. D. is recorded, and the note has since been forgotten in a dusty file in the company archives. With the benefit of hindsight, what is remarkable about Rao's exercise in utopian thinking was just how much he got right. In the late 1940s and early 1950s, TISCO management did take concrete steps to finally bring order and coherence to both industrial relations and urban planning. A collective bargaining agreement was indeed signed with the TWU in 1956, only four years after Rao's predicted date. Industrial psychologists, management consultants, architects, and other foreign experts descended on Jamshedpur to offer new solutions to the old problem of implanting a modern enterprise in a rural and tribal setting. Yet, Rao failed to anticipate just how fraught the path to industrial peace would be. Collective bargaining was by no means accepted by all ranks of management. Authority continued to be exercised through a combination of carrot and stick, blending imported ideas and homegrown solutions. Workers, too, came to resent the 1956 agreement, leading to one of the most violent strikes in Jamshedpur's history two years later. Bureaucratic structures created in accordance with the principles of scientific management, such as the personnel department and a series of company information courses, appeared hollow and superficial to many. Despite urban planners' best efforts, Jamshedpur remained a spatially segregated and deeply unequal city.

The postwar period marked the high point of the cult of expertise at TISCO, when the resolution of the eternal conflict between capital and labor seemed within reach. Some scholars take seriously the company's experiments in importing scientific management from the West. TISCO stood apart from other Indian employers due to its slavish dependence on foreign experts for "new information on methods and control systems," which enabled a clear shift from coercion to co-optation.[2] Others characterize TISCO policy as an unchanged "feudal" paternalism rooted in an indigenous "precapitalist culture," subordinating workers by alternating between naked violence and the charismatic authority of the employer as traditional king or patriarch.[3] Neither interpretation fully captures extensive debates within the managerial hierarchy about which specific measures should be implemented at any given time, nor the connection between TISCO as a single company and the group as a whole. Paternalism and technocracy worked in tandem to create a hybrid labor control regime that survived throughout the second half of the twentieth century.

Accounts of scientific management usually begin with Frederick Winslow Taylor's time-motion studies and with Henry Ford's automobile assembly line, which aimed to turn human beings into machines and corporations into bureaucracies. Yet, this vision was never hegemonic anywhere in the world. In Ford's own factories at Highland Park and River Rouge, "skilled mechanics and foremen not beholden to outside efficiency experts" ran the shop floor with a free hand. They had the authority to speed up and slow down production according to their best judgment, not the ticking of a time piece—and that was just how Ford wanted it. His company lacked a formal organization chart, more representative of Max Weber's notion of "charismatic" leadership rather than Alfred Chandler's managerial corporation.[4] In France, the tire maker Michelin was seen as an evangelist for Taylorism but substantially modified its precepts by offering workers with "cradle-to-grave" support in the form of generous *oeuvres sociales* (welfare works).[5] In Germany, the steelmakers Krupp and Thyssen blended the feudal, autocratic tradition of the employer as *Herr im Hause* (master in the house) with sophisticated accounting and surveillance systems.[6] In China, the Dongya corporation mixed "Confucian paternalism and Chinese nationalism with Western Christianity, 'scientific' management, hygienic practice, consumer capitalism, industrialism, and modern discipline" in pursuit of their own "Industrial Eden."[7] Personalized bonds between employers and workers were a defining feature of industrial modernity everywhere, as the abstractions of the market were "embedded" in social relations in myriad ways.[8]

In India and other "traditional" societies, the mixture of paternalism and technocracy appears again and again in the guise of an exception—when it was, in fact, the rule. The challenge is to explain the balance between these forces and how it came about as a result of flows of expertise and exchanges of ideas between experts and managers. Concepts were deployed in highly specific and often contradictory ways. In Jamshedpur, the notion of the *adivasi* (aboriginal/tribal) "coolie" as innately unsuited for industrial discipline was used first to stall and then to justify the implementation of quasi-Taylorist measures. Among the upper echelons of management in Bombay, constructing a distinct Tata tradition involved both routinized bureaucratic procedures and an idealized past radiating the charismatic aura of the founder, Jamsetji Tata. The need to reconcile modern industry with "primitive" labor and codify a humane corporate ethos stemmed from changing political circumstances. In the 1950s, the Nehruvian state exclusively claimed the mantle of development, leaving private enterprise in a precarious position. Selectively drawing on transnational networks of knowledge production, as they had done in the realm of philanthropy, the Tatas sought to put their house in order and to belatedly live up to the promise of a different kind of capitalism.

Halfway to Utopia

Notions of indigeneity and difference had long been used by Tata managers to insist, against the advice of visiting experts like the Webbs, that little could be done to provide more amenities and services for workers. Urban planning provides one of the clearest illustrations of the tug-of-war between management and expertise in Jamshedpur. The company had failed to follow any kind of rationalizing or scientific master plan, due in no small part to the legal challenges of land acquisition, while slums proliferated on the outskirts and housing stock remained woefully inadequate. In early 1942, Chairman J. R. D. Tata forcefully pointed out these deficiencies. Jamshedpur had failed to live up to the pastoral Garden City ideal deemed most appropriate for company towns worldwide and advocated by the founder. "If we want the town to develop as a harmonious whole and retain the best features of a modern garden city," J. R. D. wrote, "we must ensure that the elevation of all *pucca* [solid] buildings put up in the town should be of pleasing appearance, and have common architectural features." To this end, he advocated employing an outside expert to prepare a master plan for Jamshedpur's growth over the coming twenty-five years.[9]

That expert turned out to be Otto Koenigsberger, a Jewish refugee from Hitler's Germany who emigrated to India at the beginning of the war and established a thriving architectural practice in Mysore and Bangalore. Through his maternal uncle, the physicist Max Born, Koenigsberger came to know Homi Bhabha, then lecturing at the Indian Institute of Science—a reminder of the importance of philanthropy in cultivating networks of expertise. Koenigsberger's commissioned work for the institute, including the aeronautical engineering department and the TISCO-supported metallurgy department, pioneered what came to be known as "tropical architecture." His buildings were rarely more than one-story tall and designed to increase circulation of air in a hot climate. Departing from existing colonial models, they were both recognizably modernist and organically suited to local conditions.[10] Whereas J. R. D. continued to refer to Jamshedpur as a "picturesque" Garden City, Koenigsberger had a more ambitious agenda in mind. But his *Jamshedpur Development Plan*, completed in 1945, reveals the limits of expertise when confronted with realities on the ground. The original sin of erecting the bungalows and officers' quarters near the plant, which forced workers to live farther and farther away, could not be corrected. The sedimentary accumulation of past infrastructures and the influx of Partition refugees crowding in temporary settlements served to check the planner's utopian impulses. As Koenigsberger put it, "an ideal solution according to theoretical postulations" was out of reach in Jamshedpur. This was not the Soviet steel city of Magnitogorsk, where the "virgin steppe" gave planners an infinite canvas for experimentation.[11]

Koenigsberger's creative attempt to overcome these limitations was the introduction of the "neighborhood unit," a self-contained group of houses with an open space at the center for residents to live, shop, and play (Fig. 5.1). Originating in the United States, the concept was appropriately modified. The Indian variant was larger, leaving room for up to 2,000–3,500 houses or 10,000–18,000 residents. Koenigsberger believed the neighborhood unit was ideally suited to India because it mimicked the imagined village community. Jamshedpur's first planner, F. C. Temple, had made a similar argument in support of the hexagonal "coolie town" at Sonari (see Chapter 2). Koenigsberger also acknowledged the imperative to control labor and preserve existing social hierarchies, albeit more reluctantly than Temple. "Theoretically," he explained, "it would be desirable that each Neighborhood Unit in Jamshedpur should be composed of people of all social classes, highly paid officers, technicians, clerks, skilled workers, coolies, and sweepers." But since "cultural differences and contrasts in the style of living are still too great for such an attempt . . . the 19th century style social grouping must therefore be accepted as a necessary part of the Jamshedpur plan."[12] Tellingly, Koenigsberger never proposed "segregated residential areas" before or after this commission, suggesting this was a deliberate compromise with his patron's demands.[13]

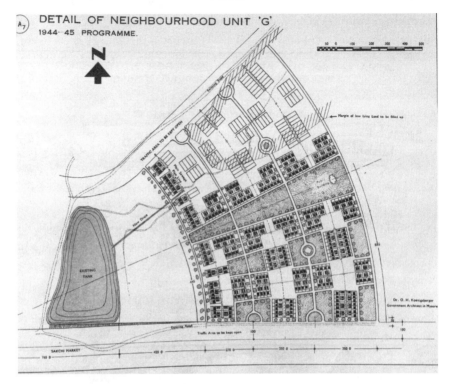

FIG. 5.1. Neighborhood unit in Otto Koenigsberger's *Jamshedpur Development Plan,* 1945. Courtesy Architectural Association Archives, London.

Pleased with Koenigsberger's work, J. R. D. Tata arranged for him to draw up another plan for Mithapur, the Tata Chemicals township under construction on the western coast of Gujarat. Unlike Jamshedpur, Mithapur offered a true tabula rasa for experimentation. With the bitter struggles over retrenchment at TISCO in mind, J. R. D. held that a "town of about 5,000 should be quite sufficient for all the labour force required and that we should not employ too many men."[14] By contrast, for Koenigsberger, the aim was to "turn the place from a labour camp . . . into a living organism with individuality and character, into a place which its citizen [*sic*] own with pride and to which they like to return in their leisure hours." He planned for twenty thousand residents, four times the number J. R. D. wanted. To counteract the emerge of Jugsalai-like slums in neighboring villages, he proposed acquiring additional land within a 1.5-mile radius of the plant and providing opportunities for workers to cultivate small plots. Combining "agriculture with industrial labor" would prevent complete dependence on the company. Refusing to compromise on the composition of neighborhood units, Koenigsberger stressed an "equal share of labour class and middle class in the housing of the town." He believed this would be more appropriate for Mithapur because chemical production was more "highly mechanized" than steelmaking and "by the nature of its processes requires qualified technicians rather than primitive cooly labour."[15] In reality, Tata Chemicals ended up relying on manual "coolie" labor every bit as much TISCO and most other Indian employers did.

Koenigsberger's plans for Jamshedpur and Mithapur were more than routine corporate commissions beholden to the logic of labor control. They held special significance for the infrastructural needs of independent India. In 1948, Koenigsberger was appointed director of housing for the Ministry of Health by Prime Minister Nehru and tasked with coordinating post-Partition refugee resettlement. At the beginning of his tenure, Koenigsberger made arrangements to publicize the *Jamshedpur Development Plan* in view of its obvious "value to the nation."[16] Private company towns would serve as a model for the so-called new towns, a broad category encompassing refugee settlements like Gandhidam in Gujarat and Faridabad in Haryana, new state capitals like Bhubaneswar in Orissa (also planned by Koenigsberger) and Chandigarh in Punjab, and eventually the steel cities of Rourkela, Bhilai, and Durgapur. Austere and functional, new towns were meant to "train newcomers for productive work," whether they were refugees or migrants from the countryside, becoming a "symbol of self-confidence and hope" for the postcolonial nation.[17] Although this voluntarist and participatory ethic reflected both Gandhian and Nehruvian ideals, it also drew on older anxieties about the peculiarities of Indian industrial modernity.

New towns, like their private company town antecedents, were precariously suspended between the past and the future. In the interwar period, Jamshedpur had exemplified the same rapid compression of historical time that "sped up progress into an imminent age."[18] But planners' fascination with village communities as spaces of natural vigor, ethnic purity, and fixed social order, from Temple's hexagons to Koenigsberger's neighborhood units, meant resisting the formation of "wholly urban subjectivities."[19] The Ford Foundation–sponsored Delhi Master Plan, completed in 1960, embraced segregation by class and caste in neighborhood units for the sake of upholding "place-based community."[20] Jamshedpur had long been a key site for the circulation and adaptation of transnational expertise in India. Its successes and failures in this regard would become the nation's as well.

The Measure of the Worker

Koenigsberger's "tropical architecture" was only one of several transnational disciplinary innovations directed at the problems of Indian industrial modernity, particularly mass migration from the village to the city. Industrial psychology was another, seeking to reform the minds of displaced migrant workers rather than merely changing their surroundings. Its pioneer in India was Narendra Nath Sengupta, who came of age during the *swadeshi* movement in Bengal and studied in the laboratory of German psychologist Hugo Münsterberg at Harvard.[21] Münsterberg was at the forefront of a shift away from the mechanistic focus of Taylorism on the body in motion toward a scientific exploration of the human mind in the laboring process. He championed scientific recruitment through vocational aptitude testing, among other methods.[22] Sengupta built on his mentor's work, establishing the Indian Psychological Association (IPA) in 1925 and the associated *Journal of Indian Psychology* one year later. Far from a "derivative" project, the development of the discipline in India was an act of "nationalist assertion" in a universalist frame, drawing on indigenous intellectual resources such as the Bhagavad Gita and the Upanishads and the latest in European thought. In the inaugural issue of the journal, Sengupta argued that India "must share her burden of contribution to the unraveling of the mysteries of psychic life, to the development of Psychology as a science."[23] Radhakamal Mukerjee, with whom Sengupta coauthored *Introduction to Social Psychology* (1928), endeavored to do the same for political economy.[24] Both found in Jamshedpur an ideal laboratory for social scientific knowledge production.

M. N. Banerji, Sengupta's student and successor as IPA president, conducted the first series of efficiency and fatigue studies of the TISCO workforce, over a decade after they were first proposed by the visiting London School of Economics (LSE) experts. Banerji's research team took a set of three hundred measurements of grip strength (using an instrument known as a dynamometer) and reaction time (using a Vernier chronoscope) in different departments of the steel plant, from the sheet mills to the blast furnaces. Results showed that "the measures of Reaction Time before and after work give a more reliable index of the onset of fatigue than those by the Dynamometer" and that workers in the sheet mills suffered more from fatigue than those in other departments. Banerji made no concrete suggestions for improvement of factory conditions, taking great care "not to create suspicion or distrust in the minds of the worker and the owner."[25] But this type of limited physiological inquiry was on its way out, to be replaced by a more holistic psychological approach considering mind and body together. Assumptions that workers everywhere could be studied using the same techniques also gave way to more relativistic and contextual perspectives.

Around the same time, social scientists in the Anglophone world were turning their attention from individual efficiency to the "inter-subjective relations of the workplace."[26] In Britain, fatigue studies of the kind conducted by Banerji were deemed to "lack theoretical coherence." Group "morale" emerged as an intangible yet essential determinant of healthy industrial relations.[27] Australian-born psychologist Elton Mayo's Hawthorne studies, conducted in a Western Electric plant near Chicago in the mid-1920s, demonstrably proved the importance of social ties among workers as a means of enhancing productivity. This was a clear departure from both Taylorism and the rival tradition of Quaker businessman and philanthropist Seebohm Rowntree, whose investigations showed that workers were primarily motivated by pay incentives. The Hawthorne studies became canonical due to Mayo's self-promotional skills and his connections to an expanding network of private consultants. He told managers what they wanted to hear—namely, that increasing workers' pay was less effective than fostering community in the factory; conveniently, the latter also happened to cost less.[28] Partly on the basis of Mayo's work, American corporations began to be reimagined as "democratic sociocultural institutions" structured around small groups, not efficiency-maximizing individuals.[29]

The transition to "group" thinking was a decidedly transnational phenomenon, but in India, it was driven by a particular set of anxieties. In the report of the Royal Commission on Labour (1931) and anthropologist Margaret Read's evocative lay version, Indian workers were depicted as passive victims of a fundamental clash between dynamic Western "individualism" and a static Eastern civilization "based on agriculture, on community life, on established custom." The experience of migration and factory labor left them "bewildered" and mired in a "fog of apathy." Denied agency and even consciousness, migrant workers were seen as "the prey of forces which they do not understand, of forces which are just as impersonal and relentless as the waves of the sea on a sandbar."[30] Deflecting criticisms that the commission wanted to "set the path of Indian labour along the path of Western trades unionism," Read was at pains to show that the "group spirit" of caste, kinship, and locality was irreversibly breaking down and had to be rebuilt.[31] In a similar vein, Clifford Manshardt and the faculty at the Tata Institute of Social Sciences (TISS) diagnosed labor unrest not as an expression of class conflict but as psychological "maladjustment" (see Chapter 3).

Articles in the *Indian Journal of Psychology*, and the discipline as a whole, thus came to explain Indian workers' feelings of alienation as a function of the erosion of caste and kinship. Follow-up studies in Jamshedpur by D. L. Sharma contrasted the strong "superego" of individuals in the village community with the rootlessness of urban life. "In the new environment in which he transplants himself," the TISCO worker "finds that all these factors, family, religion, economic and social, the combination of which formed the superego are either absent or working against him."[32] Rejecting purely class-based explanations, Sharma insisted that "the difficulties of the workers are deeper and psychological rather than what people generally think them to be or what sometimes the workers themselves put them forward to be."[33] Only the properly trained investigator could uncover their subconscious grievances. The struggles of industrial labor at Jamshedpur were framed as an intractably Indian phenomenon rooted in the process of migration from the village to the city—an old concern dressed up in new scientific garb.

These ideas found an institutional home within TISCO with the creation of the personnel department, a watershed moment in the history of the company. In a confidential proposal drafted in 1943, J. R. D. Tata admitted that management had "little cause for self-congratulation or for feeling complacent." If the workers felt "frequently discontented and mistrustful, and hostile towards us," he wrote, "I think we must assume that the fault lies with us and not with them." The lack of a "personal touch" and of "mutual trust and friendly understanding" could be addressed by "finding means of associating in some way labour with management." To this end, the proposed department would absorb the existing welfare and safety departments and labor employment bureau, as well as introducing a "Bureau of Industrial Psychology and Efficiency, incorporating Statistical and Research sections."[34] It would collect data on worker selection, vocational and aptitude tests, physical environment, periods of rest, and "the posture and movement of the worker at his task."[35] But this was no mere fact-finding bureaucracy. The personnel department was also tasked with overseeing massive reductions in a workforce inflated by the wartime production boom. J. R. D. believed there was "no more urgent problem for us to tackle" than "the excessive size of our labour force at Jamshedpur," which harmed productivity, efficiency, and morale.[36] Retrenchment and rationalization had been at the root of the strikes of the late 1920s, but the sheer scale of the attempted reductions was unprecedented. Integrating industrial psychology into the operational structure of the company was both a practical necessity and a natural outcome of the vernacularization of the discipline in India.

Implementation of J. R. D.'s proposal proceeded slowly. In 1946, TISCO approached the National Institute for Industrial Psychology in London to find an expert "who could undertake a scientific classification, analysis, and point-rating of jobs." To aid in labor recruitment, the company secured the services of the colonial government's new Employment Selection Bureau, headed by Brigadier H. Vinden.[37] In his work with the Indian Army during the war, Vinden brought the universalizing methods of scientific selection to an otherwise conservative and tradition-bound institution. The aptitude tests he used to screen recruits were replicas of the tests used in Britain, paying no mind to prevailing stereotypes of "martial races." He faced heavy criticism from both old-guard civil servants and Indian nationalists, who advocated relying on "local knowledge" for their own very different reasons.[38] TISCO made little progress on this front, showing how difficult it was to transfer already contested techniques from the military and civil service to an industrial setting. A suitable psychologist could not be obtained from London, and Vinden's bureau was disbanded within a few months of independence.

Meanwhile, the labor situation on the ground in Jamshedpur rapidly deteriorated. Workers were dissatisfied with the revised wage and bonus structure introduced after the war, while the "morale of the Officers was shaken and everywhere there was a spirit of indiscipline."[39] With management hopelessly divided on how to respond, J. R. D. decided to call upon "a fresh and expert mind"—his friend John Moore, head of the consulting firm IBCON in India.[40] IBCON began as an offshoot of the international consultancy headed by Charles Bedaux, an eccentric French-born American businessman who devised a new standard unit of work measurement known as the B. A modified version of Taylor's "unit-time" method, the B gained widespread acceptance in British management circles in the interwar period. Bedaux's colorful personal life and dubious political allegiances, notably his association with the Duke of Windsor and accusations of collaborating with the Nazis, eventually dented his appeal.[41] India was one of the few places where the Bedaux system had more of a lasting influence than Taylorism. IBCON began its investigations in Jamshedpur more or less in secret. Given that "labour has got management on the run," it was imperative that the unions did not "get a wrong impression" that Moore was there to push reductions on a mass scale.[42]

In January 1948, TISCO officially hired IBCON on a three-year contract to establish an industrial engineering department and to undertake an analysis of "potentials" and "incentives for higher production and reduced personnel." Bonus pay was linked with a series of standardized output indices, varying by department.[43] Moore submitted a "Memorandum on the Deployment of Labour" in 1950, calling for "a final overall reduction" of as many as ten thousand workers, or 25 percent of the total. The fallout of this drastic cost-cutting measure was couched in the language of the new social scientific consensus. The "problems which will arise are largely psychological for each individual" and should be dealt with on a case-by-case basis by the personnel department, not as a matter for collective bargaining.[44] But Moore's advice was not always heeded. Following the Bedaux method, the memorandum proposed a universal standard of "equivalent men" to measure productivity, using the low-skilled *khalasi* (lifting operator) as a basic "man-unit." J. R. D. protested that this would give the unions the impression that only a few highly skilled and well-paid employees could be retrenched to cut costs, rather than starting at the bottom with the most expendable workers.[45] Expertise and managerial discretion diverged yet again.

For their part, workers were under no illusions about the consultants' prescriptions. They were rightly baffled by the complex systems of incentives and grades but intuitively understood the new institutions as structures of domination.[46] Under the fiery Congress leader Abdul Bari, the company-recognized TWU initially welcomed scientific recruitment methods, even threatening a strike if the company continued to delay the introduction of the personnel department.[47] However, once the particulars of the retrenchment scheme became clear, the department became a target. The Tata Mazdoor Sabha, a non-recognized union led by the Congress Socialists, passed a resolution in 1951 calling for its immediate abolition.[48] Management secured the necessary cover to implement the reductions only when the more accommodating Michael John took over the leadership of the TWU after Bari's death.

Moore and IBCON went on to advise other Tata companies on ways to reduce costs and raise productivity. At Tata Chemicals in Mithapur, they proposed reductions of 25 percent in labor and 35 percent in the clerical staff over a period of three to five years, along with the establishment of an industrial engineering division to provide training in time-motion studies. The Empress Mills at Nagpur were told to drastically reduce clerical staff from 417 to 186.[49] Connections between Tata companies allowed experts to test and refine their interventions, as Koenigsberger did when planning Jamshedpur and Mithapur.

But expertise was often subordinated to management's predetermined plans, as Moore discovered when suggesting the "equivalent men" unit. Despite the continuing lip service paid to industrial psychology and scientific management as cutting-edge disciplines, notions of Indian difference and ruling with a firm hand took precedence.

Forging Industrial Peace

In the early 1950s, the leadership in Bombay House initiated a comprehensive restructuring of labor relations across all companies, with TISCO in Jamshedpur as a point of departure. Its main architect was Minoo Masani, a trained lawyer and former trade unionist who moved from the public relations department to advise the chairman on industrial relations. In February 1953, Masani opened the First Tata Personnel and Labour Officers' Conference in Bombay by proposing the creation of a centralized department of industrial relations within a year's time.[50] He invited John Marsh, director of the Industrial Welfare Society in London, to prepare a meticulous two-week information course for TISCO supervisory staff as a first step. However, in his speech at the conference, Marsh advocated strengthening existing welfare programs rather than "jumping too quickly into the full flush of personnel management as practised in the West." The destructive effects of industrialization on the joint family system, as well as the "survival" of "regional prejudices" among Jamshedpur's heterogeneous workforce, would have to be addressed. Going against the latest trends in management thinking, Marsh even suggested replacing the position of industrial psychologist with a chief welfare officer.[51]

Masani's centralizing efforts faced a barrage of objections at the conference. Tata managers worried about their role under the new system: would personnel officers correspond directly with their respective departments, or would they have to go up the chain of command in each company? Union representatives viewed personnel officers as inherently "political agents" serving the interests of management and called for unmediated collective bargaining. G. D. Ambekar of the Congress Party–affiliated Indian National Trade Union Congress (no member of the Communist-affiliated All India Trade Union Congress was invited) maintained that "the institution of the P.O. is a failure and should be allowed to die out. He has no place in the Indian set-up." Surprisingly, some managers shared these objections. Young Russi Mody of TISCO also insisted that collective bargaining should be given a chance to work at the company level.[52] He went so far as to say that "it would be better if the expenditure on welfare activities was reduced and the money spent on better wages as in the United States." This argument met with the familiar objection that "workers in India were not educated enough to spend their money in a proper way, and until such time as they could be shown the proper way of living, the need for welfare activities would remain."[53] This was a near-verbatim reprise of the debates between B. J. Padshah and S. K. Sawday in the mid-1920s (see Chapter 2). Back then, even hardliners like Sawday begrudgingly accepted the desirability of raising wages no matter how the workers spent them. But reactionary paternalism lived on.

The son of a prominent Tata Sons director, Russi Mody began his career as a labor officer in the TISCO mines in 1947, earning a reputation for charismatic, hands-on leadership. One early incident speaks to his understanding of labor control as both disciplinary and dialogic. Surrounded by a "howling mob" of workers, Mody stood his ground, engaged with them, and promised to look into their complaints. The results were near-miraculous: "Gradually, the howling subsided, the tension eased, and the men slowly withdrew from their state of frenzy. They were sitting before me keen to listen and act as I bade them."[54] The story may well come across as a textbook illustration of paternalism, but Mody was in fact a powerful insider voice in favor of reform. Shortly after his participation in the First Personnel and Labour Officers' Conference, he was dispatched to Mithapur to compile a report on growing unrest at Tata Chemicals. A personnel department staffed by officers trained in Jamshedpur had been established after a short-lived strike in April 1952, but workers were "demoralised" and did not feel "part and parcel of the enlightened Tata Policy on Labour." Mody observed that "a situation like this 26 years ago would have been ideal from the Management's point of view and possibly much good might have resulted from adopting a paternalistic attitude and making some concessions on your own." But times had changed, and business was on the defensive as trade unions fell under the spell of a resurgent Communist Party. Mody proposed immediately recognizing the Congress-affiliated union to halt the Communists' inroads and then entering into negotiations.[55]

Mody's report from Mithapur seemed to have decisively tilted the scales toward "a more modern and up-to-date concept of management" in the group.[56] In January 1956, TISCO and the TWU finally signed a comprehensive collective bargaining agreement, paving the way for the company's two-million ton program (TMP) expansion. At the Second Tata Management Conference later that year, Masani hailed it as "a landmark in the history of industrial relations in this country."[57] A three-tiered consultative machinery came into being, consisting of twenty-seven joint departmental councils, a joint works council, joint town council, and joint consultative council at the top level, each staffed by representatives of management and the union.[58] Management assured Michael John and the TWU that "there will be no retrenchment of existing employees" and promised to offer higher wages "in recognition of the increased labour productivity and the larger profits resulting from the plant expansion programme." But the precise amount and timing of this wage increase were conditional on the implementation of another "job evaluation" survey by IBCON. Significantly, town employees were given their own joint council but were excluded from the wage bargain. John had expressed his opposition to this clause but did not press the point for fear of a breakdown in negotiations.[59]

The triumph of collective bargaining proved short lived. The agreement gambled on bringing the union into the fold, a strategy entirely dependent on the TWU maintaining its legitimacy among the workers. As during the late 1920s, the impetus for resistance came from the very lowest ranks. In May 1957, the staff of the health department and "certain categories of lower-paid employees" in the town division went on strike to protest their exclusion from the promised wage increases in the agreement. Lower-caste sweepers "went round in small batches shouting slogans near General Offices" and "asking the clerical staff to show sympathy by stopping work." They threw "nightsoil" in the store accounts department and in the houses of employees who remained at their posts. Management reported that "a power vacuum has been created in the town with the sweepers and others having no definite affiliations," a state of affairs ripe for exploitation by the Communist-led Jamshedpur Mazdoor Union (JMU).[60]

This small strike was one of many warning signs that all was not well at TISCO. Supervisors openly confessed "that they did not understand the departmental incentive scheme themselves or the reasons for setting the high standard." The company information courses proposed by Marsh and other training sessions had only partially changed managerial attitudes. All that could be said was that "there was much less shouting than before."[61] A memorandum submitted by Resident Director M. K. Powvala observed, "There is at present next to no communication between workmen and supervisors in the Steel Company. The Personnel Dept. does not appear to possess the confidence of the workers. In these circumstances, when any of them want help, comfort and guidance, they do not turn to the management but look elsewhere." This "elsewhere" was the JMU, which was gaining in strength and popularity as workers came to view the TWU leadership as compromised. Alarmed, Powvala warned J. R. D. Tata that "sitting round a table with the representatives of the workers was not the final solution. Work on the shop floor was very necessary, and this must be insisted upon. . . . I got the feeling that our officers really do not believe in it."[62] The sense of unease and anticipation was palpable.

By the autumn of 1957, Masani had left Tata to concentrate on his political career, winning a seat in Parliament as an independent. But he continued to serve the group from afar by forming an independent consulting company, Personnel and Productivity Services (PPS), which assumed the intermediary role of standardizing best practices across group companies.[63] In November, PPS conducted a confidential assessment of labor relations at TISCO, confirming management's worst fears of widespread discontent. Rather than going back to the negotiating table, Masani's main suggestion was to "assert leadership over the men." He advised that "John Moore should not, as originally contemplated, hand over to the Union President a note embodying the Company's proposals regarding job evaluation and rationalisation of the wage structure." In effect, the TWU would be kept in the dark about the implications of the agreement they had signed. Masani predicted that "a showdown may become inevitable in the middle of 1958." Recent disputes, including at Mithapur, had shown that "certain intractable problems are more easily solved at the end of a stoppage than without it. . . . The time to implement the job evaluation scheme and the rationalization of the wage structure will be when the men return to work in a more chastened mood."[64] Mody had drawn exactly the opposite lesson from the experience at Mithapur. Tata managers retreated into a familiar defensive posture. Bereft of fresh ideas to breathe life into the cumbersome bureaucratic structures they had created, they hoped a show of strength and resolve would suffice to bring the workers to heel.

Annus Horribilis, 1958

Masani's prediction of an impending showdown at Jamshedpur proved eerily prescient. Galvanized by the election of trade unionist Kedar Das to the Bihar Legislative Assembly from Jamshedpur in the 1957 elections, the Communists mobilized workers throughout the steel and mining belt of eastern India. As employers were making record profits and wages stagnated, Jamshedpur and other company towns remained "private properties of the Companies, almost their private 'Empires,'" thundered veteran leader S. A. Dange.[65] On May 12,

1958, the JMU spearheaded a one-day strike that led to a complete plant shutdown. TISCO intelligence reports described how the strike was "excellently organized," with "mass picketing at strategic places" and the "men carrying square pink cards whilst the numerous cars or taxis they used bore red flags." Inside the plant, JMU leaders "organized the men into batches and marched out with red flags shouting slogans."[66] The TWU was powerless to stop them, and management responded violently. On the night of May 20, police fired into demonstrators and the army was called to Jamshedpur, reportedly by Chief Personnel Officer and ex–civil servant R. S. Pande.[67] Support from the Bihar state and central governments was crucial in regaining control by early June. Nehru viewed the Communist actions in Jamshedpur and elsewhere as "a stab in the back of the nation" designed to undermine the Second Five-Year Plan, and committed to cracking down on labor through a new code of discipline.[68]

In conjunction with the foreign exchange crisis, labor unrest was a key factor in private capital's tentative rapprochement with the state. The Jamshedpur strike was also thoroughly enmeshed in Cold War geopolitics. The timing could not have been worse for TISCO, which had staked the success of the TMP expansion on World Bank financing and was gravely concerned about its reputation in the United States. *Business Week* reported that contractors of the American steelmaker Kaisers working on the TMP were specifically targeted by the strikers, at the precise moment when the Soviets were racing ahead with the construction of the Bhilai plant. The *Wall Street Journal* published an article ominously titled "Reds on the Rise: They Gain in Influence in India as New Feuds Split Nehru's Party." Through the offices of Tata Inc. in New York, TISCO moved quickly to counter such negative coverage, enlisting the US consul-general in Calcutta and the director of information at the World Bank in the propaganda campaign.[69] In July, the public relations department issued *The Story of a Strike*, which put forward the company's official line: the strike was a planned political "conspiracy" by the Communists to capture the "Ruhr of India" and had nothing to do with genuine economic grievances.[70] Letters of support and requests for copies of the booklet trickled in from small businesses and political pressure groups, including the Oriental Carpet Manufacturers of Amritsar and the Kerala Anti-Communist Front.[71]

Discerning observers questioned the company line. The American economic historian Morris David Morris, far from a leftist firebrand, was in Jamshedpur in the spring of 1957 teaching at the Xavier Labour Relations Institute. He fell ill and observed the town employees' agitation from his bed in the Tata Memorial Hospital. Partly on the basis of his firsthand experience, he published the first academic analysis of the strike in the *Economic Weekly* in November 1958. Morris puzzled over the sudden disruption of an "apparently peaceful, harmonious environment." To date, TISCO had "made extensive use of industrial consultants, time-and-motion studies, job evaluation programmes, incentive schemes, and all the other devices in the arsenal of Western practice." In doing so, the company "accomplished what so many social scientists despair of seeing achieved in India, not only the creation of a stable, disciplined industrial labour force but also the development of a responsible voluntary collective bargaining between management and labour." Morris rejected political conspiracy as the sole explanation for why this promising trend had run aground. The Communists "built on dissatisfactions that were widespread," seizing on the weaknesses of the 1956 agreement in particular. The TWU had failed to put it to a democratic vote before the membership, leading workers to suspect that the union leadership did not have their interests at heart. Most damningly, Morris charged management with only adopting foreign expertise in a superficial manner "because it is impressively Western," all the while remaining firmly wedded to the "paternalism that has historically characterized TISCO policy."[72]

Behind the public relations facade, the strike reanimated internal debates about the balance between technocracy and paternalism within the group. M. D. Madan, the TISCO deputy director of education and social services and one of the ringleaders of the Quit India strike in 1942, described the incoherence of the company's attitude to expertise in terms strikingly similar to the assessment by Morris:

> In Jamshedpur we are not afraid to experiment and not afraid to say we made a mistake. In a way our little weakness for "foreign experts" (the more "foreign" the better!) is itself evidence of our humility and our anxiety to do the right thing. The obvious is never quite obvious to us unless we have paid a heavy fee to somebody from the other end of the world to come and tell us so. On the other hand, deep down within us we are proud enough to go our own way when we disagree with the "expert." We have one unanswerable reason, in such an eventuality, why his advice cannot be put into practice: "Conditions in India are so very different, don't you know!"[73]

A few days into the 1958 strike, Madan wrote an impassioned personal letter to the chairman, urging him to admit that "the workmen of Jamshedpur have given you an unambiguous message: 'Mr. John does not represent us.'" As a fellow Parsi and devoted servant of the company for many years, Madan took the liberty of chiding J. R. D. for having "often allowed your loyalties to your friends to outweigh your loyalty to greater things." His solution was to fully commit to collective bargaining by revoking the TWU's official recognition, sitting down with the JMU, and dropping the overblown Cold War rhetoric about the dangers of Communism. After all, Madan wryly concluded, "if Dwight Eisenhower can speak to Nikita Kruschev [sic], Jehangir Tata can speak to Kedar Das and probably a lot more effectively."[74] TISCO management had not always listened to Madan, but he believed that this time his advice would fall on receptive ears. He would be sorely disappointed.

The Third Personnel and Labour Officers' Conference opened on January 5, 1959, providing an ideal venue to conduct a postmortem on the strike. Masani, taking the chair once again, spent a great deal of time dissecting Morris's criticism. He conceded that the personnel department was "a dream that failed" but only because it "became much too cooperative, or, let us say, sympathetic with the union leadership." Masani laid the greater share of the blame on the TWU, which had let down management by failing to control the workers. Unions in India were too "political," too vulnerable to capture by outsiders, and too quick to take recourse to the law. By signing the 1956 agreement, management had gambled on collective bargaining and lost. Masani argued instead that Tata should pursue measures appropriate for "a situation where there are no trade unions worthy of the name"—namely, withholding official recognition and refining the "internal machinery" that dealt with workers directly.[75] The veteran Royist unionist V. B. Karnik agreed that personnel officers were essential "in creating a feeling of belonging amongst the workers," but they should do so through direct face-to-face contact, not as cogs in a well-oiled bureaucratic machine.[76]

Paternalism remained a useful fallback option when the advice of experts proved unpalatable or when collective bargaining broke down. Experts had arguably sown the seeds of their own irrelevance by attempting to vernacularize their disciplines. For example, industrial psychologists who dwelled on Indian difference unwittingly reinforced managements' tendency to favor the status quo. The story of postwar industrial relations at TISCO is not one of definite change, from coercion to consent, nor one of a seamlessly executed "carrot and stick" or "divide and rule" strategy. It is a story of recurring conflicts between competing ideas and practices, unfolding in a range of new institutional actors and sites, from consultancies like IBCON and PPS to the personnel and management conferences. Genuine voices of dissent, like Madan's, remained in the wilderness.

Cultivating the Corporate Self

In the mid-1950s, Tata faced an identity crisis, evident both in the vacillations over labor policy and the fraught relationship with the Nehruvian state. In the life cycle of the modern corporation, such moments of instability are often the catalyst for a return to the past through a combination of internal "collective nostalgia" and "historical revisionism" in relation to external political events.[77] Half a century after the founder's death, there was little institutional memory of the early days, which allowed a growing chorus of insider critics like Madan and Darookhanavala (Padshah's former protégé who attacked the Bombay Plan) to claim that the group had strayed from its roots. A new generation of managers would have to be inculcated in a shared corporate identity through the creation of a usable past.

The first step in this direction was taken by Tata director John Matthai, freshly returned from an unhappy stint as finance minister. In 1952, he proposed assembling a book on "the progress of industrial development and organisation in India of which Tatas would form the main skeleton." This kind of task would have normally been entrusted to the public relations department, but Matthai envisioned a "high class exercise in economic scholarship" that would "avoid any appearance of propaganda."[78] The research work was carried out by the Tata Sons Department of Economics and Statistics (DES), which had also assisted with preparing the Bombay Plan and issued the *Tata Quarterly*, a highly regarded review of economic trends and financial data. The DES became the custodian of the firm's records, typing up tens of thousands of documents that form the bedrock of the group's archives today. Its mandate was to use these records to produce a "sober, straightforward factual narrative" that only implicitly brought out "what private enterprise and the managing agency system have done and still can do if run with a full sense of responsibility." While not glossing over mistakes and setbacks, it was equally important to "not embarrass or compromise our position in the context of present or future activities."[79]

The final outline of *The House of Tata*, completed in November 1954, began with a general overview of the Indian economy in the colonial period and was organized thematically, with subheadings dealing with finance, personnel, philanthropy, and so on. Unlike typical corporate hagiographies, the book aspired to make an independent intellectual contribution to Indian business history. Comments by Tata directors on the manuscript highlighted overlooked aspects of the group's past without neglecting the demands of the present. For example, A. D. Shroff observed that "for a long time, side by side with manufacturing activity, Tatas also carried on trade." After the failure of Tata & Co. and its exit from East Asia in the early 1930s, the group withdrew from this sphere (see Chapter 1). Since the group was attempting to revive global connections in the postwar period by "investing in concerns which are interested in trade besides industrial activity," Shroff believed "adequate reference should be made also to this matter."[80] Soon-to-be deputy chairman Naval Tata summarized the thesis of the book in light of political developments: "Tatas through their benevolent activities propagated socialism to strengthen capitalism."[81] The notion of Tata as "socialist" was a transparent concession to contemporary Nehruvian rhetoric as well as particular to Naval—J. R. D. never used such language. However it was presented, the project of knowing one's history had a clear telos: to enhance the group's legitimacy as a global and national institution.

The second step in the process of constructing a shared corporate identity was the Tata Staff College, opened in 1956 on the lush grounds of the Turf Club in Poona. In his inaugural speech to the second session of the college, Matthai explained its dual purpose. Managers from different group companies would "get together and develop a corporate sense" in order to ensure the survival of the Tata "tradition." In the process, they would become effective public advocates for business "as means of rendering service to the country," countering the socialist agenda of the ruling Congress Party. As the public sector expanded and the government provided an ever-greater share of industrial finance, the control of diversified conglomerates like Tata over individual companies weakened. Moreover, the rise of state-run educational bodies such as the Indian Institutes of Management (IIMs) and Indian Institutes of Technology (IITs) threatened to make their privileged role as providers of expertise and technical training obsolete as well. Rather than pioneering new industries, as in the colonial period, Tata was now destined to "fulfil a very important purpose, namely, to provide the *right atmosphere* and the *right tradition* which is a very important thing now a days, because there is a great deal of criticism against the way in which business is being run."[82] The mission of the college was to reconstruct that tradition, which was far from self-evident, and imbue it with new meaning.

Instruction was modeled on the Administrative Staff College at Henley, founded by celebrated British management consultant Lyndall Urwick in 1945 to bring together best practices from business, civil service, and the military. Tata adapted the "syndicate method" in use at Henley, consisting of "experiential learning" through lectures and small-group discussions. The focus was not on specialized technical knowledge but on "personal development" broadly conceived, imbuing incoming managers with a common purpose, sense of fellowship, and the appropriate "attitude and demeanor" of a leader. Due to the group's decentralized nature, the college aimed to perfect the "arts of self-government," in the terminology of French philosopher Michel Foucault, creating "reliable, responsible proxies for direct personal control from headquarters."[83] Events in Jamshedpur, where the chain of command was falling apart, undoubtedly confirmed the necessity of learning to govern at a distance.

At the same time, the college paid close attention "the cultural side of life," taking inspiration from MIT and Caltech as models of "general education" in addition to Henley. Among the suggested speakers at the eighth session of the college in 1962 were the filmmaker Satyajit Ray and the author R. K. Narayan. Course subjects ranged from economics and labor relations to art, science, and "topical" issues such as space exploration. Participants could draw on a wide array of resources, including the DES and the TISS library in Bombay.[84] The newly established Tata Computer Centre, which eventually became Tata Consultancy Services (TCS), gave talks on the use of electronic data processing, the next frontier of information sharing within the group.[85] However, in this rarefied environment, a "tendency to think 'TATA' rather than to think 'Indian'" became noticeable. The college could bring Tata managers together but not necessarily equip them with the tools to effectively run their companies. To guard against this possibility, Masani's PPS was commissioned to devise a more rigorous course in "executive development."[86] In 1966, the college was formally renamed the Tata Management Training Centre (TMTC).

The third and arguably most successful identity construction initiative was the Tata Administrative Service (TAS), which helped fill "senior executive posts." TAS and TMTC became two stages in the trajectory of an aspiring Tata manager: recruitment from prestigious educational institutions, especially IITs and IIMs, followed by integration into everyday corporate culture. Diverse types of candidates were considered: the "quiet scholar" and "the extroverted 'many-splendoured' Executive who thinks that the world rotates because he walks," the "public school boy" and the "under-privileged" striver, the engineer and the humanities graduate. TAS officers mostly ended up with jobs in Tata companies, although a few took up positions with the World Bank, the United Nations, and the Ford Foundation. The *Illustrated Weekly of India* ranked TAS at the very top of the "plum jobs in the private sector," above oil companies, chartered accountants, and banks.[87] For an entire generation of educated elites from the 1960s to the 1980s, TAS contributed to an enduring image of the group as a byword for integrity and excellence in a corrupt society—the only worthy rival to the lumbering behemoth of the state. In the 1920 *Bombay Chronicle* exposé, the Tatas had been criticized for failing to nurture *swadeshi* talent by developing "a great Indian Industrial Tata Service" as a parallel bureaucracy to the British Raj (see Chapter 1). That vision had at last become reality.

Taken together, these various initiatives institutionalized scientific management at the top of the hierarchy to a greater extent than in the realm of labor relations. As J. R. D Tata noted in a speech to TAS officers in 1966, the "tremendous upsurge of interest in scientific management" in India since the war, inspired by the advances of the British and American militaries in recruitment, selection, and psychological testing, had been slow to permeate the private sector. Twenty years on, the personnel and management conferences, TMTC, and TAS marked "the beginning of a new era in the field of management." But they also looked to the past and the group's unique nation-building role. "To understand Tatas' approach and what we stand for," J. R. D. said, it was necessary to go back to the founder's "uncompromising honesty, vision of a New India, dedication to such vision, will power and determination to succeed in face of any odds." In urging young managers to follow Jamsetji's lead, J. R. D. was not asking them to "abide by outmoded ideas of 19th century paternalism" but to seek inspiration from history through the reinvention and reproduction of tradition. "If there is today such an intangible yet living entity that we call the 'House of Tata,'" he concluded, "it is largely due to the magic of his name and the principles and traditions he laid down for us."[88] Paternalism and technocracy could be reconciled in the person of the founder, whose example would sustain the group in trying times.

Jamsetji's mythic aura became much more powerful after his death, available as a free-floating signifier to resolve tensions within the group or meet new political challenges. In part due to the protracted evolution of its corporate culture over several decades, Tata stands out among comparable business dynasties. Henry Ford's charismatic authority was deeply ingrained in the operations of his company during his lifetime. The subordination of profit to productivity was a clear directive from the top, reflected in everything from account books to labor regimes.[89] In the South African mining giant Anglo American, "collective nostalgia" operates in a particular racial and imperial register, summoning a bygone era of smoke-filled clubs and exclusive private schools. Founder Ernest Oppenheimer's nation-building claims and professed connection to the land are analogous to Jamsetji's but sit uncomfortably alongside the globalized nature of the mining business.[90] The construction of Tata's identity and tradition in the 1950s smoothed over the contradictions of belonging to the nation and the world.

Steel Pastoral

The efforts to create a coherent managerial ethos described so far, both in the boardroom and on the shop floor, were largely internal to the group. Externally, a diffuse and multifaceted public relations campaign articulated the wider social purpose of the large corporation in the shadow of the state. In particular, the celebration of TISCO's achievements freely drew on the discourse of Nehruvian developmentalism by linking industry with social progress. Commissioned paintings and photographs reproduced in advertisements underscored the vital nation-building role played by private capital, creating a new industrial modernist aesthetic in the process. Like philanthropy, artistic production was shaped by semiautonomous networks of influence and did not necessarily serve the group's economic interests. But art made the case for Tata more vividly than any other medium.

In 1948, when the debates over industrial policy reached a fever pitch, Masani's public relations department issued the illustrated pamphlet *Sixty Years: The Story of Tatas,* authored by essayist Aubrey Menon. It opened with the anxious voice of an ordinary worker confessing to "feeling small because Tatas is so big." His concerns were immediately assuaged by an appeal to patriotism: "You are not only an employee, you are not only a worker. You are above everything else an Indian. . . . If India is poor you are poor; if India has no freedom, you have no freedom; if India has no food, you starve." The pamphlet then described, with the aid of colorful drawings of key events in Tata history and black-and-white photographs of smokestacks, power-generating stations, and airliners, how "Tatas have put power in the hands of every Indian—the power to make Nature serve them."[91] This formulation echoed Vivekananda's praise of Jamsetji for "placing into the hands of Indians this knowledge of Nature . . . that by having the knowledge, they might have power over her" (see Chapter 3). The group's disparate ventures were reduced to one critical imperative: the conquest of nature through modern science and technology. The postcolonial citizen's freedom to share in the fruits of national development had been won not only by political sacrifice but also by the spirit of economic *swadeshi* Tata claimed as its own. The steel company was the highest embodiment of that spirit.

Throughout the colonial period, TISCO produced relatively few promotional materials beyond advertisements of its products in specialized trade journals. That changed in 1943, when the Ministry of Information and Broadcasting suggested the inclusion of the Jamshedpur works in a series of industrial films meant to serve as war propaganda. The resulting treatment, drafted by the company's sales department in Calcutta and titled "The Harnessed Giant," began by connecting the technological sophistication of the steel plant with the long tradition of iron ore mining by *adivasis* in the region: "The film opens with a view of an Aboriginal furnace and shows the men who made Iron centuries ago. After a close-up, we see a group of Aborigines carrying baskets of ore. . . . The Commentary tells us that ore is the basis of Iron & Steel. Should show ore arriving at Steel Works."[92] The film was never produced, but the symbolic juxtaposition between the primitive and the modern would recur in subsequent visual and textual representations of labor in Jamshedpur, notably in the works of the painter Walter Langhammer, the photographer Sunil Janah, and the anthropologist Verrier Elwin.

A former university professor of art in Vienna, Walter Langhammer came to Bombay on the eve of World War II to escape Nazi persecution (his wife, Kathe, was Jewish). Along with fellow German émigrés Rudi von Leyden and Emmanuel Schlesinger, his arrival in Bombay revitalized a staid and derivative art scene. The trio mentored the emergent Progressive Artists Group and served as a bridge between their radical experimentation and older sensibilities. Despite their suspicion of capitalism, the Progressives responded to the urbane cosmopolitanism of Bombay's business elite and benefited from its generous patronage.[93] The Taj Hotel hosted numerous exhibitions, and Homi Bhabha's Tata Institute of Fundamental Research held one of the largest and best collections in the city. Chairman J. R. D. Tata provided guaranteed advertising revenue and office space in the Army and Navy Building at Kala Ghoda to *Marg* magazine, edited by famed novelist Mulk Raj Anand. *Marg* helped spread awareness of modern art and architecture among the culturally discerning middle classes, featuring an eleven-page spread of Koenigsberger's *Jamshedpur Development Plan* in its inaugural issue.[94] Artistic patronage was inseparable from public relations. At one time, the public relations department even planned to merge *Marg* with the Tata art department to form a dedicated in-house advertising agency.[95]

In 1944, TISCO invited Langhammer to Jamshedpur, where he stayed for three months and produced five 16″ × 24″ oil paintings: three panoramic views of the factory and two depictions of workers in the blooming mill and open-hearth furnace.[96] One of the landscapes, for which he was paid Rs. 1,000, hung in TISCO's central office in Jamshedpur. It was also reproduced in company calendars and the *Times of India Annual* in 1947, the year of independence, to illustrate an article on "Industrial India."[97] There was little, if any, precedent in the subcontinent for this kind of art. Large factories had existed for nearly a century, but most paintings of or about work took peasants or artisanal craftsmen as their subjects. Langhammer aimed to re-create the sensory experience of the steel plant while domesticating its harsh and alien environment, tempering the shock of the cold, machine-driven future with warm colors and thick brushstrokes.[98] His paintings display the essential characteristics of what visual historian John Stilgoe has termed the "industrial zone aesthetic" in the early twentieth-century United States—namely, a "fascination with angular forms, a middle distance of water or unoccupied land, and towering structures wreathed in a haze of half-smoke, half-steam."[99] Whereas in the American tradition humans were largely absent from the idealized industrial landscape, Langhammer dwelled on the romantic and heroic figure of the worker (Fig. 5.2).

Langhammer's muscular subjects are oversized, bent at sharp angles as the painter's brush captures them midway through a fierce battle with the fires of the furnace. Their faces are shrouded, giving no immediate clue as to religion, caste, or ethnicity. At first sight, the message is a simple one—man masters machine, and industry tames nature. A clear undercurrent of danger runs through the compositions, creating the conditions of possibility for heroic action and noble self-sacrifice. Like the early nineteenth-century colonial painters of the so-called Company school, Langhammer highlighted action and motion rather than static categorization.[100] The deliberately simple titles of the paintings (*Steel Worker*) aspired to universality, but Langhammer's representational choices were constrained by the realities of the production process (workers had to wear masks to protect themselves) and identity was always there beneath the surface.

Similar imagery could be used to convey more specific meanings. The figure of the masked worker battling the furnace also appeared in TISCO's wartime

FIG. 5.2. Walter Langhammer, *Steel Worker*, oil on canvas, ca. 1944. Tata Steel Art Collection. Courtesy Centre for Excellence, Tata Steel, Jamshedpur.

"Men of Steel" advertising campaign, which celebrated the harmonious blending of different ethnicities in the factory. The "sons of men who forged their crude blades over open fire" in the "rugged frontier hills" have gone on to "deftly control masses of molten steel for mammoth machinery," one such advertisement proudly states (Fig. 5.3).[101] The campaign implicitly acknowledged the widespread practice of occupational segregation in Indian industry (with Bengalis serving as clerks, Punjabis as foremen, "rugged" Pathans as furnace operators, and so on), recasting it in accordance with the nationalist ideal of unity in diversity. Without the accompanying text, Langhammer's painting could stand in for any factory anywhere in the world. With just a hint of context, which no Indian viewer could miss, the meaning of the painting changes. An entire social history of industrialization is brought to bear on the canvas.

The pioneering Bengali photojournalist Sunil Janah explored some of the same ground in another medium. Having made his name with a harrowing series of photographs of the Bengal Famine in 1943–1944, Janah was initially a member of the Communist Party of India but later became a freelancer taking on industrial commissions from both state and private enterprises.[102] He captured Nehru's "temples of modern India," from the state-owned steel plants at Bhilai and Rourkela to the hydroelectric dam at Bhakra-Nangal, as

MEN OF STEEL 2.

From the rugged frontier hills—sons of men who forged their crude blades over open fire—today deftly control masses of molten steel for mammoth machinery to fashion into tools of war and peace. A new generation is arising in India—Men of Steel.

ALWAYS
EVERYWHERE
STEEL
FOR STRENGTH

TATA STEEL

ISSUED BY THE TATA IRON & STEEL CO. LTD., HEAD SALES OFFICE: 102-A, CLIVE STREET, CALCUTTA

FIG. 5.3. "Men of Steel," Tata Iron and Steel Co. advertisement, 1942. Courtesy Centre for Excellence, Tata Steel, Jamshedpur.

well as spending a significant part of his career making close-up portraits of *adivasis*. In both settings, Janah was fascinated by the juxtaposition of the primitive and the modern. "Very often, the contrast between these simple folk from the forests and the structures and symbols of modern industry in which they were employed made interesting pictures," he recalled in the introduction to his book *The Tribals of India*. True to his earlier political radicalism, Janah stressed the diversity and inclusivity of the nation while subjecting it to subtle critique. He wished to bring attention to *adivasis* as the forgotten original inhabitants or "earliest natives" of India and as the true builders of the nation through their labor.[103]

The interplay of nationalism and socialism has been the dominant frame of analysis of Janah's industrial photography, obscuring his debt to an older way of seeing the factory. One image of a distant, barely visible human figure in a Gandhi cap framed by a massive vessel in the TISCO melting shop seems to indicate the erasure of labor by machinery, as in Stilgoe's "industrial zone aesthetic."[104] Indeed, engineers and managers are often reduced to "tiny specks in the distant horizon," while the clean and orderly lines of the monumental machines dominate the visual field.[105] However, nearly all his images of *adivasi* workers are resolutely focused on the human body and its resilience through labor, suggesting a more complex and agonistic relationship with technological modernity.[106] Janah's photograph of trainees in the TISCO machine shop, their well-lit, studious faces and alert bodies occupying the center of the frame, conveys a fragile, grounded sense of hope that contrasts with both Nehruvian developmentalist optimism and the heroic proletariat in the socialist realist tradition (Fig. 5.4).

Although Janah departed from Langhammer's comparatively abstract and romanticized view of the factory, his interest in the body at work neatly dovetailed with the company's public relations strategy. A 1961 newspaper spread prepared by leading agency J. Walter Thompson in Calcutta transposed Janah's evocative image of the trainees into a rough line drawing. The accompanying text, titled "Let the Indian learn to do things for himself" (Jamsetji Tata's words), offered encouraging statistics about advances in technical training in the nation's engineering colleges and national laboratories (Fig. 5.5).[107] The circulation of Janah's photographs formed part of a rich discourse of the Tata steel plant as the proving ground for the future of modern industry in India, dating back to the interwar period (see Chapter 2). Artists and photographers in the 1950s rediscovered the trope of the "machine in the garden" in its vernacular guise, not as a disruptive paradox but as a generative contradiction. India's most ostensibly primitive people would be transformed into productive laboring subjects and citizens, while simultaneously imbuing cold and impersonal machinery with their vitality and virility.

On the occasion of TISCO's golden jubilee in 1957, the anthropologist Verrier Elwin, a close friend and collaborator of Janah, was commissioned to

FIG. 5.4. Sunil Janah, *Young Trainees at a Machine Shop, Tata Iron & Steel Co., Jamshedpur, Bihar,* photograph, 1950s. © Sunil Janah. Courtesy Arjun Janah, http://suniljanah.org.

write a glossy illustrated history of the company.[108] The choice appears surprising, but it was dictated by entrenched networks of patronage and influence. Elwin was a heterodox anthropologist, whose political allegiances shifted from Gandhian constructive work to advocacy of tribal cultural and religious autonomy.[109] The Bombay business elite, including Purshotamdas Thakurdas and the cotton baron J. P. Patel, funded Elwin's research and supported the

FIG. 5.5. "Let the Indian Learn to Do Things for Himself," Tata Iron and Steel Co. advertisement, 1961. Courtesy Centre for Excellence, Tata Steel, Jamshedpur.

Tribal Art and Research Unit (TARU), with which Janah was associated as well.[110] The Tatas had steadfastly backed Elwin for over two decades. He had been a research associate at TISS, and a grant from the Dorabji Tata Trust enabled the publication of his ethnographic study *The Baiga* (1939).[111] Elwin's next book, *The Agaria* (1942), was on the tribal iron smelters of the Central Provinces. It was dedicated to J. R. D. Tata, "partly as a token of your friendship and partly because of your relationship to the great iron-works of which the Agaria furnaces were the first and primitive foreshadowing. . . . On every ground, therefore, it is your book."[112]

The Agaria was a heartfelt plea for the preservation of a dying lifestyle threatened by the relentless advance of modern industry. Elwin blamed the "interests of big business on one side and sheer ignorance and carelessness on the other" for the decline of Agaria smelting.[113] In doing so, he recapitulated early nationalist polemics against the destruction of indigenous manufacture under colonial rule. For example, M. G. Ranade's canonical 1892 essay on the subject lamented that "the native furnaces have stopped work" under the onslaught of competition from factory iron.[114] This stance cannot be easily reconciled with Elwin's effusive praise for Tata. It is quite possible that J. R. D. himself never read the book and was unaware of the possible contradiction.[115] But even if he had read it, he might not have found much to object to. A close reading of the text reveals that Elwin took great care to exempt TISCO from blame. Since the plant at Jamshedpur had not been located in the Central Provinces, the Agarias were spared for a time.[116] More importantly, TISCO was a *swadeshi* industry that connected the primitive tribe to the modern Indian nation through the "magic" substance of iron. The Agarias already had "more to do with the outside world than some other aboriginals" and were not inherently opposed to technology. Invoking the well-worn trope of the train intruding into a pastoral idyll, Elwin reported their fascination with "iron and fire and coal combined in a gigantic moving furnace."[117] The book installed TISCO as the rightful heir to the Agarias' legacy and mechanized steelmaking as the fullest realization of their ancient craft.

A TISCO advertisement from the same year as Elwin's book, issued in advance of the completion of the Howrah Bridge in Calcutta using company steel, makes this point explicitly: "Knowledge gained some thousands of years ago paved the way to present-day achievements." In the narrative below, the Agarias perform a pioneering role analogous to that of the Tatas, bringing "the law of plenty to the jungle" through their iron—a miniature Industrial Revolution, but one that took place "in days gone by." There is little room for the Agaria in the present except as a relic and symbol of placid coexistence with nature (Fig. 5.6).[118] The appearance of the advertisement around 1942, before independence and Nehruvian developmentalism, indicates that it is responding to a different set of concerns and anxieties originating in the foundational moment of dispossession. The claim of continuity between traditional and modern knowledge was potentially subversive and destabilizing to the company's legitimacy in the region. To this day, the Agarias or Asuras in Jharkhand maintain that Tata had stolen the secrets of their manufacturing process and grown fabulously wealthy at their expense, later refusing them jobs in the plant. Activists keep alive ancestral tales of the time when "men with big cameras, who were Tata employees, would spy on our methods of identifying the right ore, lighting furnaces and smelting."[119]

The overlap between Elwin's ethnographic research and his promotional work for TISCO is evident in *The Story of Tata Steel*, the commissioned volume he produced for an honorarium of Rs. 10,000. Elwin reproduced almost ver-

FIG. 5.6. "Knowledge Gained Some Thousand Years Ago," Tata Iron and Steel Co. advertisement, ca. 1942. Courtesy Centre for Excellence, Tata Steel, Jamshedpur.

batim from his earlier book a passage on "the protective power of iron" in Agaria folktales, recounting how the Tatas were asked by local *adivasis* to produce "magic iron."[120] The same apocryphal story appears in the memoirs of General Manager John L. Keenan, who ascribes the request to a "learned Brahmin." For Keenan, the hard-nosed American, it is an example of the quaint but inappropriate use of the "suggestion box" scheme, one of the many scientific management techniques that failed to catch on in India.[121] For Elwin, it is salutary proof of TISCO as an organic outgrowth from Indian soil. He absolved the company of any wrongdoing in the matter of displacing local inhabitants or impoverishing the surrounding region, claiming that villagers had "warm memories of Tata visitors" bringing "new prosperity into their homes." Above all, Elwin was at pains to show how the Tata steel plant had induced a temporal leap from primitive to modern: "Few stories are more romantic than that of the growth of little Sakchi in an area whose inhabitants lived by scratching the soil and extracting a few hundred-weight of iron from tiny furnaces, to the great modern town, ideally planned and provided with most of the things that make life worth living."[122]

The Story of Tata Steel was published in February 1958, a few months before the Communist-led strike. Meant for "mass distribution to the employees and shareholders" of the company, its function was to boost internal morale and to score a political point. As J. R. D. Tata's foreword put it, TISCO "has provided a living and dynamic answer to the charge that private enterprise 'cannot deliver the goods,' is only inspired by selfish motives and does not serve the needs of the people."[123] The book included full-color plates of smiling *adivasis* working in the company's mines and reproductions of Langhammer's paintings of Jamshedpur and a photograph of the golden jubilee celebrations identical to one of Janah's images. The utopia dreamed by the typist Rao, with which this chapter began, was realized only in the imagination. While Jamshedpur was engulfed in violence and political intrigue, these artistic and literary works provided the comforts of an alternative history, where private industry fulfilled the nation's cherished hopes for development and social progress, and where men met machines on equal terms.

6

The Social Responsibilities of Business

In early January 1942, from the confines of the Deoli detention camp in the deserts of Rajputana, the Congress Socialist leader Jayaprakash (JP) Narayan acknowledged receipt of several books sent by his friend Minoo Masani for a "little intellectual spring-cleaning." He reported finishing Peter Drucker's *The End of Economic Man* (1939) and pronounced Arthur Koestler's *Darkness at Noon* (1940) "most revealing and stimulating."[1] JP had landed in prison as a result of his underground campaign against the British during World War II. For him, as for many others bearing the brunt of the colonial state's repression, incarceration was a transformative experience. Books were often the medium through which they refashioned their political selves.[2] Through daily acts of solitary reading and reflection, JP began to question his commitment to Marxism, which dated back to his studies in the United States during the 1920s. For his part, Masani had already become disillusioned with the Soviet Union after a visit in 1935, coinciding with the onset of Stalin's purges. The seeds of doubt sown during that trip were confirmed after reading the works of former "fellow travelers" Koestler, André Gide, and James Burnham. By sending JP their writings, Masani hoped to persuade his old comrade to abandon orthodox Marxism for a more ideologically flexible democratic socialism.[3]

At first, JP refused to budge: "You know, I do not owe allegiance to the established Church, and in that regard I am a Protestant, but yet my faith in the original doctrines of the founders remains unshaken, and I do not see an alternative. Much of the disillusioned thought of the present period merely [dries?] itself up in the sands of liberalism."[4] Yet the regular stream of books that kept flowing in eventually had the desired effect. JP was particularly impressed with James Burnham's *The Managerial Revolution* (1941), which foretold the coming of an all-encompassing totalitarian and technocratic ruling elite and collapsed the distinctions between Nazi Germany, the Soviet Union, and the United States. JP pronounced Burnham "one of the most clear-headed authors I have read" on the "problem of democracy and economic planning, jokingly asking Masani, "Are all ex-Trotskyists clear-headed?"[5]

Why was JP so attracted to writers like Burnham and Drucker, and how was this inveterate critic of capitalism drawn into the defense of free enterprise? Burnham was influenced by the classic New Deal–era study *The Modern Corporation and Private Property* (1932) by Adolf A. Berle Jr. and Gardiner Means, which showed that capitalism in its most advanced phase was characterized by the "separation of ownership and control" and the rise of a distinct managerial class. Burnham took this conclusion further, arguing that the inevitable result of the process would be a slide into a totalitarian dystopia. Shedding his Trotskyist past, he moved to the far right of the political spectrum and became a guiding light of the postwar conservative movement in the United States. Austrian-born philosopher Drucker also read Berle and Means but followed a different path, reinventing himself as a management guru. In *The Concept of the Corporation* (1946), he set out to prove that large corporations "could act as responsible leaders in the new industrial age," principally as a bulwark against the state. Drawing on and departing from his contemporary Karl Polanyi's critique of laissez-faire liberalism, Drucker embraced the "responsible" corporation as a positive manifestation of capitalism's increasing "embeddedness" in social relations.[6]

As in the United States, Indian thinkers with diverse backgrounds and political convictions found common ground in their quest for a middle way between unfettered capitalism and totalitarian statism. Many abandoned Marx for Gandhi, the indigenous political icon of mass struggle who sought to overcome class conflict through the conceptual innovation of "trusteeship." But the "indigenization" or "soft vernacularization" of Marxism was far from a smooth process.[7] As the exchanges between JP and Masani indicate, it was often experienced as a traumatic rupture. Changing one's mind about Marxism required a radical refashioning of the intellectual self—a secular conversion from one "absolutist passion" to another. The fierceness with which many ex-Marxists condemned their former belief system mirrored their initial devotion to the cause.[8] Although JP remained ambivalent about big business throughout his long career, Masani was a zealous convert who worked tirelessly to advance its interests in his work with the Tatas.

The historiographies of anticommunist and anticolonial thought remain largely separate, and together even more distant from the study of capitalists as social and political actors. Foregrounding intellectual conversion allows an alternative genealogy of neoliberalism in India to emerge from debates about the meaning of socialism. The study of neoliberalism is no longer confined to the Anglo-American policy bundle of deregulation, privatization, and fiscal austerity implemented by Ronald Reagan and Margaret Thatcher in the 1980s under the intellectual guidance of Milton Friedman and the Chicago school of neoclassical economics. In the early postwar years, neoliberals gathered under the auspices of the Mont Pelerin Society recognized the failure of self-regulating markets and advocated a variety of political and legal-institutional mechanisms to protect them from the pressures of mass democracy.[9] As a post-colonial nation and a "mixed economy" with a robust private sector and a government ostensibly committed to "socialism," India served as an ideal proxy and test case for the refinement of neoliberal ideas.[10] At the same time, "a wide variety of socialisms" were in dialogue with neoclassical economics throughout the world, through experiments such as Yugoslav worker self-management (much admired by Masani and JP) and Hungarian "goulash communism." In India, as in Eastern Europe and Latin America, socialists initially participated in the intellectual and political project of pitting markets against the state, only to find their ideas co-opted, distorted, or marginalized.[11]

Masani and JP's engagement with the transnational intellectual debates in the late 1940s, initially mediated by the circulation of books across prison walls, would continue to unfold after independence in a most unlikely setting—the boardrooms of private companies. Indian political leaders wrestled with the big questions of the age, particularly the organization of society in a Cold War world divided by competing ideologies and superpower conflict. The concept of "socially responsible" business was one of many answers to these questions. The ethical burden of relieving poverty and promoting development in part-nership with the state, expressed most clearly in the Bombay Plan, was su-perseded by the imperative of fighting dishonest practices such as tax evasion and "black marketing" by the mid-1960s. Reclaiming "socialism" from its do-mestication and appropriation by the Nehruvian state, JP and the Gandhians viewed themselves as engaged in a "moral battle against corruption in society." If necessary, they were willing to circumvent the ballot box through direct mass mobilization.[12] Capitalists like J. R. D. Tata, who might have otherwise been among the targets of the Gandhians' crusade, emphasized their ability and willingness to self-regulate. By positing corruption and red tape rather than monopoly or inequality as the worst evils affecting the Indian economy, they claimed the moral high ground against an impersonal bureaucratic state. Gandhian and socialist critiques of the state only served to reinforce business conduct as a key terrain of political struggle.

It is tempting to view the concept of "social responsibility" in this period as a forerunner to the recent practice of corporate social responsibility (CSR). By virtue of their reliance on technocratic and managerial expertise, the Tatas are commonly assumed to have been the "uncontested" leaders of a shift from old-style philanthropy to modern CSR—all part of unbroken tradition of putting service above profits.[13] Such an approach obscures the specific historical context in which the concept was first articulated, as well as the radical possibilities it once contained and how they were lost. Another temptation is to disregard "social responsibility" entirely as a superficial rhetorical veil concealing the pursuit of crude self-interest. But no idea or concept can be derived solely from "the material situation of a particular class or social group," in this case Indian big business, nor can it be understood "in abstraction from its linguistic form." "Social responsibility" was a new "political language" carefully crafted and deployed to address a perceived crisis of legitimacy.[14]

In times of transition, ideas are a resource mobilized by economic agents for collective action and institution building.[15] "Social responsibility" was meant to confront the twin challenges of the "managerial revolution" and the rise of the welfare state. It was the product of numerous compromises and strategic alliances barely held together by force of personality and circumstance. It was also an idea very much of its time, made possible by the intersection of Gandhian thought with diffuse networks of heterodox economists, Quaker entrepreneurs, and other figures on the margins of the postwar Keynesian consensus. By the late 1970s, "social responsibility" had outlived its usefulness as the Indian state entered into a partnership with big business to boost productivity and discipline labor. This was also the moment when CSR took on its current form as a narrow, technocratic tool kit for ameliorating companies' impact on surrounding communities, shedding the pretense of systemic change.

Reinventing Trusteeship

During the independence struggle, Mohandas K. Gandhi performed the exceptional feat of leading a mass movement of workers and peasants without frightening big business. Against sustained criticism from the left, he rejected expropriation and the redistribution of property, demanding instead the spiritual regeneration of the rich in the spirit of the gift (*dan*) and nonpossession (*aparigraha*). Individual capitalists, Gandhi believed, held their wealth "in trust" for the benefit of society at large. He claimed to have derived this theory of "trusteeship" from a variety of sources, including Andrew Carnegie's "Gospel of Wealth," John Ruskin's political economy, and the ancient Upanishads. Both vernacular and universal, it was similar to the hybrid disciplinary innovations of *swadeshi* intellectuals Benoy Kumar Sarkar, Radhakamal Mukerjee, and Narendra Nath Sengupta (see Chapters 2 and 5). A lawyer by training, Gandhi was also influenced by nineteenth-century legal thought, in particular the principle of fiduciary obligation to one's trustees in the works of Henry Maine and F. W. Maitland.[16]

Trusteeship was both a "provocative theoretical construct" reconciling ethics and economics and an "effective mechanism in political mobilization" to persuade businessmen to support the Congress.[17] Gandhi developed close personal and financial relationships with Jamnalal Bajaj and G. D. Birla, who helped fund his campaigns for *khadi* (homespun cloth), village industries, and untouchable uplift, as well as his *ashrams* (self-contained communities) at Sabarmati and Wardha. The close relationship between Birla and Gandhi has been described as one of "patron" and "publicist," with Birla gaining spiritual and social prestige in return for financial support.[18] However, Gandhi's true disciples were in a minority among businessmen. The Tatas remained largely distant from the Gandhian movement before independence and made no claim to practicing trusteeship except indirectly through the ownership of the main holding company by philanthropic trusts. Even in this respect, they claimed an independent affinity to the Ford and Carnegie Foundations without Gandhi's conceptual intermediation.

As a radical pressure group within the nationalist mainstream, the Congress Socialists opposed Gandhi and scorned trusteeship as a fig leaf for perpetuating the inequities of capitalism. JP Narayan even authored a scathing critique titled "The Shark, a Trustee for the Minnow." As Masani later recalled, "When Mahatma Gandhi described [trusteeship] as his pattern of socialism, I, in my Marxist or semi-Marxist superiority, thought how out of date and antediluvian he was."[19] Yet, soon after Gandhi's assassination in 1948 and the outbreak of the Cold War, transnational intellectual exchanges around anticommunism suddenly rendered trusteeship more relevant than ever as India's contribution to the search for a middle path. Masani proudly noted that the Yugoslav dissident Milovan Djilas had also turned to Gandhi in his rebellion against Marx and the "new class" of elite Communist bureaucrats. During a visit to Yugoslavia in the 1950s, Masani observed that the experiments in worker self-management there followed Gandhi's ideas developed in India decades earlier.[20] Trusteeship was attractive, indeed globally export-able, because it was designed to transform capitalism without destroying it:

> What the theory of trusteeship comes to is that the State allows the present owners of property to continue in possession only on condition that they use the property for the benefit and profit of the entire community. Any property owner who uses his property primarily for private profit would be removed from possession on the ground of breach of trust. In other words, it is a conception in which the capitalist is defunctionalised. . . . The value of the concept of "trusteeship" is not in its finality but rather in its elasticity as a transition technique. It stresses the ethical and social value of attempting to undo the wrong of the anti-social use of property before destroying or liquidating the wrong-doer.[21]

This notion of an "anti-social use of property" lies at the heart of business-men's subsequent critique of corruption and their self-fashioning as ethical subjects. Masani and JP hoped to convert trusteeship from a vehicle for nationalist political mobilization to a fundamental principle of corporate organization in independent India.

The Cold War solidified the incipient alliance between Gandhi's followers and big business. JP was appointed president of the Indian Committee of the Congress for Cultural Freedom (CCF), while Masani edited its magazine *Freedom First*. The CCF had been established in 1950 by the first generation of hardline anti-Stalinist converts, led by Koestler and Burnham, as a way of countering Soviet influence among artists, writers, and intellectuals in Europe and the Third World. With the covert backing of the US Central Intelligence Agency (CIA), the CCF chose to cultivate the democratic non-Communist left and gradually distanced itself from hardliners like Koestler and Burnham. In India, the popularity of Nehru's nonaligned stance and widespread suspicion of the United States posed uniquely difficult challenges.[22] Gandhism, understood primarily in ethical and spiritual terms, was useful but not perfectly suited to anticommunist politics. The CCF-sponsored Indian literary magazine *Quest* occasionally critiqued the Gandhian program as religiously obscurantist and a "romantic return to the past."[23]

If the CCF had limited success in India overall, Masani secured a firmer foothold for its agenda in the world of business. Chairman J. R. D. Tata was particularly receptive to the message of the hardliners. During Burnham's visit to Bombay for the inaugural meeting of the Indian CCF in 1951, Masani arranged for them to meet. Against criticisms in the press, J. R. D. insisted that Burnham was far from "a fascist, cold-blooded or otherwise," insisting that Indians should be grateful to him and Koestler for being "amongst the first to open our eyes to the true facts, meanings and objectives of world communism."[24] J. R. D.'s position in this matter was not a function of his class interest. He actively and willingly engaged in exchanges of ideas facilitated by Masani and had to persuade his fellow businessmen to take a more assertive stance against the dangers posed by the Nehruvian state.

Masani also arranged for the chairman to meet JP Narayan in June 1954, during JP's visit to Bombay to collect donations for the *bhoodan* (gift of land) and *sampattidan* (gift of wealth) campaigns. The brainchild of Vinayak Narahari (Vinoba) Bhave, Gandhi's anointed spiritual successor and JP's guru, *bhoodan* was an ambitious program of voluntary land redistribution. Vinoba traveled across India on foot persuading villagers to collectively pool and share their land in order to stave off agrarian unrest without state intervention. Congress governments at the national and provincial level tolerated *bhoodan* as a more palatable alternative to legal expropriation, even as Vinoba and JP hailed its truly radical potential.[25] *Sampattidan* was a closely related program encouraging wealthy individuals to donate a fixed portion of their income to Gandhian organizations. JP viewed *sampattidan* not as another form of charity but as "a first step towards the goal of trusteeship." Given the proliferation of tax evasion and other corrupt practices under the managing agency system, JP believed that the voluntary alienation of wealth would create more substantive institutional change than mere legal reform. As he explained to one sympathetic industrialist, "If the Managing Agency system is abolished by law, I would be pleased. But I would be much more pleased if the Managing Agents voluntarily relinquished their privileges and became trustees."[26]

JP expected a favorable hearing from J. R. D. Tata, but the two men's ideas about the meaning and purpose of trusteeship turned out to be very different. At first, J. R. D. proudly announced that he would contribute one-sixth of his net personal income for five years as *sampattidan* and that the Tata Trusts would make a series of donations to the *bhoodan* campaign.[27] In his annual chairman's statement to the Tata Iron and Steel Company (TISCO) board in August 1954, J. R. D. cited the "great socialist leader" JP's attack on the welfare state as an instrument of totalitarianism, evidently delighted to have found common ground with a prominent critic of the government.[28] Yet, he soon faced a swift backlash from many of his friends and colleagues in Bombay.

The veteran Congress politician and labor leader Kanji Dwarkadas privately warned J. R. D. that *bhoodan* was "a kind of dope, which sends people to sleep." As a fickle ex-Marxist turned Gandhian following the political winds, JP was not to be trusted: "He wobbles all the time and he does not know his own mind. . . . The only thing Jai Prakash is interested in is himself." As for trusteeship, Dwarkadas said it was nothing more than an insidious cover for a socialist program in which "there cannot be any words like charity, philanthropy, or generosity; you are a plunderer with all the money you had got and you have no right to keep it with you!"[29]

Such criticisms made an impression on J. R. D., who protested to JP that he had been made the face of a movement whose ultimate aim he could not possibly share. JP replied that he was "extremely sorry for having put you in an embarrassing position" of making a public commitment "to end the capitalist system that you represent." Betraying a certain naïveté, he did not think that J. R. D. would be "so keen to preserve that system." He had taken at face value Tata's claim to be a more enlightened business: "If even the Gandhian revolution, in which the capitalists play such an honourable and constructive and forward role, is not acceptable *even to men such as you*, then God alone save the capitalists, and with them the non-capitalists too!"[30] It was clear that the two men had completely misunderstood each other. J. R. D. viewed *sampattidan* as a purely charitable cause, in line with the Tata Trusts' pledge to support various nation-building activities by voluntary organizations. He could not agree that it implied surrendering the right of private enterprise to exist in its present form, even theoretically. He bluntly told JP that they did not share the same "understanding of the role of the capitalist system or its place in history." Gandhism was commendable for its emphasis on decentralization and might work well in rural areas. But it was unsuited to "a modern, highly industrialised society" in which only large-scale mass production and consumption could raise standards of living. Vinoba and JP's quest was doomed to fail, J. R. D. concluded, because it could not harness "the urge for private ownership—whether of a piece of land, a cow, a house, a motorcar or a bank account."[31] The alliance between Gandhians and big business threatened to break down almost as soon as it had been forged.

Behind the scenes, Masani moved quickly to smooth over the philosophical and political differences revealed in this frank exchange of views by ensuring that Tata's contributions to *bhoodan* were perceived as fully consistent with Gandhian precepts. Masani advised JP to inform trade unions in Jamshedpur that "the practice already followed by Mr. Tata over a number of years of allocating to public causes of a charitable nature a proportion of his income which is in excess of the minimum requirements of Sampattidan, entitled him to be considered a Sampattidani." The J. R. D. Tata Trust made it known that the chairman's donations came from his own personal income and were not simply a routine charitable act.[32] Vinoba told JP that the underlying tenets of their movement were "freedom from government and freedom from exploitation" but that "we should keep our mind open for mutual discussion and leave ourselves free to make adjustments" when dealing with private donors. J. R. D. then wrote a respectful and conciliatory note to Vinoba, declaring the concept of trusteeship "one which each of us should seek to implement in whatever way is possible."[33] This eased but did not eliminate tensions. When Vinoba proposed the extension of *sampattidan* to industries more generally, rather than individuals, the Tata Sons board of directors decided that the group "should keep out of this movement."[34] Gandhians and businessmen may have shared "freedom from government" as a basic value, but they continued to disagree about "freedom from exploitation."

Apart from publicly associating the Tatas with the Gandhian movement, Masani sought to implant the idea of trusteeship into the operations of the group during his tenure. At the Tata Staff College, trainees pored over the distinction between a "fully socialist economy" and a "mixed economy," which they were told had "arisen out of the Gandhian thinking." If private enterprises were run as if they were trusts, "the institution of the industrialists need not be destroyed." A "change in values" was sufficient to erase the prevailing stigma of profit seeking. College syllabi included Howard R. Bowen's *Social Responsibilities of the Businessman* (1953) and Peter Drucker's *The Practice of Management* (1954).[35] The group's history and ethos were aligned with both indigenous Gandhian ideas and transnational currents of management thought. Naval Tata argued that "long before Gandhi's preachings," Jamsetji "established in India a firm foundation of trusteeship capital by setting aside a substantial part of his wealth as a national bequest." He framed the evolution of modern corporations into "impersonal institutions" no longer "dominated by single individuals, but by thousands of professional technocrats," as an opportunity to realize the trusteeship ideal.[36] The tension between capitalism as a system of wealth creation and the Gandhian call for the voluntary abdication of economic power, which had so troubled J. R. D. in his correspondence with JP, was deliberately minimized.

In a speech titled "The Management Man as Trustee," delivered at the Tata Staff College in 1960, Masani reiterated the significance of the separation between ownership and control, derived from Berle and Means via Drucker. The new expert managerial class, comprised of "people who run enterprises like the Tata Trusts, the directors and the senior executives of Tata Industries and the various Tata enterprises," was still in its infancy in India but would, in time, to ensure that the private sector lived up to its obligations to society. Tata had taken the lead in reconciling labor and capital through scientific management and the application of collective bargaining. The next step was to devise a wide-ranging code of conduct applicable to everything from the production of consumer goods to the reinvestment of profits. Masani warned, "One of the charges made against the Indian businessmen is that even if they are clean they mix with those who are not clean. Are good businessmen prepared to dissociate themselves as businessmen from those who are letting down the way of life in which they believe?"[37]

In order to present a united front against the state, Indian capitalists first had to put their own house in order. Trusteeship could act as a litmus test to separate those who were "clean" from those who were not, and as a set of first principles to enable the construction of a mutual understanding of "social responsibility." This set the largest houses such as Tata, which most closely approximated Drucker's ideal-typical managerial corporation, on a collision course with the thousands of small traders and manufacturers whose unscrupulous practices were seen as undermining the legitimacy of private enterprise as a whole. Through both internal reforms of management practice and external public relations campaigns, Tata had taken the lead in crafting an image of big business as a respectable, modernizing, quasi-public institution essential to economic life in India. It would now try to encourage others to live up to that image.

Fighting for Free Enterprise

The ascent of Gandhian trusteeship by the late 1950s as the preferred rhetoric to defend business interests displaced an earlier mobilization around the plight of the "middle classes." On the basis of the Constitution's guarantee of "economic justice" to all Indian citizens, the postcolonial state had chosen to retain the system of extensive price and commodity controls introduced by the colonial government to deal with shortages during World War II. Even as the wartime boom led to record profits, three or four times higher than what appeared on official tax documents, draconian criminal laws and the intrusive bureaucracy needed to enforce them created new categories of "socio-economic crimes," including "hoarding, black-marketeering, tax evasion, food adulteration and illegal trading in licences and permits."[38] In this way, both public and private corruption exploded, giving birth to a new political language that could be used against electoral opponents or business rivals.[39]

Traders in cloth and food grains, many of whom had been loyal supporters of the Congress, were hardest hit by the postwar continuation of controls. Organizations such as the Bengal Trades Association, affiliated with the Bengal Chamber of Commerce, vociferously protested against the state's "appeasement of both capital and labour, all-through at the expense of the middle classes and the cultivators." They denounced controls on sugar and cotton yarn as a conspiracy to enrich millowners at the expense of traders and pointed to the reluctance of revenue authorities to investigate tax evasion among the largest houses. This was in keeping with earlier criticisms of the Bombay Plan as unrepresentative of the interests of the entire business community.[40] Sensing the mood of anger, Purshotamdas Thakurdas moved a resolution on "The Plight of the Middle Classes" at the annual session of the Federation of Indian Chambers of Commerce and Industry (FICCI) in March 1950, calling for an end to controls on consumer goods and the restoration of normal channels of trade. The classes in question were defined as the "professional and technical men, employees of Governments and local authorities, traders and merchants, shop assistants and clerks and vast mass of small shop-keepers" who together comprised the "backbone" of Indian commercial society. Thakurdas's speech in support of the resolution stressed the ethical as well as the economic consequences of the controls regime. A "deliberate moral degradation in the business sphere of India" had taken place due to the "anti-social behavior" of a few "black sheep." But the "sins of the few" should not be extended to the majority, which still clung to "old traditions of business ethics."[41]

Not all FICCI leaders were convinced by this argument. G. D. Birla, who remained close to Nehru personally and to the Congress Party politically, countered that it was only "at the higher level that the normal trade channel has ceased to exist." Even though food was indeed distributed through inefficient ration shops, other commodities were largely unaffected. He went so far as to assert that "many new employments have been created due to controls."[42] Thakurdas was aghast. Through their intimate knowledge of markets, middlemen in grain, sugar, and cotton performed a "vital, essential and cheap service" by linking producers and consumers. Controls had thrown them out of work, creating widespread unemployment and weakening the nation's economy.[43] At one level, this exchange reflected long-standing conflicts pitting industrialists against merchants, the city against the country, and the state against the market. Birla's defense of controls exposed a divided business community unsure of how to respond to the growing involvement of the state in economic life. Birla was reluctant to take a more confrontational stance, partly because his interests in Calcutta were most threatened not by Nehru but by the rising Communist Party. Most Marwari and Gujarati businessmen followed him down the path of accommodation with the Congress. By contrast, the Tatas and other groups based in Bombay were more willing to take an oppositional stand. Neither side cared very much about the concerns of the small traders. Indeed, big business was not opposed to the continuation of controls on producer goods such as iron and steel, cement, and coal.[44] Ever the mediator, Thakurdas calibrated the language of the FICCI resolution to appeal to all factions. In time, most businessmen would come to speak of a decline in "values" and the need to confront "antisocial" elements through self-regulation, appropriating public anxieties about corruption and directing them against the state.

The Forum of Free Enterprise was the first attempt to build a unified platform for business to collectively influence public opinion. It was the brainchild of A. D. Shroff, the Tata director most responsible for the strategy of circumventing the state in the pursuit of foreign capital and an inveterate opponent of the Congress left since the 1930s (see Chapter 4). The forum launched an aggressive campaign "to educate the public about the mistaken policy of the ruling party and to satisfy the country that the attempt to establish a Socialist State is not calculated to serve the best interests of the hundreds of millions inhabiting this country."[45] Shroff and his associates, including Masani and the eminent jurist Nani Palkhivala, went on speaking tours and circulated pamphlets on planning, annual budgets, nationalization of industries, and other pressing economic issues of the day. The forum was ostensibly an apolitical think tank, funded by small donations in order to counter rumors of covert CIA funding.[46] Business leaders themselves were not enthusiastic participants, at least in public. As the "License-Permit Raj" was taking shape, they kept their distance from the forum in order to preserve their privileged access to the upper echelons of the state bureaucracy. Placed on the back foot after criticizing the five-year plans, J. R. D. Tata was not yet willing to jeopardize his relationship with Nehru and "reacted by withdrawing into a shell." FICCI and Birla's faction wanted nothing to do with the forum from the start, ensuring it could never speak for the entire business community.[47] Shroff later bemoaned the "moral cowardice the business men of India suffered from at the time I sponsored the Forum of Free Enterprise in 1956."[48]

The forum steered clear of the language of Thakurdas's resolution in support of the "middle classes," which highlighted the efficiency of markets and the importance of trade and consumer goods to the national economy. Instead, "free enterprise" emphasized the autonomy of business as a collective agent and its capacity to direct the economy in opposition to the regulatory and redistributive state. This language originated in the United States, specifically in the coordinated assault on the New Deal in the 1930s by chambers of commerce and affiliated organizations such as the American Enterprise Institute and the Foundation for Economic Education.[49] Its closest Indian antecedent was the corporatist vision of the Bombay Plan, shorn of any concessions to the primacy of the state in planning. Recognizing the limited political resonance of "free enterprise" outside the United States, forum spokesmen chose to couch their antistatist message in the language of socialism and Gandhian trusteeship. They appealed to India's "rich heritage of spiritual past and Gandhian ideals," quoting the Mahatma alongside the Austrian economists Hayek and von Mises. Socialism, in their definition, was "a way of life, representing certain ethical values which cannot be imposed from above dictates of Government or by merely nationalizing industries."[50] By adopting "the enemy's political vocabulary," they spoke back to the state in its own terms, while simultaneously committing themselves to a transnational Cold War project of defending capitalism from the menacing threat of Communism.[51]

The forum, just like the earlier campaign on behalf of the middle classes, could not succeed alone. Collective action was impossible without the participation of the majority of the business community. To this end, Shroff drafted a code of conduct setting out the mutual responsibilities of producers, consumers, shareholders, and workers. It began by condemning "hoarding, black-marketing and profiteering" as "anti-social and evil," a familiar complaint that had come to encapsulate the case for self-regulation.[52] Masani skillfully used the code to convince his Gandhian friends to see the forum as their ally. In January 1959, a seminar took place in Bombay under the auspices of the Akhil Bharat Sarva Seva Sangh, the apex Gandhian organization controlled by Vinoba. The Sangh called for "radical change in the character of industry and commerce," reiterating the distinction between *sampattidan* and ordinary charity. Masani could not resist the urge to test those in attendance, including JP, U. N. Dhebar, and Shankarrao Deo, by "reading from [Shroff's] Code without saying what it was to ask if this is what they understood by the application of trusteeship in practice." When they all "said that it was beautifully put," Masani triumphantly revealed that "it was from that 'horrible reactionary organization' which they have imagined the Forum of Free Enterprise to be!"[53] This bit of showmanship was meant to bolster the forum's legitimacy by associating codification of business ethics with the ideals of trusteeship. Corporate social responsibility was an adversarial political language, requiring both an external Other (the state) and an internal enemy (unscrupulous traders). Big business was de facto socially responsible, inherently embodying a cosmopolitan, technocratic, and managerial ethos. The Gandhians would unwittingly reproduce these divisions, playing into Masani's hands and constricting their utopian horizons.

In Search of a Code

In late 1964, JP Narayan decided to convene the Seminar on the Social Responsibilities of Business in New Delhi, with a view to "discovering the first steps toward practical trusteeship."[54] He began by issuing a public statement calling for the imposition of a broad-based code of conduct in the private sector, thereby fueling ongoing factional conflicts. In the statement, JP pointed to a recent instance of price gouging by flour millers in Calcutta as an example of "how woefully has the business community failed to exert any manner of internal discipline upon its erring members." In response, the chairman of the Federation of Mofussil Traders Organisations of West Bengal complained against singling out "small and middle-class businessmen" while big industrialists were left alone to prosper.[55] Having moderated his public support of Nehru, G. D. Birla now took the side of the traders, accusing JP of never bothering to meet and listen to their concerns before smearing them in the press.[56] J. R. D. Tata, on the other hand, sought to absolve big business of the sins of the many. The root cause of "profiteering" and "antisocial acts," according to him, lay in the "woefully low ethical and civic standards in our country." Traders, most of whom belonged to close-knit ethnic and religious communities, were taught "since childhood, to ensure the safety, health, and material prosperity of the family ahead of any other duty" and thus saw nothing wrong in hoarding or tax evasion.[57] JP felt "rather depressed" by this hostile reaction, thinking J. R. D. would "appreciate the non-ideological approach" and likening him to Nehru in conflating his own virtues with the institutions to which he belonged.[58] It fell to the second tier of Tata managers and executives to express the business point of view at the seminar.

JP worked closely with Masani to draw up an eclectic list of invitees, reflecting the latest transnational currents of economic and managerial thought. Nani Palkhivala, an expert on tax policy and spokesman for the Forum of Free

Enterprise, and Colonel Leslie Sawhny, J. R. D.'s brother-in-law, would represent Tata. From abroad, Masani floated the names of Milton Friedman (who had recently visited India), E. F. Schumacher (chief economist of the National Coal Board in the UK and an adviser to the Planning Commission), John Marsh (who had assisted Masani in implementing scientific management at TISCO), A. A. Berle (coauthor of *The Modern Corporation and Private Property*), and the ubiquitous Peter Drucker.[59] India was fast becoming a battleground in a global war of ideas about the prospects of the mixed economy model, with the neoliberal Friedman on one side and mainstream New Deal liberals like Berle and J. K. Galbraith on the other. Each side viewed India through the prism of its respective ideological lens.[60] Within India, too, Masani's list aroused suspicion on all sides of the political spectrum. J. R. D. Tata objected to "the idea of foreigners, mainly from countries where the understanding of social responsibilities has evolved much ahead of ours, being invited for such a discussion, *as it will expose our weaknesses!*"[61] Tarlok Singh, member of the Planning Commission, worried that the seminar was "not sufficiently indigenous perhaps in its roots and purposes and that in practice it may be a little external, escapist or even superficial."[62] Both presumed, for different reasons, that imported expertise was ill suited to the Indian context.

The seminar categorically rejected this distinction between foreign and indigenous ideas. Masani and JP detected a deep resonance between Gandhian trusteeship and related experiments in advanced industrial economies. Two prominent participants in the seminar from Britain were George Goyder, a newsprint manufacturer and advocate of reforming corporate governance, and Ernest Bader, a Swiss-born Quaker entrepreneur who converted his chemicals company into a worker-owned "commonwealth." Like Gandhi, Goyder drew on Maine's and Maitland's nineteenth-century legal theories to posit a shift in corporate law from contract to "the personality of the organized group." Since the introduction of the joint-stock form, he found, the "personality or essence of a company resides in its Memorandum and Articles of Association." But in the existing paradigm, directors were "trustees" of the shareholders alone, having no legally defined responsibilities to workers, consumers, and the community at large. In *The Future of Private Enterprise* (1951), Goyder proposed the introduction of a general objects clause in companies' memoranda of association to specify these additional responsibilities, leading up to the guarantee of worker representation on an equal standing to shareholders.[63] Bader was an embodiment of the practical, bottom-up approach, giving concrete expression to Goyder's ideas by transferring 90 percent of the share

capital of his chemicals company to the workers. Bader was directly influenced by Gandhian trusteeship, which he discovered through the radical
Labour Member of Parliament Wilfred Wellock. Together, they launched
the Association for the Democratic Integration of Industry (Demintry) to
promote the ideals of common ownership. Bader visited India for the first
time in 1958, staying with JP at his *ashram* in Bihar and delivering speeches
to *bhoodan* workers. To assuage Tarlok Singh's and J. R. D.'s concerns about
the relevance of foreign expertise, JP pointed to his long-standing association
with Bader and Goyder and their shared vision.[64]

The Seminar on Social Responsibilities of Business took place at the India
International Centre in New Delhi over six days in March 1965. Discussions
centered on the definition of trusteeship and its contemporary relevance. M. L.
Dantwala, an agricultural economist and former confidant of Gandhi who had
originally drafted the six fundamental principles of trusteeship, revealed that
the great man himself had been open to making them more conciliatory toward
business. U. N. Dhebar, another veteran Gandhian activist, pointed out that
trusteeship as currently formulated "had in view only the problems of an agro-
industrial society and not those of a technological society." Economist R. K.
Hazari found it to be a "rather negative" concept. He thought "traditional
norms of social responsibility" as practiced by Indian business families and
castes, were "based on paternalism" and not applicable to large firms that had
"developed a corporate conscience." Masani, speaking on behalf of big business, put forward the broadest possible definition: "free enterprise reinforced
by social objectives was trusteeship." Questions of ownership were excluded
from the discussion, while JP insisted that the focus of the seminar was on
"voluntary measures" and not state regulation.[65] The very flexibility and open-
endedness of trusteeship, which could bring thinkers with such different
backgrounds and beliefs around the same table, also limited its intellectual
coherence.

The formal declaration issued by the seminar at the conclusion of proceedings staked a middle ground, avoiding political implications and presenting
"social responsibility" as a natural outgrowth of the advent of managerial capitalism. Clause 4 read:

> Every business has an over-riding responsibility to make the fullest
> possible use of its resources, both human and material, as has each
> individual. An enterprise is a corporate citizen. Like a citizen it is

esteemed and judged by its actions in relation to the community of which it is a member, as well as by its economic performance. Management has the main responsibility today for developing the corporate enterprise which is everywhere replacing the family and family business as the unit of work in a technological society.[66]

Following Goyder's proposals, the declaration went on to recommend the inclusion of "a specific statement of these responsibilities" in the memorandum of association of public and private companies and a regular social audit to assess compliance. A standing committee was formed and a regional seminar on the same theme convened in Calcutta in March 1966. In his inaugural speech at the Calcutta seminar, JP reflected on the limitations of his earlier campaigns, conceding that "the Sampattidan programme of the Sarvodaya movement was a very crude and unrealistic step towards the goal of Gandhian trusteeship." Experiments such as the Scott Bader Commonwealth revealed that "much more has been done" abroad than in India to make trusteeship a reality.[67]

Meanwhile, business groups in Bombay renewed their self-regulation drive, which had stagnated due to the political marginalization of Shroff's Forum of Free Enterprise. In April 1965, Ramkrishna Bajaj, then serving as president of the Maharashtra Chamber of Commerce, invited J. R. D. Tata to help draft "a detailed code of fair practices." Ramkrishna was the younger son of the Marwari industrialist Jamnalal Bajaj, one of Gandhi's most devoted followers, but he did not always see eye to eye with the contemporary Gandhian movement.[68] J. R. D. made his participation conditional on a punitive system of sanctions as a means of enforcement. The result was a new organization, the Fair Trade Practices Association (FTPA).[69] The first meeting took place in September, with Bajaj, textile and chemicals manufacturer Arvind Mafatlal, and P. A. Narielwala of the Tatas in attendance. They drew up a "retailers' pledge" committing signatories to "charge consumers a just and fair price," "not withhold or suppress goods, with a view to indulging in black marketing," "not deal in smuggled goods," and generally uphold the "high standards of business ethics."[70] Bajaj also joined the standing committee charged with implementing the Delhi declaration, recognizing the two initiatives as complementary.

Despite its membership growing to around two hundred by 1968, the FTPA never spoke for the majority of the business community. FICCI officially maintained that voluntary sanctions were unenforceable and that regulation was best left to the government. Some members felt the association went too far and others that it was essentially toothless body. J. R. D. wanted to see it actively "ostracise those who are known to offend its principles," which invariably meant smaller retail traders and not big business houses. Significantly, tax evasion found no mention in the list of core principles.[71] Only Tata companies that dealt in consumer goods, such as TELCO, TOMCO, Voltas, and the mills, joined the FTPA. Even if a company did become a member, "it should not consider itself tied down to the Association's views and should be prepared to take an independent stand in respect of prices and distribution."[72] The FTPA laid bare the inadequacy of collective action, hamstrung by companies' exceptionalism and tendency to look out for their own interests first and foremost.

The standing committee tasked with implementing the Delhi declaration held its next meeting in September 1969. The list of participants was nearly identical to the FTPA leadership: Bajaj, Arvind Mafatlal, Nani Palkhivala, and S. P. Godrej among the businessmen, with the addition of JP Narayan and Masani. In accordance with George Goyder's proposal at the seminar, they set out to draft a "General Purposes Clause or Declaration on Social Objectives to be placed before companies and trade unions," inspired by TISCO's "statement on social objectives" and the Johnson & Johnson "Credo." Holding up an Indian company and an American multinational as models reaffirmed the convergence of indigenous and foreign best practices. But the committee's imagination was limited by what companies like TISCO were already doing, such as welfare provision and profit sharing. Observing the proceedings from afar, Goyder realized that his ideas had failed to translate in India. True social responsibility, he maintained, would not rest "on profit sharing but on the regular purchase of the shares of all public companies by Trustees on behalf of the workers in the company on the lines so successfully carried out by the Sears Roebuck Company of Chicago."[73] For him, worker association was a cornerstone of true Gandhian trusteeship. Businessmen predictably abandoned it in the aftermath of the Delhi seminar because it would have required a fundamental restructuring of the corporate form.

Another recommendation of the seminar, the social audit, met with a similar fate. Any systematic assessment of compliance raised the thorny problem of enforcement. The possibility of the government making it "compulsory in due course" had to be avoided at all costs. A team of "sociologists, economists, scientists, and management men" from the Tata Institute of Social Sciences

(TISS) and the Indian Institute of Management (IIM), Ahmedabad, was entrusted with preparing a detailed report on the social audit in early 1971.[74] The joint TISS-IIM report drastically limited the scope of the audit from the beginning, focusing on only "voluntary actions" and excluding "tax laws, Company Law, Industrial development regulations, foreign exchange regulations, excise laws, etc." Administering the audit would be left to independent experts connected with the Tata philanthropic institutions, who were powerless to adjudicate the most divisive issues.[75]

Looking back on the cumulative effect of these initiatives at the end of the decade, J. R. D. Tata could not hide his disappointment: "The adoption of a code of conduct and membership of the Fair Trade Practices Association has not, I fear, had as significant an impact on the public mind as we hoped it would." The fault lay with the government for failing to "differentiate between those who honestly serve the community and those who exploit it," but perhaps business had to change course as well. The chairman began to contemplate a different strategy of "direct relief and reconstruction," including building "model villages" and encouraging "slum clearance and the resettlement of squatters." Paternalism resurfaced in his call to "let industry established in the countryside 'adopt' the village in their neighbourhood."[76] True to form, JP enthusiastically embraced the idea, suggesting that TISCO and TELCO might adopt the entire Singhbhum District but was told that this would cost too much.[77] Even as the Gandhians held out hope that it would spark transformative change, the concept of "social responsibility" never lived up to its promise. As the state turned toward legally curbing the size and market power of business groups and as Tata reached the nadir of its political influence, the struggle on behalf of free enterprise required a more forceful defense of the virtues of "bigness" itself.

Big Is Beautiful

Beyond the boardrooms and seminar halls, the 1960s were a treacherous time for Indian business. Rapid growth as a result of the five-year plans and a loosely applied licensing policy over the previous decade were offset by the shock of the Mundhra and Dalmia-Jain insider trading scandals, which exposed grave deficiencies in corporate governance.[78] The far-reaching *Report of the Committee on Prevention of Corruption*, which presented its findings in 1964 (the year of Nehru's death), said very little about the private sector. Acknowledging that "the growth of monopolies, the rise of a managerial class and intricate institutional mechanisms" had enabled a range of undesirable behaviors, including insider trading, tax evasion, abuse of licenses, real estate speculation, and cornering of markets, the report nonetheless failed to present any detailed statistics to understand the real scope of these problems and did not make any concrete policy recommendations to address them. FICCI refused to meet with the committee, while the few businessmen in Calcutta and Bombay who agreed to be interviewed could only vaguely suggest empowering "trade organisations" to identify black sheep and relaxing licensing restrictions even further.[79] Big business held the line and successfully protected its gains, but that was about to change.

In 1966, the young economist R. K. Hazari, professor at the University of Bombay, consultant to the Planning Commission, and participant in the Delhi seminar the year before, published a landmark report titled *The Structure of the Corporate Private Sector*. Using a wealth of quantitative data newly made available by disclosures under the revised Companies Act, Hazari systematically mapped the structure and operations of the country's twenty largest business groups. He found a "clear and significant increase in concentration of economic power" between 1951 and 1958. The top two groups, Tata and Birla, controlled "nearly one-fifth of the gross capital stock of all non-government public companies," while the share of the top four had increased from 20.44 percent to 25.66 percent. Despite creating a robust public sector, epitomized by the state-run steel plants and other large public companies, Hazari concluded that the Nehruvian licensing regime failed in its constitutionally mandated objective of bringing about a "wider diffusion of economic power" in India.[80] Hazari also painstakingly mapped the full array of techniques used by groups to expand and consolidate. Tata Sons held low equity stakes in the companies under its control, relying on the trusts, a large number of passive shareholders such as banks and nationalized insurance companies, and direct investments by companies in others "vertically related to them" (e.g., TISCO and its captive collieries). By contrast, Birla had no single holding company, not even "a solar system in which each planet has its own satellites." Instead, "circular chains of investment which return to their starting points" allowed companies to "indirectly purchase their own shares" and cover the tracks of the controlling interest.[81]

Hazari reached nuanced and measured conclusions, admitting that concentration itself was not necessarily harmful—TISCO, for one, was an efficient and productive enterprise that "delivered the goods." He did not advocate breaking up business groups, a proposition that was "legally, impossible and, on economic grounds, unwise." Precisely because it was so difficult to tell which companies were part of groups in the first place, government regulators were destined to lose "the race against private legal ingenuity" as new methods of concealing ownership and control would be devised. Nor could the groups be nationalized wholesale if their composition was so uncertain. Even in France and the United Kingdom, only individual companies or entire sectors like coal or steel had been taken over. Given India's urgent need for faster economic growth, a "complete embargo" on the groups' expansion "would be suicidal." In the final analysis, Hazari proposed evening the scales by promoting the public sector as a countervailing force and encouraging the creation of independent small and medium businesses through discriminatory licensing and industrial finance.[82]

The government of the new Prime Minister, Nehru's daughter Indira Gandhi, followed the spirit, if not always the letter, of Hazari's recommendations. After the 1967 elections, Mrs. Gandhi (as she was conventionally referred to) broke with the old guard of the Congress and redefined herself as a champion of the poor with the support of the left parties. In 1969, she nationalized the entire banking sector, followed by the abolition of the managing agency system and the passage of the Monopolies and Trade Restrictive Practices (MRTP) Act, which established a fixed ceiling on group assets. As industrial productivity went into sharp decline and the economy sputtered, she also eroded the independence of the Planning Commission and centralized decision making on licensing in her own office with the help of the Ministry of Finance. A planned expansion of Tata Chemicals was held up in the midst of these power struggles, signaling to the Tatas that their interests were no longer safe in New Delhi.[83]

At the same time, Mrs. Gandhi promised to relax licensing restrictions if the private sector lived up to its social responsibilities. Masani, who had contested the elections on behalf of the pro-business Swatantra Party, brought the Delhi seminar and the recent meeting of the FTPA in Bombay to her attention as evidence of good faith reforms. The prime minister was unimpressed, stating that the seminar "did not make much positive impact on the business community" and that more progress could be made on "the avoidance of tax evasion and conspicuous consumption and rigorous enforcement of proper standards of quality, particularly in respect of food and drugs through voluntary action."[84] The latter was the ostensible mandate of the FTPA, but tax evasion remained a taboo subject. If anything, the onerous disclosure requirements under the MRTP Act incentivized concealment of assets and further recourse to "black money" and byzantine corporate structures—much as Hazari had predicted.[85] The prime minister's triumphant reelection campaign in 1971, using the slogan *Garibi Hatao!* (Abolish Poverty!), strengthened her hand and seemed to pose an existential threat to big business.

As relations with the government worsened, J. R. D. Tata's public statements grew more caustic and combative, alternating between righteous anger and genuine exasperation. At a meeting with the Planning Commission in August 1968, he sarcastically dismissed the entire premise of regulation: "As the head of the largest industrial group in the private sector, I must be possessed of a tremendous concentration of economic power. As I wake up every morning, I carefully consider to what purpose I shall apply my great powers that day. Shall I crush competitors, exploit consumers, fire recalcitrant workers, topple a Government or two?"[86] In a more serious vein, J. R. D. observed that Indian business groups may have been dominant in the domestic market, but they remained quite small relative to their peers in industrialized countries. The burden of the MRTP Act fell hardest on those who held the key to solving the nation's problems. Growth could be most quickly and efficiently delivered by the likes of the Tatas, as Hazari had recognized. In another speech, he denounced reporting requirements about the relationship between different Tata companies seeking licenses as "an inexcusable waste of time" and "a form of undeserved harassment."[87] Giving the Tatas a freer hand necessarily entailed restricting and disciplining others. For J. R. D., this line of attack was consistent with an evolutionary narrative of the capitalist system culminating in large managerial corporations, influenced by his reading of Burnham and Drucker. As he explained, "Bigness is an inherent and inevitable consequence of the manner in which the modern world, and life in that world, has developed. But bigness in business and industry is more than matched by bigness in Government, in trade unions, in consumer power. We are today, and increasingly, moving deeper into the age of bigness."[88] J. R. D.'s favorite argument against monopoly legislation remained the danger posed by the excessive size of the public sector vis-à-vis the private sector, not the reverse.

However, if "bigness" was desirable, it could be achieved in partnership with the state. In 1972, a year after Mrs. Gandhi's reelection, J. R. D. was invited to record his views on the future development of the economy in general and ways to spur productivity in particular. The door to the prime minister's office remained slightly ajar to big business, much to the dismay of her Communist allies. In the so-called Tata Memorandum, J. R. D. connected the critique of monopoly legislation with the self-regulating drive of the FTPA and the Delhi seminar, arguing that the issue of concentration of economic power "has been given excessive prominence because of the misdeeds of a few groups or individuals." Rather than blanket restrictions on the size or market dominance of groups, licensing policy should be determined on a case-by-case basis. Those who were found guilty of "such anti-social activities as blackmarketing, tax evasion, illegal foreign exchange transactions, profiteering, bribery and corruption" should be refused. Others like the Tatas, "whose past record and known practices and policies were consistently above reproach," should be given the green light for expansion. At the end of the memorandum, J. R. D. resurrected the "joint sector" enterprise idea implemented at Air India International, which he had first proposed to Nehru as a catch-all solution in the early 1950s (see Chapter 4). Because TISCO could not raise the required capital to double its capacity, the government would create a new company and hold up to 51 percent equity, while entrusting day-to-day management entirely to a private partner. This very same mechanism could then be used to open up existing nationalized companies such as the Shipping Corporation of India and the Indian Oil Company to private capital.[89] In effect, J. R. D. demanded a policy specifically targeted to benefit his group and its particular strengths. It was an audacious plea for partnership that rested not on competition and the free market but on the co-option and subordination of the state to the productive powers of big business.

The Communist Party of India issued a sharp rebuttal to the memorandum, pointing out the extraordinary nature of the proposal and its implications. After winning the elections on a pro-poor and anti-monopoly platform, Mrs. Gandhi's government was now "showing all the characteristics of its class nature" by inviting the foxes into the henhouse. Having failed to displace her at the ballot box, the Tatas wished to "completely corner all the funds of the public-sector financial institutions and the state funds" and divert them "to their industrial networks," re-creating the managing agency system by another name. The government would assume the main financial burden for "joint sector" ventures and agree to discipline labor, while giving up control of management—a lose-lose proposition. The *Communist Reply to Tata Memorandum* perceptively noted that the Tatas "made a special case for themselves in the form of a little exceptionalism," claiming "relaxation in their favour on merit." This was "an obvious dig at the Birlas, their class brothers but rivals."[90] Industries Development Minister C. Subramanian favorably referred to the memorandum when discussing the nationalization of the Indian Iron and Steel

Company (IISCO), indicating an alarming retreat on the part of the government. The Communists urged an intensification of anti-monopoly legislation, calling for the top seventy-five business groups to be broken up and "completely excluded from new licenses."[91] The productivity crisis, worsened by rising inflation as a result of the global oil shock in 1973, ensured this scenario never came to pass. Amid all the bluster and bravado, J. R. D. and Mrs. Gandhi were now engaged in a true dialogue, circling each other's positions and coming closer to a meeting point. The rapprochement took place in unexpected circumstances, as India was plunged into full-blown authoritarianism for the first time since independence.

Emergency Days

As part of its overtures to the prime minister after the 1971 elections, big business pledged to show concrete results in improving the lives of workers, consumers, and communities surrounding their sites of operation. Social responsibility came full circle, returning to its roots in philanthropy and social work, shadowing the state rather than confronting it. Utopian trusteeship made its last stand at a conference convened by Vinoba Bhave in September 1973 at Gandhi's old *ashram* in Wardha, Maharashtra. Although Vinoba adopted a quietist posture, JP was steadily making his way back into active politics. The widening gulf between guru and disciple was reflected in their diverging attitudes toward big business. JP's characteristically modest proposal to establish "a Board of Trustees for companies with a paid-up capital of over 50 lakhs" was roundly rejected at the Wardha conference, along with all other "elaborate legislation." With Vinoba's blessing, it was agreed that trusteeship could only "come from within" and be manifested as "a voluntary spontaneous gesture." The language suited businessmen's pursuit of "community service and development" as a way to visibly demonstrate the contributions of the private sector to society.[92] The social audit, workers' association with management, and other incipiently structural reforms fell by the wayside.

Instead, Ramkrishna Bajaj announced the formation of yet another association, Business for Social Progress (BSP). The draft constitution of BSP stated that it was meant to "promote and propagate the ideals and objectives" of the Delhi declaration. Three programs would be carried out "on an experimental basis," starting with the city of Bombay and extending to rural areas: mobile hospitals, subsidized lunch packets, and the construction of low-cost housing for "500 middle class and lower class families" living in *zopadpattis* (slums).[93] Whereas the Forum of Free Enterprise had a primarily ideological mission and the FTPA stood for codification and self-regulation, BSP redefined "social responsibility" as a set of targeted projects carried out by individual business houses, rendering its associational character obsolete in the process. J. R. D. Tata soon decided to scrap the BSP's weak draft constitution altogether. In March 1975, he informed Bajaj that "in order to move quickly," BSP's proposed work in Bombay would be carried out by just two groups, Tata and Mahindra. The demolition of informal dwellings and resettlement to the outskirts of the city would be undertaken in cooperation with the Ministry for Urban Development, because providing services such as primary education and vocational training to slum dwellers "would recognize the inevitability of the continued existence and growth of the illegal occupation of city land."[94] Not only had businessmen abandoned meaningful collective action, but they were also now seemingly willing to act as proxies for the state.

Three months to the day after BSP's announcement, Mrs. Gandhi proclaimed the imposition of a state of emergency in response to widespread social and political unrest. JP Narayan had emerged as her chief adversary, issuing a call for "total revolution" at the head of the student movement in Bihar. Civil liberties were suspended, the press was censored, political opponents (including JP) were jailed by the thousands, and the government launched a coordinated drive to raise productivity and impose economic and social discipline. Under the direction of the prime minister's son Sanjay, slum clearance and compulsory sterilization to check population growth became development priorities. Both had been endorsed by consultants from the Ford Foundation and other international organizations and practiced at local and provincial levels since the mid-1960s. The exceptional moment of the Emergency merely brought coercion out in the open, shedding the procedural cloak of constitutional democracy.[95] Violent means were used to displace the urban population, culminating in the infamous police massacre of Muslim residents near the Turkman Gate in Old Delhi in April 1976.[96]

Although the extent of state repression at this time is well known, businessmen were at times more uncompromising in carrying out its developmental agenda. In Bombay, the chief minister informed a delegation from the Tatas that the priority of the state government was "slum improvement," not wholesale demolition. He refuted the Tatas' assertion that a majority of slum dwellers were "bootleggers, smugglers, and anti-social" elements; in fact, "75 per cent of the residents were industrial workers." Would it not be better, the chief minister asked, for textile mills and other companies in the city to strengthen their welfare programs? J. R. D. Tata countered by citing his "experience in Jamshedpur" of observing uncontrolled slum growth in periph-eral villages like Jugsalai. He refused to spend any money on the project unless the government used "Mobile Police Squads to remove the zopadpattis and to abort any attempts to create them." Leela Moolgaokar, a social worker and the wife of the TELCO chairman, went further by connecting resettlement with family planning. She proposed that "couples could be warned that in case of every extra child, over the number of three, they would have to pay a rent of Rs. 10 per child per month for residing in the improved colony."[97]

Tata also had a long history of supporting family planning. In the early 1950s, when he first became an outspoken advocate for the cause, J. R. D. was firmly opposed to compulsory sterilization, declaring himself "shocked to the core" at the idea. Instead, he favored scientific solutions such as oral contraceptive pills and intrauterine devices, as well as a "sustained campaign of educational propaganda."[98] Throughout the 1960s, Tata companies carried out a mix of different measures, including cash incentives for vasectomies of up to Rs. 200 per employee (equivalent to around $26 or $160 adjusted for inflation). On a visit to TELCO in Jamshedpur, journalist Taya Zinkin marveled at the scale of the effort and how thoroughly it had been ingrained in company culture: "The charts which showed the number of TELCO employees who had been sterilized looked like production charts. . . . The names of those who volun-teered were given wide publicity; they were interviewed, photographed and made as much fuss of in the TELCO journal as if they had been Stakhano-vites in the Soviet Union." At neighboring TISCO, where persuasion was gen-tler and incentives were lower at just Rs. 50 per worker, the results were less impressive. Zinkin concluded that "obviously what India needs is more of TELCO's salesmanship."[99] What India got was a more openly coercive cam-paign at the top that nonetheless functioned very much like a market on the ground. The traffic in sterilization certificates carried out by *dalals* (brokers) and individual "motivators" in Delhi calls into question simplistic notions of agency and complicity.[100] As in the case of the land market in Jamshedpur, corporations were acting like states and vice versa.

Along with the majority of big business, J. R. D. supported the Emergency as a welcome return of law and order and a check on labor unrest. To be sure, views inside Bombay House were sharply divided, with Nani Palkhivala in favor of taking a strong stand against Mrs. Gandhi's unconstitutional actions. But J. R. D. openly praised the government's "refreshingly pragmatic and result-orientated approach," telling the *New York Times* and other newspapers that he was pleased the trains were running on time and he could finally leave his house without fearing "strikes, boycotts, demonstrations." Empty talk of "human rights and freedom," he maintained, was "not in the interests of 600 million people for whom no freedom of right matters more today than freedom from want and the right to work and earn a decent living."[101] This attitude came as a surprise to many, although it perhaps should not have. Tata executives' speeches in the early 1970s were replete with calls for a firmer authoritarian hand and condemnations of mass democracy. Naval Tata blamed the productivity crisis on "indiscipline amongst labour ranks," insisting that "maintenance of discipline, whether at home, in the school, in the factory or the farm, is a basic requirement for orderly development." As long as the government did not espouse "the an nihilation of the entrepreneur in an extreme form of socialism," its precise "political ideology" was irrelevant. J. R. D. went further by favoring the installation of a technocratic despotism governed by "Cabinets of experts."[102] Viewed in this light, the Emergency fulfilled businessmen's deepest fantasies about the proper role of the state—namely, "to inoculate capitalism against the threat of democracy."[103] It is also worth recalling the Bombay Plan authors' admiration for the Soviet Union, too easily dismissed as an artifact of wartime planning mania rather than an expression of a consistent underlying worldview.

In theory, the descent into authoritarianism and Mrs. Gandhi's continuing demonization of "big money" and "powerful classes" should have brought the conflict between capital and the state into the open. Superficially, the Emergency appeared to be a textbook illustration of the worst-case scenario of "extreme socialism" feared by Naval Tata. In fact, the political language of the state came to mirror that of its erstwhile detractors. The Planning Commission boasted of the "crack down on economic offenders—black marketeers, profiteers and smugglers," sounding very much like the FTPA. Strikes and lockouts plummeted, licensing and monopoly restrictions were relaxed, and corporate assets rose faster than ever before (Tata's grew by 66.6 percent between 1972 and 1977). By taking upon itself the task of managing the economy, the state paradoxically set out to achieve what businessmen had always demanded—namely, disciplining labor and reducing (bureaucratic but not corporate) corruption. In the process, its own legitimacy came to depend on the support of business, both large and small, and a nascent middle class.[104] The conceptual bundle of classical liberalism, democratic socialism, and Gandhian trusteeship cultivated by businessmen over the years fell apart, to be replaced by a neoliberal "state and business alliance for economic growth."[105]

Meanwhile, JP Narayan found himself in prison for the first time since the heady days of the Quit India movement, when he had renounced Marx for the Mahatma. At the end of his life, he became an underground revolutionary once again. Unable to explain the failure of mass resistance to the Emergency, he returned to the staunch anticommunism of his conversion phase, seeing "the Russians through the CPI and their Trojan horses within Congress" as the hidden hand behind the throne. But this time, there would be no retreat from politics into spiritualism and voluntarism. Suffering from ill health and consumed by bitterness and despair, JP threw his weight behind a grand electoral coalition to defeat Mrs. Gandhi, which crucially included the parties and organizations of the Hindu right, the Jana Sangh and the militant Rashtriya Swayamsevak Sangh (RSS).[106] His nonpolitical efforts to remake Indian society, not least by transforming capitalism through trusteeship, had led nowhere.

The Afterlives of CSR

The Emergency was lifted in January 1977, with little warning or explanation. For all her authoritarian tendencies, Mrs. Gandhi craved the validation of popular support and fully expected to get it. Big business responded by generously contributing to her campaign, with the Tatas reportedly giving Rs. 75 lakhs. The opposition Janata coalition decisively won the elections that spring, taking advantage of public discontent with the excesses of the Emergency to form independent India's first non-Congress government. Constitutional democracy was procedurally restored, but economic policy was thrown into chaos as representatives of socialist, agrarian, and conservative factions within Janata divided up ministerial portfolios among them. For Tata and other business groups, there was no turning back. J. R. D. continued to use the rhetoric typical of the Emergency, warning the new government that "the sense and substance of freedom it has brought back to the country will not be allowed to be used to cause loss of production and of wages without just cause through indiscipline and disruptive action."[107] The new industries minister was the veteran socialist trade union leader George Fernandes, an icon of resistance for his leadership of the 1974 railway strike and subsequent imprisonment. He was also an old enemy of the Tatas, publicly condemning J. R. D. for his support of the Emergency in his first speech before FICCI: "600 million people held a view contrary to that of this great leader of industry on such profound matters as the Magna Carta, freedom of thought and freedom from want."[108]

The Janata manifesto revived the issue of the "concentration of economic power," promising to "to steer clear of the evils of Capitalism and State Capitalism" and championing small-scale and cottage industries. Fernandes set his sights on TISCO as a plum target for nationalization in connivance with Minister for Steel Biju Patnaik, a shrewd politician and business rival of the Tatas. Confident that "1979 is not 1969" and that the public's newfound "fear of Government's abuse of authority" would lead to a swift backlash, Tata publicists orchestrated an effective press campaign against Fernandes. Familiar exceptionalist arguments resurfaced, with one pamphlet proclaiming that TISCO's "70-year old tradition and 106.7 per cent efficiency has touched an emotive nerve in our people." The pamphlet also inverted the conventional understanding of industrial democracy, positing the corporation as more accountable than the state: "The director of a Company, however powerful, can be questioned at shareholders' meetings, but how do you hold a faceless bureaucrat responsible?" In the *Illustrated Weekly of India*, economist Prem Shankar Jha pointed out that "in the name of 'socialism'" the Janata government sought "to destroy the most socialised part of private industry," turning a "blind eye" to the real culprits: "the smuggler, the bootlegger, the blackmarketing trader and the tax-evading manufacturer." Prime Minister Morarji Desai's intervention squashed Fernandes's proposal and TISCO carried on.[109] Never again did business groups have to defend themselves by claiming they were "socialized" enterprises. The political salience of monopolies, tax evasion, and "black money" also faded away in the euphoria of liberalization and explosive economic growth over the following decades.

Pressures on business to engage with the rural sector grew steadily regardless of who was in power. In July 1977, a few months after Janata came into office, TISCO managing director Russi Mody was informed of a policy shift "from industrial to rural development as a way of tackling our massive unemployment programme." At the group level, the chairman requested "that companies take a hard look at their existing community development and village extension programmes, if any, and see what they can do to refurbish them."[110] Other groups established initiatives such as the Birla Rural Development Association (1978), the Narottam Lalbhai Rural Development Fund (1978), the C. C. Shroff Self Help Centre (1978), and the Birla Agricultural Farm and Newata Mandal Village Project (1979).[111] TISCO followed suit by registering the Tata Steel Rural Development Society (TSRDS) as a nongovernmental organization (NGO) under the Societies Act, rather than as a constituent department of the company, with the mission of improving "earning opportunities" in the countryside. TSRDS paid special attention to *adivasi* welfare, sponsoring basic literacy classes, technical training, medical care, and cultural activities. Family planning remained a priority even after the

Emergency. In addition to the employee bonus, Rs. 100 "cash rewards" for voluntary sterilization were offered in villages covered by the scheme, despite warnings to "proceed with caution in this, primarily Adivasi region."[112]

TSRDS marked a return to an earlier paternalist mode of philanthropic engagement, building on the Rural Welfare Board's work in the early 1950s as much as it heralded the rise of professionalized NGOs in the 1980s and 1990s. For Tata, "social responsibility" began as an externally oriented political language, deployed to justify the very existence of private capital in postindependence India. It was then internalized as a territorial mandate to provide services in rural areas surrounding factories and mines. Rather than serving as a marker of business self-evidently coming into its own as an embedded social actor, what we have come to know as CSR today was shaped by diverse forces and pressures, from global flows of knowledge and expertise to domestic political upheavals. Its complex and contradictory origins, as well as its unrealized futures, have since been lost.

Epilogue

Tata was at the forefront of several major transitions in the history of Indian capitalism: from the oceanic world of long-distance trade to industrialization and the exploitation of resources in the interior for the sake of national development; from paternalism to industrial relations and scientific management; and from charitable gifting to institutionalized corporate social responsibility (CSR). During the colonial period, the group survived by insisting on a clear separation between economic and political *swadeshi*, deftly navigating the unsteady terrain between empire and nation. After independence, Tata mobilized extraterritorial financial connections and political alliances to resist encroachment on its domains by the state. Managers and experts also developed a professionalized and technocratic corporate culture to keep the group together. Above all, the secret to Tata's extraordinary continuity and resilience lay in its ability to selectively perform quasi-sovereign functions—at times acting like a state, at other times in direct opposition to state aims.

The end point of each transition, however contested or incomplete, was reached in the late 1970s. Tata was firmly ensconced within the territory of the nation-state, resuming expansion after the Emergency dampened the regulatory zeal of the state. The group as a whole was not yet looking outward to global markets in a sustained manner, despite the continuing importance of connections to the United States in a Cold War context. The Tata Iron and Steel Company (TISCO) maintained full control over Jamshedpur and the surrounding mines, successfully avoided nationalization, and bought a tenuous industrial peace through a settlement with the pliant company union. A large and stable permanent workforce enjoyed ample benefits, including a system of ethnic quotas and the guarantee of employment to family members. Farther afield from Jamshedpur, model villages and community development projects enacted a narrow vision of CSR, unmoored from the radical potential of Gandhian trusteeship but powerful enough to bolster the legitimacy of the steel company in the region.

Since the early 1980s, the unraveling of this status quo has been dramatic. Tata held on at top of the corporate ladder and enjoyed a good relationship with both Congress and non-Congress governments, while slowly regaining control of its constituent companies. The group had evolved into a loose "commonwealth" led by entrenched "satraps" like Russi Mody at TISCO and Darbari Seth at Tata Chemicals, operating with little effective oversight from Bombay. Jehangir Ratanji Dadabhoy's (J. R. D.'s) successor Ratan Tata, who assumed the chairmanship of the group in 1990, brought it back together through a wave of share buybacks and centralizing initiatives, including a unified brand identity, quality control program, and code of conduct.[1] Meanwhile, a new breed of aggressive tycoons such as the Ambanis, who owed their ascent to more intimate connections with the state, emerged as rivals. Infrastructural and consumer needs in textiles, petrochemicals, telecommunications, pharmaceuticals, automobiles, and information technology multiplied avenues for expansion. The abolition of monopoly controls and rapid economic growth after the reforms of 1991 produced more "churn" than ever in the rankings of the top groups. The regional, community, and (to a lesser extent) caste profile of the Indian business community substantially changed, leaving Tata a venerable legacy house no longer at the cutting edge of entrepreneurship.[2] A perceptible change in values accompanied this shift, as the gloves of "social responsibility" came off and capitalists embraced wealth creation for its own sake. Mukesh Ambani's twenty-seven-story personal residence Antilia, valued at $2 billion and towering over some of the world's worst slums in Mumbai, symbolized the extravagance of the times. The austere Ratan Tata wryly commented, "It makes me wonder why someone would do that. . . . That's what revolutions are made of."[3]

Back to the Nation?

The era of liberalization saw the return of older conflicts, of questions seemingly long settled. As before, Tata responded to political and economic instability by looking outward, leveraging the group's core strengths in technology and finance to claim a key stake in India's "reglobalization." Despite losing the initiative to Birla in setting up joint ventures abroad during the 1960s and 1970s, Tata's long history of collaboration with foreign capital and expertise positioned the group well to take advantage of new opportunities.[4] Tata Consultancy Services (TCS) stood out as a success story in this regard, proving especially adept at circumventing draconian restrictions on foreign exchange. With the help of Tata Inc., the group's New York branch, TCS made inroads in the United States, forming a partnership with IBM's rival Burroughs to bring computers to India in 1973. Recalling the strategy used to obtain the World Bank loan for TISCO, Tata Inc. struck a deal with Citibank to service a loan at a lower interest rate than the one offered by government institutions. The company also recruited talented Indian software engineers to offer low-cost data processing services to American companies, giving rise to the "off-shoring" model that would come to dominate the industry. Under the charismatic leadership of F. C. Kohli, TCS became the group's most profitable and innovative arm.[5]

As trade barriers came down, a wave of high-profile acquisitions by Tata companies proclaimed Indian capitalism's triumphant "arrival" on the world stage it had ostensibly abandoned after independence.[6] The first was the purchase of the tea brand Tetley, a staple in every British cupboard, in 2000. Then Tata Steel bought the Anglo-Dutch giant Corus, which included the remnants of the privatized British Steel, in 2007. It was the largest overseas acquisition by an Indian company up to that point, won after a fierce bidding war. Despite the exorbitant price tag of $12 billion, Tata leadership believed that owners of iron ore were destined to become "the OPEC of the steel industry" in a cutthroat corporate landscape.[7] Tata Steel could afford to outbid its closest competitor, the Brazilian Companhia Siderúrgica Nacional, by raising money with the assistance of Western banks (Credit Suisse, ABN-Amro, and Deutsche Bank). The necessary loans were secured through subsidiaries in the United Kingdom, Singapore, and the Netherlands, which played the same intermediary role between Indian capitalism and global finance that Tata Limited and Tata & Co. had in the early twentieth century.[8]

The news of the Corus takeover was initially greeted with jubilation in the Indian media and business circles as "the empire striking back" and "a delicious reversal of fortune: a once-proud civilization, having fallen to the humiliations of colonization, is now buying out the hallowed corporations of the West."[9] One year later, Tata Motors followed suit with the acquisition of British carmaker Jaguar Land Rover (JLR) for $2.5 billion from the American giant Ford. This deal was depicted as another form of poetic justice, since Tata Motors had been offered for sale to Ford in the late 1990s while at a low ebb. In a further sign of global economic realignment, JLR's turnaround relied on the demand for luxury cars in China.[10] The parallel entry of TCS in the Chinese market prompted explicit comparisons to the early days of the opium trade. Critical commentators presumed that Tata "would once again prove a reliable intermediary for powerful foreigners looking to extract profit from Chinese labor." Ratan Tata heralded the dawn of a new Asian age, with "China being the factory of the world and India perhaps being the IT or high-end services of the world."[11]

Hopes of inverting the master-subject colonial script, with Asian economic dynamism fueling global growth and reinvigorating a moribund industrial Europe, proved short lived. Tata's business empire was stretched too far and buckled under the strains imposed by the financial crisis of 2007–2008. The Corus acquisition turned out to be a poisoned chalice. Tata Steel lost its competitive advantage derived from holding captive mines in India and risked becoming "ore deficient" on volatile global markets. A botched leadership transition, sagging demand, and relentless competition from cheap Chinese steel conspired to make Corus a "drag on the company."[12] Tata Steel was now responsible for the livelihoods of workers not only in Jamshedpur but also in faraway places such as Port Talbot in South Wales with their own proud industrial history.[13] As these communities struggled to cope with job losses and dwindling pensions, Tata found it difficult to live up to its new responsibilities and maintain a healthy bottom line. Throughout early 2016, Tata Steel sold off smaller units in piecemeal fashion while promising to keep the main steel plant at Port Talbot open. That summer, plans to find a buyer stalled due to an unexpected tectonic political shift: Britain's vote to exit the European Union.[14]

Back in the group headquarters at Bombay House, senior Tata leadership grew bitterly divided over how to proceed, with Chairman Cyrus Mistry pitted against his predecessor Ratan Tata, who had overseen the Corus and JLR acquisitions. The son of the largest individual shareholder in the group but not a member of the Tata family, Mistry began his term in 2012 with the goal of reconfiguring the group's strategy to stay competitive and relevant. For Mistry, this meant dealing with the "legacy hotspots" of Ratan's reign, chiefly the Corus albatross and the troubled Nano small car project, by downsizing and consolidating ("cutting the flab") if necessary. Ratan promised to give Mistry room to breathe as he took charge of the Tata Trusts, which still held 66 percent of the shares in the main holding company Tata Sons. Although legally prohibited from influencing the operation of the group, the trustees began to exercise behind-the-scenes pressure as they lost confidence in Mistry's performance. Ratan and his allies came to believe that under Mistry, "the drive towards profit was overpowering the aim to build the institution" of the group, which remained "reputationally and financially very important to India."

The conflict culminated in Mistry's shock dismissal in October 2016 and a protracted legal battle to remove him from the boards of individual Tata companies.[15]

The ensuing public scandal severely tarnished the group's reputation, while bringing its history into sharp focus. Mistry's allegations of undue interference and insider trading by the trusts led to an investigation by the income tax authorities. Sounding remarkably like an anti-corporate activist, Mistry argued that "the Trusts belong to the people and must be administered by the government." The trustees defended themselves using the logic of the market, pointing to their fiduciary obligation to ensure the "value" of their stake in the holding company Tata Sons "didn't go down" through mismanagement.[16] Exposing the blurred boundaries between philanthropy and economy, the conflict reflected widespread global anxieties about the power and influence of big foundations bankrolled by the super-rich, or "philanthrocapitalism."[17] The very arrangement that lay at the heart of Tata's distinct ethos led to a breakdown in corporate governance. It was no longer clear, if it ever was, who called the shots in the group: Tata Sons, the trusts, or the shareholders of the companies?

The scandal also called Tata's nation-building character into question. The Parsi businessman Nusli Wadia, an erstwhile close friend of Ratan turned key ally of Mistry, emphatically stated that "it is not the role of your company to save jobs in the UK nor to support its pension funds" but to seek out "the most profitable growth opportunities which are quite obviously better served by investing in India." For Ratan, the group could neither go back on its commitments to the British government, which would not be consistent with the Tata ethos, nor give up its hard-won global foothold. Wadia played the nationalist card in response, claiming that it was "ironic that the founder Jamsetji Tata started Tata Steel to fight British steel and now Ratan Tata is trying to save British steel by deploying huge resources at the cost of Tata Steel India."[18] The internecine family disputes between Dorabji and R. D. Tata over foreign expansion in the aftermath of the 1920–1921 crisis reappeared in new guises. No longer kept secret, they were splashed onto the front pages of the newspapers and endlessly replayed on 24/7 television channels, Twitter threads, and blog posts.[19] As before, the nation-state and domestic markets offered a safe haven from the unforgiving winds of globalization. At the time of writing, the unprecedented worldwide economic contraction caused by the COVID-19 pandemic is likely to push Tata even deeper within the borders of the nation.[20]

A Fading Utopia

Even as its future grows more precarious, the group's past continues to matter greatly. When the Corus deal was first announced in 2007, the Tatas were introduced to the British public as representatives of a unique "brand of caring capitalism." Workers who felt "nervous" at the prospect of the takeover were told they "need look no further than Jamshedpur" to realize they had nothing to fear.[21] A 2015 British Broadcasting Corporation (BBC) radio and television documentary presented by Zareer Masani, Minoo Masani's son, promised to unlock the secrets of Tata by recounting a familiar history of ethical business practice: "This concept of a benevolent employer caring for its employees' needs and for the wider community, a virtual state within the state, has made Tata a household name for trust and integrity across the Indian subcontinent."[22]

At first sight, the view from Jamshedpur appeared less gloomy than the view from Port Talbot. After 1991, Tata Steel downsized nearly half its permanent workforce in the name of global competitiveness, ended the guarantee of employment to family members, and scaled back spending on civic and welfare amenities. Yet the "historical languages of paternalism," never abandoned despite the turn to scientific management, proved resilient enough to legitimize the mass casualization of labor.[23] Affluent middle-class residents continued to enjoy municipal services of much higher quality than the rest of the country. Indeed, it is commonly said Jamshedpur is one of the few cities in India where one can drink water straight from the tap. The decision to spin off the Town Division into a separate company, the Jamshedpur Utilities and Services Corporation (JUSCO), was hailed by the business press as a model for how private companies can deliver "world-class" urban services.[24] But pockets of misery amid plenty remained, markers of entrenched spatial segregation and the fragmented sovereignty of the company dating back to the colonial period. The lack of democratic self-government served as a lightning rod of criticism and claims making from below.

Local activist Jawaharlal Sharma, the son of an ex-TISCO employee, took up the cause of the *bastis* (slums or informal settlements) where low-caste workers lived in precarious conditions. The irregular distribution of municipal services by the company and the exclusion of *bastis* from the leasehold area violated their basic rights without redress in the absence of an elected municipality. After the publication of TISCO's first voluntary social audit in 1980, Mr. Sharma initiated a correspondence with Chairman J. R. D. Tata on various issues missing from the audit, including electricity, sanitation, housing, health care, pollution, and corruption among contractors. Appealing to J. R. D. both as a rights-bearing subject to a sovereign authority and through the language of paternalism, he invoked the fictive kinship of the steel company as one big multigenerational family: "In fact I consider myself as a TISCO SON [sic]." More importantly, he fought to resurrect the broader utopian possibilities of the social audit, which JP Narayan and the Gandhians had once advocated as a transformative measure. He accused the chairman of not making "any effort to give share holdership to workers, businessman, and common people of the society," which would "full fill [sic] the dream of the great founder J. N. Tata's view of trusteeship."[25]

Repeatedly rebuffed and ignored by the company, Mr. Sharma turned to the courts. In 1988, he filed and won a public interest litigation (PIL) in the Supreme Court, arguing that the Constitution guaranteed a "third vote" (for local as well as state and national government) to every citizen. Before the court could implement the order, middle-class residents rose in protest against what they perceived as the needless surrender of the best-run city in India to a lawless and corrupt Bihar state government. Tata Steel launched an extensive public relations campaign playing on and amplifying their fears. One thirteen-year-old girl simply stated, "If we get a municipality here, there will be mosquitos and dirt."[26] Buoyed by a wave of public support, the company won a stay order against the notification in the Patna High Court. Mr. Sharma expressed both sadness and genuine surprise at the attitude of his fellow citizens: *"Jamshedpur mein kya* slavery mind *mein hai* (What slavery of the mind there is in Jamshedpur). . . . People said, 'I don't want my rights.'"[27] Yet, he continued his fight as investigative journalists published exposés of life in Jamshedpur, uncovering data on air and water quality, giving poorer residents a voice, and keeping the spotlight on his legal cases.[28] In 2019, after another round of petitions and appeals to the Jharkhand High Court, the state government agreed to formally designate Jamshedpur as an "industrial township."[29] Exploiting a loophole in Article 243Q of the Constitution, originally designed to facilitate the creation of special economic zones (SEZs), this compromise enabled Tata Steel to retain substantial administrative powers and deny the residents of Jamshedpur their right to a "third vote."[30] For Mr. Sharma, it is no substitute for a democratically elected municipality, but it may represent the end of the road.

Elsewhere in India, Tata companies faced more overt resistance as they rapidly expanded in the wake of liberalization. In 1996, Tata Steel first attempted to establish a second integrated steel plant in Gopalpur, Orissa. As tensions

over worker buyouts rose, union politics took a violent turn with the assassination of a veteran Tata Workers' Union leader (allegedly by members of a
rival faction). Senior management hoped to wipe the slate clean and start over,
building a "new corporate culture" with a plant staffed by Jamshedpur's "cream
of the crop." But Gopalpur was a poor choice of location. Land could only be
acquired by force and displaced villagers mobilized in protest. The project was
eventually abandoned, but the company did not learn from its mistakes. At
the next proposed site in Kalinganagar, also in Orissa, twelve *adivasis* (aboriginals / tribals) were killed and thirty-seven injured in a police firing in
2006.[31] That same year, at Singur in West Bengal, fierce protests over land
acquisition stalled a proposed Tata Motors plant to manufacture the innovative Nano, a miniature, low-cost "people's car." The project shifted to Gujarat,
the Tatas' ancestral homeland, following a generous offer of land and tax concessions by then–chief minister and future prime minister Narendra Modi.
Echoing J. R. D.'s support of Indira Gandhi's push for growth during the
Emergency, Ratan Tata praised Modi as a "visionary" leader and "an extremely
easy person to deal with."[32]

These incidents were portrayed in business-friendly literature as rare blem-
ishes on Tata's stellar record of business ethics, or blamed on the political
machinations of "vested interests."[33] Critics viewed them as predictable out-
comes of the untrammeled forward march of exploitative capitalism, aided and
abetted by a repressive state apparatus.[34] Surprisingly, the critical view even
made its way into popular culture. In Prakash Jha's *Chakravyuh* (2012), a mainstream Bollywood film depicting Naxalite Maoist insurgents in the tribal
belt, Tata featured along with Birla and Ambani in a controversial song accusing corporations of exploiting the nation for their own benefit and fueling
their "engine" with the blood of the common man.[35] Reflecting on the group's
vulnerable public image, some old Tata hands detected a creeping malaise
within company culture. One former insider argued that, unlike the generation of Russi Mody and J. R. D. Tata, senior leadership was afraid to go into
communities and persuade them of the benefits industrial projects can bring.
With more of a "personal touch," perhaps Tata would have been welcomed in
Singur and Kalinganagar.[36]

Such declinist narratives are compelling but obscure profound structural
changes in Indian and global capitalism. Direct territorial control through
"village adoption" in the 1960s and 1970s gave way to professionalization and
devolution through nongovernmental organization partnerships and the use
of rigorous quantitative metrics. The emphasis on individual empowerment

through income generation and access to markets has a less pedagogical and disciplinary tone than earlier interventions to "uplift" rural populations but serves as a convenient justification to evade the cost burden of direct service provision.[37] As steelmaking has become increasingly automated, the aspirations of displaced villagers for upward mobility through factory employment can no longer be met. Tata and other companies in eastern India sponsor skills-building and job placement programs in retail or construction, often with little success.[38] This is consistent with CSR practices in extractive industries around the world, from the oil fields of Argentina to the diamond mines of South Africa. Rather than fulfilling its stated aim of helping individuals become "self-sufficient people, autonomous from the company," CSR generates new relationships of interdependence and moral obligation that sustain corporate power and legitimacy in different ways.[39]

Back in Jamshedpur, Tata Steel managers draw on a deep reservoir of goodwill and trust when they link the town's fate with the steel company's profitability. But in the same breath, they raise the specter of Detroit as a possible alternative future, as if to say, *Après nous, le déluge.*[40] The company decisively moved away from a "Jamshedpur-centric model" once the Kalinganagar plant opened in 2015. Proprietary townships with full provision of municipal services were never meant to be replicated at future sites.[41] Some activists and critics believe that Jamshedpur itself will cease to be a space of production within a decade or so, proving useful to Tata Steel only for speculation in land.[42] Jamshedpur is arguably no longer the crown jewel of industrial modernity in India, just another place where a shrinking, specialized workforce makes steel. But it is still standing and has not yet become another charismatic ruin of deindustrialization like Detroit and its ill-fated Amazonian outpost Fordlandia, which receded into the jungle along with the memory of the prosperity and progress it was meant to bring.[43] No matter if or when the factory gates shut, Jamshedpur will continue to exercise enormous symbolic power as an embodiment of the promises and disappointments of capitalism. As the humble typist A. Gowtama Rao once foresaw, "in eras and eons to come it is given for Jamshedpur to bear the fervid testimony of the stature of our material civilization."[44]

Appendix

List of Estates and Lands (undated, probably 1904–1905)

Note: Monetary value is expressed as rupee/anna/paisa, with one anna equal to 1/16 of one rupee and one paisa equal to 1/64 of one rupee.

EXECUTORS OF THE LATE MR. J. N. TATA

Elphinstone Estate Godown (14,170/1/9)

Coorla Chawl (5,455/8/9)

Navsari House (8,028/10/9)

Government Land at Navsari (5,394/12/9)

Danti Land at Navsari (6,711/1/3)

Dadar Lands (22,212/5/-)

Anik Gam (70,899/6/3)

Nasik Lands (3,735/13/9)

Dumas Bungalow (12, 931/-/-)

Punchgani Lands & Bungalow (51,319/3/11)

"Harrow on the Hill" Ootacamund (33,020/5/9)

Jew Property (26,867/8/1)

Maher Property (31,093/10/3)

Silk Factory (14,707/4/1)

Bangalore Bush Farm (11,073/5/1)

Mahi Lands (10,743/10/-)

Coorla Dongi Agar (33,659/7/3)

Anik Gam Tanks etc. (50, 000 / - / -)

Matunga Lands (208,223 / 5 / 7)

Khar Road Property (22,155 / 5 / 8)

Bandora Estate (333,356 / 11 / -)

Mody Bay Stables (1,509 / 9 / 2)

Wellington Lines Plot No. 14 (103,280 / 15 / 11)

Coran Lands (2,625 / 5 / 9)

Marole Lands (5,137 / 15 / 2)

Daroli Lands (2,628 / 6 / 11)

Naru Agar (1,722 / 11 / 2)

Sion Lands (9,806 / 11 / 7)

Versava Lands (794 / 8 / 9)

Dharavi Lands (26,648 / 15 / 4)

Naigam Lands (2,210 / 9 / 8)

Mount Villas (70,979 / 2 / 3)

Worlee & Sirree Property (Girdharidas Ganshamdas) (139,666 / 9 / -)

TATA SETTLEMENT NO. I

Bellair (142,100 / 9 / 1)

Belle Vue (49,456 / 8 / -)

Panorama House (94,194 / 8 / 6)

Round Ice House (52,857 / 12 / -)

Parel Tank Road Chawl (83,486 / 7 / 3)

Esplanade House (563,395 / - / -)

alterations etc. (65,623 / 6 / 2)

Navsari Family House (25,000 / - / -)

Land at Chinchpugly Bungalow No. 25 (41,419 / 7 / 3)

TATA SETTLEMENT NO. 2

Jubilee Buildings (139,702 / 13 / -)

Albion Terrace Ferzandari Land (760,111 / 14 / -)

Vacant Land at Wagheshri (108,156 / 15 / 9)

Chawl Land at Wagheshri (6,217 / 11 / 6)

MESSRS. R. D. TATA & R. J. TATA

Plot No. 70 Building Hornby Rd. (28,935 / 15 / 5)

Plot No. 74 Building Hornby Rd. (29,127 / 10 / 1)

Navsari Building (424,699 / 1 / -)

MR. R. J. TATA

Plot No. 16/17 Wellington Lines (106,485 / 14 / 5)

Plot No. 19/20 Wellington Lines (25,933 / 15 / 2)

Santa Cruz Bungalow (21,776 / 14 / 7)

Poona Bungalow (10,651 / 7 / -)

Matheran Bungalow (28,924 / 6 / 3)

Navsari Vajifa & Menageri (41,653 / 14 / 10)

THE BOMBAY UNITED BUILDING CO. LTD.

Arthur House Wellington Lines No. 5 (115,000 / - / -)

Wellesley House Wellington Lines No. 6 (135,770 / - / -)

Grey Lands Marine Lines No. 2 (54,100 / - / -)

Red Lands Marine Lines No. 6 (54,100 / - / -)

Bright Lands Marine Lines No. 5 (63,500/-/-)

Colaba Causeway Plot No. 11C (92,508/-/10)

THE INDIAN HOTELS CO. LTD.

Taj Mahal Hotel (2,894,574/15/8)

Wellington Mews (359,174/5/2)

Greens Mansions (383,617/11/9)

Source: Tata Central Archives, Fire-Proof File No. 8 (FP8).

Notes

Archive Abbreviations

AA   Architectural Association Archives, London
IOR   India Office Records, British Library, London
LSE   London School of Economics Archives
MSA   Maharashtra State Archives, Mumbai
NAI   National Archives of India, New Delhi
NARA   National Archives and Records Administration, College Park, Maryland
NMML   Nehru Memorial Museum and Library, New Delhi
TCA   Tata Central Archives, Pune
TIFR   Tata Institute of Fundamental Research Archives, Mumbai
TNA   The National Archives, Kew
TSA   Tata Steel Archives, Jamshedpur

Introduction

1. TCA, TS-2004-NO-03-VOL-38-MAR-PG-07; Arundhati Roy, "Capitalism: A Ghost Story," *Outlook,* March 26, 2012.

2. Richard Eaton, *The Rise of Islam and the Bengal Frontier, 1204–1760* (Berkeley: University of California Press, 1993), 162–164.

3. Aman Nath and Jay Vithalani, with Tulsi Vatsal, *Horizons: The Tata-India Century, 1904–2004* (Mumbai: India Book House, 2005), 337.

4. Gjertje Baars and André Spicer, "Introduction: Why the Corporation?," in *The Corporation: A Critical, Multi-Disciplinary Handbook,* ed. Gjertje Baars and André Spicer (Cambridge: Cambridge University Press, 2017), 1–5; Shoshana Zuboff, *The Age of Surveillance Capitalism: The Fight for a Human Future at the New Frontier of Power* (New York: Public Affairs, 2019); Barbara Freese, *Industrial-Strength Denial: Eight Stories of Corporations Defending the Indefensible, from the Slave Trade to Climate Change* (Berkeley: University of California Press, 2020).

5. James Crabtree, *The Billionaire Raj: A Journey through India's New Gilded Age* (New York: Crown/Tim Duggan Books, 2018), 8–15; Lucas Chancel and Thomas Piketty, "Indian Income Inequality, 1922–2015: From British Raj to Billionaire Raj?," *Review of Income and Wealth* 65, no. S1 (November 2019): S33–S62.

6. Joseph Schumpeter, "The Process of Creative Destruction," in *The Entrepreneur: Classic Texts by Joseph A. Schumpeter,* ed. Markus C. Becker, Thorbjørn Knudsen, and Richard Swedberg (Stanford, CA: Stanford University Press, 2011), 313–319.

7. Data for 1931 taken from Claude Markovits, *Indian Business and Nationalist Politics 1931–1939: The Indigenous Capitalist Class and the Rise of the Congress Party* (Cambridge: Cambridge University Press, 1985), appendix 1, 190. For 1958, see R. K. Hazari, *The Structure of the Corporate Private Sector: A Study of Concentration, Ownership and Control* (Bombay: Asia Publishing House, 1966), 17. For 1991 and after, see Gita Piramal, "Big Business and Entrepreneurship," *Seminar* 528 (August 2003); J. Dennis Rajakumar and John S. Henley, "Growth and Persistence of Large Business Groups in India," *Journal of Comparative International Management* 10, no. 1 (2007): 13–16.

8. Andrew Ross, *Fast Boat to China: High-Tech Outsourcing and the Consequences of Free Trade* (New York: Vintage, 2007), 138.

9. Claude Markovits, "The Tata Paradox," in *Merchants, Traders, Entrepreneurs: Indian Business in the Colonial Era* (London: Palgrave Macmillan, 2008), 152–157; Amiya Bagchi, "Multiculturalism, Governance, and the Indian Bourgeoisie," in *Capital and Labour Redefined: India and the Third World* (London: Anthem Press, 2002), 309–316; Tirthankar Roy, *Company of Kinsmen: Enterprise and Community in South Asian History, 1700–1940* (New Delhi: Oxford University Press, 2010), 111–114.

10. Omkar Goswami, *Goras and Desis: Managing Agencies and the Making of Corporate India* (Gurgaon: Penguin Random House, 2016); Blair Kling, "The Origins of the Managing Agency System in India," in *Entrepreneurship and Industry in India, 1800–1947,* ed. Rajat Kanta Ray (New Delhi: Oxford University Press, 1992); Maria Misra, *Business, Race and Politics in British India* (Oxford: Clarendon Press, 1999); Gijsbert Oonk, "Motor or Millstone? The Managing Agency System in Bombay and Ahmedabad, 1850–1930," *Indian Economic and Social History Review* 38, no. 4 (2001): 419–452.

11. Gareth Austin, Carlos Dávila, and Geoffrey Jones, "The Alternative Business History: Business in Emerging Markets," *Business History Review* 91, no. 3 (2017): 563–564; Patrick Fridenson and Kikkawa Takeo, eds., *Ethical Capitalism: Shibusawa Eiichi and Business Leadership in Global Perspective* (Toronto: University of Toronto Press, 2017).

12. Octavio Paz, *In Light of India,* trans. Eliot Weinberger (New York: Harvest, 1995), 7–8; Simin Patel, "Cultural Intermediaries in a Colonial City: The Parsis

of Bombay, c. 1860–1921" (DPhil thesis, Balliol College, University of Oxford, 2015), 115–117, 158–160; Vibhuti Patel, "The Other Taj," *The Hindu*, October 29, 2011.

13. Markovits, *Indian Business and Nationalist Politics*, 19–21, 35, 127. Because the Tata Iron and Steel Company (TISCO) was heavily dependent on government orders for rails in its early years, tariff policy has been the major area of analysis. See Amiya Kumar Bagchi, *Private Investment in India 1900–1939* (Cambridge: Cambridge University Press, 1972), 5; Vinay Bahl, *The Making of the Indian Working Class: A Case of the Tata Iron and Steel Company, 1880–1946* (New Delhi: Sage, 1995), 36–39.

14. Sven Beckert, *Empire of Cotton: A Global History* (New York: Knopf, 2014), 418–423; Charles A. Jones, *International Business in the Nineteenth Century: The Rise and Fall of a Cosmopolitan Bourgeoisie* (Brighton, UK: Wheatsheaf Books, 1987), 85–86.

15. Austin, Davíla, and Jones, "Alternative Business History," 539–544, 554–555; Kevin Hjortshøj O'Rourke and Jeffrey G. Williamson, introduction to *The Spread of Modern Industry to the Periphery since 1871* (Oxford: Oxford University Press, 2017), 1–12.

16. Robert Vitalis, *When Capitalists Collide: Business Conflict and the End of Empire in Egypt* (Berkeley: University of California Press, 1995), xi–xvi, 10–11, 21–23; Sherene Seikaly, *Men of Capital: Scarcity and Economy in Mandate Palestine* (Stanford, CA: Stanford University Press, 2016), 8–11.

17. Carter J. Eckert, *Offspring of Empire: The Koch'ang Kims and the Colonial Origins of Korean Capitalism, 1876–1945* (Seattle: University of Washington Press, 2014), xii–xviii, 58–67, 125–126.

18. Brett Sheehan, *Industrial Eden: A Chinese Capitalist Vision* (Cambridge, MA: Harvard University Press, 2015), 1–15.

19. Markovits, "The Tata Paradox," 159–163.

20. TCA, FP29A/II/JN Tata Obituaries and Press Clippings, copy of translation of an extract from the monthly magazine *Udyam* for the month of October 1930.

21. Steven Press, *Rogue Empires: Contracts and Conmen in Europe's Scramble for Africa* (Cambridge, MA: Harvard University Press, 2017), 7–8; William Dalrymple, *The Anarchy: The East India Company, Corporate Violence, and the Pillage of an Empire* (London: Bloomsbury, 2019); Steve Coll, *Private Empire: Exxon-Mobil and American Power* (New York: Penguin Books, 2012).

22. Joshua Barkan, *Corporate Sovereignty: Law and Government under Capitalism* (Minneapolis: University of Minnesota Press, 2013), 4.

23. Philip J. Stern, *The Company-State: Corporate Sovereignty and the Early Modern Foundations of the British Empire in India* (New York: Oxford University Press, 2011), 6, 208–213; Julia Adams, *The Familial State: Ruling Families and Merchant*

Capitalism in Early Modern Europe (Ithaca, NY: Cornell University Press, 2005), 20–21, 58.

24. Gayatri Chakravorty Spivak, *A Critique of Postcolonial Reason: Toward a History of the Vanishing Present* (Cambridge, MA: Harvard University Press, 1999), 220–222. I thank Alejandra Azuero-Quijano for this reference.

25. Manu Goswami, *Producing India: From Colonial Economy to National Space* (Chicago: University of Chicago Press, 2004), 7–19.

26. M. G. Ranade, "Indian Political Economy," in *Essays on Indian Economics* (Madras: G. A. Natesan, 1920), 31.

27. Markovits, "The Tata Paradox," 158.

28. Andrew Sartori, "Global Intellectual History and the History of Political Economy," in *Global Intellectual History*, ed. Samuel Moyn and Andrew Sartori (New York: Columbia University Press, 2013), 126–127. On "deglobalization," see Tirthankar Roy, *India in the World Economy: From Antiquity to Present* (Cambridge: Cambridge University Press, 2012), 224–231.

29. Ritu Birla, "Vernacular Capitalists and the Modern Subject in India: Law, Cultural Politics, and Market Ethics," in *Ethical Life in South Asia*, ed. Daud Ali and Anand Pandian (Bloomington: Indiana University Press, 2010), 83–100.

30. Sandra Halperin, "Nationalism Reconsidered: The Local / Trans-Local Nexus of Globalisation," *Studies in Ethnicity and Nationalism* 9, no. 3 (2009): 466–476.

31. Karl Polanyi, *The Great Transformation: The Political and Economic Origins of Our Time* (Boston: Beacon, 1957), 10–12.

32. William G. Roy, *Socializing Capital: The Rise of the Large Industrial Corporation in America* (Princeton, NJ: Princeton University Press, 1997), 12–13.

33. Ida M. Tarbell, *The History of the Standard Oil Company*, vol. 1 (New York: McClure, Phillips, 1904), vii–viii.

34. Chinmay Tumbe, "Recent Trends in the Business History of India," *Business History Review* 93 (2019): 153–159; Medha Kudaisya, "Mercantile Communities, Business and State in Twentieth-Century India: State of the Field," *South Asia: Journal of South Asian Studies* 39, no. 1 (2016): 262–270; Tirthankar Roy, *A Business History of India: Enterprise and the Emergence of Capitalism from 1700* (Cambridge: Cambridge University Press, 2018), 1–20.

35. Interview with archivist, Tata Central Archives, Pune, January 15, 2014; Priyanka Sangani, "At Tatas, Sage Advice an Archival Inheritance," *Economic Times,* February 18, 2017.

36. Dinah Rajak, "Corporate Memory: Historical Revisionism, Legitimation and the Invention of Tradition in a Multinational Mining Company," *PoLAR: Political and Legal Anthropology Review* 37, no. 2 (November 2014): 259–260.

37. Jones, *International Business in the Nineteenth Century,* 24.

38. Arun Kumar, "Making History: Archives, Historiography, and Their Silences," Best Paper, CMS Division, *Academy of Management Proceedings* no. 1 (2016): 1–3.

39. Kudaisya, "Mercantile Communities, Business and State," 265–266; Ritu Birla, *Stages of Capital: Law, Culture, and Market Governance in Late Colonial India* (Durham, NC: Duke University Press, 2009), 24–27.

40. Purnima Bose and Laura E. Lyons, "Introduction: Toward a Critical Corporate Studies," in *Cultural Critique and the Global Corporation,* ed. Purnima Bose and Laura E. Lyons (Bloomington: Indiana University Press, 2010), 3–9.

41. See, inter alia, R. M. Lala, *The Creation of Wealth: The Tatas from the 19th to the 21st Century* (New Delhi: Penguin, 2006), *For the Love of India: The Life and Times of Jamsetji Tata* (New Delhi: Penguin, 2004), *Beyond the Last Blue Mountain: A Life of J. R. D. Tata* (New Delhi: Penguin, 2003), *The Romance of Tata Steel* (New Delhi: Penguin, 2007); Rudrangshu Mukherjee, *A Century of Trust: The Story of Tata Steel* (New Delhi: Penguin, 2008); Philip Chacko and Christabelle Noronha, *Salt of the Earth: The Story of Tata Chemicals* (Chennai: Westland, 2014); Harish Bhat, *Tata Log: Eight Modern Stories from a Timeless Institution* (New Delhi: Penguin, 2012); Morgen Witzel, *Tata: The Evolution of a Corporate Brand* (New Delhi: Penguin, 2010); Peter Casey, *The Greatest Company in the World? The Story of Tata* (New Delhi: Penguin, 2014); Shashank Shah, *The Tata Group: From Torchbearers to Trailblazers* (New Delhi: Penguin, 2018); Girish Kuber, *The Tatas: How a Family Built a Business and a Nation* (Noida: HarperCollins India, 2019).

42. Ann Stoler, *Along the Archival Grain: Epistemic Anxieties and Colonial Common Sense* (Princeton, NJ: Princeton University Press, 2009), 20.

43. Emma Rothschild, "Arcs of Ideas: International History and Intellectual History," in *Transnationale Geschichte: Themen, Tendenzen und Theorien,* ed. Gunilla Budde, Sebastian Conrad and Oliver Janz (Göttingen, Germany: Vandenhoeck & Ruprecht, 2006), 224–225.

44. Jeffrey R. Fear, "Constructing Big Business: The Cultural Concept of the Firm," in *Big Business and the Wealth of Nations,* ed. Alfred D. Chandler Jr., Franco Amatori, and Takashi Hikino (Cambridge: Cambridge University Press, 1997), 561–569.

45. Marina Welker, *Enacting the Corporation: An American Mining Firm in Post-Authoritarian Indonesia* (Berkeley: University of California Press, 2014), 1–4.

1. Becoming Swadeshi

1. D. E. Wacha, *The Life and Life-Work of J. N. Tata,* 2nd ed. (Madras: Ganesh, 1915), 4, 16–17; F. R. Harris, *Jamsetji Nusserwanji Tata: A Chronicle of His Life,* 2nd ed. (London: Blackie, 1958), 9–10.

2. Sven Beckert, *Empire of Cotton: A Global History* (New York: Knopf, 2014), 272–273.

3. Max Weber, *General Economic History*, trans. Frank H. Knight (New York: Collier Books, 1961), 260–264. Midcentury sociologists did go on to ascribe Weberian "industrial rationality" to the Parsis, deriving it from the "abstract values" of the Zoroastrian religion. See Robert Kennedy, "The Protestant Ethic and the Parsis," *American Journal of Sociology* 68, no. 1 (July 1962): 11–20.

4. Wacha, *Life and Life-Work of J. N. Tata*, 8.

5. Claude Markovits, *Indian Business and Nationalist Politics 1931–1939: The Indigenous Capitalist Class and the Rise of the Congress Party* (Cambridge: Cambridge University Press, 1985), 75–76, 189; Beckert, *Empire of Cotton*, 423. By contrast, smaller marketeers and traders consistently backed the Congress and were said to constitute the real "national bourgeoisie" (see Chapter 4). A. D. D. Gordon, *Businessmen and Politics: Rising Nationalism and a Modernising Economy in Bombay, 1918–1933*, Australian National University Monographs on South Asia No. 3 (Delhi: Manohar, 1978), 1.

6. Amiya Kumar Bagchi, *Private Investment in India 1900–1939* (Cambridge: Cambridge University Press, 1972); Rajat Kanta Ray, *Industrialization in India: Growth and Conflict in the Private Corporate Sector, 1914–47* (Delhi: Oxford University Press, 1979); Morris David Morris, "Indian Industry and Business in the Age of *Laissez Faire*," in *Entrepreneurship and Industry in India, 1800–1947*, ed. Rajat Kanta Ray (Delhi: Oxford University Press, 1992), 197–227.

7. How these trading companies became "something of a side-show in relation to the firm's manufacturing ventures" remains unexplored. Claude Markovits, "The Tata Paradox," in *Merchants, Traders, Entrepreneurs: Indian Business in the Colonial Era* (London: Palgrave Macmillan, 2008), 157. See also Sunil Kumar Sen, *The House of Tata, 1839–1939* (Calcutta: Progressive Publishers, 1975), 9.

8. Gordon, *Businessmen and Politics*, 2–3; Thomas A. Timberg, *The Marwaris: From Jagat Seth to the Birlas* (New Delhi: Penguin / Allen Lane, 2014).

9. Ritu Birla, *Stages of Capital: Law, Culture, and Market Governance in Late Colonial India* (Durham, NC: Duke University Press, 2009), 19–20, 166–176.

10. Tirthankar Roy, *Company of Kinsmen: Enterprise and Community in South Asian History, 1700–1940* (New Delhi: Oxford University Press, 2010), 117–120, 129.

11. Ross Bassett, *The Technological Indian* (Cambridge, MA: Harvard University Press, 2016), 8–10, 49–55.

12. TCA, FP30, Some Side-Lights and Reminiscences of Late Mr. J. N. Tata by Jamshedji E. Saklatvala, 7; T53-DES-T20-IMPORTANT-EXTRACTS-DHARAVI-2, Note on Tata History, August 1910.

13. IOR E/4/841, India Office Financial Department to Governor-General in Council, January 28, 1857. Bushire was the most important port city in the Persian Gulf. As a point of connection between the long-distance maritime and

overland caravan trades, it became a strategic target for the East India Company. Willem Floor, "Bushehr: Southern Gateway to Iran," in *The Persian Gulf in Modern Times: People, Ports, and History,* ed. Lawrence G. Potter (London: Palgrave Macmillan, 2014), 182–187.

14. Harris, *Jamsetji Nusserwanji Tata,* 2–6.

15. Tirthankar Roy, "Trading Firms in Colonial India," *Business History Review* 88, no. 1 (2014): 18–19.

16. Sanjay Subrahmanyam and C. A. Bayly, "Portfolio Capitalists and the Political Economy of Early Modern India," *Indian Economic and Social History Review* 25, no, 4 (December 1988): 401–424.

17. Richard J. Grace, *Opium and Empire: The Lives and Careers of William Jardine and James Matheson* (Montreal: McGill-Queen's University Press, 2014), 339–343.

18. Asiya Siddiqi, "The Business World of Jamsetjee Jeejeebhoy," *Indian Economic and Social History Review* 19, nos. 3 and 4 (1982): 301–324; Madhavi Thampi and Shalini Saksena, *China and the Making of Bombay* (Mumbai: K. R. Cama Institute, 2009), 28–29, 59; Jesse Palsetia, *The Parsis of India: Preservation of Identity in Bombay City* (Leiden, the Netherlands: Brill, 2001), 52–57; Charles A. Jones, *International Business in the Nineteenth Century: The Rise and Fall of a Cosmopolitan Bourgeoisie* (Brighton, UK: Wheatsheaf Books, 1987), 48–55, 80–82.

19. Christine Dobbin, *Urban Leadership in Western India: Politics and Communities in Bombay City, 1840–1885* (Oxford: Oxford University Press, 1972), 16–19.

20. Rusheed R. Wadia, "Bombay Parsi Merchants in the Eighteenth and Nineteenth Centuries," in *Parsis in India and the Diaspora,* ed. John R. Hinnells and Alan Williams (Abingdon, UK: Routledge, 2008), 124–128; Roy, *Company of Kinsmen,* 113–114.

21. Siddiqi, "Business World of Jamsetjee Jeejeebhoy," 323–324.

22. TNA, C 16/290/N34, *Narrondas, J. N. Tata et al. v. Springfield* (1865), Bill of Complaint.

23. Originally from the small town of Bisau in Rajasthan, Cheniram Jesraj started one of the few Marwari trading firms in Bombay in 1880. The majority settled in Calcutta. Thomas A. Timberg, "Three Types of the Marwari Firm," *Indian Economic and Social History Review* 10, no. 1 (January 1973): 18.

24. Jairus Banaji, "Seasons of Self-Delusion: Opium, Capitalism and the Financial Markets," *Historical Materialism* 21, no. 2 (2013): 3–9.

25. Harris, *Jamsetji Nusserwanji Tata,* 6–7.

26. For a reassessment of Premchand Roychand's life and career, see Lakshmi Subramanian, *Three Merchants of Bombay: Doing Business in Times of Change* (New Delhi: Penguin/Allen Lane, 2012), chapter 4.

27. Harris, *Jamsetji Nusserwanji Tata,* 10–11.

28. IOR, L/MIL/17/17/38, *Report from the Select Committee on the Abyssinian Expedition* (1870), v–xx. I thank Claude Markovits for this reference.

29. See, for example, "The Ugly Face of Tata," International Campaign for Justice in Bhopal, February 20, 2007, https://www.bhopal.net/the-ugly-face-of-tata/; Arun Kumar, "Making History: Archives, Historiography, and Their Silences," Best Paper, CMS Division, *Academy of Management Proceedings* no. 1 (2016): 4.

30. Harris, *Jamsetji Nusserwanji Tata,* 12–13; Sen, *House of Tata,* 8–9.

31. Hong Kong Legislative Council No. 21, March 25, 1887, https://www.legco.gov .hk/1886–87/h870325.pdf.

32. Tirthankar Roy, "Embracing the World: Parsis after the China Trade," in *Across Oceans and Flowing Silks: From Canton to Bombay 18th–20th Centuries,* ed. Pheroza J. Godrej and Firoza Phuntakey Mistree (Mumbai: Spenta Multimedia, 2013), 65–66.

33. Harris, *Jamsetji Nusserwanji Tata,* 38–39. The French established the first mechanized spinning mill in India at Pondicherry in the 1830s for this purpose, but it failed to stand up to British competition. Beckert, *Empire of Cotton,* 172.

34. Harris, *Jamsetji Nusserwanji Tata,* 52–59; TCA, T53-DES-T59S-MIS-NOTES-1, Notes on the History of the Swadeshi Mills.

35. NAI, Finance Department, Statistics and Commerce Branch, A Proceedings, Nos. 427–429 (September 1894), Protest by Messrs. Tata & Sons against any measure which will have the effect of imposing an excise duty on cotton goods produced in India.

36. Hiroshi Shimizu, "The Indian Merchants of Kobe and Japan's Trade Expansion into Southeast Asia before the Asian-Pacific War," *Japan Forum* 17, no. 1 (2005): 28–29.

37. Harris, *Jamsetji Nusserwanji Tata,* 92–95.

38. Harris, *Jamsetji Nusserwanji Tata,* 96–98; Sen, *House of Tata,* 24–25.

39. TCA, Box 539, T53/PRD/Old Records/Misc/7, Tata & Sons to the Editor of the *Indian Textile Journal,* February 21, 1894. The letter went on to point out that of the 15,700 bales of cotton shipped to Japan, only 5,300 belonged to Tata & Co.

40. M. G. Ranade, "Iron Industry—Pioneer Attempts," in *Essays on Indian Economics* (Madras: G. A. Natesan, 1920), 150–157.

41. Daniel R. Headrick, *The Tentacles of Progress: Technology Transfer in the Age of Imperialism, 1850–1940* (Oxford: Oxford University Press, 1988), 281–283, 294–298.

42. Tirthankar Roy, "Did Globalisation Aid Industrial Development in Colonial India? A Study of Knowledge Transfer in the Iron Industry," *Indian Economic and Social History Review* 46, no. 4 (2009): 580–581.

43. On Jamsetji's relationship with the early Congress, see Harris, *Jamsetji Nusser-wanji Tata*, 247–250. Apart from a single recorded donation of Rs. 500 in 1889, the precise extent of his financial support remains unknown. NAI, Dadabhai Naoroji Papers, J. N. Tata to Naoroji, November 27, 1889. I thank Dinyar Patel for providing me with a copy of this letter.

44. The Tata & Sons mining department kept a close eye on the progress of the Yawata works. TSA, Box 546, Appendices (1902), British Consular Report on the Capital Expenditure of the Imperial Japanese Government Iron Works.

45. TCA, T30/DES History Project 1, Naoroji to J. N. Tata, December 9, 1898.

46. Ranade, "Iron Industry," 170; Manu Goswami, *Producing India: From Colonial Economy to National Space* (Chicago: University of Chicago Press, 2004), 210–215.

47. Chikayoshi Nomura, *The House of Tata Meets the Second Industrial Revolution: An Institutional Analysis of Tata Iron and Steel Co. in Colonial India* (Singapore: Springer Nature, 2018), 41.

48. TCA, FP, J. N. Tata-Dadabhai Naoroji Correspondence, Naoroji to J. N. Tata, September 16, 1902.

49. NAI, Dadabhai Naoroji Papers, J. N. Tata to Naoroji, September 19, 1902. Courtesy of Dinyar Patel.

50. Barbara Ramusack, *The Indian Princes and Their States* (Cambridge: Cambridge University Press, 2004), 79–80, 186–187.

51. Bagchi, *Private Investment in India*, 213–215.

52. Sen, *House of Tata*, 38–39; Rudrangshu Mukherjee, *A Century of Trust: The Story of Tata Steel* (New Delhi: Penguin, 2008), 18–20.

53. Nomura, *House of Tata*, 75–78, 126–127.

54. Vinay Bahl, *The Making of the Indian Working Class: A Case of the Tata Iron and Steel Company, 1880–1946* (New Delhi: Sage, 1995), 72–73.

55. TCA, T30/DES History Project 2, B. J. Padshah to Bezonji Dadabhai, February 20, 1905.

56. Bagchi, *Private Investment in India*, 292–293. On racial barriers between British and Indian business, see also Maria Misra, *Business, Race and Politics in British India* (Oxford: Clarendon Press, 1999), and Amartya Sen, "The Pattern of British Enterprise in India 1854–1914: A Causal Analysis," in *Entrepreneurship and Industry in India, 1800–1947*, ed. Rajat Kanta Ray (Delhi: Oxford University Press, 1992), 117–118, 123–126.

57. John Gallagher and Ronald Robinson, "The Imperialism of Free Trade," *Economic History Review*, n.s., 6, no. 1 (1953): 1–15. On the geographical preferences of City of London financiers in this period, see P. J. Cain and A. G. Hopkins, "Gentlemanly Capitalism and British Expansion Overseas II: New Imperialism, 1850–1945," *Economic History Review*, n.s., 40, no. 1 (1987): 1–26.

58. TSA, File No. 93 (vii), R. D. Tata to Sassoon David, February 5, 1907.

59. TCA, Box 539, T53/PRD/Old Records of Various Companies/8/Tata Limited London, B. J. Padshah to R. D. Tata, March 15, 1907.

60. TCA, T30/DES History Project 2, Padshah to R. D. Tata, October 2, 1906.

61. TCA, FP41A, J. N. Tata to H. A. Crump, Secretary (Revenue Department) to the Chief Commissioner, Central Provinces, April 1, 1901.

62. TCA, T53-DES-T34-MINUTES-01, W. L. Harvey, Secretary to the Government of India, to Messrs. Tata & Sons, August 9, 1905; Bahl, *Making of the Indian Working Class*, 76–77.

63. NAI, Commerce & Industry Department, Geology and Minerals Branch, C Proceedings, No. 3 (November 1907), Note by J. F. Finlay, October 8, 1907.

64. TCA, T53-DES-T34-MINUTES-01, Minutes of Conference in London between Mr. Robert Miller, Managing Director, and Messrs. Tata, Perin and Weld, March 16, 1905; Sen, *House of Tata*, 38–39, 46.

65. Nomura, *House of Tata*, 104–105.

66. TCA, T53-DES-T34-MINUTES-01, Tata Iron and Steel Company (TISCO) Board Meeting, May 23, 1912.

67. TCA, T53-DES-T34-MINUTES-02, TISCO Board Meeting, April 27, 1916.

68. TCA, FP41, J. N. Tata to Richmond Ritchie, Secretary to Lord George Hamilton, May 10, 1901.

69. Sunila Kale, "Structures of Power: Electrification in Colonial India," *Comparative Studies of South Asia, Africa and the Middle East* 34, no. 3 (2014): 455–457; Pierre Lanthier, "L'électrification de Bombay avant 1920. Le projet de Jamsetji N. Tata," *Outre-Mers* 89, nos. 334–335 (2002): 216–217, 220.

70. TCA, FP41, Padshah to Tata & Sons, 21 December 1906; S. M. Rutnagur, *Electricity in India* (Bombay: Indian Textile Journal, 1912), 9–12.

71. Kale, "Structures of Power," 462–465.

72. TCA, T53-DES-T20-IMPORTANT-EXTRACTS-DHARAVI-1, C. F. De Nordwall to B. J. Padshah, December 1, 1904; Lanthier, "L'électrification de Bombay," 220.

73. TCA, T53-DES-T20-IMPORTANT-EXTRACTS-DHARAVI-2, Edward Miller to D. J. Tata, July 24, 1905; FP, B. J. Padshah Correspondence, R. D. Tata to Padshah, July 27, 1905.

74. TCA, T53-DES-T20-IMPORTANT-EXTRACTS-DHARAVI-2, Tata Sons & Co. to Bombay Hydro-Electric Syndicate, London, October 25, 1907; Bombay Hydro-Electric Syndicate to Tata Sons & Co., January 10, 1908.

75. TCA, T53-DES-T20-IMPORTANT-EXTRACTS-DHARAVI-2, Sakhawat Hussain, P.S. to the Ruler of Bhopal, to Tata Sons & Co., October 4, 1910.

76. TCA, T30/DES History Project 1, D. J. Tata to Lalubhai (Samaldas), July 5 (?), 1925.

77. Lanthier, "L'électrification de Bombay," 230–233.

78. TCA, T53-DES-TATA INDUSTRIAL BANK LTD-1, TISCO's Brief Resume of Mr. Burjorji Padshah's Career.

79. TCA, FP, D. J. Tata Correspondence, D. J. Tata to Padshah, August 11, 1905.

80. TCA, FP, B. J. Padshah Correspondence, Padshah to R. D. Tata, June 21, 1906.

81. Roy, *Company of Kinsmen*, 120.

82. TCA, T30/DES History Project 2, Padshah to R. D. Tata, August 24, 1906.

83. TCA, T30/DES History Project 2, Padshah to R. D. Tata, August 24, 1906.

84. TCA, Box 539, T53/PRD/Old Records/Misc/8, Padshah to R. D. Tata, March 15, 1907.

85. TSA, File No. 93 (i), Agents (Tata Sons), Bombay, to Tata Limited, London, June 27, 1907.

86. TCA, FP, D. J. Tata Correspondence, D. J. Tata to R. D. Tata, November 5, 1913. Meherbai came from an elite Parsi family. Her father Hormusji Bhabha was inspector general of education in the princely state of Mysore. See Geraldine Forbes, *Women in Modern India* (Cambridge: Cambridge University Press, 1996), 75–76.

87. TNA, MUN 4/512, B. B. Cubbitt, War Office, to India Office, December 20, 1916; H. O. Manse, Brig.-Gen., to Sir E. Moir, December 30, 1916.

88. TSA, Box 45, File No. 2, H. Treble to A. J. Bilimoria, January 6, 1916.

89. NAI, Indian Munitions Board (Chemicals & Minerals), A Proceedings, Nos. 1–86 (July 1919), File No. M.-375, C. A. Innes, Controller of Munitions, Madras, to R. D. Bell, Controller of Industrial Intelligence, June 28, 1918; TCA, T53-DES-T20-BO-2, Tata Hydro-Electric Power Company Board Meeting, October 28, 1915.

90. Bagchi, *Private Investment in India*, 303–306; Markovits, *Indian Business and Nationalist Politics*, 11–12.

91. TCA, T53-DES-T34-MINUTES-2, TISCO Board Meetings, October 18, 1917, August 15, 191(8?), November 7, 1918.

92. TSA, Box 45, File No. 2, Padshah to Treble, May 15, 1916.

93. Headrick, *Tentacles of Progress*, 291–292.

94. Nomura, *House of Tata*, 108–120.

95. MSA, Revenue No. 625, Pt. III (1919), Tata Sons to A. F. L. Brayne, Under Secretary to the Government of Bombay, Revenue Department, September 27, 1918; Tata Sons to P. J. Mead, Chief Secretary to the Government of Bombay, May 23, 1919.

96. MSA, Revenue No. 625, Pt. I (1919), J. W. Meares, Chief Engineer, Hydro-Electric Survey of India, to W. J. J. Howley, Chief Engineer, Public Works (Irrigation) Department, Madras Presidency, June 16, 1919; TCA, T53-DES-T20-TP-BO-1, Tata Power Company Board Meeting, November 19, 1920.

97. MSA, Revenue No. 625, Pt. II (1919), Thomas M. Ainscough, Trade Commissioner, to George Carmichael, Member of Council of the Governor of Bombay, July 18, 1918.

98. MSA, Revenue No. 625, Pt. III (1919), Tata Sons to A. F. L. Brayne, September 27, 1918; Tata Sons to P. J. Mead, May 23, 1919.

99. TSA, File No. 601(iii), Arrangement made with the General Electric Company in 1916, May 17, 1922.

100. NAI, Commerce & Industry (Industries), A Proceedings, Nos. 7–22 (July 1919), Note by A. H. Ley on the recommendations of the Indian Industrial Commission, September 18, 1918.

101. Clive Dewey, "The Government of India's 'New Industrial Policy,' 1900–1925: Formation and Failure," in *Economy and Society: Essays in Indian Economic and Social History*, ed. K. N. Chaudhuri and Clive Dewey (Delhi: Oxford University Press, 1979), 216–217, 221–231; Partha Sarathi Gupta, "State and Business in India in the Age of Discriminatory Protection, 1916–1939," in *Power, Politics and the People: Studies in British Imperialism and Indian Nationalism*, ed. Sabayasachi Bhattacharya (London: Anthem Press, 2002), 114–115, 126–127.

102. TCA, FP, B. J. Padshah Correspondence, Padshah to R. D. Tata, July 23, 1918.

103. TCA, FP, B. J. Padshah Correspondence, Padshah to R. D. Tata, July 23, 1918.

104. TCA, T53-DES-TATA INDUSTRIAL BANK LTD-1, Resume of Padshah's Career.

105. TCA, T30/DES History Project 1, Padshah to Tilden Smith, September 3, 1920.

106. TCA, T30/DES History Project 2, Extract from a Circular (Private and Confidential for Friends Only) regarding the proposed Industrial Bank, issued by Tata Sons & Co., November 5, 1917.

107. TNA, BT 58/80/COS/9684, Tata Industrial Bank Ltd. (Companies particulars as to Directors of 1917), August 12, 1921.

108. TCA, T53-DES-T71-BO-1, Minutes of the Meetings of the Board of Directors, Tata Limited, December 11, 1917.

109. TCA, T53-DES-TATA INDUSTRIAL BANK LTD-2, Notes on Tata Industrial Bank, n.d.

110. TCA, T53-DES-TATA INDUSTRIAL BANK LTD-1, "Tata Industrial," *Commerce*, June 24, 1920.

111. Gordon, *Businessmen and Politics*, 85–86, 109.

112. TCA, T53/PRD/Old Records/Misc/4, Speech by R. D. Lam at farewell function, Taj Mahal Hotel, March 27, 1946.

113. Adam Tooze has described this crisis as "probably the most underrated event in twentieth-century world history," foreclosing radical possibilities of social transformation in the aftermath of World War I. See Adam Tooze, *The Deluge: The Great War, America and the Remaking of the Global Order, 1916–1931* (New

York: Viking, 2014), 353–362. On the effects of the crisis on India beyond the Tatas' experience, see Gordon, *Businessmen and Politics*, 176–177.

114. London Metropolitan Archives, CLC/B/140/KS04/02/02/020, Kleinwort Benson Group Papers, Client Correspondence, Tata Limited to Kleinworts Sons & Co., April 18, 1921; R. D. Tata to National Bank of India, December 24, 1920.

115. TCA, T53-DES-T71-1, Treble to B. F. Madon, December 29, 1921.

116. TCA, T53-DES-T71-1, N. M. Muzumdar to Nowroji Saklatvala, December 17, 1924; "Cotton Transactions—Memorandum by Mr. Muzumdar," January 3, 1925.

117. TCA, T53-DES-T71-1, Tata Sons & Co., Case for the Opinion of Counsel, January 1, 1917.

118. TCA, T53-DES-T71-1, File No. 374, Proposed reconstruction of Tata Ltd., London (Shares).

119. Nomura, *House of Tata*, 183–189.

120. TCA, FP, D. J. Tata Correspondence, D. J. Tata to R. D. Tata, January 26, 1924.

121. TCA, FP-NO-029B-JNT-RDT-OBITUARY-1920-04-12-PG-01, "The House of Tatas: Its Future and India's Prosperity, a Danger to Jamshedji's Life-Work," *Bombay Chronicle*, April 12, 1920. The Tata Administrative Services would realize this vision only after independence (see Chapter 5).

122. TCA, FP-NO-029A-PART1-JNT-RDT-OBITUARY, "The Tatas and Mr. Padshah," *Bombay Chronicle*, April 16, 1920.

123. TCA, T53-DES-TATA INDUSTRIAL BANK LTD-2, Notes on Tata Industrial Bank, n.d.

124. Bassett, *Technological Indian*, 49–55.

125. TSA, File No. L-5, Pt. I, S. M. Marshall to Tata Sons, November 6, 1920.

126. TCA, T53-DES-T34-MINUTES-03, TISCO Board Meeting, January 3, 1919; TISCO General Meeting No. 14, June 9, 1921. For a detailed history of the JTI, see Aparajith Ramnath, *The Birth of an Indian Profession: Engineers, Industry, and the State, 1900–47* (New Delhi: Oxford University Press, 2017), 183–200.

127. TSA, Box 54, File No. A-53, "Notes on Substitution of European by Indian Labour," January 20, 1925; Box 13, File No. 13(iii), R. D. Tata to Motilal Nehru, January 27, 1924.

128. TCA, T53-DES-T34-MINUTES-06, TISCO Board Meeting, January 6, 1928.

129. TSA, File No. 601(vii), Agreement between TISCO and Truscon Steel Co. (1920–1922), John Peterson to S. M. Marshall, October 13, 1920; "A Tata Contract," *Bombay Chronicle*, October 16, 1920.

130. TCA, T53-DES-T34-MINUTES-04, TISCO Memorandum to the Government of India, October 13, 1923.

131. Bahl, *Making of the Indian Working Class*, 172–173.
132. TCA, T53-DES-T20-TP-BO-1, Tata Power Company Board Meeting, February 21, 1953; TNA, T/190/248, The Power and Traction Finance Company, Limited to Secretary, October 23, 1922; Merz and McLellan, Consulting Engineers, to W. J. Sainsbury, Trade Facilities Act Advisory Committee, October 27, 1922.
133. TNA, T 190/248, Allan M. Smith, Broadway House, to Laning Worthington Evans, General Post Office, November 9, 1923; T 190/249, Ref. No. 784A, September 23, 1924.
134. TCA, T30/DES History Project 1, John Peterson to R. Tilden Smith, March 20, 1925.
135. TCA, T53-DES-T20-TATA-HYDRO-ELECTRIC-COR-1, C. P. Perin to N. B. Saklatvala and J. D. Ghandy, June 21, 1927.
136. TCA, T30/DES History Project 1, Perin to Ghandy, June 21, 1927; TCA, T53-DES-T20-TATA HYDRO ELECTRIC-COR-1, H. Gibbs to Perin, July 22, 1927.
137. TCA, T53-DES-T20-TATA HYDRO ELECTRIC-COR-1, Saklatvala to Ghandy, July 18, 1929; T53-DES-T20-BO-2, Tata Hydro-Electric Power Company Board Meeting, August 21, 1929; T53-DES-T20-ANNUAL REPORT-CHAIRMAN-SPEECH-1, Notes on Tata power companies, October 21, 1952.
138. TCA, T53-DES-T20-BO-2, Tata Hydro-Electric Power Company Board Meeting, August 21, 1929.
139. T53-DES-T20-TATA HYDRO ELECTRIC-COR-1, Resolution before the Bombay Municipal Corporation tabled by Dr. J. N. Choksy, October 8, 1929.
140. Markovits, *Indian Business and Nationalist Politics*, 28, 140–141.
141. IOR, L/PS/15/41, File H219/1918, Conyngham Greene, British Embassy, Tokyo, to A. J. Balfour, October 14, 1918.
142. TNA, FO 917/2703, Certified copy of probate and will, R. D. Tata, in the High Court of Judicature at Bombay, September 26, 1927. On Bejan Tata's life, see Mishi Saran, "A House for Mr. Tata," in *Traveling In, Traveling Out: A Book of Unexpected Journeys*, ed. Namita Gokhale (Noida: HarperCollins India, 2014).
143. TCA, T53-DES-RDT-1, Tata Sons Ltd. File No. 240 re: R. D. Tata & Co., Ltd. (Liquidation).
144. TCA, T53-DES-T34-MINUTES-11, R. Mather to A. R. Dalal, July 6, 1935; J. C. Mahindra to Dalal, August 19, 1936.
145. TCA, T53-DES-RDT-1, Tata Sons Ltd. File No. 240 re: R. D. Tata & Co., Ltd. (Liquidation).
146. TCA, T53-DES-RDT-1, Tata Sons Ltd. File No. 240 re: R. D. Tata & Co., Ltd. (Liquidation).

147. TSA, File No. 46(iii), N. B. Saklatvala to D. J. Tata, July 11, 1930.

148. Geoffrey Jones, *Merchants to Multinationals: British Trading Companies in the Nineteenth and Twentieth Centuries* (Oxford: Oxford University Press, 2000), 237–239.

149. TCA, T53-DES-RDT-1, Tata Sons Ltd. File No. 240 re: R. D. Tata & Co., Ltd. (Liquidation).

150. TCA, T53-DES-RDT, copy of a letter from Mr. Brijmohan Lakshminarayan, Bombay, to M/s. Tata Sons Ltd., February 22, 1932.

151. TCA, T53-DES-T59C-BO-3-0042-46, Extract from the Minutes of the Meetings of the Board of Directors of the Central India Spinning Weaving & Manufacturing Co. Ltd., February 14 and April 20, 1933; Gordon, *Businessmen and Politics,* 111–112.

152. Omkar Goswami, "*Sahibs, Babus,* and *Banias*: Changes in Industrial Control in Eastern India, 1918–50," *Journal of Asian Studies* 48, no. 2 (1989): 289–309.

153. Dietmar Rothermund, "A Vulnerable Economy: India in the Great Depression, 1929–1939," in *South Asia and World Capitalism,* ed. Sugata Bose (New Delhi: Oxford University Press, 1990), 307–316; Markovits, *Indian Business and Nationalist Politics,* 43–44, 59–63.

154. Dwijendra Tripathi, *The Oxford History of Indian Business* (New Delhi: Oxford University Press, 2004), 270; Markovits, *Indian Business and Nationalist Politics,* 52, 93–94.

155. Chikayoshi Nomura, "Selling Steel in the 1920s: TISCO in a Period of Transition," *Indian Economic and Social History Review* 48, no. 1 (2011): 83–116.

156. NAI, Industries & Labour (Industries), File No. I-258 (1931), R. C. Pandit, Bihar and Orissa Chamber of Commerce, to the Secretary, Federation of Indian Chamber of Commerce and Industry, July 4, 1931.

157. TCA, T53-DES-T34-MINUTES-09, TISCO General Meeting, August 23, 1933.

158. IOR, L/F/7/254, Extract from Official Report of the Legislative Assembly Debates, re: Freight Agreement between the Tata Iron and Steel Company, Limited, and the Bengal-Nagpur Railway, August 1934.

159. TCA, T53-DES-T34-MINUTES-08, TISCO Board Meeting, August 5, 1932; Note on Ottawa Conference, August 6, 1932.

160. Nasir Tyabji, *Forging Capitalism in Nehru's India: Neocolonialism and the State, c. 1940–1970* (New Delhi: Oxford University Press, 2015), 14.

2. Governing Land and Labor

1. Louis Bromfield, introduction to John L. Keenan, *A Steel Man in India* (New York: Duell, Sloan and Pierce, 1943), xi–xiii.

2. Margaret Crawford, *Building the Workingman's Paradise: The Design of American Company Towns* (London: Verso, 1995), 6–7.

3. Rosemary Wakeman, *Practicing Utopia: An Intellectual History of the New Town Movement* (Chicago: University of Chicago Press, 2016), 1–16.

4. Nitin Sinha, *Communication and Colonialism in Eastern India: Bihar, 1760s–1880s* (London: Anthem, 2012), xviii–xx.

5. K. Sivaramakrishnan, *Modern Forests: Statemaking and Environmental Change in Colonial Eastern India* (Stanford, CA: Stanford University Press, 1999), 35–37.

6. Manu Goswami, *Producing India: From Colonial Economy to National Space* (Chicago: University of Chicago Press, 2004), 52–55; Eesvan Krishnan, "Private Speculations and the Public Interest: N. C. Kelkar's Land Acquisition Bill," *Socio-Legal Review* 8, no. 2 (2012): 87–90.

7. John L. Comaroff, "Colonialism, Culture, and the Law: A Foreword," *Law & Social Inquiry* 26, no. 2 (April 2001): 306.

8. Daniel R. Headrick, *The Tentacles of Progress: Technology Transfer in the Age of Imperialism, 1850–1940* (Oxford: Oxford University Press, 1988), 286.

9. TCA, FP36, D. J. Tata to J. N. Tata, September 25, 1902; Shapurji Saklatvala to J. N. Tata, October 6, 1902; Report of Mr. Shapurji's second visit to Hyderabad, October 10, 1902.

10. Sivaramakrishnan, *Modern Forests*, 20–21, 35–37. This definition of "political society" encompasses "the local structures of government and those aspects of civil society that have extra-local political reach," such as "headmanship, police and judicial roles of landlords, and labour contractors."

11. Ravi Ahuja, *Pathways of Empire: Circulation, Public Works and Social Space in Colonial Orissa, c. 1780–1914* (Hyderabad: Orient Blackswan, 2009), 273.

12. On Bose's conflicted identity as a "colonial nationalist geologist," supportive of Tata's efforts but critical of modern industrialization in general, see Pratik Chakrabarti, *Western Science in Modern India: Metropolitan Methods, Colonial Practices* (Ranikhet: Permanent Black, 2004), 262–263.

13. Tulsi Ram Sharma, *The Location of Industries in India* (Bombay: Hind Kitabs, 1946), 92–97.

14. R. M. Lala, *The Romance of Tata Steel* (New Delhi: Penguin, 2007), 11–18; Rudrangshu Mukherjee, *A Century of Trust: The Story of Tata Steel* (New Delhi: Penguin, 2008), 14–22.

15. Satya Brata Datta, *Capital Accumulation and Workers' Struggle in Indian Industrialisation: The Case of the Tata Iron and Steel Company, 1910–1970* (Stockholm: Almqvist & Wiksell International, 1986), 6, 21.

16. TSA, Land Acquisition File No. 2 (1907), Tata Sons to H. J. McIntosh, Commissioner of Chota Nagpur, December 23, 1907. See also Y. B. Vishwakarma, *Industrialization and Tribal Ecology: Jamshedpur and Its Environs* (Jaipur: Rawat Publications, 1991), 37–38.

17. Vinita Damodaran, "Indigenous Agency: Customary Rights and Tribal Protection in Eastern India, 1830–1930," *History Workshop Journal* 76, no. 1 (2013): 95–101.

18. Detlef Schwerin, "The Control of Land and Labour in Chota Nagpur, 1858–1908," in *Zamindars, Mines and Peasants*, ed. Dietmar Rothermund and D. C. Wadhwa (New Delhi: Manohar, 1978), 36–38, 61–64.

19. Faisal Chaudhry, "A Rule of Proprietary Right for British India: From Revenue Settlement to Tenant Right in the Age of Classical Legal Thought," *Modern Asian Studies* 50, no. 1 (2016): 365–366; Andrew Sartori, *Liberalism in Empire: An Alternative History* (Berkeley: University of California Press, 2014), 47–60.

20. IOR, V/27/314/120, Final Report of the Survey and Settlement of Pargana Dhalbhum in the District of Singhbhum (1906–11), Appendix, H. McPherson, Secretary to the Government of Bihar and Orissa, Revenue Department, to Secretary to the Government of India, Department of Revenue and Agriculture, November 14, 1912.

21. IOR, V/27/314/120, Final Report, 8. On the Chota Nagpur Encumbered Estates Act, which allowed for the temporary seizure and control of insolvent *zamindars'* property, see D. C. Wadhwa, "Zamindars in Debt," in *Zamindars, Mines and Peasants*, ed. Dietmar Rothermund and D. C. Wadhwa (New Delhi: Manohar, 1978), 132–133.

22. IOR, V/27/314/120, Final Report, 15, 21–22; Dwijendra Tripathi, *The Oxford History of Indian Business* (New Delhi: Oxford University Press, 2004), 130.

23. TSA, Land Acquisition File No. 3 (1908, Pt. I), F. H. Eggar, Solicitor to Govt., to the Commissioner of Chota Nagpur, April 21, 1908.

24. TSA, Land Acquisition File No. 3 (1908, Pt. I), Morgan & Co. to F. H. Eggar, Solicitor to Govt., June 26, 1908.

25. TSA, Land Acquisition File No. 5 (1908, Pt. III), Morgan & Co. to Messrs. Tata Sons & Co., July 14, 1908.

26. This view was expressed to me in a series of interviews conducted with social activists in Jamshedpur and Ranchi, April 2014.

27. TSA, Land Acquisition File No. 4 (1908, Pt. II), W. O. Renkin to The Tata Iron & Steel Co., Bombay, September 7, 1908.

28. IOR, L/PJ/6/7805 (File 3804), The Chota Nagpur Tenancy Bill, 1908, 13.

29. TSA, Land Acquisition File No. 3 (1908, Pt. I), The Tata Iron and Steel Co. Ltd. to The Chief Secretary to the Government of Bengal, Revenue Department, February 3, 1908; Land Acquisition File No. 4 (1908, Pt. II), W. O. Renkin to Tata Iron & Steel Co., October 30, 1908; Maya Dutta, *Jamshedpur: The Growth of the City and Its Regions* (Calcutta: The Asiatic Society, 1977), 6–7.

30. TSA, Land Acquisition File No. 4 (1908, Pt. II), W. O. Renkin to Tata Iron & Steel Co., October 27, 1908.

31. Dietmar Rothermund, "The Coalfield—An Enclave in a Backward Region," in *Zamindars, Mines and Peasants*, ed. Dietmar Rothermund and D. C. Wadhwa (New Delhi: Manohar, 1978), 2–12, 18. See also Dilip Simeon, "The Currency of Sentiment: An Essay on Informal Accumulation in Colonial India," in *Corrupt Histories*, ed. Emmanuel Kreike and William Chester Jordan (Rochester, NY: University of Rochester Press, 2006), 407–408.

32. TSA, Land Acquisition File No. 7 (1911), Morgan & Co. to Messrs. Tata Sons & Co., March 21, 1911.

33. TSA, Land Acquisition File No. 8 (1912), Tata Iron & Steel Co. to The Deputy Commissioner of Singhbhum, September 16, 1912.

34. TSA, Land Acquisition File No. 11 (1917), Tata Iron & Steel Co. Ltd. vs. Sital Prosad, Title Suit No. 431 of 1917, in the Court of the Musnif at Chaibassa, District Singhbhum, written statement on behalf of the defendant.

35. TSA, Land Acquisition File No. 11 (1917), Opinion of K. Chowdry, Legal Adviser.

36. TSA, Land Acquisition File No. 11 (1917), T. W. Tutwiler to Tata Iron & Steel Co., Bombay, June 28, 1917.

37. TSA, Land Acquisition File No. 11 (1917), R. D. Tata to The General Manager, Sakchi, July 5/6, 1917.

38. TSA, Land Acquisition File No. 12 (1918, Pt. I), General Manager to Tata Iron & Steel Co., Bombay, February 28, 1918.

39. Matthew Hull, *Government of Paper: The Materiality of Bureaucracy in Urban Pakistan* (Berkeley: University of California Press, 2012), 173–174.

40. TSA, Land Acquisition File No. 13 (1918, Pt. II), Note on Land Acquisition Application, March 12, 1918; Dutta, *Jamshedpur*, 15–16; Vishwakarma, *Industrialization and Tribal Ecology*, 120.

41. TSA, Land Acquisition File No. 12 (1918, Pt. I), Draft of the Preliminary Acquisition Agreement, General Manager's Letter no. 306, January 19, 1918.

42. TSA, Land Acquisition File No. 13 (1918, Pt. II), A. Garrett, Deputy Commissioner of Singhbhum to The Commissioner of the Chota Nagpur Division, Ranchi, August 22, 1918.

43. TSA, Land Acquisition File No. 13 (1918, Pt. II), A. Garrett, Deputy Commissioner of Singhbhum to The Commissioner of the Chota Nagpur Division, Ranchi, August 22, 1918.

44. Bodhisattva Kar, "Nomadic Capital and Speculative Tribes: A Culture of Contracts in the Northeastern Frontier of British India," *Indian Economic and Social History Review* 53, no. 1 (2016): 41–67.

45. Fernando Coronil, *The Magical State: Nature, Money, and Modernity in Venezuela* (Chicago: University of Chicago Press, 1997), 76–83.

46. MSA, Revenue (B Branch), File No. B-117, Pt. VI (1920), W. F. Hudson, Collector of Poona, to Revenue Department, Bombay, February 22, 1921. Unlike gold, flowing water was held to be *res communes* (owned by no one and of use to all) in English law. Andreas Malm, *Fossil Capital: The Rise of Steam Power and the Roots of Global Warming* (London: Verso, 2016), 117–118.

47. IOR, Mss Eur E251/22, Papers of Sir Maurice Hallett, Report of the Jamshedpur Committee, 22.

48. TSA, Land Acquisition File No. 12 (1918, Pt. I), Memorandum, June 11, 1918.

49. TCA, T53-DES-T34-MINUTES-3-020-21, TISCO Board Meeting, November 4, 1919.

50. Many localities in other parts of India were deliberately listed as notified areas or even villages rather than cities in order to avoid higher taxation. William J. Glover, "The Small Town in Colonial Punjab," unpublished paper kindly shared by the author.

51. IOR, Mss Eur D296/2, Municipal Administration at Jamshedpur, Note by John Peterson, proposals sanctioned by Board of Directors, November 24, 1925.

52. F. C. Temple, *Report on Town Planning,* Jamshedpur Social Welfare Series (Bombay: Commercial Press, 1919), 5–11; Amita Sinha and Jatinder Singh, "Jamshedpur: Planning an Ideal Steel City in India," *Journal of Planning History* 10, no. 4 (2011): 268–270.

53. IOR, Mss Eur D296/2, F. C. Temple to John Peterson, October 19, 1925.

54. IOR, Mss Eur D296/2, Note by M. G. Hallett, Commissioner, November 6, 1927.

55. TCA, T30/DES History Project 1, John Peterson to S. Sinha, Member, Executive Council, Govt. of Bihar & Orissa, January 2, 1924.

56. IOR, Mss Eur D296/2, Deputy Commissioner, Singhbhum, to F. C. Temple, October 18, 1927.

57. Coronil, *Magical State,* 107–108.

58. TCA, T53-DES-T34-MINUTES-11-004, TISCO Board Meeting, January 25, 1936; Peter Adey, *Aerial Life: Spaces, Mobilities, Affects* (Oxford: Wiley-Blackwell, 2010), 87. See also Priya Satia, *Spies in Arabia: The Great War and the Cultural Foundations of Britain's Covert Empire in the Middle East* (Oxford: Oxford University Press, 2008), and Vazira Fazila-Yacoobali Zamindar, "Altitudes of Imperialism," *The Caravan,* July 31, 2014.

59. TSA, Box 779, Jamshedpur Town Planning Scheme by P. G. W. Stokes (1937), 5; Sinha and Singh, "Jamshedpur," 270.

60. Dutta, *Jamshedpur,* 32–36; Vishwakarma, *Industrialization and Tribal Ecology,* 131.

61. TSA, Box 698, What I Have Seen in Jamshedpur by S. Modak (1969), 2.

62. Jugsalai remains a source of subversion to this day due to the presence of a free press, which does not exist in Jamshedpur proper. Interview with R. S.

Agrawal, editor of *Uditvani*, a Hindi-language daily newspaper based in Jugsalai, April 2014.

63. TSA, General Manager's Correspondence File No. GM-169, Pt. I, Note on Road Bridge over the Subarnarekha, January 9, 1935.

64. TSA, General Manager's Correspondence File No. GM-169, Pt. I, J. R. D. Tata to General Manager, January 10, 1935.

65. TCA, T53-DES-T34-MINUTES-09, TISCO Board Meeting, April 20, 1934.

66. David A. Johnson, "Land Acquisition, Landlessness, and the Building of New Delhi," *Radical History Review* 108 (Fall 2010): 107.

67. TSA, Land Acquisition File No. 10 (1915), Note by K. Chowdry, Legal Adviser, November 1, 1915.

68. Walter Hauser, ed., *Swami Sahajanand and the Peasants of Jharkhand: A View from 1941* (New Delhi: Manohar, 1995), 189–191.

69. Asoka Kumar Sen, *Representing Tribe: The Ho of Singhbhum under Colonial Rule* (New Delhi: Concept Publishing, 2011), 71–72.

70. TSA, Box 721, Report on the Revisional Survey and Settlement of Pargana Dhalbhum in the District of Singhbhum (1934–1938), 14, 24–27.

71. TSA, General Manager's Correspondence File No. GM-172, Pt. I, J. J. Ghandy, General Manager, to S. K. Sinha, Prime Minister for Home Affairs, Patna, February 15, 1938.

72. Prabhu Mohapatra, "Coolies and Colliers: A Study of the Agrarian Context of Labour Migration from Chotanagpur, 1880–1920," *Studies in History* 1, no. 2 (1985): 278–298.

73. Sen, *Representing Tribe*, 119–123. For a critical reflection on the term "coolie," in its historical and pejorative sense as well as a positive identity to be recuperated, see Gaiutra Bahadur, *Coolie Woman: The Odyssey of Indenture* (Chicago: University of Chicago Press, 2014), xix–xxi.

74. Vinay Bahl, *The Making of the Indian Working Class: A Case of the Tata Iron and Steel Company, 1880–1946* (New Delhi: Sage, 1995), 101–109; Partha Sarathi Gupta, "Notes on the Origin and Structuring of the Industrial Labour Force in India, 1880–1900," in *Power, Politics and the People: Studies in British Imperialism and Indian Nationalism*, ed. Sabayasachi Bhattacharya (London: Anthem Press, 2002), 337–338; Rajnarayan Chandavarkar, *The Origins of Industrial Capitalism in India: Business Strategies and the Working Classes in Bombay, 1900–1940* (Cambridge: Cambridge University Press, 1994), 150.

75. Quoted in Lala, *The Romance of Tata Steel*, 8. On the influence of Ebenezer Howard's utopian model of the "garden city" on company towns at the turn of the century, see Crawford, *Building the Workingman's Paradise*, 70–72, and Helena Chance, *The Factory in a Garden: A History of Corporate Landscapes from the Industrial to the Digital Age* (Manchester, UK: Manchester University Press, 2017), 41–44.

76. TCA, T53-DES-T34-MINUTES-1-127, TISCO Board Meeting, November 19, 1914.

77. Kim P. Sebaly, "The Tatas and University Reform in India, 1898–1914," *History of Education: Journal of the History of Education Society* 14, no. 2 (1985): 133.

78. LSE, Passfield Papers 10.2.1, B. J. Padshah to Director, Indian Institute of Science, May 19, 1910; Unsigned proposal sent to Ratan Tata, May 28, 1910.

79. José Harris, "The Webbs, the Charity Organisation Society and the Ratan Tata Foundation: Social Policy from the Perspective of 1912," in *The Goals of Social Policy*, ed. Martin Bulmer, Jane Lewis, and David Piachaud (London: Unwin Hyman, 1989), 28–29, 33–40; Ralf Dahrendorf, *LSE: A History of the London School of Economics and Political Science, 1895–1995* (Oxford: Oxford University Press, 1995), 124–126.

80. G. R. Searle, *The Quest for National Efficiency: A Study in British Politics and Political Thought, 1899–1914* (Berkeley: University of California Press, 1971), 90–92.

81. Beatrice Webb's Diary, "Taj Hotel, Bombay, 10 to 15 April 1912," in *Sidney and Beatrice Webb: Indian Diary*, ed. Niraja Gopal Jayal (New Delhi: Oxford University Press, 1990), 198–199; Nicholas Owen, "British Progressives and Civil Society in India," in *Civil Society in British History: Ideas, Identities, Institutions*, ed. José Harris (Oxford: Oxford University Press, 2003), 166–171.

82. Harris, "The Webbs, the Charity Organisation Society and the Ratan Tata Foundation," 45, 53–54. For an illustrative example, see V. de Vesselitsky, *Expenditure and Waste: A Study in War-Time* (London: G. Bell, 1917). By privileging the first-hand voices of working-class women in East London, this and other research carried out by the LSE department served as a bridge between late-Victorian social investigation and the more ethnographic approach animating postwar studies such as Michael Young and Peter Wilmott's *Family and Kinship in East London* (1957). See also Lise Butler, *Michael Young, Social Science, and the British Left, 1945–1970* (Oxford: Oxford University Press, 2020), 119–126.

83. LSE, Central Filing Registry 652A, Padshah to Urwick, December 7, 1917.

84. Harris, "The Webbs, the Charity Organisation Society and the Ratan Tata Foundation," 46–47.

85. TSA, Industrial Relations File No. L-57, Pt. II, Note on Bhopal State, May 3, 1919.

86. TSA, Box 752, The Medical Service in the Welfare Work at Sakchi by Sidney Webb, 1–2. On eugenics and the Webbs' notion of "degeneracy," see Searle, *The Quest for National Efficiency*, 61–63.

87. TSA, Box 752, Memorandum on Fatigue by Edward J. Urwick & L. T. Hobhouse, 1–3.

88. Government-owned railway workshops had already adopted the eight-hour day before TISCO. Bahl, *Making of the Indian Working Class*, 117; Datta, *Capital Accumulation and Workers' Struggle*, 122–124.

89. TSA, Box 752, Fatigue: Positive Suggestions by Edward J. Urwick, 1–5.

90. Priyanka Srivastava, *The Well-Being of the Labor Force in Colonial Bombay: Discourses and Practices* (London: Palgrave Macmillan, 2017), 50–55.

91. TSA, Box 743, Report on Investigations with regard to Social Welfare Work at Jamshedpur by Dr. Harold H. Mann (1919), 102–107.

92. TSA, Box 743, Report on Investigations with regard to Social Welfare Work at Jamshedpur by Dr. Harold H. Mann (1919), 92–101. Emphasis mine.

93. TSA, Box 775, File C-4, Minutes of the 10th Meeting of the Permanent Welfare Committee, June 2, 1919.

94. TSA, Box 775, File C-4, Padshah to A. J. Billimoria, March 25, 1919.

95. TSA, Box 743, Report on Social Welfare Work at Jamshedpur, 5–7, 16–17, 32–34.

96. TSA, Box 775, File C-4, Padshah to Tata Iron & Steel Co., Bombay, March 25, 1919.

97. Srivastava, *The Well-Being of the Labor Force*, 94–95.

98. TCA, T53-DES-T34-MINUTES-01, TISCO Board Meeting, June 23, 1915.

99. F. C. Temple, *Report on Town Planning*, Jamshedpur Social Welfare Series (Bombay: Commercial Press, 1919), 12–13. The hexagonal layout still exists in Sonari and is clearly visible from the air. However, the plots were later subleased for construction of conventional single and double-storied brick houses, a reality far from Temple's idealized village. Sinha and Singh, "Jamshedpur," 279.

100. Rudolf Müller, "The City of the Future: Hexagonal Building Concept for a New Division," *Österreichische Wochenschrift für den öffentlichen Baudienst* XIV (1908), trans. Eric M. Nay (1995), http://urbanplanning.library.cornell.edu /DOCS/muller.htm; Eran Ben-Joseph and David Gordon, "Hexagonal Planning in Theory and Practice," *Journal of Urban Design* 5, no. 3 (2000): 237–265.

101. TSA Box 762, Jamshedpur—The Birth and First Twenty Years of an Industrial Town in India by F. C. Temple (1928), 285.

102. TSA, Box 698, What I Have Seen in Jamshedpur, 4.

103. E. P. Thompson, "Time, Work-Discipline, and Industrial Capitalism," *Past & Present* 38, no. 1 (1967): 56–97.

104. Dipesh Chakrabarty, *Rethinking Working-Class History: Bengal 1890 to 1940* (Princeton, NJ: Princeton University Press, 1989), 69–73. Using the example of the Calcutta jute mills, Chakrabarty argues that employers were, along with workers, part of a "precapitalist, inegalitarian culture marked by strong primordial loyalties." For a critique, see Vivek Chibber, *Postcolonial Theory and the Specter of Capital* (London: Verso, 2013), 103–119, 144–145.

105. Aditya Sarkar, *Trouble at the Mill: Factory Law and the Emergence of Labour Question in Late Nineteenth-Century Bombay* (Oxford: Oxford University Press, 2018), 137.

106. Srivastava, *The Well-Being of the Labor Force*, 7–9, 133–136.

107. TSA, Industrial Relations File No. L-8, Tata Iron & Steel Co. to The Secretary, Board of Industries & Munitions, Simla, November 30, 1920.

108. Janaki Nair, *Women and Law in Colonial India: A Social History* (New Delhi: Kali for Women, 1996), 104–106, 112–115; Dhiraj Kumar Nite, "Work, Family and the Reproduction of Life: The Phase of Early Industrialization in the Jharia Coalfields, 1890s–1940s," in *Labour Matters: Towards Global Histories*, ed. Marcel van der Linden and Prabhu Mohapatra (New Delhi: Tulika Books, 2009), 84–96; Srivastava, *The Well-Being of the Labor Force*, 163–166. Employers' appeals to indigeneity and difference carried the day. The revised Factory Act of 1922 did not mandate maternity benefits, and the Mines Act of 1923 did not ban women's employment underground.

109. TSA, Industrial Relations File No. L-9, Office note on the decision of the Metallurgical Conference at Jamshedpur, November 30, 1920.

110. TSA, Industrial Relations File No. L-9, Padshah to S. M. Marshall, December 2, 1920.

111. TSA, Industrial Relations File No. L-9, Padshah to A. W. Dods, December 1, 1920.

112. TSA, Industrial Relations File No. L-9, S. K. Sawday to Padshah, December 6, 1920.

113. TCA, T53-DES-T34-MINUTES-03, S. N. Haldar and N. C. Chatterjee to T. W. Tutwiler, March 1, 1920.

114. Chikayoshi Nomura, *The House of Tata Meets the Second Industrial Revolution: An Institutional Analysis of Tata Iron and Steel Co. in Colonial India* (Singapore: Springer Nature, 2018), 171–179; Bahl, *Making of the Indian Working Class*, 208–234.

115. TCA, T53-DES-T34-MINUTES-03, Extract from Mr. Tutwiler's address to strikers, March 1, 1920.

116. TSA, Industrial Relations File No. L-4, Pt. II, "Jamshedpur Strike: Agitation and the Riots," *Times of India*, March 30, 1920.

117. Nomura, *House of Tata*, 208–215; Dilip Simeon, *The Politics of Labour under Late Colonialism: Workers, Unions and the State in Chota Nagpur, 1928–1939* (New Delhi: Manohar, 1995), 41–42.

118. Simeon, *The Politics of Labour*, 57–59; Bahl, *Making of the Indian Working Class*, 254–255.

119. TSA, Box 82, Report by S. K. Sawday, September 5, 1927, 9–11. On Taylorism in interwar Europe, see Anson Rabinbach, *The Human Motor: Energy, Fatigue, and the Origins of Modernity* (Berkeley: University of California Press, 1992),

276–277; Charles S. Maier, "Society as Factory," in *In Search of Stability: Explorations in Historical Political Economy* (Cambridge: Cambridge University Press, 1987), 23–38.

120. Nomura, *House of Tata*, 240–242; Chikayoshi Nomura, "TISCO's Strikes in 1927–29: An Initial Step towards a Shopfloor Democracy," NIHU Program Contemporary India Area Studies (INDAS) Working Paper no. 11 (March 2013), 71.

121. Chakrabarty, *Rethinking Working-Class History*, 89–90.

122. Margaret Read, *The Indian Peasant Uprooted: A Study of the Human Machine* (London: Longmans, Green, 1931), 38.

123. Read, *The Indian Peasant Uprooted*, 185.

124. Chandavarkar, *The Origins of Industrial Capitalism*, 335–338, 395–396.

125. TSA, Box 546–50, Appendices (1902), Extract from Von Schwartz Report.

126. TCA, Box 998, Tata Staff College Refresher Course (October–November 1960), Factory and Community: The Tata Steel Works at Jamshedpur by M. D. Madan, 5.

127. Quoted in Sharma, *The Location of Industries*, 192–195.

128. Kris Manjapra, *Age of Entanglement: German and Indian Intellectuals across Empire* (Cambridge, MA: Harvard University Press, 2014), 150–152.

129. Radhakamal Mukerjee, *The Indian Working Class*, 3rd ed. (Bombay: Hind Kitabs, 1951), 239–242.

130. Benoy Kumar Sarkar, "Rationalization in Indian Cotton Mills, Railways, Steel Industry & Other Enterprises," Economic Brochures for Young India (Calcutta: Oriental Press, 1930), 137.

131. Benoy Kumar Sarkar, *Creative India: From Mohenjo-Daro to the Age of Ramakrsna-Vivekananda* (Lahore: Motilal Banarsi Dass, 1937), 430.

132. Datta, *Capital Accumulation and Workers' Struggle*, 25–27.

133. Mukerjee, *Indian Working Class*, ix–x.

134. Sarkar, "Rationalization," 129–130.

135. Martin Orans, "A Tribal People in an Industrial Setting," *Journal of American Folklore* 71, no. 281 (1958): 428.

136. Leo Marx, *The Machine in the Garden: Technology and the Pastoral Ideal in America* (Oxford: Oxford University Press, 1964), 25–26, 220–229.

137. Simeon, *The Politics of Labour*, 52.

138. IOR L/PJ/6/1979, File 1753, Riot at Jamshedpur, Singhbhum District, Bihar & Orissa, originating in fake rumours of the kidnapping of children, May–June 1929.

139. Ahuja, *Pathways of Empire*, 32–33, 46–47, 288–289.

140. Jonathan Parry, "The Sacrifices of Modernity in a Soviet-Built Steel Town in Central India," in *On the Margins of Religion*, ed. Frances Pine and João de Pina-Cabral (Oxford: Berghahn, 2008), 234–240, 251–255.

3. Worlds of Philanthropy

1. TCA, FP-NO-029B-JNT-RDT-OBITUARY, Excerpt from *Hindi Punch*, Bombay, May 22, 1904.

2. Pierre Bourdieu, "Symbolic Capital," in *The Logic of Practice*, trans. Richard Nice (Stanford, CA: Stanford University Press, 1990), 119–120.

3. Marcel Mauss, *The Gift: The Form and Reason for Exchange in Archaic Societies*, trans. W. D. Hall (New York: Norton, 2000), 65–69; Harry Liebersohn, *The Return of the Gift: European History of a Global Idea* (Cambridge: Cambridge University Press, 2010), 158–163.

4. Ritu Birla, "C = f(P): The Trust, 'General Public Utility,' and Charity as a Function of Profit in India," *Modern Asian Studies* 52, no. 1 (2018): 136–141.

5. Sumathi Ramaswamy, "Giving Becomes Him: The Posthumous Fortune(s) of Pachaiyappa Mudaliar," *Modern Asian Studies* 52, no. 1 (2018): 39–47.

6. Preeti Chopra, *A Joint Enterprise: Indian Elites and the Making of British Bombay* (Minneapolis: University of Minnesota Press, 2011), 14–17.

7. Jesse Palsetia, "Merchant Charity and Public Identity Formation in Colonial India: The Case of Jamsetjee Jejeebhoy," *Journal of Asian and African Studies* 40, no. 3 (2005): 204–207; Carey A. Watt, "Philanthropy and Civilizing Missions in India c. 1820–1960," in *Civilizing Missions in Colonial and Postcolonial South Asia*, ed. Carey A. Watt and Michael Mann (London: Anthem, 2011), 273–279.

8. Filippo Osella, "Charity and Philanthropy in South Asia: An Introduction," *Modern Asian Studies* 52, no. 1 (2018): 12–17.

9. Skip Worden, "The Role of Religious and Nationalist Ethics in Strategic Leadership: The Case of J. N. Tata," *Journal of Business Ethics* 47, no. 2 (2003): 151–155; Gareth Austin, Carlos Dávila, and Geoffrey Jones, "The Alternative Business History: Business in Emerging Markets," *Business History Review* 91, no. 3 (2017): 563–564.

10. Ritu Birla, "Vernacular Capitalists and the Modern Subject in India: Law, Cultural Politics, and Market Ethics," in *Ethical Life in South Asia*, ed. Daud Ali and Anand Pandian (Bloomington: Indiana University Press, 2010), 98–99.

11. Arun Kumar, "Pragmatic and Paradoxical Philanthropy: Tatas' Gift Giving and Scientific Development in India," *Development and Change* 49, no. 6 (2018): 1425–1431.

12. Kumar, "Pragmatic and Paradoxical Philanthropy," 1439.

13. N. S. B. Gras, "A Great Indian Industrialist: Jamsetji Nusserwanji Tata, 1839–1904," *Bulletin of the Business Historical Society* 23, no. 3 (1949): 150.

14. Inderjeet Parmar, *Foundations of the American Century: The Ford, Carnegie, and Rockefeller Foundations in the Rise of American Power* (New York: Columbia University Press, 2012), 7–11, 28; Corinna R. Unger, "Towards Global Equilibrium: American Foundations and Indian Modernization, 1950s to 1970s,"

Journal of Global History 6, no. 1 (2011): 121–126; John Krige and Helke Rausch, "Introduction—Tracing the Knowledge: Power Nexus of American Philanthropy," in *American Foundations and the Coproduction of World Order in the Twentieth Century*, ed. John Krige and Helke Rausch (Göttingen: Vandenhoeck & Ruprecht, 2012), 16–20.

15. Dwijendra Tripathi, "Colonial Syndrome and Technology Choices in Indian Industry," in *Chinese and Indian Business: Historical Antecedents*, ed. Medha Kudaisya and Ng Chin-keong (Leiden, the Netherlands: Brill, 2009), 123–133.

16. F. R. Harris, *Jamsetji Nusserwanji Tata: A Chronicle of His Life*, 2nd ed. (London: Blackie, 1958), 154–168.

17. Harris, *Jamsetji Nusserwanji Tata*, 245–246.

18. "Plague and Inoculation, Lecture by Mr. W. M. Haffkine," *Times of India*, July 13, 1901; Deepak Kumar, "'Colony' under a Microscope: The Medical Works of W. M. Haffkine," *Science, Technology & Society* 4, no. 2 (1999): 251–254; Rajnarayan Chandavarkar, "Plague Panic and Epidemic Politics in India, 1896–1914," in *Epidemics and Ideas: Essays on the Historical Perception of Pestilence*, ed. Terence Ranger and Paul Slack (Cambridge: Cambridge University Press, 1992), 228–230.

19. TCA, T53-DES-T59C-BO-1, Bezonji Dadabhoy to Deputy Commissioner, Nagpur, September 6 and 17, 1899; "Inoculation in Mills, Successful Operations," *Times of India*, June 21, 1906.

20. "The Bubonic Plague in Bombay: Mills, Houses, and Shops Still Closed," *Times of India*, April 3, 1897; Sheetal Chhabria, *Making the Modern Slum: The Power of Capital in Colonial Bombay* (Seattle: University of Washington Press, 2019), 117–128; Aditya Sarkar, "The Tie That Snapped: Bubonic Plague and Mill Labour in Bombay, 1896–1898," *International Review of Social History* 59, no. 2 (2014): 181–214.

21. TCA, FP30, Some Side-Lights and Reminiscences of Late Mr. J. N. Tata by Jamshedji E. Saklatvala, 5–14.

22. TCA, FP41, J. N. Tata to E. F. Law, Finance Member, Viceregal Council, February 2, 1903.

23. TCA, FP41, Memo. Respecting the Growth of Egyptian Cotton in India by J. N. Tata, 1–9. See also Sven Beckert, *Empire of Cotton: A Global History* (New York: Knopf, 2014), 168–169, 421.

24. TCA, FP30, Side-Lights and Reminiscences, 15; D. E. Wacha, *The Life and Life-Work of J. N. Tata*, 2nd ed. (Madras: Ganesh, 1915), 102; NAI, Foreign (Frontier), Nos. 79–85, Pt. A (August 1905), Major H. L. Showers, Political Agent, Kalat, to Government of India, Foreign Department, February 3, 1905.

25. Wacha, *Life and Life Work of J. N. Tata*, 103.

26. Asiya Siddiqi, "The Business World of Jamsetjee Jeejeebhoy," *Indian Economic and Social History Review* 19, nos. 3 and 4 (1982): 301–302; Christine Dobbin,

Urban Leadership in Western India: Politics and Communities in Bombay City,
1840–1885 (Oxford: Oxford University Press, 1972), 12–13; Rajnarayan Chandavarkar, *The Origins of Industrial Capitalism in India: Business Strategies and the*
Working Classes in Bombay, 1900–1940 (Cambridge: Cambridge University
Press, 1994), 62–63.

27. TCA, FP6, J. N. Tata to Curzon, May 6, 1901. On Indian propertied elites'
opposition to urban reconstruction projects by the Bombay Improvement Trust
in this post-plague period, see Prashant Kidambi, *The Making of an Indian Me-*
tropolis: Colonial Governance and Public Culture in Bombay, 1890–1920 (Aldershot,
UK: Ashgate, 2007), 84–85.

28. TCA, FP30, Side-Lights and Reminiscences, 8.

29. Kim P. Sebaly, "The Tatas and University Reform in India, 1898–1914," *His-*
tory of Education: Journal of the History of Education Society 14, no. 2 (1985):
118–119.

30. TCA, Box 450, Shankari Prasad Basu, "Vivekananda, Nivedita, and Tata's Research Scheme," *Prabuddha Bharata* (October 1978): 414.

31. B. V. Subbarayappa, *In Pursuit of Excellence: A History of the Indian Institute of*
Science (New Delhi: Tata McGraw-Hill, 1992), 21.

32. TCA, Box 450, Basu, "Vivekananda, Nivedita, and Tata's Research Scheme,"
418–419.

33. Sebaly, "The Tatas and University Reform," 120–121; Subbarayappa, *In Pursuit*
of Excellence, 22–24.

34. IOR, L/PJ/6/554, Legislative No. 8, Henry H. Fowler to the Governor General of India in Council, April 26, 1894.

35. Ritu Birla, *Stages of Capital: Law, Culture, and Market Governance in Late Colo-*
nial India (Durham, NC: Duke University Press, 2009), 93–95.

36. IOR L/PJ/6/339, File 260, Extract from the Abstract of the Proceedings of
the Governor-General in Council, January 12, 1893.

37. Lawrence Friedman, *Dead Hands: A Social History of Wills, Trusts, and Inheri-*
tance Law (Stanford, CA: Stanford University Press, 2009), 128–137; IOR,
L/PJ/6/367, File No. 290, Note by J. A. Sinclair, Government Advocate,
Punjab, July 6, 1893.

38. IOR, L/PJ/6/367, File No. 290, Government of Bengal to Home Department,
November 15, 1893.

39. IOR, L/PJ/6/367, File No. 290, North-West Provinces Government to Home
Department, October 7, 1893.

40. IOR, L/PJ/6/554, Note of conference with Mr. Tata, October 30, 1900.

41. Leilah Vevaina, "Good Deeds: Parsi Trusts from 'the Womb to the Tomb,'"
Modern Asian Studies 52, no. 1 (2018): 241–250.

42. IOR, L/PJ/6/554, Minute by A. H. L. Fraser, June 3, 1899.

43. IOR, L/PJ/6/554, Note in J. & P. Committee, June 30, 1899.

44. Jivanchandra Mukerji, *Raja Gokuladasaji ka jivana-carita* (Bombay: Srivenkatesvara Stima Press, 1929), 82–83; Birla, *Stages of Capital*, 113–114. See also Philip McEldowney, "Colonial Administration and Social Developments in Middle India, the Central Provinces, 1861–1921" (PhD diss., University of Virginia, 1980), chapter 8.

45. Subbarayappa, *In Pursuit of Excellence*, 53–54.

46. TCA, T30/DES History Project 1, D. J. Tata to Bazonji (?), October 30, 1905.

47. TCA, Box 450, Basu, "Vivekananda, Nivedita, and Tata's Research Scheme," 451.

48. Olivier Zunz, *Philanthropy in America: A History* (Princeton, NJ: Princeton University Press, 2011), 11–16; Friedman, *Dead Hands*, 148–151.

49. IOR, L/PJ/6/274, File No. 608, The Charitable Endowments Act, 1890, clause 2.

50. Birla, *Stages of Capital*, 101.

51. IOR, L/PJ/6/554, Note, November 6, 1900.

52. IOR, L/PJ/6/554, Note of conference with Mr. Tata, October 30, 1900.

53. Manu Bhagavan, *Sovereign Spheres: Princes, Education and Empire in Colonial India* (New Delhi: Oxford University Press, 2003), 23, 69–75.

54. NAI, Foreign & Political Department, Internal Branch, A Proceedings, Nos. 131–133 (April 1907), Note by J. M. Macpherson in the Legislative Department, September 6, 1906.

55. An enclave directly administered by the Government of India, the Civil and Military Station was itself a zone of exception. Conflicts over jurisdiction would continue until the end of the colonial period, as nationalists active in the old city often "escaped the long arm of the law" by seeking refuge in the station. Janaki Nair, *The Promise of the Metropolis: Bangalore's Twentieth Century* (New Delhi: Oxford University Press, 2005), 74.

56. NAI, Foreign Department, Internal Branch, A Proceedings, No. 1 (December 1907), Note by G. Fell in the Home Department, July 27, 1907; Note by T. W. Richardson in the Legislative Department, October 7, 1907.

57. Subbarayappa, *In Pursuit of Excellence*, 76–77; Suresh Chandra Ghosh, "The Genesis of Curzon's University Reforms, 1899–1905," in *New Perspectives in the History of Indian Education*, ed. Parimala Rao (Hyderabad: Orient Blackswan, 2014), 263–264.

58. Sebaly, "The Tatas and University Reform," 120–126, 132–135.

59. NAI, Commerce & Industry (Industries), Nos. 7-22, Pt. A (June 1919), C. A. Innes, Director of Industries, Madras, to Secretary to Government, Revenue (Special) Department, January 20, 1919.

60. Shirish Kavadi, "State Policy, Philanthropy, and Medical Research in Western India, 1898–1962" (PhD thesis, University of Mumbai, 2011), 235–253, 333–369. I thank the author for generously sharing the full text with me.

61. TNA, FD 1/4198, Dorabji Tata to Government of Bombay, July 25, 1922.

62. IOR, L/PS/11/106, File 2499/16, "Japan and India: An Interview with Sir Rabindranath Tagore," *India*, July 21, 1916.

63. Brij Mohan Dattatreya 'Kaifi,' "A Mirror for India," trans. Christopher Shackle, in *Nationalism in the Vernacular: Hindi, Urdu, and the Literature of Indian Freedom*, Shobna Nijhawan (Ranikhet: Permanent Black, 2010), 111.

64. Pratik Chakrabarti, *Western Science in Modern India: Metropolitan Methods, Colonial Practices* (Ranikhet: Permanent Black, 2004), 287–288.

65. Benoy Kumar Sarkar, *Creative India: From Mohenjo-Daro to the Age of Ramakrsna-Vivekananda* (Lahore: Motilal Banarsi Dass, 1937), 540–544.

66. Quoted in Subbarayappa, *In Pursuit of Excellence*, 19.

67. David L. White, "From Crisis to Community Definition: The Dynamics of Eighteenth-Century Parsi Philanthropy," *Modern Asian Studies* 25, no. 2 (1991): 314–318; Jesse Palsetia, *The Parsis of India: Preservation of Identity in Bombay City* (Leiden, the Netherlands: Brill, 2001), 45–46.

68. TCA, Box 539, T53/PRD/Old Records of Various Companies/3, Deed of Constitution, October 10, 1892, and Addendum, January 28, 1893; Wacha, *Life and Life Work of J. N. Tata*, 46.

69. TCA, Box 178, RJT/PERS/LEG/WILL/1, Copy of will of Sir Ratanji J. Tata, March 20, 1913.

70. TCA, Box 178, DJT/PROP/WILL/2, Copy of Sir D. J. Tata's will, March 12, 1932.

71. TCA, Box 178, DTT/Pers/Prop/Leg/Wills/BO/OPT/1/Trust Papers, S. F. Markham to Lady Ratan Tata, July 12, 1933; Note by N. M. Muzumdar on Markham's letter, September 15, 1933.

72. TNA, FD 1/3319, Report by R. Row, September 14, 1932; Shirish Kavadi, "Lady Tata Memorial Trust and Leukaemia Research in Europe, 1932–53," *Economic and Political Weekly* 49, no. 45 (November 2014): 69–71; Kumar, "Pragmatic and Paradoxical Philanthropy," 1432–1433.

73. TCA, Box 212, RTT/PHIL/Mis/Clipp/Article/3, *Parsi Prakash* excerpt, 1909, translated by Marzban J. Giara; Richard G. Fox, *Gandhian Utopia: Experiments with Culture* (Boston: Beacon, 1989), 140; Isabel Hofmeyr, *Gandhi's Printing Press: Experiments in Slow Reading* (Cambridge, MA: Harvard University Press, 2013), 28.

74. TCA, Box 212, RTT/COR/Mahatma Gandhi/1, R. J. Tata to M. K. Gandhi, November 18, 1910.

75. TCA, Box 212, RTT/PHIL/Mis/Clipp/Article/3, *Parsi Prakash* excerpts, May 22, 1906 and September 11, 1913, translated by Marzban J. Giara. Over half of Parsi overseas charitable donations went to Britain by the early twentieth century, with Tata one of the most visible benefactors. A decline set in during the interwar years as political tensions rose. See John Hinnells, "The

Flowering of Zoroastrian Benevolence: Parsi Charities in the 19th and 20th Centuries," in *Papers in Honour of Professor Mary Boyce*, ed. Harold Walter Bailey, Adrian David H. Bivar, Jacques Duchesne-Guillemin, and John R. Hinnells (Leiden, the Netherlands: Brill, 1985), 285–288.

76. Sraman Mukherjee, "New Province, Old Capital: Making Patna Pataliputra," *Indian Economic and Social History Review* 46, no. 2 (2009): 261–276; Nayanjot Lahiri, *Finding Forgotten Cities: How the Indus Civilization Was Discovered* (Ranikhet: Permanent Black, 2005), 106–112.

77. TCA, FP30, Side-Lights and Reminiscences, 7.

78. TCA, FP, D. J. Tata Correspondence, D. J. Tata to R. D. Tata, July 15, 1902.

79. TCA, FP, D. J. Tata Correspondence, J. N. Tata to D. J. Tata, July 18, 1902.

80. Tanya M. Luhrmann, *The Good Parsi: The Fate of a Postcolonial Elite in a Postcolonial Society* (Cambridge, MA: Harvard University Press, 1996), 163–166; Mitra Sharafi, "Judging Conversion to Zoroastrianism: Behind the Scenes of the Parsi Panchayat Case (1908)," in *Parsis in India and the Diaspora*, ed. John Hinnells and Alan Williams (Abingdon, UK: Routledge, 2008), 159–170; Palsetia, *The Parsis of India*, 227–245.

81. Luhrmann, *The Good Parsi*, 93.

82. TCA, Box 178, RJT/PERS/LEG/WILL/1, Copy of will of Sir Ratanji J. Tata.

83. TCA, Box 178, DJT/PROP/WILL/2, Copy of Sir D. J. Tata's will.

84. TCA, Box 212, RTT/PHIL/Mis/Clipp/Article/3, *Parsi Prakash* excerpts, May 3 and July 11, 1908, translated by Marzban J. Giara.

85. IOR, L/PJ/6/1224, File 768, Note by Judicial & Public Department, India Office, February 5, 1913.

86. *Lady Tata: A Book of Remembrance* (Bombay: Commercial Printing Press, 1932); Mrinalini Sinha, *Specters of Mother India: The Global Restructuring of an Empire* (Durham, NC: Duke University Press, 2006), 152–154.

87. Godrej Archives, Mumbai, MS06-01-94-53, MS200800885, Jt. Hon. Secretary, Z. A. Agre. Committee, November 15, 1918.

88. Jamshed Sorab Vatcha, "Charity Causing Degeneration among Parsis?," *Times of India*, May 14, 1932; Simin Patel, "Cultural Intermediaries in a Colonial City: The Parsis of Bombay, c. 1860–1921" (DPhil thesis, Balliol College, University of Oxford, 2015), 233–235; Luhrmann, *The Good Parsi*, 135–149.

89. Letter from Meherbai Tata to Miss Serenbai Maneckjee Cursetjee, March 3, 1931, in *Lady Tata: A Book of Remembrance*, 138–139.

90. TCA, Box 178, DTT/Pers/Prop/Leg/Wills/BO/OPT/1/Trust Papers, Minutes of Dorabji Tata Trust Meeting, September 20, 1935.

91. Jal F. Bulsara, *Parsi Charity Relief and Communal Amelioration* (Bombay: Sanj Vartaman Press, 1935), 4–5; Hinnells, "The Flowering of Zoroastrian Benevolence," 279–281; Luhrmann, *The Good Parsi*, 135–137. For a comparative example

of how corporate philanthropy in the 1930s racialized poverty and dissemi-
nated eugenic anxieties, focusing on the category of "poor whites" in South
Africa, see Tiffany Willoughby-Herard, *Waste of a White Skin: The Carnegie
Corporation and the Racial Logic of White Vulnerability* (Berkeley: University of
California Press, 2015).

92. TCA, Box 212A, RTT/MIS/Clipp/Articles/York House/2, Talk by
Mr. P. P. Mistri to Members of the Inter-departmental Conference, November
1945.

93. Sebaly, "The Tatas and University Reform," 135.

94. Clifford Manshardt, *Pioneering on Social Frontiers in India* (Bombay: Lalvani
Publishing House, 1967), 79–81.

95. Manshardt, *Pioneering on Social Frontiers*, 8–11.

96. Seth Koven, *Slumming: Sexual and Social Politics in Victorian London*
(Princeton, NJ: Princeton University Press, 2006), 228–230; Prashant Kidambi,
"From 'Social Reform' to 'Social Service': Indian Civic Activism and the Civi-
lizing Mission in Colonial Bombay c. 1900–1920," in *Civilizing Missions in
Colonial and Postcolonial South Asia*, ed. Carey A. Watt and Michael Mann
(London: Anthem, 2011), 227–231; Priyanka Srivastava, *The Well-Being of the
Labor Force in Colonial Bombay: Discourses and Practices* (London: Palgrave
Macmillan, 2017), 129–134.

97. Clifford Manshardt, *The Social Settlement as an Educational Factor in India*
(Calcutta: YMCA Press, 1931), 7–8, 76–77.

98. TCA, Box 198, DTT/PHIL/TISS/FP/4, Report by Clifford Manshardt for
the establishment of TISS, 27–29.

99. Alice O'Connor, *Social Science for What? Philanthropy and the Social Question
in a World Turned Rightside Up* (New York: Russell Sage Foundation, 2007),
26–41; Zunz, *Philanthropy in America*, 18–19.

100. TCA, Box 199, DTT/PHIL/TISS/Mis/1, Clifford Manshardt to the
Trustees of the Sir Dorabji Tata Trust, May 15, 1935.

101. Manshardt, *Pioneering on Social Frontiers*, 88–89.

102. Manshardt, *Social Settlement*, 76–77.

103. TCA, Box 203, DTT/PHIL/TISS/CLIP/1940–85, "Education and Social
Change: Relationship Explained," *Evening News,* June 21, 1940.

104. TCA, Box 201, DTT/PHIL/TISS/CLIP/1935–1937, J. M. Kumarappa,
"Training for Social Efficiency: The School's New Role," *Times of India,* December 18, 1936.

105. TCA, Box 202, DTT/PHIL/TISS/CLIP/1937–1940, "More Spent for God
than for Man: Appalling Tragedy of Social Disorganisation," *Bombay Sentinel,*
March 17, 1938.

106. TCA, Box 203, DTT/PHIL/TISS/CLIP/1940–1985, J. M. Kumarappa,
"How to Prevent Family Disintegration: Making Use of New Sciences,"

Illustrated Weekly of India, May 12, 1940. On the relationship between political economy and the reform of marriage laws in the late colonial period, see Eleanor Newbigin, *The Hindu Family and the Emergence of Modern India: Law, Citizenship and Community* (Cambridge: Cambridge University Press, 2013).

107. Richard Overy, *The Morbid Age: Britain between the Wars* (London: Allen Lane, 2009).

108. O'Connor, *Social Science for What?,* 52–56.

109. Barbara Weinstein, *For Social Peace in Brazil: Industrialists and the Remaking of the Working Class in São Paulo, 1920–1964* (Chapel Hill: University of North Carolina Press, 1997), 73–74.

110. Kumar, "Pragmatic and Paradoxical Philanthropy," 1435–1436.

111. TCA, Box 195, DTT/PHIL/FP/6, DES report on the Tata Memorial Hospital.

112. Kavadi, "State Policy, Philanthropy, and Medical Research," 411–412.

113. TNA, FD 1/3521, N. M. Muzumdar and H. S. Patel to Dr. Paterson, Christie Hospital, Manchester, September 1933; Luis A. Campos, *Radium and the Secret of Life* (Chicago: University of Chicago Press, 2015), 49–52, 242–243; Siddhartha Mukherjee, *The Emperor of All Maladies: A Biography of Cancer* (New York: Scribner, 2010), 73–79.

114. TCA, Box 207, DTT/PHIL/TMH/FP/1A, Meeting of the Trustees of the Sir Dorabji Tata Trust, August 23, 1935.

115. TCA, Box 207, DTT/PHIL/TMH/FP/1A, Meeting of the Trustees of the Sir Dorabji Tata Trust, August 23, 1935, Supplementary Minutes.

116. TCA, Box 195, DTT/PHIL/FP/6, DES report on the Tata Memorial Hospital; Kavadi, "State Policy, Philanthropy, and Medical Research," 413–421.

117. Jahnavi Phalkey, *Atomic State: Big Science in Twentieth-Century India* (Ranikhet: Permanent Black, 2013), 173–174. Tensions between the brothers suggest that atomic and medical research were not always perfectly complementary. Although Ernest supported the experimental treatments, John's demand for isotopes placed a significant burden on the laboratory's capabilities. See Michael Hiltzik, *Big Science: Ernest Lawrence and the Invention That Launched the Military-Industrial Complex* (New York: Simon & Schuster, 2015), 161–164.

118. Phalkey, *Atomic State,* 153n37–38.

119. Phalkey, *Atomic State,* 65, 111–114; Robert S. Anderson, *Nucleus and Nation: Scientists, International Networks, and Power in India* (Chicago: University of Chicago Press, 2010), 65–74.

120. Indira Chowdhury, "Fundamental Research, Self-Reliance, and Internationalism: The Evolution of the Tata Institute of Fundamental Research, 1945–47," in *Science and Modern India: An Institutional History, c. 1784–1947,* ed. Uma Das Gupta (New Delhi: Pearson Longman, 2011), 1103–1104.

121. TCA, Box 195, DTT/PHIL/TIFR/FP/7, Historical note on TIFR prepared by Homi J. Bhabha for the Prime Minister, January 1, 1954; TIFR, J. J. Bhabha to H. J. Bhabha, February 26, 1944.

122. TCA, Box 194, DTT/PHIL/TIFR/FP/1, H. J. Bhabha to Sorab Saklatvala, March 12, 1944.

123. TCA, Box 194, DTT/PHIL/TIFR/FP/1, A Note on Trust Policy by R. Choksi, April 10, 1944; Note to the Trustees in connection with Dr. H. J. Bhabha's scheme, April 14, 1944.

124. TCA, Box 195, DTT/PHIL/TIFR/Mis/2, J. R. D. Tata to Ness Wadia, June 22, 1945; Wadia to J. R. D. Tata, July 28, 1946.

125. Phalkey, *Atomic State*, 131–138, 231–233, 272–274; Anderson, *Nucleus and Nation*, 169–180.

126. TCA, Box 196, DTT/PHIL/TIFR/Mis/12, Speech by Dr. S. S. Bhatnagar at the foundation stone laying ceremony, January 1, 1954.

127. TCA, Box 195, DTT/PHIL/TIFR/FP/7, Historical note on TIFR; Indira Chowdhury, *Growing the Tree of Science: Homi Bhabha and the Tata Institute of Fundamental Research* (New Delhi: Oxford University Press, 2016), 64–68.

128. TIFR, D-2004-00467-TIFR-ARCH-DIR-PER-NAOROJI-KAD, H. J. Bhabha to K. A. D. Naoroji, March 16, 1949.

129. Chowdhury, *Growing the Tree of Science*, xxx–xxxii, 74–76.

130. Anderson, *Nucleus and Nation*, 177–179.

131. TIFR, D-2004-00187-TIFR-ARCH-DIR-PER-BHABA-JJ, Philip Spratt, "The Scientist's Responsibility," *Freedom First*, June 1953; David Engerman, *The Price of Aid: The Economic Cold War in India* (Cambridge, MA: Harvard University Press, 2018), 149–151.

132. TIFR, D-2004-00241-TIFR-ARCH-DIR-PER-CHOKSI-RD, H. J. Bhabha to R. D. Choksi, May 10, 1951.

133. Houghton Library, Harvard University, bMS Eng 1176 (36–39), D. D. Kosambi to Agnes Conklin, December 20, 1950.

134. TIFR, D-2004-00390-TIFR-ARCH-DIR-PER-KOSAMBI-DD4, Professor D. D. Kosambi and the Riemann Hypothesis, August 23, 1960; D-2004-00391-TIFR-ARCH-DIR-PER-KOSAMBI-DD5, H. J. Bhabha to Kosambi, May 16, 1962; Chowdhury, *Growing the Tree of Science*, 166–169, 220–224; Ramakrishna Ramaswamy, "Integrating Mathematics and History: The Scholarship of D. D. Kosambi," in *Unsettling the Past: Unknown Aspects and Scholarly Assessments of D. D. Kosambi*, ed. Meera Kosambi (Ranikhet: Permanent Black, 2012), 387–388.

135. TCA, Box 195, DTT/PHIL/FP/6, DES note on TIFR; TIFR, D-2004-00660-TIFR-ARCH-DIR-PER-VESUGAR, P. J. Vesugar to P. D. Bharucha, TMH Superintendent, April 25, 1951; Bharucha to Vesugar, May 8, 1951.

136. TIFR, D-2004-00001-TIFR-ARCH-DIR-HJB-CORRESP-GEN-3, H. J. Bhabha to Irène Joliot-Curie, April 28, 1947; Bhabha to Frederick James, November 20, 1947.

137. TCA, Box 207, DTT/PHIL/TMH/FP/3, H. J. Bhabha to R. Choksi, December 16, 1961.

138. TCA, Box 187, DTT/PHIL/IIPS/Mis/1, DES note on Indian Institute of Population Studies; K. C. K. E. Raja to John Matthai, February 14, 1955.

139. Unger, "Towards Global Equilibrium," 125–139.

140. Matthew Connelly, *Fatal Misconception: The Struggle to Control World Population* (Cambridge, MA: Harvard University Press, 2008), 168–174.

141. TCA, J. R. D. Tata Correspondence, MF34, J. R. D. Tata to Lady Rama Rau, October 15 and November 25, 1952; MF35, J. R. D. Tata to Mary Ward, December 31, 1952.

142. TCA, Box 195, DTT/PHIL/FP/6, DES note on Tata Trusts.

143. TCA, Box 179, DTT/PHIL/DON/3, Note by J. R. D. Tata, June 27, 1946; Note by R. Choksi, July 4, 1946.

144. TCA, Box 195, DTT/PHIL/FP/6, DES note on Tata Trusts.

145. Alice O'Connor, "The Politics of Rich and Rich: Postwar Investigations of Foundations and the Rise of the Philanthropic Right," in *American Capitalism: Social Thought and Political Economy in the Twentieth Century*, ed. Nelson Lichtenstein (Philadelphia: University of Pennsylvania Press, 2006), 233–246.

146. Deepali Gupta, *Tata vs. Mistry: The Battle for India's Greatest Business Empire* (New Delhi: Juggernaut, 2019), 31–33, 166.

147. TCA, Box 207, DTT/PHIL/TMH/FP/2, R. Choksi to K. C. K. E. Raja, September 25, 1951.

148. TCA, Box 195, DTT/PHIL/FP/6, DES note on Rural Welfare Board; Box 180, DTT/PHIL/Fin/1/Trust Report for the years 1959–1961, The Sir Dorabji Tata Trust: Report for the year ended the 31st December 1959, Appendix A.

149. TCA, Box 998, Rural Welfare Board, report by Allie C. Felder, Cooperation League of the USA, AIA-Rockefeller.

150. Kumar, "Pragmatic and Paradoxical Philanthropy," 1440–1442.

151. TCA, Box 195, DTT/PHIL/FP/6, DES note on Tata Trusts.

4. National Capitalists, Global Wars

1. TSA, File No. L-145, Pt. I, Wadia Gandhy & Co. to M. N. Roy, March 24, 1944.

2. Kris Manjapra, *M. N. Roy: Marxism and Colonial Cosmopolitanism* (New Delhi: Routledge, 2010), 125–129.

3. NMML, M. N. Roy Papers, Subject File No. 4, V. M. Tarkunde to M. N. Roy, July 29, 1944.

4. NMML, Purshottamdas Thakurdas Papers, File No. 239 (Part 4), Lala Shri Ram to Purshotamdas Thakurdas, August 24, 1942.

5. TSA, File No. L-145, Pt. I, Ardeshir Dalal to B. R. Ambedkar, May 15/16, 1944; NMML, M. N. Roy Papers, Subject File No. 3, Tarkunde to Roy, April 21, 1944.

6. NMML, M. N. Roy Papers, Subject File No. 4, Roy to Muthiah Mudaliar, July 13, 1944; Tarkunde to Roy, July 20, 1944.

7. TSA, File No. L-145, Pt. II, J. D. Choksi to S. Khambatta, Wadia Gandhy & Co., December 27, 1946; File No. L-145, Pt. I, Roy to Plaintiffs in the High Court of Judicature at Bombay, Suit No. 574 of 1944, September 1, 1947.

8. This historiographical gap has been addressed by two richly detailed studies, Yasmin Khan, *The Raj at War: A People's History of India's Second World War* (London: Bodley Head, 2015), and Srinath Raghavan, *India's War: World War II and the Making of Modern South Asia* (New York: Basic Books, 2016).

9. Chirashree Das Gupta, *State and Capital in Independent India: Institutions and Accumulation* (Cambridge: Cambridge University Press, 2016), 60.

10. Aditya Mukherjee, *Imperialism, Nationalism and the Making of the Indian Capitalist Class, 1920–1947* (New Delhi: Sage, 2002), 397–404. Emphasis in original. See also Manali Chakrabarti, "Why Did Indian Big Business Pursue a Policy of Economic Nationalism in the Interwar Years? A New Window to an Old Debate," *Modern Asian Studies* 43, no. 4 (2009): 984–988.

11. Vivek Chibber, *Locked in Place: State-Building and Late Industrialization in India* (Princeton, NJ: Princeton University Press, 2003), 87–91, 134–147. For a critique, see David Lockwood, *The Indian Bourgeoisie: A Political History of the Indian Capitalist Class in the Early Twentieth Century* (London: Tauris, 2012), 94–95, 183–187.

12. TISCO's support for protective tariffs in the 1930s thus proves how even a firm "not especially inclined towards industrial activism and still less towards nationalist politics" was drawn to the Congress. Lockwood, *The Indian Bourgeoisie*, 106–111.

13. Kamal Aron Mitra Chenoy, *The Rise of Big Business in India* (New Delhi: Aakar, 2015), 88–90.

14. Robert Vitalis, *When Capitalists Collide: Business Conflict and the End of Empire in Egypt* (Berkeley: University of California Press, 1995), 13–18.

15. James Brennan and Marcelo Rougier, *The Politics of National Capitalism: Peronism and the Argentine Bourgeoisie, 1946–1976* (Philadelphia: University of Pennsylvania Press, 2009), 9–11, 62–63.

16. David Engerman, *The Price of Aid: The Economic Cold War in India* (Cambridge, MA: Harvard University Press, 2018), 2–8.

17. Benjamin Zachariah, *Developing India: An Intellectual and Social History* (Delhi: Oxford University Press, 2005), 96; Partha Sarathi Gupta, "State and

Business in India in the Age of Discriminatory Protection, 1916–1939," in *Power, Politics and the People: Studies in British Imperialism and Indian Nationalism*, ed. Sabayasachi Bhattacharya (London: Anthem Press, 2002), 150–151.

18. Claude Markovits, *Indian Business and Nationalist Politics 1931–1939: The Indigenous Capitalist Class and the Rise of the Congress Party* (Cambridge: Cambridge University Press, 1985), 109–112, 135–139.

19. Michael Kidron, *Foreign Investments in India* (London: Oxford University Press, 1965), 36, 58.

20. TCA, T53-DES-T14-MINUTE-1, Notes on the Chemical Scheme, January to July 1937; J. A. D. Naoroji to Chairman, November 20, 1937.

21. TCA, T53-DES-T14-MINUTE-1, Notes by J. A. D. Naoroji, July 27, 1932, and A. R. Dalal, September 8, 1938.

22. TCA, T53-DES-T14-MINUTE-1, Kapilram Vakil to J. R. D. Tata, April 1 and 13, 1939.

23. TCA, T53-DES-T14-MINUTE-1, Naoroji to N. B. Saklatvala, September 11, 1937.

24. TSA, File No. L-145, Pt. I, The Steel Company and Messrs. Tata Sons, Ltd. vs. M.N. Roy and another, Notes on the allegations contained in Appendix (1) of the Written Statement, November 20, 1944.

25. NMML, M. N. Roy Papers, Subject File No. 3, Sheo Pujan Singh to Roy, August 14 and 22, 1942.

26. TSA, File No. GM-178, Pt. II, C. K. Rao et al. to General Manager, May 9, 1942. On anxieties about the sexual threat posed by soldiers to respectable Indian womanhood, see Khan, *The Raj at War*, 149–151.

27. TSA, File No. L-145, Pt. I, Maneck Homi to Roy, August 22, 1942.

28. NMML, M. N. Roy Papers, Subject File No. 3, Statement on Tata's Strike, Indian Federation of Labour, October 25, 1942.

29. Rajnarayan Chandavarkar, "The War on the Shopfloor," *International Review of Social History* 51, no. S14 (2006): 265–266, 275.

30. Ross Bassett, *The Technological Indian* (Cambridge, MA: Harvard University Press, 2016), 117–120, 153–162.

31. TSA, File No. L-147, Pt. I, Address to the Employees of the Tata Iron & Steel Company by Sir Ardeshir Dalal, August 28, 1942; File No. L-145, Pt. I, The 1942 Strikes at Jamshedpur, Summarised from Mr. Mahanty's Confidential Reports.

32. NMML, Subject File No. 2, M. N. Roy to Reginald Maxwell, September 10, 1942.

33. TSA, File No. L-145, Pt. I, J. J. Ghandy to the Tata Iron & Steel Co., Bombay, November 17, 1944.

34. TSA, File No. L-147, Pt. II, P. H. Kutar to A. A. Bryant, Works Manager, April 24, 1946.

35. Raghavan, *India's War*, 321.

36. TSA, File No. L-145, Pt. I, Notes on the allegations contained in Appendix (1) of the Written Statement; File No. L-147, Pt. I, P. H. Kutar to General Manager, August 24, 1942.

37. Vinay Bahl, *The Making of the Indian Working Class: A Case of the Tata Iron and Steel Company, 1880–1946* (New Delhi: Sage, 1995), 359–374.

38. Indivar Kamtekar, "The Shiver of 1942," *Studies in History* 18, no. 1 (2002): 85–86, 99–101.

39. TSA, File No. L-147, Pt. I, Translation of a two-page leaflet titled *Bande Mataram*, August 31, 1942; Translation of a Hindi printed leaflet signed Bharatiya Mazdoor Sangh (Indian Labour Federation), October 14, 1942; File No. L-145, Pt. I, Mahanty's Confidential Reports.

40. NMML, Homi Mody Papers, Speeches and Writings No. 309, Business opportunities during the war.

41. TCA, A. D. Shroff Papers, Box 401, ICI/ADS/35, Shroff to Homi Mody, June 11, 1940.

42. Kenton J. Clymer, *Quest for Freedom: The United States and India's Independence* (New York: Columbia University Press, 1995), 58–59.

43. NMML, Thakurdas Papers, File No. 281, FICCI Press Communiqué, April 26, 1942.

44. NMML, Thakurdas Papers, File No. 281, Thakurdas to Birla, April 18, 1942; Birla to Thakurdas, April 22, 1942.

45. Clymer, *Quest for Freedom*, 48–50.

46. For instances of this assumption, see Lockwood, *The Indian Bourgeoisie*, 154–155; Kidron, *Foreign Investments in India*, 65–66.

47. TNA, BT 87/88, Report of the American Technical Mission to India, August 1942, 24–29.

48. TCA, T53-DES-T34-MINUTES-12, TISCO Board Meeting, December 10, 1942.

49. TSA, File No. L-145, Pt. I, Appendix (1), Statement by Rajaram Pandey, Constituted Attorney of Defendant No. 1, November 8, 1944; Notes on the allegations contained in Appendix (1) of the Written Statement.

50. TNA, WO 32/10269, D.C.I.G.S. Note, September 16, 1942; India Office to P. J. Grigg, Secretary of State for War, September 28, 1942; Clymer, *Quest for Freedom*, 174–175.

51. G. Bernard Noble and E. R. Perkins, eds., *Foreign Relations of the United States: Diplomatic Papers*, 1942, Vol. I, General; The British Commonwealth; The Far East (Washington, DC: Government Printing Office, 1960), Document 539, Memorandum of Conversation by the Adviser on Political Relations (Murray), April 24, 1942.

52. TNA, WO 32/10269, H.M. Consul-General, New York, to Government of India, Supply Department, September 26, 1942; TCA, T53-DES-T34-

MINUTES-12, TISCO Board Meeting, February 11, 1943; Clymer, *Quest for Freedom*, 77–81.

53. Khan, *Raj at War*, 151–152.

54. TCA, Box 339-339A, JRDT/AVI/A2/CHMN/CLIPP/5, Translation of an article appearing in a German newspaper *Nachtausgabe*, Berlin, ca. March 1944.

55. Purshottamdas Thakurdas et al., *Memorandum Outlining a Plan of Economic Development for India* (Harmondsworth, UK: Penguin, 1944).

56. Medha Kudaisya, *Tryst with Prosperity: Indian Business and the Bombay Plan of 1944* (Gurgaon: Penguin Random House, 2018), 38, 112.

57. M. R. Masani, *Picture of a Plan* (Bombay: Geoffrey Cumberledge, Oxford University Press, 1945), iii.

58. Ritu Birla, "Capitalist Subjects in Transition," in *From the Colonial to the Post-colonial: India and Pakistan in Transition*, ed. Dipesh Chakrabarty, Rochona Majumdar, and Andrew Sartori (New Delhi: Oxford University Press, 2007), 244–253.

59. Zachariah, *Developing India*, 255–257; Chibber, *Locked in Place*, 96–97; Kudaisya, *Tryst with Prosperity*, 45, 71–72.

60. IOR, L/I/1/1061, File 462.83(f), G. S. Bozman, Department of Information and Broadcasting, New Delhi, to A. H. Joyce, India Office, London, June 2, 1944; B. S. Saklatvala to Information Officer, India Office, July 4, 1944; Kudaisya, *Tryst with Prosperity*, 126–128.

61. Masani, *Picture of a Plan*, i.

62. Sugata Bose, "Instruments and Idioms of Colonial and National Development: India's Historical Experience in Comparative Perspective," in *International Development and the Social Sciences*, ed. Frederick Cooper and Randall Packard (Berkeley: University of California Press, 1998), 53; D. Parthasarathy, "Planning and the Fate of Democracy: State, Capital, and Governance in Post-Independence India," in *State Capitalism, Contentious Politics and Large-Scale Social Change*, ed. Vincent Kelly Pollard (Leiden, the Netherlands: Brill, 2011), 89–90.

63. Gurcharan Das, introduction to Kudaisya, *Tryst with Prosperity*, xv–xvi.

64. The consensus view in the essays collected in Sanjaya Baru and Meghnad Desai, eds., *The Bombay Plan: Blueprint for Economic Resurgence* (New Delhi: Rupa Publications, 2018).

65. Respectively in Mukherjee, *Imperialism, Nationalism and the Indian Capitalist Class*, 435–436; Nasir Tyabji, *Forging Capitalism in Nehru's India: Neocolonialism and the State, c. 1940–1970* (New Delhi: Oxford University Press, 2015), 52–53; Chibber, *Locked in Place*, 89–90.

66. Tirthankar Roy, *A Business History of India: Enterprise and the Emergence of Capitalism from 1700* (Cambridge: Cambridge University Press, 2018), 147–148.

67. Quoted in Kudaisya, *Tryst with Prosperity*, 136.

68. NMML, Thakurdas Papers, File No. 291 (Part 1), Jones to Thakurdas, February 12, 1944.
69. NMML, Thakurdas Papers, File No. 291 (Part 2), Singhania to Thakurdas, February 20, 1944.
70. M. D. Darookhanavala, *The Indian Politeia* (Bombay: Lakhani Book Depot, 1949), 19–20.
71. Masani, *Picture of a Plan*, 60–61; Kudaisya, *Tryst with Prosperity*, 106–109.
72. IOR, L/E/8/2637, A. G. Wagholikar, "The Two Plans," *Independent India*, April 16, 1944; Manjapra, *M. N. Roy*, 132–133.
73. P. A. Wadia and K. T. Merchant, *The Bombay Plan: A Criticism* (Bombay: Popular Book Depot, 1946), 1–16.
74. IOR, L/I/1/1061, File 462.83(f), An Examination of the Bombay "Plan of Economic Development for India" by T. E. Gregory, May 17, 1944; Zachariah, *Developing India*, 97–99.
75. IOR, L/I/1/1061, File 462.83(f), Secretary of State to Governor-General, May 27, 1944.
76. IOR, L/E/8/2637, Extract from *The Economist*, March 11, 1944.
77. Zachariah, *Developing India*, 131.
78. IOR, L/E/8/2637, Note by Secretary of State, March 27, 1944.
79. IOR, L/E/8/2637, Notes on Gregory's memorandum, April 22 and 30, 1944.
80. NMML, Thakurdas Papers, File No. 291 (Part 1), Thakurdas to Matthai, December 13, 1943.
81. TCA, JRDT/AVI/A2/CHMN/CLIPP/5, Note initialed J. R. D. T., 1943.
82. Wadia and Merchant, *The Bombay Plan: A Criticism*, 9–12, 18–19.
83. IOR, L/I/1/1061, File 462.83(f), Examination by T. E. Gregory.
84. TCA, JRDT/AVI/A/31, J. R. D. Tata to Matthai, December 21, 1948; NMML, Thakurdas Papers, File No. 239 (Part 7), Thakurdas to Birla, December 12, 1946; Chenoy, *Rise of Big Business*, 150–155.
85. Chibber, *Locked in Place*, 147.
86. NMML, Thakurdas Papers, File No. 291 (Part 2), The Bombay Plan: Lecture II by Dr. Gyanchand, October 1944; Kudaisya, *Tryst with Prosperity*, 110.
87. IOR, L/E/8/2637, Tata Plan of Economic Development in India (1944), Extract from Reuter Message, April 11, 1944.
88. TCA, JRDT/Mis/8, J. R. D. Tata, Post-War Disposal of Sterling Balances, December 11, 1942.
89. IOR, L/E/8/2637, Office Note, February 29, 1944; Kudaisya, *Tryst with Prosperity*, 144–145.
90. TCA, T53-DES-T14-MINUTE-2, Tata Chemicals Board Meeting, September 14, 1945.
91. Kidron, *Foreign Investments in India*, 69–70; Mukherjee, *Imperialism, Nationalism and the Indian Capitalist Class*, 367.

92. TCA, JRDT/Mis/5, J. R. D. Tata to K. A. D. Naoroji, June 6, 1945.

93. TCA, JRDT/Mis/7, J. R. D. Tata to Shroff, March 14, 1945.

94. TCA, A. D. Shroff Papers, Box 425, ICI/ADS/215, Shroff to J. R. D. Tata, March 19, 1945.

95. TCA, T53-DES-AVI-A3-BO-2, Extracts from a speech of Mr. J. R. D. Tata before the Rotary Club, Bombay, on Air Mail Services in India, March 1933; A. Sen, *Five Golden Decades of Indian Aviation: Tata's Memorable Years* (Bombay: Aeronautical Publications of India, 1978), 29–42; Murad Fyzee, *Aircraft and Engine Perfect: The Story of J. R. D. Tata Who Opened Up the Skies for His Country* (New Delhi: Tata-McGraw Hill, 1991), 12–13.

96. Sen, *Five Golden Decades*, 53–55; Aashique Ahmed Iqbal, "Sovereign Skies: Aviation and the Indian State 1939–53" (DPhil thesis, University of Oxford, 2017). I thank the author for generously providing me a copy of the relevant excerpts.

97. TCA, JRDT/AVI/A3/1, G. V. Bewoor to B. W. Figgins, Tata Air Lines, September 12, 1946.

98. TCA, JRDT/AVI/A3/1, J. R. D. Tata to G. D. Birla, August 23, 1946.

99. TCA, JRDT/AVI/A3/1, Birla to J. R. D. Tata, September 23, 1946.

100. NMML, Homi Mody Papers, Correspondence No. 140, M. R. Masani to Mody, January 30, 1948; Chenoy, *Rise of Big Business*, 112–117.

101. Chibber, *Locked in Place*, 134–144.

102. Chenoy, *Rise of Big Business*, 135–139; Engerman, *Price of Aid*, 33.

103. NARA, RG59/LF57D373/B2, Department of State, Memorandum of Conversation on American Economic Aid for India, June 6, 1949.

104. TNA, DO 142/56, Trade Commissioner, New Delhi, to Under Secretary, Export Production Department, Board of Trade, January 30, 1948; Note on a meeting of the East India Association and Overseas League, April 27, 1948; P. Harris, Board of Trade, to Trade Commissioner, New Delhi, May 5, 1948.

105. TNA, DO 142/68, A. C. B. Symon to G. H. Baxter, Commonwealth Relations Office, April 5, 1948.

106. IOR, L/E/8/7570, L. Harrison to G. Bowen, Board of Trade, August 20, 1949; Bowen to J. Thomson, Commonwealth Relations Department, October 6, 1949.

107. TCA, A. D. Shroff Papers, Box 400, ICI/ADS/25, Shroff to C. D. Deshmukh, June 5, 1950.

108. Robert J. McMahon, *The Cold War on the Periphery: The United States, India, and Pakistan* (New York: Columbia University Press, 1995), 41–57.

109. NMML, G. D. Birla Papers, File No. 2, Birla to Nehru, March 31, 1948.

110. TNA, DO 142/76, Note on International Bank Loan to India; U.K. High Commissioner, New Delhi, to Commonwealth Relations Office, April 14, 1950.

111. Aditya Balasubramanian and Srinath Raghavan, "Present at the Creation: India, the Global Economy, and the Bretton Woods Conference," *Journal of World History* 29, no. 1 (2018): 91–92.

112. TNA, DO 142/76, Tata Purchases in U.S., August 28, 1948.

113. TCA, JRDT/COR/MF1, J. R. D. Tata to J. J. Ghandy, September 10, 1947.

114. TCA, JRDT/COR/MF29, J. R. D. Tata to D. K. Daji, November 12, 1951.

115. Sen, *Five Golden Decades*, 55.

116. Gita Piramal, *Business Legends* (New Delhi: Penguin Books, 1998), 428–429.

117. TCA, JRDT/AVI/A3, Speech by Jagjivan Ram on the occasion of the inaugural ceremony of the Indian Airlines, New Delhi, August 1, 1953.

118. TCA, JRDT/COR/MF35, Views of the departmental heads at an informal meeting convened by the Chairman, December 11, 1952.

119. TCA, Box 334, JRDT/AVI/A/2/2, Speech to Air India shareholders, June 22, 1953; JRDT/COR/MF36, J. R. D. Tata to Birla, March 24, 1953.

120. TCA, JRDT/Mis/1, Nehru to J. R. D. Tata, November 28 and December 17, 1953.

121. TCA, JRDT/Mis/1, J. R. D. Tata to K. C. Reddy, December 28, 1953.

122. NMML, T. T. Krishnamachari Papers, File No. 8A, C. D. Deshmukh to Nehru, October 7, 1952; Engerman, *Price of Aid*, 81–84.

123. NMML, T. T. Krishnamachari Papers, File No. 8A, Krishnamachari to Nehru, September 2 and November 2, 1954.

124. TNA, DO 35/8526, E. A. Midgley to F. Doy, Board of Trade, September 6, 1954.

125. Kidron, *Foreign Investments in India*, 93; Chenoy, *Rise of Big Business*, 217.

126. TCA, A. D. Shroff Papers, Box 426, ICI/ADS/229, Shroff to J. R. D. Tata, October 8, 1954.

127. TNA, DO 35/852, U.K.H.C. to Commonwealth Relations Office, September 11, 1954; Note on discussion with Mr. T. T. Krishnamachari, September 10, 1954; Midgley to Doy, September 13, 1954.

128. Kidron, *Foreign Investments in India*, 319.

129. Engerman, *Price of Aid*, 118.

130. TCA, JRDT/AVI/A3/1, E. T. Warren to J. R. D. Tata, January 5, 1955.

131. Taya Zinkin, *Challenges in India* (London: Chatto & Windus, 1966), 106–113.

132. NARA, RG59/LF62D43/B24, The Three Government Steel Plants in India, January 12, 1959.

133. Ved Mehta, *Portrait of India* (New York: Farrar, Strauss, and Giroux, 1970), 293–296.

134. Oscar Sanchez-Sibony, *Red Globalization: The Political Economy of the Soviet Cold War from Stalin to Khrushchev* (Cambridge: Cambridge University Press, 2014), 131–137; Zinkin, *Challenges in India*, 105–106.

135. Engerman, *Price of Aid*, 129–130.

NOTES TO PAGES 134-139

136. Zinkin, *Challenges in India*, 130–131.
137. Sanchez-Sibony, *Red Globalization*, 138–140.
138. NARA, RG59/LF60D449/B9, U.S. Loan Aid for Expansion of Tata Iron and Steel Company, May 24, 1955.
139. NARA, RG59/LF60D449/B9, Memorandum of Conversation, February 23, 1956.
140. Robert J. Mcmahon, William F. Sanford, and Sherrill B. Wells, eds., *Foreign Relations of the United States, 1955–57*, Vol. X, Foreign Aid and Economic Defense Policy (Washington, DC: Government Printing Office, 1987), Document 14, Memorandum of Discussion at the 273d Meeting of the National Security Council, Washington, DC, January 18, 1956.
141. NARA, RG59/LF60D449/B9, Charles D. Withers, Office of South Asian Affairs, to Cedric M. Seager, Office of Near East, South Asia and Africa Operations, International Cooperation Administration, January 24, 1957; McMahon, *Cold War on the Periphery*, 230.
142. NARA, RG59/LF60D449/B9, Complaints and Fears of U.S. Businessmen with Respect to India, January 7, 1957.
143. Sanchez-Sibony, *Red Globalization*, 165–169; McMahon, *Cold War on the Periphery*, 258–259.
144. McMahon, *Cold War on the Periphery*, 233–236; Kidron, *Foreign Investments in India*, 120–127, 178–179; Chenoy, *Rise of Big Business*, 230–231.
145. Engerman, *Price of Aid*, 160–167; Das Gupta, *State and Capital*, 103–107.
146. Kidron, *Foreign Investments in India*, 315.

5. Between Paternalism and Technocracy

1. TSA, General Manager's Correspondence, File No. GM-180, Shape of Things to Come—Jamshedpur as in the year 1954 by A. Gowtama Rao, May 1944; Rao to J. R. D. Tata, October 7, 1944.
2. Vinay Bahl, *The Making of the Indian Working Class: A Case of the Tata Iron and Steel Company, 1880–1946* (New Delhi: Sage, 1995), 91–92, 355–356; Satya Brata Datta, *Capital Accumulation and Workers' Struggle in Indian Industrialisation: The Case of the Tata Iron and Steel Company, 1910–1970* (Stockholm: Almqvist & Wiksell International, 1986), 99.
3. Blair Kling, "Paternalism in Indian Labor: The Tata Iron and Steel Company of Jamshedpur," *International Labor and Working-Class History* 53 (1998): 71–72; Dipesh Chakrabarty, *Rethinking Working-Class History: Bengal 1890 to 1940* (Princeton, NJ: Princeton University Press, 1989), 107–114.
4. Stefan Link, "The Charismatic Corporation: Finance, Administration, and Shop Floor Management under Henry Ford," *Business History Review* 92, no. 1 (2018): 85–115.

5. Stephen L. Harp, *Marketing Michelin: Advertising and Cultural Identity in Twentieth-Century France* (Baltimore: Johns Hopkins University Press, 2001), 201–224.

6. Jeffrey R. Fear, *Organizing Control: August Thyssen and the Construction of German Corporate Management* (Cambridge, MA: Harvard University Press, 2005), 715–742; Harold James, *Krupp: A History of the Legendary German Firm* (Princeton, NJ: Princeton University Press, 2012), 178–187.

7. Brett Sheehan, *Industrial Eden: A Chinese Capitalist Vision* (Cambridge, MA: Harvard University Press, 2015), 8–9.

8. James Vernon, *Distant Strangers: How Britain Became Modern* (Berkeley: University of California Press, 2014), 15, 124–125; Vivek Chibber, *Postcolonial Theory and the Specter of Capital* (London: Verso, 2013), 112–119, 144–145.

9. TSA, General Manager's Correspondence, File No. GM-178, Pt. I, Note by J. R. D. Tata on Future Development of Jamshedpur, January 26, 1942.

10. Rachel Lee, "Constructing a Shared Vision: Otto Koenigsberger and Tata & Sons," *ABE Journal: Architecture beyond Europe* 2 (2012), https://doi.org/10.4000/abe.356; Vandana Baweja, "Messy Modernisms: Otto Koenigsberger's Early Work in Princely Mysore, 1939–41," *South Asian Studies* 31, no. 1 (2015): 1–26.

11. Otto Koenigsberger, *Jamshedpur Development Plan* (Bombay: Tata Iron and Steel Company, 1945), 1–8; Rhodri Liscombe, "In-dependence: Otto Koenigsberger and Modernist Urban Resettlement in India," *Planning Perspectives* 21, no. 2 (2006): 9–12.

12. Koenigsberger, *Jamshedpur Development Plan*, 10–13; Amita Sinha and Jatinder Singh, "Jamshedpur: Planning an Ideal Steel City in India," *Journal of Planning History* 10, no. 4 (2011): 271–273. On the difficulties of applying the neighborhood unit model elsewhere in India, see Sanjeev Vidyarthi, "Inappropriately Appropriated or Innovatively Indigenized? Neighborhood Unit Concept in Post-Independence India," *Journal of Planning History* 9, no. 4 (2010): 260–276.

13. Rachel Lee, "From Static Master Plans to 'Elastic Planning' and Participation: Otto Koenigsberger's Planning Work in India (1939–1951)," in *Proceedings of the 16th International Planning History Society* 16, no. 1 (2014): 613.

14. TCA, T53-DES-T14-1, Notes of visit of Chairman, Dr. Matthai, and discussions, February 14, 1946.

15. AA, Otto Koenigsberger Papers, Box 11, Plan for Mithapur submitted to Messrs. Tata Chemicals Ltd.

16. AA, Koenigsberger Papers, Box 4, Public Edition of the Jamshedpur Development Plan, February 2, 1948; Lee, "Constructing a Shared Vision."

17. Otto Koenigsberger, "New Towns in India," *Town Planning Review* 23, no. 2 (1952): 100–101.

18. Rosemary Wakeman, *Practicing Utopia: An Intellectual History of the New Town Movement* (Chicago: University of Chicago Press, 2016), 4.

19. William J. Glover, "The Troubled Passage from 'Village Communities' to Planned New Town Developments in Mid-Twentieth-Century South Asia," *Urban History* 39, no. 1 (2012): 110.

20. Matthew Hull, "Communities of Place, Not Kind: American Technologies of Neighborhood in Postcolonial Delhi," *Comparative Studies in Society and History* 53, no. 4 (2011): 757–790.

21. Benoy Sarkar, "The Making of Naren Sengupta, the Pioneer of Experimental Psychology in India," *Indian Journal of Psychology* 19, nos. 3 and 4 (March and June 1944): 125–129.

22. Anson Rabinbach, *The Human Motor: Energy, Fatigue, and the Origins of Modernity* (Berkeley: University of California Press, 1992), 255–256.

23. N. N. Sengupta, "Psychology, Its Present Development and Outlook," *Indian Journal of Psychology* 1, no. 1 (January 1926): 19; Aria Laskin, "The Indian Psychological Association, the Birth of the Modern Discipline and 'the Destiny of One Nation,' 1905–1947," *Modern Intellectual History* 10, no. 2 (2013): 420–424; Kris Manjapra, *Age of Entanglement: German and Indian Intellectuals across Empire* (Cambridge, MA: Harvard University Press, 2014), 213–216.

24. Radhakamal Mukerjee and Narendra Nath Sen-Gupta, *Introduction to Social Psychology: Mind in Society* (Boston: Heath, 1928).

25. M. N. Banerji, "Investigations in Industrial Psychology," *Indian Journal of Psychology* 9, nos. 3 and 4 (July and October 1934): 49–54; M. N. Banerji, "Reaction Time as an Indicator of Onset of Fatigue," *Indian Journal of Psychology* 10, nos. 1–3 (January–July 1935): 69–71.

26. Nikolas Rose, *Governing the Soul: The Shaping of the Private Self* (London: Routledge, 1990), 69–70; Rabinbach, *The Human Motor*, 274–275, 287.

27. Daniel Ussishkin, "The 'Will to Work': Industrial Management and the Question of Conduct in Interwar Britain," in *Brave New World: Imperial and Democratic Nation-Building in Britain between the Wars*, ed. Laura Beers and Geraint Thomas (London: Institute of Historical Research, 2011), 103–104.

28. Michael Weatherburn, "Human Relations' Invented Traditions: Sociotechnical Research and Worker Motivation at the Interwar Rowntree Cocoa Works," *Human Relations* 73, no. 7 (2020): 899–923.

29. Daniel Immerwahr, *Thinking Small: The United States and the Lure of Community Development* (Cambridge, MA: Harvard University Press, 2015), 31–34. Taylor's followers were more committed to industrial democracy and trade union power than Mayo's, despite the latter's self-styled humanistic approach. Chris Nyland and Kyle Bruce, "Democracy or Seduction? The Demonization of Scientific Management and the Deification of Human Relations," in *The Right and Labor in America: Politics, Ideology, and Imagination*, ed. Nelson Li-

chtenstein and Elizabeth Tandy Shermer (Philadelphia: University of Pennsylvania Press, 2012), 43–57.

30. Margaret Read, *The Indian Peasant Uprooted: A Study of the Human Machine* (London: Longmans, Green, 1931), 2–3, 183–184.

31. Institute of Education Library and Archives, University College London, Margaret Read Papers, R/B/1, Discussion of "The Halfway House in India" by Prof. J. E. G. de Montmorency, *Asiatic Review* (April 1932).

32. D. L. Sharma, "Psychological Mechanism of the Morale of Industrial Workers," *Indian Journal of Psychology* 25, nos. 1–4 (January–December 1950): 130–133.

33. D. L. Sharma, "Adjustment Problems of Industrial Workers," *Indian Journal of Psychology* 23, nos. 1–4 (January–December 1948): 34.

34. TSA, Industrial Relations File No. 103-F, J. R. D. Tata, Proposal for the Creation of a Personnel Department at Jamshedpur, July 29, 1943.

35. TSA, Industrial Relations File No. 103-F, J. J. Bhabha, "Proposed Form and Functions of a Personnel Department," July 29, 1943.

36. TSA, Industrial Relations File No. 103-F, J. R. D. Tata, Labour Policy, November 2, 1945.

37. TSA, Industrial Relations File No. L-146, Tata Workers Union General Subjects (1941–1946). J. R. D. Tata to R. Mather, September 20, 1946.

38. Erik Linstrum, *Ruling Minds: Psychology in the British Empire* (Cambridge, MA: Harvard University Press, 2016), 125–134.

39. TCA, T53-DES-T34-MINUTES-13-034-36, TISCO Board Meetings, May 19 and June 19, 1947.

40. TCA, T53-DES-T34-MINUTES-13-049, TISCO Board Meeting, September 25, 1947.

41. Michael R. Weatherburn, "Scientific Management at Work: The Bedaux System, Management Consulting, and Worker Efficiency in British Industry, 1914–48" (PhD diss., Imperial College London, 2014); Matthias Kipping, "Consultancies, Institutions and the Diffusion of Taylorism in Britain, Germany and France, 1920s to 1950s," *Business History* 39, no. 4 (1997): 68–75.

42. TCA, J. R. D. Tata Correspondence, MF1, J. R. D. Tata to J. J. Ghandy, September 24, 1947.

43. TCA, T53-DES-T34-MINUTES-13-049, TISCO Board Meeting, January 29, 1948.

44. TSA, Industrial Relations File No. 103-H, Pt. I, J. J. Ghandy to J. R. D. Tata, March 27, 1950.

45. TSA, Industrial Relations File No. 103-H, Pt. I, Minutes of the discussion in the Chairman's room, May 23, 1950.

46. Datta, *Capital Accumulation and Workers' Struggle*, 96–102.

47. TSA, File No. 94 (ii), Tata Workers' Union (Public Meeting) and Notes on Liaison Report, May 26, 1946.

48. TSA, Industrial Relations File No. 103-E, Resolutions of the Tata Mazdoor Sabha meeting, September 23, 1951.

49. TCA, T53-DES-T59C-AGM-1-0036-37, Central India Mills File C-L2 (II), Our Labour Officer's notes and reports on Labour matters, 1949; T53-DES-T14-3-03, Tata Chemicals Board Meeting, June 29, 1951.

50. TCA, Box 874, First Tata Personnel and Labour Officers' Conference, First Session: Labour Legislation, February 9, 1953; Company Information Course: Draft of Two Weeks Training Programme for TISCO Supervisors, prepared by Mr. John Marsh.

51. John Marsh, *The Road to Management and Worker Co-Operation in Indian Industry*, The Third Sir Ardeshir Dalal Memorial Lecture (Jamshedpur: Proceedings of the Society for the Study of Industrial Medicine, 1953), 5–11; TCA, Box 874, First Tata Personnel and Labour Officers' Conference, Third Session: Proposed Central Department of Industrial Relations, February 10, 1953.

52. TCA, Box 874, First Tata Personnel and Labour Officers' Conference, Third Session, and Fourth Session: Relations with the Trade Unions, February 10, 1953.

53. TCA, Box 874, First Tata Personnel and Labour Officers' Conference, Sixth Session: Welfare, February 11, 1953.

54. S. N. Pandey, *Human Side of Tata Steel* (New Delhi: Tata McGraw-Hill, 1989), 27–29.

55. TCA, T53-DES-T14-MINUTE-3, Report on labour conditions at Mithapur, February 4, 1953; Note on General Labour Situation in Mithapur prepared by Mr. Russi Mody, April 1953.

56. TSA, Box 874, Second Tata Management Conference (1956), Inaugural Address by J. R. D. Tata.

57. TSA, Box 874, Second Tata Management Conference (1956), Note on progress made and action taken by M. R. Masani.

58. TSA, File No. 103-B14-A, A talk given by Sir Jehangir Ghandy at a meeting of Chairmen of Joint Departmental Councils and other Executives of the Company, August 14, 1957.

59. *The Story of a Strike: May 1958, The Communist Bid for Power in Jamshedpur* (Calcutta: Tata Iron and Steel Company Limited, 1958), Appendix I: Clauses of the Agreement signed in January 1956 between The Tata Iron & Steel Co. Ltd. and the Tata Workers' Union, 59–60; TSA, File No. 103-C-1, Pt. I, J. J. Ghandy to J. R. D. Tata, May 9, 1957.

60. TSA, File No. 103-C-1, Pt. I, S. M Dhar to J. J. Bhabha, May 22, 1957; Ghandy to Tata, May 9, 1957; Confidential report on Town Division (Fourth Day of Stay-in-Strike), May 4, 1957.

61. TSA, File No. 103-Q, Extract from the Minutes of the meeting of the Committee of Management, October 23, 1957.

62. TSA, File No. 103-Q, Memorandum for the Committee of Management, sd. M. K. Powvala, August 20, 1957; Powvala to J. R. D. Tata, August 22, 1957.

63. TCA, Box 106, TS/TI/DIR/SO/MRM/1/1957–1962, M. R. Masani to J. R. D. Tata, January 13, 1958.

64. TCA, Box 106, TS/TI/DIR/SO/MRM/1/1957–1962, Personnel & Productivity Services Confidential Note, sd. M. R. Masani, November 18, 1957; Confidential note prepared by Mr. H. N. Nanjundiah of Personnel & Productivity Services for personal information of Sir Jehangir Ghandy, based on his visit to Jamshedpur on October 3, 4, 5, and 8, 1957.

65. TSA, File No. 103-C-3, Pt. III, A Brief note on the Jamshedpur and Burnpur Iron and Steel Workers by S. A. Dange, M. P., May 8, 1958.

66. TSA, File No. 103-C-3, Pt. III, M. K. Powvala to J. R. D. Tata, May 13, 1958.

67. TSA, File No. 103-C-2-A, "Inside Story behind TISCO's Dadagiri," *Blitz*, June 14, 1958.

68. Chirashree Das Gupta, *State and Capital in Independent India: Institutions and Accumulation* (Cambridge: Cambridge University Press, 2016), 139; TSA, File No. 103-C-3, Pt. III, J. R. D. Tata to Nehru, May 3, 1958; "Nehru Denies Use of Troops to Break Jamshedpur Strike," *Indian Express*, August 13, 1958.

69. TSA, File No. 103-C, U.S. Press Reports on the Strike, June 25, 1958; File No. 103-C-3.11-18, Dilip Mukerjee to J. J. Bhabha, September 4, 1958; File No. 103-C-3, Pt. III, Mukerjee to Bhabha, May 2, 1958.

70. J. J. Ghandy, foreword to *The Story of a Strike*.

71. TSA, File No. 103-C, C. Constantinides to J. R. D. Tata, August 12, 1958; B. Wellingdon to Managing Director, Tatas, January 29, 1959.

72. TSA, File No. 103-C, Morris D. Morris, "Order and Disorder in the Labour Force: The Jamshedpur Crisis of 1958," *Economic Weekly*, November 1, 1958.

73. TCA, Box 998, Tata Staff College Refresher Course (October–November 1960), Factory and Community by M. D. Madan; Kling, "Paternalism in Indian Labor," 84.

74. TSA, File No. 103-C-3, Pt. IV, M. D. Madan to J. R. D. Tata, May 16, 1958.

75. TCA, Box 874, Third Tata Personnel and Labour Officers' Conference (1959), Union Relations in Tata Enterprises: Review and Outlook by M. R. Masani.

76. TCA, Box 874, Third Tata Personnel and Labour Officers' Conference (1959), Towards Sounder Management-Labour Relations, Speaker: V. B. Karnik, Chairman: P. N. Krishna Pillai.

77. Dinah Rajak, "Corporate Memory: Historical Revisionism, Legitimation and the Invention of Tradition in a Multinational Mining Company," *PoLAR: Political and Legal Anthropology Review* 37, no. 2 (November 2014): 261; Marina Welker, *Enacting the Corporation: An American Mining Firm in Post-Authoritarian Indonesia* (Berkeley: University of California Press, 2014), 55–56.

78. TCA, T53/DES History Project 1, John Matthai to J. R. D. Tata, April 14, 1952; M. R. Masani to Y. S. Pandit, May 17, 1952; Matthai to Pandit, May 24, 1952.

79. TCA, T53/DES History Project 1, Outline of the proposed Monograph on the Tata Organization, sd. John Matthai, November 18, 1954.

80. TCA, T53/DES History Project 1, Mr. A. D. Shroff's comments on the draft of The House of Tata.

81. TCA, T53/DES History Project 1, Mr. N. H. Tata's comments on the draft of The House of Tata.

82. TCA, Box 998, Tata Staff College Inaugurals and Closings, Report on Sixth Session (1956–1961), A Talk by Dr. John Matthai on the opening day of the Second Session of the Tata Staff College, December 5, 1956; Emphases mine.

83. Swapnesh K. Masrani, Linda Perriton, and Alan McKinlay, "Getting Together, Living Together, Thinking Together: Management Development at Tata Sons 1940–1960," *Business History* (2018), https://doi.org/10.1080/00076791 .2018.1458840.

84. TCA, Box 998, A Talk by Dr. John Matthai; Tata Staff College Eighth Session (July–August 1962), V. D. Raje to D. Malegamwala, July 26, 1962. Around the same time, the MIT curriculum provided a model for the integration of the sciences and humanities at IIT Kanpur and the Birla Institute of Technology and Science at Pilani. Ross Bassett, *The Technological Indian* (Cambridge, MA: Harvard University Press, 2016), 236.

85. Bassett, *Technological Indian*, 250–254.

86. TCA, Box 998, Tata Staff College Inaugurals and Closings, Report on Sixth Session (1956–1961), R. D. Choksi to J. R. D. Tata, January 9, 1958.

87. TCA, TAS files, Report on the Tata Administrative Service, 1956–1974.

88. TCA, TAS files, 1966-06-06-0001-8, Points for Chairman's Talk to TAS Officers on the occasion of the Inauguration of the Tata Management Training Center in Poona, January 6, 1966.

89. Link, "The Charismatic Corporation," 92–97.

90. Rajak, "Corporate Memory," 264–273.

91. Aubrey Menon, *Sixty Years: The Story of Tatas* (Bombay: Commercial Printing Press, 1948), 2, 32.

92. TSA, General Manager's Correspondence, File No. GM-178, Pt. II, H. Vincent Murray, Sales Manager, to The Agent, TISCO, October 19, 1943.

93. Karin Zitzewitz, *The Art of Secularism: The Cultural Politics of Modernist Art in Contemporary India* (New York: Oxford University Press, 2014), 71–86; Georgina Maddox, "Benevolent Benefactors," in *Mumbai Modern: Progressive Artists' Group 1947–2013* (New Delhi: Delhi Art Gallery, 2013).

94. Rachel Lee and Kathleen James-Chakraborty, "*Marg* Magazine: A Tryst with Architectural Modernity," *ABE Journal: Architecture beyond Europe* 1 (2012), https://doi.org/10.4000/abe.623.

95. TCA, Box 540, T53/PRD/Mis/3, F. S. Mulla to P. A. Narielwala, June 10, 1954.

96. Tata Steel Art Collection Catalog, W. Langhammer, *The Steel Worker* (Acc. No. MUM-BH-851), *Steel City* (MUM-BH-855), *Steel Worker* (MUM-BH-857), *Steel Works* (MUM-BH-858), *Steel City* (MUM-NM-891). Obtained through the kind courtesy of Jenny Shah.

97. TSA, General Manager's Correspondence, File No. GM-179, Pt. II, J. J. Bhabha to Advertisement Manager, *Times of India*, August 23, 1946; S. Nanavati to Bhabha, August 24, 1946; Bhabha to Nanavati, November 8, 1946.

98. Priya Maholay-Jaradi, "Art from the Heart," in *Lasting Legacies: Special Commemorative Issue* (Mumbai: Tata Review, 2004).

99. John Stilgoe, "Moulding the Industrial Zone Aesthetic: 1880–1929," *Journal of American Studies* 16, no. 1 (1982): 5–24.

100. Rebecca M. Brown, "Colonial Polyrhythm: Imagining Action in the Early 19th Century," *Visual Anthropology* 26, no. 4 (2013): 269–297.

101. TSA Box 424–437, Advertisements, item no. 205.

102. Ranu Roychoudhuri, "Documentary Photography, Decolonization, and the Making of 'Secular Icons': Reading Sunil Janah's Photographs from the 1940s through the 1950s," *BioScope: South Asian Screen Studies* 8, no. 1 (2017): 63–64.

103. Rashmi Varma, "Prior to Erasure: Looking for Adivasis in Photographs," in *Political Aesthetics: Culture, Critique and the Everyday,* ed. Arundhati Virmani (London: Routledge, 2015), 117–118, 121; Sunil Janah, *The Tribals of India* (New Delhi: Oxford University Press, 1993); Sunil Janah, *Photographing India* (New Delhi: Oxford University Press, 2013).

104. Rebecca M. Brown, *Art for a Modern India, 1947–1980* (Durham, NC: Duke University Press, 2009), 127–130; Emilia Terracciano, *Art and Emergency: Modernism in Twentieth-Century India* (London: Tauris, 2017), 118–120.

105. Atreyee Gupta, "Developmental Aesthetics: Modernism's Ocular Economies and Laconic Discontents in the Era of Nehruvian Technocracy," in *Water Histories of South Asia: The Materiality of Liquescence*, ed. Sugata Ray and Venugopal Maddipati (London: Routledge, 2020), 192–197.

106. Roychoudhuri, "Documentary Photography," 70–74.

107. TSA, Box 427–437, Advertisements, item no. 64.

108. They met in 1946 when Janah was commissioned to do feature on *adivasis* for the picture agency Tropix in Calcutta. Elwin's help was also acknowledged in the foreword to Janah's *The Tribals of India*. See Varma, "Prior to Erasure," 117, and Sunil Janah, "Shadowing a Philanthropologist," *The Times Higher Education Supplement* 1398 (August 20, 1999).

109. Ramachandra Guha, *Savaging the Civilized: Verrier Elwin, His Tribals, and India* (Chicago: University of Chicago Press, 1999), 103–109. For a critique of Elwin's romantic primitivism, which arguably laid the groundwork for the

advance of Hindu nationalism in tribal areas, see Archana Prasad, *Against Ecological Romanticism: Verrier Elwin and the Making of an Anti-Modern Tribal Identity* (Gurgaon: Three Essays Collective, 2003), 2–8, 92–98.

110. Other patrons included M. A. Master, Birla Brothers, J. K. Mehta, Chunilal Mehta, Anandilal Podar, Shri Ram, and R. G. Saraiya. NMML, Thakurdas Papers, File No. 337, List of donors to Dr. Verrier Elwin.

111. TCA, J. R. D. Tata Correspondence, E-9, Verrier Elwin to John Murray, July 23, 1943.

112. TCA, J. R. D. Tata Correspondence, E-9, Elwin to J. R. D. Tata, November 6, 1940.

113. Verrier Elwin, *The Agaria* (Calcutta: Oxford University Press, 1942), 239–244.

114. M. G. Ranade, "Iron Industry—Pioneer Attempts," in *Essays on Indian Economics* (Madras: G. A. Natesan, 1920), 152.

115. Guha, *Savaging the Civilized,* 119–120.

116. Elwin, *The Agaria,* xxiv–xxv.

117. Elwin, *The Agaria,* 14–15.

118. TSA, Box 427–437, Advertisements, item no. 506.

119. Suditpo Mullick, "Heavy Metal," *The Caravan,* November 30, 2017.

120. Verrier Elwin, *The Story of Tata Steel* (Bombay: Commercial Printing Press, 1958), 4–5; NMML, Verrier Elwin Papers, Correspondence No. 7–8, J. J. Bhabha to Elwin, November 15, 1956; Correspondence No. 193–194, Bhabha to Elwin, May 13 and 28, 1957.

121. John L. Keenan, *A Steel Man in India* (New York: Duell, Sloan and Pierce, 1943), 126.

122. Elwin, *The Story of Tata Steel,* 33–58.

123. J. R. D. Tata, foreword to Elwin, *The Story of Tata Steel,* 6–7.

6. The Social Responsibilities of Business

1. NAI, M. R. Masani Papers, File No. III, S. No. 13, Jayaprakash Narayan to Masani, January 4, 1942.

2. David Arnold, "The Self and the Cell: Indian Prison Narratives as Life Histories," in *Telling Lives in India: Biography, Autobiography, and Life History,* ed. David Arnold and Stuart Blackburn (Bloomington: Indiana University Press, 2004), 29–31.

3. Minoo Masani, *Bliss Was It in That Dawn . . . A Political Memoir upto Independence* (New Delhi: Arnold-Heinemann, 1977), 84–85, 133, 170.

4. NAI, M. R. Masani Papers, File No. III, S. No. 12, Narayan to Masani, March 26, 1942.

5. NAI, M. R. Masani Papers, File No. III, S. No. 170, Narayan to Masani, January 20, 1945.

6. Daniel Immerwahr, "Polanyi in the United States: Peter Drucker, Karl Polanyi, and the Midcentury Critique of Economic Society," *Journal of the History of Ideas* 70, no. 3 (2009): 445–466; James Burnham, *The Managerial Revolution: What Is Happening in the World* (New York: John Day, 1941), 88–95.

7. C. A. Bayly, *Recovering Liberties: Indian Thought in the Age of Liberalism and Empire* (Cambridge: Cambridge University Press, 2011), 291–296; Benjamin Zachariah, *Developing India: An Intellectual and Social History* (Delhi: Oxford University Press, 2005), 262.

8. Susan Jacoby, *Strange Gods: A Secular History of Conversion* (New York: Pantheon, 2016), 337–356.

9. Daniel Stedman Jones, *Masters of the Universe: Hayek, Friedman, and the Birth of Neoliberal Politics* (Princeton, NJ: Princeton University Press, 2012); Angus Burgin, *The Great Persuasion: Reinventing Free Markets since the Depression* (Cambridge, MA: Harvard University Press, 2012); Quinn Slobodian, *Globalists: The End of Empire and the Birth of Neoliberalism* (Cambridge, MA: Harvard University Press, 2018).

10. Nicole Sackley, "The Road from Serfdom: Economic Storytelling and Narratives of India in the Rise of Neoliberalism," *History and Technology* 31, no. 4 (2015): 397–419.

11. Johanna Bockman, *Markets in the Name of Socialism: The Left-Wing Origins of Neoliberalism* (Stanford, CA: Stanford University Press, 2011), 5–12, 219; Johanna Bockman, "Democratic Socialism in Chile and Peru: Revisiting the 'Chicago Boys' as the Origin of Neoliberalism," *Comparative Studies in Society and History* 61, no. 3 (2019): 654–679.

12. Matthew Jenkins, "Anna Hazare, Liberalisation and the Careers of Corruption in Modern India, 1974–2011," *Economic and Political Weekly* 49, no. 33 (August 16, 2014): 41–44; Daniel Kent Carrasco, "A Battle over Meanings: Jayaprakash Narayan, Rammanohar Lohia and the Trajectories of Socialism in Early Independent India," *Global Intellectual History* 2, no. 3 (2017): 370–388.

13. Bidyut Chakrabarty, *Corporate Social Responsibility in India* (London: Routledge, 2011), 131–136; Meera Mitra, *It's Only Business! India's Corporate Social Responsiveness in a Globalized World* (Delhi: Oxford University Press, 2007), 36–38, 137–138; Shashank Shah, "Corporate Social Responsibility: A Way of Life at the Tata Group," *Journal of Human Values* 20, no. 1 (2014): 59–74.

14. Gareth Stedman Jones, "Rethinking Chartism," in *Languages of Class: Studies in English Working-Class History, 1832–1982* (Cambridge: Cambridge University Press, 1983), 93–96.

15. Mark Blyth, *Great Transformations: Economic Ideas and Institutional Change in the Twentieth Century* (Cambridge: Cambridge University Press, 2002), 6–14.

16. David Hardiman, *Gandhi in His Time and Ours: The Global Legacy of His Ideas* (New York: Columbia University Press, 2004), 82–85; Ajit K. Dasgupta, *Gandhi's Economic Thought* (London: Routledge, 1996), 118–131.

17. Chakrabarty, *Corporate Social Responsibility in India*, 72–73.

18. Leah Renold, "Gandhi, Patron Saint of the Industrialist," *Sagar: South Asia Graduate Research Journal* 1, no. 1 (1994): 16–29.

19. TCA, Box 998, Tata Staff College First Refresher Course (1960), The Management Man as Trustee by M. R. Masani; Richard G. Fox, *Gandhian Utopia: Experiments with Culture* (Boston: Beacon, 1989), 158–160.

20. Masani, *Bliss Was It in That Dawn*, 62. Numerous experiments with worker self-management were taking place across the Third World—some revolutionary, others directed by the state, and still others emerging out of labor movements. See Kristin Plys, "Worker Self-Management in the Third World, 1952–1979," *International Journal of Comparative Sociology* 57, nos. 1–2 (2016): 3–29.

21. M. R. Masani, *Socialism Reconsidered* (Bombay: Padma Publications, 1944), 52.

22. Peter Coleman, *The Liberal Conspiracy: The Congress for Cultural Freedom and the Struggle for the Mind of Postwar Europe* (New York: Free Press, 1989), 2–11, 44–45, 91–93.

23. Margery Sabin, "The Politics of Cultural Freedom: India in the 1950s," in *Dissenters and Mavericks: Writings about India in English, 1765–2000* (New York: Oxford University Press, 2002), 148–151.

24. TCA, J. R. D. Tata Correspondence, MF25, J. R. D. Tata to Frank Moraes, n.d. (May 1951?).

25. Taylor C. Sherman, "A Gandhian Answer to the Threat of Communism? Sarvodaya and Postcolonial Nationalism in India," *Indian Economic and Social History Review* 53, no. 2 (2016): 265–267; Fox, *Gandhian Utopia*, 186–188.

26. NMML, Jayaprakash Narayan Papers, 1st Instalment, Subject File No. 325A, Narayan to Shantikumar Morarji, June 22, 1955.

27. TCA, Box 355, JRDT/Mis/14, Note signed J. R. D. Tata, April 29, 1955; Masani, *Bliss Was It in That Dawn*, 168–169.

28. J. R. D. Tata, "Shedding Preconceptions," in *Keynote: J. R. D. Tata, Excerpts from His Speeches and Chairman's Statements to Shareholders*, ed. S. A. Sabavala and R. M. Lala (Bombay: Tata Press, 1986), 48.

29. TCA, Box 355, JRDT/Mis/14, Kanji Dwarkadas to J. R. D. Tata, November 24, 1954.

30. TCA, Box 355, JRDT/Mis/14, JP Narayan to J. R. D. Tata, December 24, 1954. Emphasis mine.

31. Letter from J. R. D. Tata to JP Narayan, January 4, 1955, in Arvind Mambro, R. M. Lala, and S. A. Sabavala, eds., *J. R. D. Tata: Letters*, vol. 1 (New Delhi: Rupa, 2004), 423–424.

32. TCA, Box 355, JRDT/Mis/14, Masani to JP Narayan, March 7, 1955; Note by D. R. D. Tata, April 29, 1955.

33. TCA, Box 355, JRDT/Mis/14, Vinoba Bhave to JP Narayan, n.d.; J. R. D. Tata to Vinoba, June 27, 1955.

34. TCA, Box 355, JRDT/Mis/14, Extract from the Minutes of the Agents' Meeting, April 9, 1958.

35. TCA, Box 998, Tata Staff College Refresher Course, The Role of a Corporate Citizen (October–November 1960), Supervisors' Discussion Group on What are the factors that weld together society and industry?, Social Responsibilities of Management: An Outline.

36. Naval Tata, "Trusteeship Capital," in *In Pursuit of Industrial Harmony: An Employer's Perspective* (Bombay: National Institute of Labour Management, 1976), 71–73.

37. TCA, Box 998, Tata Staff College First Refresher Course (1960), The Management Man as Trustee by M. R. Masani.

38. Rohit De, "'Commodities Must Be Controlled': Economic Crimes and Market Discipline in India (1939–1955)," *International Journal of Law in Context* 10, no. 3 (2014): 286–289; Indivar Kamtekar, "A Different War Dance: State and Class in India, 1939–1945," *Past and Present* 176, no. 1 (2002): 201–204.

39. William Gould, "From Subjects to Citizens? Rationing, Refugees and the Publicity of Corruption over Independence in UP," *Modern Asian Studies* 45, no. 1 (2011): 33–56.

40. NMML, Purshotamdas Thakurdas Papers, File No. 430, Memorandum on the present socio-economic problems affecting West Bengal and particularly the Middle-Class Traders, February 11, 1950; Tirthankar Roy, *A Business History of India: Enterprise and the Emergence of Capitalism from 1700* (Cambridge: Cambridge University Press, 2018), 147–148.

41. NMML, Purshotamdas Thakurdas Papers, File No. 430, Resolution on The Plight of the Middle Classes moved by Sir Purshotamdas Thakurdas at the 23rd Annual Session of the Federation of Indian Chambers of Commerce and Industry, March 11, 1950.

42. NMML, Purshotamdas Thakurdas Papers, File No. 430, G. D. Birla to Thakurdas, March 2, 1950.

43. NMML, Purshotamdas Thakurdas Papers, File No. 430, Thakurdas to Birla, March 6, 1950.

44. Stanley Kochanek, *Business and Politics in India* (Berkeley: University of California Press, 1974), 215–216; Nasir Tyabji, *Forging Capitalism in Nehru's India: Neocolonialism and the State, c. 1940–1970* (New Delhi: Oxford University Press, 2015), 82–85.

45. A. D. Shroff, *Free Enterprise in India* (Bombay: Forum of Free Enterprise, 1956), 2.

46. Tyabji, *Forging Capitalism*, 142–143.

47. Sucheta Dalal, *A. D. Shroff: Titan of Finance and Free Enterprise* (New Delhi: Viking, 2000), 61, 115–119; Kochanek, *Business and Politics in India*, 204–206.

48. A. D. Shroff, *Private Enterprise and Politics* (Bombay: Forum of Free Enterprise, 1962), 2.

49. Lawrence B. Glickman, *Free Enterprise: An American History* (New Haven, CT: Yale University Press, 2019), 2–18.

50. A. D. Shroff, Murarji Vaidya, and C. L. Gheevala, *A Survey of Socialism Today* (Bombay: Forum of Free Enterprise, 1961), 34–50.

51. Howard L. Erdman, *The Swatantra Party and Indian Conservatism* (Cambridge: Cambridge University Press, 1967), 197–199; Aditya Balasubramanian, "Contesting 'Permit-and-Licence *Raj*': Economic Conservatism and the Idea of Democracy in 1950s India," *Past and Present* (2020), https://doi.org/10.1093/pastj/gtaa013.

52. Dalal, *A. D. Shroff*, 119.

53. M. R. Masani, *Congress Misrule and the Swatantra Alternative* (Bombay: Manaktalas, 1966), 174–175.

54. TCA, Box 1007, JP Narayan to J. R. D. Tata, October 29, 1964.

55. NMML, Brahmanand Papers, File No. 36, Statement by JP Narayan, Kohima, November 2, 1964; S. N. Bajoria, Chairman, Paschim Banga Mofussil Byabasayee Sammelan, to Narayan, November 19, 1964.

56. NMML, Brahmanand Papers, File No. 36, G. D. Birla to JP Narayan, November 24, 1964; Narayan to Birla, December 7, 1964.

57. TCA, Box 1007, J. R. D. Tata to JP Narayan, November 16, 1964; NMML, Brahmanand Papers, Correspondence No. 491, Tata to Narayan, December 21, 1964.

58. TCA, Box 1007, JP Narayan to J. R. D. Tata, December 2, 1964.

59. NMML, Jayaprakash Narayan Papers, 1st Instalment, Subject File No. 485, M. R. Masani to Narayan, November 26, 1964 and March 23, 1965.

60. David Engerman, *The Price of Aid: The Economic Cold War in India* (Cambridge, MA: Harvard University Press, 2018), 108–109; Sackley, "The Road from Serfdom," 398–408.

61. TCA, Box 1007, J. R. D. Tata to JP Narayan, November 16, 1964.

62. NMML, Jayaprakash Narayan Papers, 1st Instalment, Subject File No. 485, Tarlok Singh to Ashoka Mehta, Dy. Chairman, Planning Commission, December 10, 1964.

63. George Goyder, *The Future of Private Enterprise: A Study in Responsibility* (Oxford: Basil Blackwell, 1951), 50–61, 93–97. The models Goyder used for inspira-

tion were the Carl Zeiss Stiftung (Foundation or Trust) in Germany and the John Lewis Partnership in Britain.

64. Susanna Hoe, *The Man Who Gave His Company Away: A Biography of Ernest Bader, Founder of the Scott Bader Commonwealth* (London: Heinemann, 1978), 108–119, 161–172; NMML, Jayaprakash Narayan Papers, 1st Instalment, Subject File No. 485, Narayan to Ashoka Mehta, January 11, 1965.

65. NMML, Jayaprakash Narayan Papers, 1st Instalment, Subject File No. 487, Summary of proceedings, Seminar on Social Responsibility of Business; Subject File No. 491, Majumdar to M. C. Bhandari, February 11, 1966; Mitra, *It's Only Business!*, 24–25, 169–170; Pushpa Sundar, *Business and Community: The Story of Corporate Social Responsibility in India* (New Delhi: Sage, 2013), 179–182.

66. TCA, Box 1007, Declaration on the Social Responsibilities of Business, New Delhi, March 15–21, 1965.

67. NMML, Jayaprakash Narayan Papers, 1st Instalment, Subject File No. 491, Address by Shri Jayaprakash Narayan at the Calcutta Seminar on Social Responsibilities of Business, March 25–27, 1966.

68. TCA, Box 72, TS/ICO/CFBP/2, Ramkrishna Bajaj to J. R. D. Tata, April 16, 1965. The following year, Ramkrishna refused JP's appeal for donations to the Bihar Relief Fund for flood victims. He justified the decision by blaming the government's "doctrinaire statist outlook" for "stifling every incentive of the business community to do anything constructive or charitable." NMML, Ramkrishna Bajaj Papers, Correspondence No. 122–27, JP Narayan to Bajaj, November 2, 1966; Bajaj to Narayan, November 8, 1966. See also M. V. Kamath, *Gandhi's Coolie: Life and Times of Ramkrishna Bajaj* (Bombay: Allied Publishers, 1988), 185–219.

69. TCA, Box 72, TS/ICO/CFBP/2, J. R. D. Tata to Ramkrishna Bajaj, May 5, 1965.

70. TCA, Box 72, TS/ICO/CFBP/2, Report of the Sub-Committee Regarding Model Code of Fair Commercial Practices, September 15, 1965.

71. TCA, Box 72, TS/ICO/CFBP/2, J. R. D. Tata to Ramkrishna Bajaj, April 1, 1966; Kochanek, *Business and Politics in India*, 207–208.

72. TCA, Box 72, TS/ICO/CFBP/2, Extract from the Minutes of the Board of Directors of Tata Industries, May 12, 1966; Note from Agents, December 16, 1966.

73. NMML, Jayaprakash Narayan Papers, 3rd Instalment, Subject File No. 46, Conference on the Social Responsibilities of Business held in the Princes Room at the Taj Mahal Hotel, Bombay, September 13, 1969; George Goyder to M. C. Bhandari, June 17, 1969. On profit sharing at Sears, see Sanford M. Jacoby, *Modern Manors: Welfare Capitalism since the New Deal* (Princeton, NJ: Princeton University Press, 1997), 108–111.

74. NMML, Jayaprakash Narayan Papers, 1st Instalment, Correspondence No. 567, Leslie Sawhny Programme of Training for Democracy to Narayan, June 3, 1970.

75. NMML, Jayaprakash Narayan Papers, 3rd Instalment, Subject File No. 402, Social Audit compiled by the Tata Institute of Social Sciences, Bombay, and The Indian Institute of Management, Ahmedabad, March 1971.

76. J. R. D. Tata, "Brakes on Growth," in *Keynote: J. R. D. Tata, Excerpts from His Speeches and Chairman's Statements to Shareholders*, ed. S. A. Sabavala and R. M. Lala (Bombay: Tata Press, 1986), 42–44.

77. TCA, J. R. D. Tata Correspondence, MF224, J. R. D. Tata to JP Narayan, November 2, 1972.

78. Kamal Aron Mitra Chenoy, *The Rise of Big Business in India* (New Delhi: Aakar, 2015), 246–247; Chirashree Das Gupta, *State and Capital in Independent India: Institutions and Accumulation* (Cambridge: Cambridge University Press, 2016), 89–93.

79. *Report of the Committee on Prevention of Corruption* (New Delhi: Ministry of Home Affairs, Government of India, 1964), 10–12, 42–45.

80. R. K. Hazari, *The Structure of the Corporate Private Sector: A Study of Concentration, Ownership, and Control* (Bombay: Asia Publishing House, 1966), 17–19.

81. Hazari, *The Structure of the Corporate Private Sector*, 47–49, 52–58.

82. Hazari, *The Structure of the Corporate Private Sector*, 357–362.

83. Medha Kudaisya, "Developmental Planning in 'Retreat': Ideas, Instruments, and Contestations of Planning in India, 1967–1971," *Modern Asian Studies* 49, no. 3 (2015): 740–749.

84. NMML, Jayaprakash Narayan Papers, 3rd Instalment, Subject File No. 403, Minoo Masani to Indira Gandhi, October 9, 1969; Indira Gandhi to Masani, November 16, 1969.

85. Gita Piramal, *Business Legends* (New Delhi: Penguin Books, 1998), 508–509.

86. J. R. D. Tata, "As I Wake Up Every Morning," in *Keynote: J. R. D. Tata, Excerpts from His Speeches and Chairman's Statements to Shareholders*, ed. S. A. Sabavala and R. M. Lala (Bombay: Tata Press, 1986), 62–63.

87. J. R. D. Tata, "Launching on an Obstacle Course," in *Keynote: J. R. D. Tata, Excerpts from His Speeches and Chairman's Statements to Shareholders*, ed. S. A. Sabavala and R. M. Lala (Bombay: Tata Press, 1986), 67–68.

88. J. R. D. Tata, "Big Can Also Be Beautiful," in *Keynote: J. R. D. Tata, Excerpts from His Speeches and Chairman's Statements to Shareholders*, ed. S. A. Sabavala and R. M. Lala (Bombay: Tata Press, 1986), 69.

89. J. R. D. Tata, *Suggestions for Accelerating Industrial Growth* (Bombay: Tata Industries Private Limited, 1972), 15–20, 21–27; Howard L. Erdman, "The Industrialists," in *Indira Gandhi's India: A Political System Reappraised*, ed. Henry C. Hart (Boulder, CO: Westview, 1976), 136–137; David Lockwood,

The Communist Party of India and the Indian Emergency (New Delhi: Sage, 2016), 61–62.

90. H. K. Vyas, *Communist Reply to Tata Memorandum* (New Delhi: Communist Party Publication, 1972), 1–9.

91. Vyas, *Communist Reply*, 31–35.

92. TCA, N. A. Palkhivala Papers, Box 596, NAP/Business for Social & Economic Progress/1973, Trusteeship: A Review of the Wardha Conference, September 14, 1973; Summary of the Discussions with Shri Vinobaji by Ramkrishna Bajaj.

93. TCA, N. A. Palkhivala Papers, Box 596, NAP/Trusts/Ramkrishna Bajaj/Misc/1, Ramrkishna Bajaj to N. A. Palkhivala, September 20, 1973; NMML, Ramkrishna Bajaj Papers, File No. 27, A meeting to study different schemes which could be undertaken under the auspices of BSP in Bombay city, July 24, 1973.

94. NMML, Ramkrishna Bajaj Papers, File No. 27, J. R. D. Tata to Bajaj, April 10, 1974 and March 27, 1975.

95. Gyan Prakash, *Emergency Chronicles: Indira Gandhi and Democracy's Turning Point* (Princeton, NJ: Princeton University Press, 2018), 269–283.

96. John Dayal and Ajoy Bose, *For Reasons of State: Delhi under Emergency* (Delhi: Ess Ess Publications, 1977), 35–65.

97. TCA, Box 460, T20/PHIL/Slum Clearance/1, Meetings with the Chief Minister and Chairman, June 10, 1975; Note by Leela Moolgaokar, June 27, 1975.

98. TCA, J. R. D. Tata Correspondence, MF29, J. R. D. Tata to Gordon Pearce, December 1, 1951.

99. Taya Zinkin, *Challenges in India* (London: Chatto & Windus, 1966), 133–134; Matthew Connelly, *Fatal Misconception: The Struggle to Control World Population* (Cambridge, MA: Harvard University Press, 2008), 225. By 1971, the group-level department of industrial health coordinated 20,000 vasectomies or tubectomies out of 125,000 employees, or 16 percent of the total (the target was 30 percent). Naval Tata, "The Population Problem and Employers," in *In Pursuit of Industrial Harmony*, 11–12.

100. Emma Tarlo, "Body and Space in a Time of Crisis: Sterilization and Resettlement during the Emergency in Delhi," in *Violence and Subjectivity*, ed. Veena Das, Arthur Kleinman, Mamphela Ramphele, and Pamela Reynolds (Berkeley: University of California Press, 2000), 250–254.

101. Ramachandra Guha, "Gentle Dents in a Worthy Idol," *The Telegraph* (Kolkata), January 6, 2007; Piramal, *Business Legends*, 509–512.

102. Naval Tata, "Pot-Holes in the Path of Industrial Peace" and "Labour Relations in a Changing Political Environment," in *In Pursuit of Industrial Harmony*, 53–54, 58–62; J. R. D. Tata, "The Presidential System," in *Keynote: J. R. D. Tata,*

Excerpts from His Speeches and Chairman's Statements to Shareholders, ed. S. A. Sabavala and R. M. Lala (Bombay: Tata Press, 1986), 124–127.

103. Slobodian, *Globalists,* 2.

104. Erdman, "The Industrialists," 125–126, 138–146; Arvind Rajagopal, "The Emergency as Prehistory of the Indian Middle Class," *Modern Asian Studies* 45, no. 5 (2011): 1010–1021.

105. Atul Kohli, "Politics of Economic Growth in India, 1980–2005, Part I: The 1980s," *Economic and Political Weekly* 41, no. 13 (April 1, 2006): 1251–1255; Das Gupta, *State and Capital,* 209–211.

106. Prakash, *Emergency Chronicles,* 306–316.

107. J. R. D. Tata, "Corrective Action on Employers," in *Keynote: J. R. D. Tata, Excerpts from His Speeches and Chairman's Statements to Shareholders,* ed. S. A. Sabavala and R. M. Lala (Bombay: Tata Press, 1986), 101.

108. TCA, Box 540, T53/PRD/Mis/8, S. A. Sabavala to George Fernandes, April 26, 1977.

109. R. M. Lala, *India Says 'NO' to Nationalisation* (Bombay: Rajaji Foundation, 1979), 1–9, 29–30; Piramal, *Business Legends,* 513–516.

110. TSA, Box 267, File No. 34, Pt. V, S. A. Sabavala to Russi Mody, July 15, 1977.

111. Mitra, *It's Only Business!,* 32–33.

112. TSA, Box 267, File No. 34AC-3, Pt. I, Rural Development Programme—Family Planning Scheme, February 11, 1980; Note by A. D. Gadgil on Community Development, Rural Development and Adivasi Welfare, June 6, 1980.

Epilogue

1. Gita Piramal, *Business Legends* (New Delhi: Penguin Books, 1998), 518–526; Morgen Witzel, *Tata: The Evolution of a Corporate Brand* (New Delhi: Penguin, 2010), 59–81; Sunil Mithas, *Dancing Elephants and Leaping Jaguars: How to Excel, Innovate, and Transform Your Organization the Tata Way* (North Potomac, MD: Finerplanet, 2014).

2. Dwijendra Tripathi, "Change and Continuity," *Seminar* 428 (October 1999); Harish Damodaran, *India's New Capitalists: Caste, Business, and Industry in a Modern Nation* (Ranikhet: Permanent Black, 2008), 3–5, 23–24; J. Dennis Rajakumar and John S. Henley, "Growth and Persistence of Large Business Groups in India," *Journal of Comparative International Management* 10, no. 1 (2007): 15–18; Tirthankar Roy, *A Business History of India: Enterprise and the Emergence of Capitalism from 1700* (Cambridge: Cambridge University Press, 2018), 232–241; Surajit Mazumdar, "Industrialization, Dirigisme and Capitalists: Indian Big Business from Independence to Liberalization," NMML Occasional Paper, History and Society New Series 7 (New Delhi: Nehru Memorial Museum and Library, 2012), 23–32.

3. James Crabtree, *The Billionaire Raj: A Journey through India's New Gilded Age* (New York: Crown/Tim Duggan Books, 2018), 30.

4. Chinmay Tumbe, "Transnational Indian Business in the Twentieth Century," *Business History Review* 91, no. 4 (2017): 667–670; Pierre Lanthier, "Tata Becoming Multinational: A Long-Term Process," *Entreprises et histoire* 90, no. 1 (2018): 82–87; Chirashree Das Gupta, *State and Capital in Independent India: Institutions and Accumulation* (Cambridge: Cambridge University Press, 2016), 109–111.

5. S. Ramadorai, *The TCS Story . . . and Beyond* (New Delhi: Penguin Portfolio, 2011), 39–57, 76–80; Ross Bassett, *The Technological Indian* (Cambridge, MA: Harvard University Press, 2016), 260–263.

6. Ravinder Kaur and Thomas Blom Hansen, "Aesthetics of Arrival: Spectacle, Capital, Novelty in Post-Reform India," *Identities: Global Studies in Culture and Power* 23, no. 3 (2016): 4–5.

7. Rudrangshu Mukherjee, *A Century of Trust: The Story of Tata Steel* (New Delhi: Penguin, 2008), 1–8; Daniel Madar, *Big Steel: Technology, Trade, and Survival in a Global Market* (Vancouver: University of British Columbia Press, 2010).

8. Dilip Hiro, *The Age of Aspiration: Power, Wealth, and Conflict in Globalizing India* (New York: New Press, 2015), 60–68.

9. Anand Giridharadas, "India Celebrates a Take-Over," *New York Times*, February 1, 2007.

10. Murali Gopalan, "Tata Motors—Rescued to the Rescue," *Hindu BusinessLine*, December 23, 2013; "Ratan Tata Was Humiliated by Ford, Reveals Colleague," *NDTV Auto*, March 16, 2015.

11. Andrew Ross, *Fast Boat to China: High-Tech Outsourcing and the Consequences of Free Trade* (New York: Vintage, 2007), 136–141.

12. Suman Layak, "Wanted: Another Lease of Life," *Business Today*, January 11, 2011; Prince Mathews Thomas, "Putting the Shine Back into Tata Steel," *Forbes India*, April 19, 2013; Ishita Ayan Dutt, "Tata Steel's Problem Child Struggles to Make Good," *Business Standard*, June 4, 2014.

13. Karl West, "Welsh Town with Steel at Its Heart Casts a Wary Eye at the Future," *The Guardian*, September 25, 2014; Karl West, "Tata Steelworkers Prepare to Strike as Gloom Descends on Port Talbot Again," *The Guardian*, June 9, 2015; Bleddyn Penny, "'The City of Steel': Port Talbot's Steel Industry, from 'Treasure Island' to Crisis," *History and Policy*, April 11, 2016.

14. Graham Ruddick and Heather Stewart, "Tata Steel to Sell Off Entire British Business," *The Guardian*, March 29, 2016; Sean Farrell, "Tata Completes Sale to Greybull, Saving Jobs and Reviving British Steel," *The Guardian*, June 1, 2016; "Brexit Jitters Could Delay Tata Steel's Port Talbot Sale," *Forbes*, July 7, 2016; Michael Pooler and Patrick McGee, "Tata Seeks a Way Out of European Steel Woes," *Financial Times*, July 19, 2016.

15. Deepali Gupta, *Tata vs. Mistry: The Battle for India's Greatest Business Empire* (New Delhi: Juggernaut, 2019), 8–9, 31–33, 46–47, 94–96; "Mistry's Elephant," *The Economist*, September 24, 2016; "Clash of the Tatas," *The Economist*, November 19, 2016; "Behind Tata-Mistry Clash, a Distinct Set of Governance Rules," *Economic Times*, December 26, 2016; Simon Mundy, "Tata in Turmoil: The Battle inside India's Biggest Business," *Financial Times Magazine*, February 15, 2017.

16. Gupta, *Tata vs. Mistry*, 89, 117–119; Suman Layak, "Trusts to Protect Value of Stake in Tata Sons: R. Venkataramanan," *Economic Times*, November 26, 2016; Satish Gupta, "Income Tax Department Asks Two Tata Trusts to Explain 'Unlawful' Investments," *Economic Times*, November 19, 2016; Rashmi Rajput, "Income Tax Department Cancels Registration of Six Tata Trusts," *Economic Times*, November 2, 2019; Ruhi Kandhari, "A Trust Deficit at Tata Trusts," *The Ken*, January 10, 2020.

17. Matthew Bishop and Michael Green, *Philanthrocapitalism: How the Rich Can Save the World* (New York: Bloomsbury, 2008); David Callahan, *The Givers: Wealth, Power, and Philanthropy in a New Gilded Age* (New York: Knopf, 2017); Anand Giridharadas, *Winners Take All: The Elite Charade of Changing the World* (New York: Knopf, 2018); Rob Reich, *Just Giving: Why Philanthropy Is Failing Democracy and How It Can Do Better* (Princeton, NJ: Princeton University Press, 2018).

18. Gupta, *Tata vs. Mistry*, 108–109, 179–180; "Corporate Gladiator Nusli Wadia Has Entered the Tata Battle—and He's Going after His Childhood Friend," *Quartz*, November 15, 2016; "Amid Typhoon Tata, Nusli Wadia Backs Cyrus Mistry," *Forbes Asia*, January 17, 2017.

19. Megha Mandavia, "Tata Sons Threatens to Sue Ex-GEC Member Nirmalya Kumar for 'Disparaging' Remarks," *Economic Times*, November 26, 2016; Saritha Rai, "Tata's Boardroom Battles Have Sparked a Twitter War," *Bloomberg*, December 1, 2016.

20. "Tata Group Survived Two World Wars, Group Ready for Any Challenge: Chairman Chandrasekaran," *Avenue Mail* (Jamshedpur), March 3, 2020.

21. Justin Huggler, "From Parsee Priests to Profits: Say Hello to Tata," *The Independent*, February 1, 2007.

22. Zareer Masani, "What Makes the Tata Empire Tick," *The Independent*, February 5, 2015; Zareer Masani and Vibeke Venema, "The Men of Steel with a Softer Side," *BBC News Magazine*, February 2, 2015. Masani's documentary, *Tata: India's Global Giant*, aired on BBC Radio 4 on February 6, 2015.

23. Andrew Sanchez, "Deadwood and Paternalism: Rationalizing Casual Labour in an Indian Company Town," *Journal of the Royal Anthropological Institute* 18 (2012): 809–810; Roy, *Business History of India*, 217; Divya Gupta, "Moral Minefield," *The Caravan*, November 1, 2011.

24. Kala S. Sridhar and Samar Verma, "A Way Out of Urban Chaos," *Hindu Business Line*, October 4, 2013; James Crabtree, "Welcome to India's Steel Citadel," *Financial Times Magazine*, November 10, 2015.

25. TSA, Box 267, File No. 34, Jawaharlal Sharma to J. R. D. Tata, September 28, 1981.

26. Barbara Crossette, "Good Government Scares a Good City in India," *New York Times*, January 22, 1991.

27. Interview with Jawaharlal Sharma, Jamshedpur, April 2014.

28. Gupta, "Moral Minefield"; Matthew Samuel and Shalini Rai, "Capitalist Punishment: How Tata Steel Killed a City," *Tehelka*, February 28, 2015; Shalini Rai, "The Real Face of Corporate Giant Tata," *Tehelka*, March 7, 2015.

29. Aniek Paul, "Battle for the Soul of Jamshedpur," *LiveMint*, August 2, 2018; "State Responds on Township Residents' Voting Rights," *Hindustan Times* (Ranchi), January 14, 2019.

30. K. C. Sivaramakrishnan, "Local Government," in *The Oxford Handbook of the Indian Constitution*, ed. Sujit Choudhry, Madhav Khosla, and Pratap Bhanu Mehta (Oxford: Oxford University Press, 2016), 568–570.

31. Interview with former TSRDS officer, New Delhi, June 2014; Gupta, "Moral Minefield"; Andrew Sanchez, "Capitalism, Violence and the State: Crime, Corruption and Entrepreneurship in an Indian Company Town," *Journal of Legal Anthropology* 1, no. 2 (2010): 165–188; Nityanand Jayaraman, "Stolen for Steel: Tata Takes Tribal Lands in India," *CorpWatch*, May 24, 2006.

32. Ananya Roy, "The Blockade of the World-Class City: Dialectical Images of Indian Urbanism," in *Worlding Cities: Asian Experiments and the Art of Being Global*, ed. Ananya Roy and Aihwa Ong (Hoboken, NJ: Wiley-Blackwell, 2011), 267–274; Sarasij Majumder, *People's Car: Industrial India and the Riddles of Populism* (New York: Fordham University Press, 2019), 19–31; Christophe Jaffrelot, "Business-Friendly Gujarat under Narendra Modi," in *Business and Politics in India*, ed. Christophe Jaffrelot, Atul Kohli, and Kanta Murali (Oxford: Oxford University Press, 2019), 215–218; Mahesh Langa, "All Hail Modi, 'a Leader of Grand Vision,'" *Hindustan Times*, January 11, 2013; "'Government Has a Vision for India': Ratan Tata's Thumbs Up to PM Modi," *Hindustan Times*, January 16, 2020.

33. Pushpa Sundar, *Business and Community: The Story of Corporate Social Responsibility in India* (New Delhi: Sage, 2013), 43; Meera Mitra, *It's Only Business! India's Corporate Social Responsiveness in a Globalized World* (Delhi: Oxford University Press, 2007), 100–101; Aveek Datta and Shutapa Paul, "'Vested Interests' to Blame, Says Tata Steel," *LiveMint*, December 22, 2009.

34. Felix Padel and Samarendra Das, *Out of This Earth: East India Adivasis and the Aluminium Cartel* (Hyderabad: Orient Blackswan, 2010); Sudeep Chakravarti,

Clear.Hold.Build: Hard Lessons of Business and Human Rights in India (Noida: Collins Business, 2014).

35. R. Jagannathan, "Chakravyuh: How India Inc Moved from Hero to Villain," *Firstpost,* September 26, 2012.

36. Interview with former TSRDS officer, New Delhi, June 2014.

37. Until the 1990s, Tata Steel spent 12 percent of PAT (profits after tax) on CSR, but the proportion subsequently declined to around 6 percent. See Jittu Singh, "Tight Rope Walk at Tata Steel: Balancing Profits and CSR," *South Asian Journal of Management* 15, no. 1 (January–March 2008): 118–136.

38. Sunila S. Kale, "From Company Town to Company Village: CSR and the Management of Rural Aspirations in Eastern India's Extractive Economies," *Journal of Peasant Studies* (2020), https://doi.org/10.1080/03066150.2020.1825290. I thank the author for kindly sharing a prepublication draft.

39. Elana Shever, *Resources for Reform: Oil and Neoliberalism in Argentina* (Stanford, CA: Stanford University Press, 2012), 169–173; Dinah Rajak, *In Good Company: An Anatomy of Corporate Social Responsibility* (Stanford, CA: Stanford University Press, 2011), 17–18.

40. Tata Steel press conference, Russi Mody Centre for Excellence Auditorium, Jamshedpur, April 1, 2014.

41. Interviews with former managing director, Tata Steel, and former vice president of Town Services, Tata Steel, Mumbai, February 2014.

42. Interviews with Xavier Dias, Ranchi, April 2014; R. S. Agrawal, Jugsalai, April 2014.

43. Greg Grandin, *Fordlandia: The Rise and Fall of Henry Ford's Forgotten Jungle City* (New York: Picador, 2010), 360.

44. TSA, General Manager's Correspondence, File No. GM-180, Shape of Things to Come, May 1944. See Chapter 5.

Acknowledgments

This book began life at Harvard University nine years ago, in a very different world. Maya Jasanoff taught me how to write, how to teach, and how to be a historian, from the simple task of asking the right questions to the subtle art of communicating ideas beyond the confines of academia. She has been a shining example of mentorship and dedication to her students, which I can only hope to emulate. Sugata Bose shaped the way I think about and approach the entire field of modern South Asian history. Sunil Amrith's generosity and enthusiasm for my study of Tata from its earliest stages made all the difference. David Engerman was an invaluable interlocutor, giving my writing a thorough and exacting read. Manu Goswami inspired my overall intellectual trajectory more than anyone else. I am grateful for her continued engagement with my work. While at Harvard, I also had the good fortune to learn from Richard Delacy, Ajantha Subramanian, Judith Surkis, Emma Rothschild, Erez Manela, and the late Roger Owen.

I owe my initial resolve to pursue an academic life to my undergraduate teachers at the University of California, Berkeley. Gene Irschick's courses first set me on the path of studying South Asia and, more importantly, showed me the possibilities of a theoretically informed perspective on the past. The late Kavita Datla was my graduate student instructor in my freshman year and then unexpectedly became a treasured colleague during my first solo teaching experience at Mount Holyoke College eleven years later. Tom Laqueur warmly encouraged my aspirations from the start. James Vernon and Tom Metcalf gave me my first taste of the graduate school experience in my senior year. I have since continued to benefit from James's wise and witty counsel.

The book was completed at the University of Maryland, College Park, where I have been assistant professor in the Department of History since 2017. My thanks go to each and every one of my colleagues for their support and advice, particularly to Phil Soergel and Peter Wien as chair and interim chair, respectively, and to my faculty mentors, David Sicilia and David Freund. Our extraordinary staff, led by Lisa Klein and Gail Russell, keeps the department running. It is a well-worn cliché for professors to say they learn from their students, but in my case, it has been absolutely true. At Maryland, I also owe a special debt to Rajshree Agarwal and the Ed Snider Center for Enterprise and Markets, which has championed my work and provided a space for community and conversation across disciplinary boundaries.

My thinking in this book has been shaped by fruitful discussions and exchanges of ideas and materials with Eric Beverley, Rebecca Brown, Carlo Caduff, Uday Chandra, Indira Chowdhury, Nick Cullather, Rohit De, David Edgerton, Ramachandra Guha, Atreyee Gupta, Sunila Kale, Shirish Kavadi, Yasmin Khan, Sunil Khilnani, Sonal Khullar, Rachel Lee, Mike Levien, Erik Linstrum, Claude Markovits, Jerry Muller, Jonathan Parry, Sumathi Ramaswamy, Tirthankar Roy, Andrew Sanchez, Andrew Sartori, Priya Satia, Glenda Sluga, Philip Stern, Carolien Stolte, Stefan Tetzlaff, Thomas Timberg, Leilah Vevaina, Michael Weatherburn, and Karin Zitzewitz.

In recent years, while it was still possible to travel freely around the globe, I have presented fragments of the book at conferences and workshops in Atlanta, Baltimore, Birmingham (UK), Boston, Chicago, Princeton, Kolkata, Kyoto, Madison, Minneapolis, New Haven, New York, Seattle, Stanford, and Sydney. I thank fellow panelists, discussants, and audience members for their stimulating questions and incisive comments.

Research for the book was made possible by a Fulbright-Nehru Fellowship and a Frederick Sheldon Traveling Fellowship, which allowed me to spend the 2013–2014 academic year in India, as well as by short-term grants from the Weatherhead Center for International Affairs, the South Asia Institute, the John Clive Fellowship, and the Program on the Study of Capitalism Research Fellowship at Harvard. Funding from the University of Maryland Department of History enabled follow-up research in 2018.

In India, I am deeply indebted to numerous archivists and librarians for their assistance and expert guidance, especially to Rajendra Prasad Narla at the Tata Central Archives in Pune, Swarup Sengupta and Jenny Shah at the Tata Steel Archives in Jamshedpur, and Oindrila Raychaudhuri at the TIFR Archives in Mumbai. In a similar vein, I thank the dedicated staff of the Nehru Memorial Museum and Library and the National Archives of India in Delhi, the Maharashtra State Archives and the Godrej Archives in Mumbai, and the West Bengal State Archives in Kolkata. Neeraj Goswami and the Fulbright–

Institute of International Education provided crucial logistical aid as I embarked on this nomadic research itinerary.

While in India, I also benefited enormously from the kindness and hospitality of many people who opened their doors and gave up their time. I sincerely thank Shernaz Cama, Amar Farooqui, Divya Gupta, Viraf Mehta, and Dilip Simeon in Delhi; Yezad Kapadia in Gurgaon; Jairus Banaji, Pheroza Godrej, and Rusheed Wadia in Mumbai; Yutika Vora and her family in Panchgani; Xavier Dias in Ranchi; and Dilith Castleton, Amit Mukherjee, Saryu Roy, Santanu Sarkar, Jawahlarlal Sharma, and Jittu Singh in Jamshedpur.

In London, I thank Ed Bottoms at the Architectural Association Archives and the staff of the British Library, the National Archives at Kew, the London School of Economics Archives, and the London Metropolitan Archives. Rusi Dalal led me on a memorable walking tour of Brookwood Cemetery in Surrey, where Jamsetji Tata and his sons are buried.

For assistance with images and permissions, I thank Merlyn Anklesaria, Mort Chatterjee and Tara Lal, Arjun Janah, Ritu Gairola Khanduri, Kirsten Pontalti, Sagar Rane, Ranu Roychoudhuri, Robert Dean Smith, and Mrinalini Vasudevan.

Parts of Chapter 1 first appeared in "Trade, Finance, and Industry in the Development of Indian Capitalism: The Case of Tata," *Business History Review* 94, no. 3: 569–592, © The President and Fellows of Harvard College 2020. Portions of Chapter 2 were first published in "'A Mass of Anomalies': Land, Law, and Sovereignty in an Indian Company Town," *Comparative Studies in Society and History* 60, no. 2: 367–389, © Society for the Comparative Study of Society and History 2018. Both are reprinted here with permission.

I thank my editor, Sharmila Sen, for taking a chance on this project and keeping the faith. It has been a pleasure to work with Heather Hughes, Stephanie Vyce, and the team at Harvard University Press. Dave Prout made a great index. Two anonymous reviewers helped improve the manuscript significantly in every respect, from empirical detail to argument and structure. Any remaining errors or omissions are entirely my own.

For their friendship and solidarity during my time at Harvard and beyond, I thank Greg Afinogenov, Ania Aizman, Aditya Balasubramanian, Mou Banerjee, Eva Bitran, Shane Bobrycki, Lowell Brower, Elise Burton, Rohit Chandra, Rishad Choudhury, Sakura Christmas, Christina Crawford, Nick Crawford, Namita Dharia, Hardeep Dhillon, Darja Djordjevic, Josh Ehrlich, Carla Heelan, Philippa Hetherington, Tom Hooker, Abbas Jaffer, Sadaf Jaffer, Neelam Khoja, Ateya Khorakiwala, Karen Kieser, Julie Kleinman, Matthew

Kustenbauder, Alix Lacoste, Kristen Loveland, Daniel Majchrowicz, Johan Mathew, Nadia Marx, Salmaan Mirza, Margot Moinester, Shaun Nichols, Rachel Orol, Arafat Razzaque, Carolin Roeder, Kathryn Schwartz, Dan Sheffield, Sarah Shortall, Josh Specht, Trevor Stark, Tara Suri, Deniz Turker, Anand Vaidya, Lydia Walker, and Delia Wendel. Hearty *salaams* and *shukriyas* to Sana Aiyar, Tariq Omar Ali, Dinyar Patel, Ben Siegel, Julie Stephens, and Gitanjali Surendran, my seniors in the South Asia field.

Other friends, near and far, have enriched my life and work in countless ways. Thank you to Lys Alcayna-Stevens, Andrew Amstutz, Hannah Archambault, David Boyk, Nina Brooks, Lise Butler, Emmerich Davies, Radhika Govindrajan, Gracie Halpern, Ashley Hayes, Leslie Hempson, Samantha Iyer, Aaron Jakes, Kiira Johal, Harry Kennard, Janhvi Maheshwari-Kanoria, Polina Mischenko, Aphrodite Papadatou, Tehila Sasson, Ileana Selejan, Holly Shaffer, Sudev Sheth, Matt Shutzer, Asheesh Siddique, Nishita Trisal, Dominic Vendell, Rashmi Viswanathan, Sam Wetherell, and Hollian Wint.

I have known Erin Mosely for exactly a decade, coinciding with the making of this book from crude prospectus to final manuscript. Her deep love and unending support has sustained me through good and bad times. She has shown me much of the world, from one Great Lakes region to another, and I owe her more than could ever be expressed here. My parents, Şerban and Andrea Raianu, gave me a childhood surrounded by books, brought me to a new country where my esoteric interest in history might be rewarded, and above all, believed that I had the wisdom to choose the right path in life. Last, the book is dedicated to my grandfather, Eugen Prahoveanu. When I was fifteen years old, he dedicated the fourth edition of his foundational textbook *Essential Economics* to me, with the wish that I would one day "become a worthy intellectual." I hope I have begun to repay that faith.

Index

Page numbers in italics indicate illustrations.